ZALE ZEVIAR

WHATEVER
HAPPENED TO
? DIVINE ?
GRACE

D0732796

WHATEVER HAPPENED TO
? **DIVINE** ?
GRACE

An Alexander Book
by Ramón Stevens

STILLPOINT
PUBLISHING

Copyright © 1988 Ramón Stevens
First Edition

All rights reserved. No part of this book may be
reproduced without written permission from the publisher,
except by a reviewer who may quote brief passages or
reproduce illustrations in a review; nor may any part
of this book be reproduced, stored in a retrieval system,
or transmitted in any form or by any means
electronic, mechanical, photocopying, recording,
or other, without written permission
from the publisher.

This book is manufactured in the United States of America.
Book design by Rostislav Eismont Design, Richmond, NH.
Typesetting by debset, Peterborough, NH.
Published by Stillpoint Publishing, a division of
Stillpoint International, Inc.,
Box 640, Meetinghouse Road,
Walpole, NH 03608.

Published simultaneously in Canada by
Fitzhenry & Whiteside Ltd., Toronto

Library of Congress Card Catalog Number: 87-063015
Stevens, Ramón
Whatever Happened to Divine Grace?
ISBN 0-913299-46-4

9 8 7 6 5 4 3 2 1

DEDICATION

**with love to Paul
who started it all**

Foreword

Deep within our lives, we can feel the challenge of change. It's the giant ground swell of energy rearranging our relationships, job opportunities, financial security and every level of health and well-being. Today's changes represent the metamorphosis of transformation, or transformed thinking. It means that we are being given the opportunity to cleanse and revitalize our bodies, minds and souls, to meet the requirements necessary for the creation of a dynamic, harmonious and peaceful 21st century.

Our current attitudes, beliefs, and intentions are being challenged to make way for new beliefs which reflect a merger of both the physical and nonphysical worlds. What was known and secure yesterday is now being internally reprocessed and re-evaluated to form a different perspective. We are changing our attitudes and beliefs because we are subtly, inwardly aware that we have an obligation to bring our truest awareness and most authentic wisdom into the upcoming millennium.

Our newly shaped beliefs and the actions that follow them are increasingly suggestive of harmony rather than cacophony, peace rather than war, personal empowerment rather than individual isolation and victimization. Old, outdated attitudes like yesterday's wardrobes are being refashioned for the times. There is a greater level of wisdom at work in our lives that is claiming a voice. It is the voice of DIVINE GRACE, which Alexander defines as:

"...the motivating power of your life and universe. Divine means the source is beyond your physical universe; grace means that the divinity rides on a loving, buoyant intent which seeks always to carry you to your own greatest fulfillment."

WHATEVER HAPPENED TO DIVINE GRACE? will enhance your own processing of change. It will offer you vital new perspectives on every aspect of your life as well as on the causes and effects of personal and global choices that have brought current political, social, moral, and cultural structures into being.

The key to enjoying and benefitting from the dynamic information in *WHATEVER HAPPENED TO DIVINE GRACE?* will be your willingness to challenge your own conscious and subconscious belief patterns. While you may agree or disagree with Alexander's views, most importantly, you will be examining your beliefs to determine whether they are still appropriate. Because your beliefs form the foundation from which your physical success and happiness grow, you can improve the quality of your physical life circumstances by your willingness to entertain new ideas.

Alexander, channeled by Ramón Stevens, has a unique voice which guides with wit and clarity, and a quiet appreciation for the struggle that accompanies being human. Each chapter is filled with new thoughts that will cause you to question "the way things really are."

As you read WHATEVER HAPPENED TO DIVINE GRACE?, you will begin to feel new energy surrounding your beliefs and a new commitment in your words. Your perspective, too, will begin to shift to encompass what has not been apparent to you before. You will see a different way to be, to teach, to share and to learn, and you will certainly feel the imminent challenge of the 21st century: to become all that you were meant to be.

Meredith Lady Young
Author,
AGARTHA: A JOURNEY TO THE STARS and
LANGUAGE OF THE SOUL

Preface

This book was dictated by a spirit entity named Alexander while I sat before my home computer. It was transmitted as a seamless whole, which I have broken down into chapters and sections. As Alexander later describes, the material was arranged and conveyed in nonverbal form, later linking with the closest approximating meaning in English and funneled through my fingers onto the computer's keyboard.

Although Alexander's humor and irreverence will soon be known to the reader, there is a marked difference between his tone while dictating *Divine Grace* and his more informal dialogues with me. To round out the reader's perception and to demonstrate that this work was not delivered on stone tablets but as part of an interactive process in which I challenged or questioned the material during the book's transmission, I have included in the Appendix a sampling of our exchanges.

I hope the material will be seen to stand on its own as an insightful and penetrating study of the state of our society. Its origin—offered by an entity beyond our physical plane—should neither lead to the material's summary dismissal nor hold it immune from challenge. Alexander makes no claim to omniscience, although his insights, in my opinion, make a significant contribution to understanding who we are and where we are headed.

From this point on, then, the words belong to Alexander.

R.S.

Table of Contents

PART FOUR
ART

PART FIVE
THE AGES OF LIFE

PART SIX
YESTERDAY, TODAY AND TOMORROW

Introduction

You begin this book couched in the comfort and familiarity of a physical world. Your senses drink in a rich and wondrous three-dimensional earth, and you sit now in your private corner, safe, secure, resting on bedrock stability.

If so inclined you could measure this book and determine its height, depth, weight, number of pages and so on. The book itself is a part of the physical earth that you know. Yet its author has no physical existence, no height or weight or complexion for you to perceive and measure.

However rich and miraculous your world seems, however unique and precious, know that its three dimensions are reflections of far vaster, deeper realities, that your world spins in but one universe of many, that the "you" who reads this book is but a fraction of your greater multidimensional existence. It is from these depths beyond the physical world that we speak to you, squeezing our thoughts into physical expression as an offering, urging you toward a more comprehensive understanding of your world, your life and the grander design in which you play a unique and precious part.

You may have been drawn to read this book because, while you sense that there is a deeper meaning and purpose to the world, to life, no institution or body of thought can fully provide you with that deeper meaning.

Science calls you an accident, the result of eons of mutational evolution, beginning with single-celled organisms and staggering haphazardly to your appearance on the earth. All this on an accidental globe circling an accidental sun in an accidental universe. For what is the universe's origin, according to science? A big bang? From whence originated the material of that first explosion? Where did it come from? Science has no answer. While you dutifully accept the conclusions and principles of your white-frocked superiors, because you have no better explanation, something gnaws at you. Life an accident? This marvelous planet an accident? Surely there is more...some deeper meaning and purpose to it all.

Religion has posited an omniscient and usually benevolent God, eternally loving but not entirely above flooding the globe to eliminate your species when its conduct fails to meet moral specifications. You are told that God is love, that He cares for every person on the planet. Why, then, are hundreds of millions starving? Is God asleep? If not, does He not care? If so, why doesn't He do something? If suffering is part of "God's plan," what kind of plan is this? What sort of God, to hatch a plan in which so many stagger from birth to death in unspeakable misery? God is love? This is God's plan? You know it cannot be; while you sense a source of divinity and power from beyond your physical earth, you cannot accept this cruel and capricious God. There must be more.

Your last great institution, after science and religion, would be government, politics. You need not take our word that this arena of your society has utterly failed you; read this morning's headlines. Any morning.

Science, religion and politics each attempts to explain the nature of reality, the source of the world, the meaning of existence. But they fail you. Life an accident? God's plan unspeakable suffering? Security through nuclear weapons? Such is nonsense, all of it; you know this, but you stumble along, mouthing the laws of science, the platitudes of religion, the slogans of politics, not knowing where else to turn.

In fact, your world is an eminently **comprehensible**, logically constructed, rationally ordered, divinely inspired corner of creation. There is not a phenomenon upon it—in either physical earth or nonphysical thought—that cannot be understood, once the few basic principles of existence are grasped. There is no mystery to life, no intent that you grope blindly through your days, careening from science to religion to politics, coming away shortchanged, empty-handed, ignorant. You are blessed with the capacity for conscious, rational thought, and thus every aspect of creation, as we shall see, is entirely comprehensible once the framework in which your world is created is understood.

In our own modest way, we hope to impart these basic principles of existence to you, to apply them to myriad aspects of your life and world, and to leave you with the mystery stripped away, replaced with knowledge and understanding, restored both to your divine origin and rational thought.

So let us begin.

PART ONE
DIVINE GRACE

CHAPTER ONE

Creation of the Physical World

Now, let us examine the smallest building block known on your plane, the atom.

Your scientists understand the atom to contain neutrons, protons and electrons, combining in various ways and bonds to create the basic building blocks of nature. From this starting point, atoms combine to form molecules, and on we go right up the scale to the blue whale.

But consider the atom. First, let us examine its properties from the standpoint of motion. Are the atom and its elements composed in a predetermined structure with the neutrons and protons and electrons all obediently lining up and counting off? Hardly. What you have is a mad dance, an entirely unpredictable one, as the electrons jump from point to point within the limits of their sphere, never stopping, never falling into any consistent pattern or ritual.

Now consider this. The smallest, most basic unit of physical matter is one entirely unpredictable, constantly spinning dance. What does this tell you about the solidity of your precious physical matter?

But to return to our atom. Where do these tiny building blocks, these minute elements, themselves come from? Are they in fact the smallest unit of physical matter, or can we divide them further and further?

The question is unanswerable in those terms. It presupposes that the origin of physical matter is physical matter, that stuff must come from stuff. This is not the case. **Intent** is the origin of physical matter.

It is as if there were an invisible membrane; on one side is the physical reality that you know, and on the other is the invisible machinery, that **intent** of All That Is*, which makes it possible. Intent is the key word. Desire, if you prefer. But in any case, it is All That Is Whose **desire** and **intent** to explore Itself in all possible manifestations create your physical world, and that intent begins at the very smallest unit of matter. An electron, then, is like the first hesitant physical manifestation of **intent** as it eases through the membrane into physical life and begins its joyful dance. There are pockets, then, gaps in that membrane which, when energized with enough **intent**, transform that intent into a unit of physical

---

*Alexander uses the common metaphysical phrase "All That Is" to avoid the negative connotations of religion's traditional word "God."

matter, an electron. It is the great thrusting desire of All That Is which oozes through and springs to life across this invisible membrane.

And once an electron has been given birth in such a manner, it calls back, sends its **own** intent back to All That Is, begging for playmates to join it in this wondrous sphere of activity, this brave new world. This makes it easier for the other units of matter to follow, as they are "denser," and therefore created by a stronger burst of intent, than the electrons. Like a game of tug of war, the electron sends back its desire to engage in the joy of physical creation; this desire helps ease creation of its brethren elements.

And so in a wondrous exchange, not only is physical matter created out of the desire of All That Is to know Itself, but also the joyful song of physical matter reaches back through "space" and "time," connects with the body of intent across that invisible membrane, and pulls more of itself into being. **Physical matter creates itself, then.** The exuberance of the atom is multiplied in the wonder of the molecule, which astonishes itself in the miracle of a single-celled organism, and on and on up the ladder to the simply unimaginably complex organism that is **you**, composed of uncountable such atoms and molecules, every one of them jumping for joy to join in partnership and create what you are.

We emphasize that the natural state of the world is one in which grace and fulfillment are the easiest paths to follow. It is much more work to bring yourself "negative" experiences, to so deny the beauty and wonder of your own beings, to turn deaf ears on the song of the molecules that compose you, that you stray from the path of fulfillment.

Much of this information is virtually inexpressible in physical terms. Understand the main points: Physical matter is created both by the intent of All That Is and by physical matter itself calling back across the frontiers of "space" to the limitless store of energy from which it springs. The essential building block of physical matter is one of random, playful energy.

Beginning with the atom, then, physical matter is "built up" as a gridwork of intent, that intent or desire of All That Is to combine and intertwine its strands of consciousness in an ever-expanding structure of matter. For each such "success," starting with the lowest single-celled organism, extending up through the botanical and reptilian ranks to what you consider the pinnacle of all creation, yourselves, endowed with the reasoning mind and immense modesty, is but the continuing creation, or playful experiment, of All That Is dabbling in the medium of physical life.

The same intent that powers and creates the atom, easing across the invisible membrane as the smallest particulate matter, then combines to form "grids" of intent that can sustain the larger physical entities. You can see how such intent must be organized in order to maintain and sustain an organism of your size. It is not enough that atom-sized bursts of intent *combine* in a random pattern, miraculously producing you or any other large mammal. In that case there would be no impetus to hold you together, and you could indeed return dust to dust whenever the atoms that compose you decide to seek greener pastures!

What you see and experience physically is always the "tip of the iceberg," an outer varnish on an inner event. In the case of physical creatures like yourselves, then, the intent of All That Is must be organized, focused. The "pattern" for your human shape is then constructed in the nonmaterial world, much as you might use a pattern to sew a dress. The nonphysical pattern for your body is composed of virtually uncountable building blocks of "intent," each assigned a particular function, each specifically directed toward the creation and sustenance of a particular part of the body.

For all your scientific investigations into the nature of life and matter, can your scientists explain how it is that a single-celled organism, which is the status of a newly impregnated egg cell, then proceeds to divide and divide and divide, with those cell divisions becoming increasingly specialized? For your beloved reason would teach that any cell reproducing itself must necessarily produce a clone. How, then, a brain cell? A liver cell? A toenail? Where do the specializations come from?

Your scientists speculate, of course, that at some point hormonal regulators come into play, "triggering" the development of differentiated cells. But this begs the question: Where do the hormones come from? Must they not be the result of some initial differentiation?

Once again, you can dissect and catalog and rip asunder as much as you wish. As long as you restrict your inquiry only to the physically perceivable, you will have all questions and no answers. For just as the atom itself is constructed, or originates, out of intent, not physical matter, so now does the body find its origin in a plane quite hidden from your probing instruments.

The blueprint for the body, then, is not contained in the genetic structure; the chromosomes simply reflect the greater origin. It is the gridwork, the structuring of intent and desire, that serves as the blueprint for the body. And that intent is then literally "fleshed out" to create the body's shape.

Now imagine the intent behind a single atom. Consider that somewhere in the universe there exists a burst of energy whose sole purpose or intent is to sustain that atom, to give it life in the physical medium. Then move up to a single molecule. Water, for example, you understand as H_2O. Two hydrogens, one oxygen. You now, therefore, have three "points of intention" combining their focus to create and sustain the larger entity of a water molecule.

Can you conceive, then, of the vast energy and intent manifesting as even a tiny babbling brook, with its billions of water molecules passing by every second? A babbling brook is a miracle in itself, but all of its elements are the same: a virtually infinite number of "points of intention" combining their physical expression, water molecules, and shoving them forward in physical space and time.

But in a complex life form, far more is involved. For you are not simply a collection of identically structured molecules slapped together in an ever-mutable shape, giving way to the contours of the physical world. You are instead composed of fantastically varied structures manifesting as organs, bones, blood and, of course, your magnificent brain. Now consider this! Consider the extraordinary organization required to put together such a creature!

A laser beam is a good physical representation to aid you in creating a physical picture of the process. Just imagine a green laser beam shooting through empty space; you see its glow, its energy, sizzling from one point to the next. Now, imagine that the source of that laser beam is the intent of All That Is to express Itself physically, and that the single laser beam will, when focused through the invisible membrane, result in the manifestation of a single atom.

Now, see the water molecule. Three beams, focusing their joint energies into the creation of such a molecule.

Now an amoeba. For such a tiny creature to appear to be anything at all, you have to peer through a microscope and magnify it many times. But just imagine how many laser beams of light and energy, given our model, would be required to create and sustain such a creature. Can you imagine the tremendous **power** and **force** sustaining such ignoble little protozoa?

Now move on up to a small organ in your body, the hypothalamus, for example. Like every organ in your body, it has a specific function necessary for the health and regulation of the body. Therefore, it is intrinsically even more complex a structure than would be a similarly sized pile of amoebas, for they are self-contained creatures, not given to worrying about anything beyond their immediate environment. But the hypothalamus, to do its job properly, must be constantly aware of the condition of the body, the condition of all its organs and systems, simultaneously! For it must make minute, imperceptible judgments and alterations in its output based upon its perception of the state of the body at any given moment.

So not only do you have the extraordinarily complex gridwork of intent required to create even a single cell of the hypothalamus, but all such cells must then combine and pool their joint intent to create the organ, which must then be telepathically aware of the condition of every other such organ in the body, which in turn are all regulated by the brain! Now, how many laser beams are we dealing with here? How much energy? The gridwork, the structure of intent required to sustain a properly functioning hypothalamus, is simply incomprehensible to the brain that regulates it!

Imagine as many energy beams as you can, crisscrossing at all angles, millions of them intersecting at a given point to create and sustain each cell of each organ of your body, communicating constantly with every other "point of intention" in the body, themselves composed of an inexpressible number of points of intention. Each human form that walks upon this earth, if you could only see it for its true form, is like a dazzling neon display, sizzling through the universe, a galaxy to other dimensions who gape at its splendor and complexity in awe and wonder.

How dare you stand before a mirror and deride such a miraculous creation! Have you any idea of the yearning, the intent, the energy required to sustain that receding hairline? the expanding paunch? the wrinkling forehead? They are miracles, every one, and to see them as anything less is the vilest blasphemy!

Do you think All That Is would expend the indescribably complex strands of energy and intent that manifest as you and then shake Its head sadly if the result failed to live up to some standard of "perfection"? Perfection, if it exists at all, does so only on your physical plane, and then only in the minds of the ignorant! For perfection, implying a state of ultimate and unsurpassable achievement or beauty, holds no fascination for All That Is, who seeks always and forever to **expand, grow** and **develop** in a never-ending cycle of joyful exuberance.

Your body, then, is your most intimate creation, for not only is it a physical manifestation of the intent of All That Is, interweaving in a gridwork of indescribably complex structure, but it is also imbued with consciousness! Were we talking about miracles before? Try this one on for size! The physical body is thus not only a "creation" from outside the physical system but is then empowered with self-direction, its own consciousness, which sets it free to explore the physical realm in the way that best suits its purposes. All That Is is no grand puppeteer, pulling the strings from above to amuse Its cosmic companions. It feeds Its intent into the wondrous medium of physical matter, then imbues it with its own miraculous consciousness, and **sets it free.**

And this is not all—not when speaking of the human expression of All That Is. For each of you is but a small expression of your own greater entity, splashing out across space and time in a variety of historical guises and situations, mirroring All That Is in your own desire to grow, develop and expand. Your reincarnational selves, then, each of which is itself set free by your greater entity to explore physical life, send back to the greater entity the sum of their experiences as a contribution to that entity's development, while each self maintains its own integrity and freedom.

Now. Do we begin to impart some small idea of the indescribably vast network of energy, intent, love and desire of which you are but the minutest representation, lovingly sustained in your own unique and inviolate path?

It was quite a leap from describing the atom to jump all the way to human form! You can determine for yourselves what a miracle a raccoon is, or a squirrel or a butterfly. For if the atom is a miracle of intent, a miracle simply by its being, then so much greater is the miracle of any self-sustaining, self-directed creature!

Man stands virtually alone on earth, then, with his reasoning abilities. We say "virtually" because you know that some animals are capable of sifting choices, of deciding whether or not to dig under the fence or to bite you on the leg. They understand the consequences of such actions and can, within limits, "choose" accordingly. But they cannot sit in a chair and daydream about floating by a desert isle on the back of a sea serpent. That is the special and unique province of the human mind.

As each reincarnational self contributes to the overall development and growth of the greater entity, so does each species on the planet contribute to the overall consciousness of the planet, its growth and development. You do not need to be a squirrel to contribute squirrelness to the earth's store of knowledge and activity; the squirrels do it for you. Fish contribute their fishness to the world; you need not spawn upstream for them. And so you—as the creature with the uniquely reasoning mind, the ability to consider past, present and future, to daydream, to plot and scheme, to love and hate—serve that role, play that part for the earth consciousness as a whole. **Every other creature on the planet benefits from your existence**, for on levels hidden from you, they depend on your unique comprehension of nature.

Over and over again we will remind you that the physical world is a representation of the great inner world. When you come to understand that the physical world is not a battleground of competing species but a community of species and organisms that both **depend upon** and **respect** each other, you begin to glimpse the great undergirdings that form your mass world in the nonphysical realm. You contribute human consciousness to the great stew of earthly life; in their own way, all other species make their unique contributions.

A true comprehension of this would represent a great leap forward in your understanding. For the world and its abundance of plant and animal life do not exist for your pleasure or at your convenience. They have their own integrity and purpose, which must be respected.

Now, you may ask, if I respect the rights of all plants and animals, what am I to eat? Rocks? But even rocks have consciousness, you say, so now I am reduced to a meager diet indeed. This misses the point. If you hunt down and consume an animal out of hunger, it understands, on levels hidden from you, that its flesh is necessary for the sustenance of yours, that in its turn it partook of the earth's bounty, and that all is a cycle. There are deep biological connections, avenues of communication, among all creatures. There is no sin, no crime, in sustaining one's life by ingesting other life. It is essential, we need not point out, for your life itself.

It is when you deny the **integrity** of your fellow creatures, and the earth, that you come into trouble. For the rules of the game are that each species, each manifestation of All That Is in whatever form, is to be accorded the respect and integrity that is its due by birthright. In your historical path, you have so emphasized the "reasoning" mind and its wondrous inventions and products that you have lost the intuitive sense of connection with the earth and its creatures. You do not feel that you are partners with the species of the earth, do you? You do not feel a kinship. You do not consider their existence unless (and this is droll) they are virtually extinct, in which case they are declared "endangered" and protected lest they disappear and you carry a burden of collective guilt! You do not realize that denying any creature's integrity lessens your own existence.

Now to return to our discussion points of earlier. Remember the extraordinary complexity of intent and cooperation required to sustain your body in the physical medium. Remember what an inexplicably, unspeakably rich and vast network of communication must be propelled across the invisible membrane to create and sustain what you are.

Let us imagine that you are able to conceive of such a structure, though with all due respect we submit that your consciousness can at best imagine only the crudest approximation of reality. But let us proceed with you imagining that complex interweaving of intention and communication that you know as you.

Now. Multiply that by five billion, the number of all humans presently on your earth. See them building families, neighborhoods, cities, countries; watch them create language, symbols, means of communication to carry a voice halfway around the globe; imagine swellings, pockets of consciousness arising in scattered parts of the globe, exploring different political, scientific and artistic fields of endeavor; perceive the rain forest, the ice cap, the high mountains and the vast seas.

If you have followed our exercise properly, and expanded your comprehension from the energy required to sustain one human being to encompass the gridworks, structures, energy, intent and desire necessary to sustain your world for even a fraction of a second, then your head would be exploding at this very moment. We trust it is not. That indicates that you are, in fact, incapable of comprehending the vastness of the hidden energy and intent that fuel your world. This is as it should be. We do not mean to talk down to you. There is no reason why you need to have such knowledge consciously. Just know that it is there.

And then consider that everything you know, your enormous, sprawling, beautiful, complex world, is but the faintest glimmer in the vast creation of All That Is, just one tiny, loving creation by the Creator of All Realities; that even your universe is but the tiniest fleck of all of Creation. We certainly do not wish to belittle your situation, nor make you feel small, unimportant or forgotten.

Let us sum up, then, by reaffirming what you are: a **unique, inviolate, divine, eternal expression of All That Is**, forever buoyed by the eternal wellsprings of desire from which you spring, never to be extinguished or forgotten, and blessed with the gift of free will and self-determination. You need not look above, below, beyond, out there, for All That Is. **Look within.**

CHAPTER TWO

Perception

We have followed the progress of the intent of All That Is as it eases across the invisible membrane to create an electron, an atom, a single-celled organism, the body's organs, you, your species and your world. You should by now have an inkling of the extraordinary and incomprehensible intent and desire that invisibly support your world.

Now. It appears to you that the world is quite solid, predictable, sturdy and secure. The chair you sit upon you do not expect to melt into candle wax without warning.

Yet, as we have already pointed out, you and your scientists understand that every physical object is composed of countless atoms; and we have dissected that particular little creature enough to show that its essential quality is randomness, a playful swirling dance. If such is the building block of physical matter, how is it that you perceive the world to be so solid?

Specialization exists everywhere in the universe—that which you know and those beyond it. The point of physical life is precisely to experience the physical impact of your thoughts, beliefs and desires, to see the seemingly immediate results extended outward onto the world. You believe that your senses **perceive** an **outer** reality; instead, they **reflect** an **inner** reality. What you perceive as the physical world is simply a **projection**, like a movie on a screen, of deeper, inner values.

No mean feat, you say, if you can swallow it at all. But just how is this accomplished?

Remember when we were speaking of the gridworks of "points of intention" that combine and form the structure for all physical matter, from the molecule to the mountain? Further explanation is now in order as to precisely what those gridworks are.

They are not simply invisible representations, or blueprints, reflecting the physical mountain or molecule. It is you, through the medium of your senses, who **perceives** a given grid of intention in such a way. Your senses, then, are bald-faced liars, convincing you that you "see" or "hear" or "touch" what in fact can never be seen or heard or touched, since in the realms where all physical worlds are created, no such senses exist.

Again, it is your **perception** of the varying grids of intention that convinces you of the solidity, stability and permanence of physical matter. Now remember what we said about how each species upon the earth contributes its own unique perception to the overall planet consciousness. We mean this quite literally. Do you suppose that the ant, the sparrow, the elephant and man all perceive a given object in the same way? Even your common sense will tell you they cannot. It is the highest arrogance to then conclude that all other species necessarily have a "distorted" or "incomplete" picture of reality, of a drabber and less richly drawn variety than what you perceive. They perceive it differently, but not less.

You must step back from your picture of the world in which you believe that the earth's objects are the permanent and enduring objects, and that your perceptions and those of other animals differ due to their limitations. Instead, only the invisible underlying gridwork of intent remains constant; the way it is **perceived** by the species of the earth differs enormously. You experience a tree in one way; an ant crawling up the bark experiences it far differently. Is the ant's perception then "wrong" when compared with yours? Is it "incomplete"? No—it is the ant's interpretation of that certain gridwork of intent that you perceive as a tree.

You believe that animals' eyesight is different from yours—for instance, that dogs and cats see only in black and white. You deduce this because the arrangement of rods and cones differs from that in your own eyes, and, again assuming that you are the pinnacle of creation, you conclude that the dogs' and cats' perception must be somehow less or diminished compared to what you perceive. Has it occurred to you that dogs and cats might have levels of perception, including sight, that are simply incomprehensible to you? You know, for example, that dogs can hear pitches you cannot. You blow a whistle, hear nothing, and the dog comes running from five yards away. Extend this same courtesy, this same appreciation for the varying modes of perception, to all species, and to all senses.

Thus, each species is given precisely those perceptors* necessary for it to experience the world the way it was intended to, and to eliminate from its awareness unnecessary or distracting data. Do you need the ant's feelers, waving about, searching for sources of food hidden from your sight? No, you jump in the car and drive to the hamburgers, using your sense of sight and the recall of your conscious mind to get you there. Thus does every other species have its peculiar and particular way of perceiving the world, of sorting the available data and perceiving as physical only that which is germane to it.

Each brand or species of consciousness has its own purpose for being. All contribute to the overall development and sustenance of the planet. While you can perceive a tree in only a certain way, All That Is benefits from the limitless variety of "interpretations" the species of the earth hold of what you consider to be a tree. It is part of the great exuberance, the wonder and delight, of All That Is in Its earthly creation that It creates the fantastically varied species of the earth precisely in order to know Itself, interpret Itself, in an infinite variety of perception.

Much of this is extremely difficult to express. On the one hand we have said that the intent of All That Is thrusts across the invisible membrane to take the form of atoms, molecules, etc. That was a simplification if you interpreted it to mean that All That Is holds a master blueprint for the objects of the world, which it then shoves into creation. Instead, closer to reality is that it is you, gazing through that invisible membrane and interpreting those grids of intention with your unique senses, who then perceive them as the objects of your physical world. You stand at that membrane as at a mirror, projecting outward your thoughts, beliefs, desires, intent, and then interpreting them as they are reflected back to you as being objects outside yourself.

By this point you might well ask, if my interpretation of this nonmaterial intent is so individualistic, so unique, why does everybody else see that chair, that tree, that bird? Why do we all agree on the shape, form and color of the world, if such qualities do not exist in deepest terms?

We remind you that every species shares a group consciousness, a group blueprint, a group understanding through which the group experience will flow.

---

*Alexander appears to have invented a word here—"perceptors"—referring to the senses as, literally, the "receptors of perception."

All human consciousness is equipped with a certain basic, given "package" of perception. This includes your five senses of sight, hearing, smell, taste and touch. You choose your deception, then, individually and en masse. Therefore, all "sane" individuals will perceive a given grid of intent as having essentially the same parameters of physical expression.

You all have heard of what has been called the "sixth sense," a broad phrase encompassing all manner of perception outside the five given physical senses. The existence of the phrase at all, the thought behind the concept, whether or not you believe such a "sixth sense" can exist, indicates your awareness as a species that there is more to the world than simply that which is physically perceivable. Those who can read auras, find water with a stick, perform acts of telepathy and clairvoyance are like pranksters ripping off the dignified shroud of the senses, exposing the inner machinery of the universe normally hidden from sight.

And consider for a moment what you believe to be the most important values in life, those that mean the most and bring you the deepest satisfaction. You might say love. Or a sense of accomplishment. The esteem of your peers. The respect of your children. Almost all persons, in whatever society, would agree that these are highly important values. Now, show me love. Sell me a half-pound of esteem. Toss me your dignity. Mail me your children's respect. You see, by laughing at these suggestions, as we hope and expect you have done, you confirm that what is truly important in life, what most matters, can never be physically expressed! The five senses, then, for all their exquisite interpretation of a physical world, are in fact meaningless when it comes to those values that give life its deepest meaning.

Your literature and art are replete with tales of those sad souls whose quest for objects, for possessions, so overruled their lives that they lost all other sources of satisfaction: family, friends and love. And are such creatures depicted at the stories' close as venerable, worthy and honorable folks? In contrast, they are seen as pathetic, pitiable and empty. Art always tells the truth (genuine art at least), and in every such story you find the spark of what we impart now, that the physical world, for all its beauty and wonder, is not the end all and be all of your existence, but simply the medium through which you live it!

The fish swims through water without pausing to consider how much it could make by selling off a few gallons to its neighbors. The bird flies through the air without staking out claims to the clouds. The animals roam the forest, and while they may set up housekeeping and guard their lair, they do not seek to own the entire forest and drive all other species out.

The fish, the bird, the tiger, then, comprehend the basic inner truth we wish to express here. Only a species that has lost its intuitive understanding of the great interplay among the species of the world, and with the world itself, would look upon the physical as the end, not the means.

We do not wish to slander all the human race, either, for certainly there are and have been cultures based on just such an intuitive sense, those based on cooperation and an easy security in the grace of nature. In your country, what you call Indians were such a people. By your standards they accomplished nothing of lasting importance but for a few scattered dwellings and cave drawings as artifacts of their civilization. Your far superior European culture has as its legacy the death-carrying nuclear megatonnage now poised beneath the lands where Indians once trod. We ask, should the final judgment day of your prophecies arrive and you stood before All That Is with the crowning achievement of your civilization and asked Its judgment, would you rather offer a pottery bowl or a nuclear warhead?

Let us return to a discussion of the source of your creation and see how it relates to your experience of physical life. As All That Is propels Itself through the invisible membrane into physical matter, to be perceived in a specialized manner by your species, It offers the world as a medium of expression, a crucible of creation in which All That Is can playfully expand and grow.

The point of physical life, the lesson learned before the reincarnational cycle can end, is that **thought creates reality**. You perceive what you want to perceive, both as a species and individually. Now, there are no value judgments on our plane, or from those "above" us. Therefore, if you wish to create a "negative" reality by projecting fears and worries out onto the physical medium, then seeing them bounce back to you faithfully expressed, there is nothing stopping you from doing so. A good parent is one who allows his/her children to experience the full brunt and consequences of their actions, not to shield them from the results. All That Is has a similar approach, except It has a broader perspective than even the most inspired parent, for in greater terms there are no "negative" experiences, only opportunities for growth.

Fear, for example, is a creation of the human mind. Those who feel it will project it and find its consequences automatically in their lives. If you fear ill health, you will get sick. If you fear poverty, you will lose your wealth. It is not the fear that drives these concepts into reality, but the fact that fear always charges, or energizes, any idea wedded to it to such an extent that it makes its physical creation that much easier.

You need not fear, so to speak, that any time you consider a possible negative outcome of an event you are automatically going to see that outcome materialized. If you consider the possibility of dying of cancer for a few moments, perhaps as a way of empathizing with those who are doing so, you need not call the ambulance out of certainty that a similar fate awaits you. Remember that the natural state of the universe is one of **grace** leading to your greatest fulfillment. It is only by prolonged and intense concentration on an idea, particularly one antithetical to your best development, that you can create such a reality. Again, there are no such judgments made on the other side of the invisible membrane, and if you so energize the concept of illness or poverty or any other unhappy condition by fearing it, visualizing it or worrying about it, then you make such a reality that much more likely.

This all ties in with the opening of our discussion, about your lovely deceptive senses and how they interpret reality for you within given parameters. The senses exist precisely to allow you to experience directly the results of your thoughts, beliefs and desires. The given spectrums of light, sound and material that you perceive are thus deliberately calculated to allow perception in those media that can best be interpreted and understood by your conscious, reasoning mind.

You exist because All That Is propelled you into being, gave you a self-directed consciousness, a form and free will. Your senses are the guideposts by which you measure the reality that you have freely created. They serve, then, as mirrors, mirrors of the soul. Your eyes do not look outward, but inward, into the source of your being, down to the root of your beliefs and desires; your ears hear not some clanging separate from and outside of yourself, but are tuned inward, receiving both the noise and harmony of your psyche.

Thought creates reality. The physical senses are the media through which you experience that basic, elemental fact. They exist to present you with a clear and undistorted picture of **who** you are, **what** you are and **where** you are at all times. They are a gift, All That Is's gift to you, through which you can know yourself.

As we have said, the human consciousness comes into being with preprogrammed parameters of perception that allow you to perceive the physical world within given spectrums and with a unique focus. Again, most people will agree that the given objects of a room or field or outdoor scene exist; they can agree on the shape, size, color and texture.

What of those whose perceptions differ? Your mental hospitals are filled with them. There are those who do not share at all what the great mass of "normal" people perceive. Are they then distorting what every "sane" person perceives, or is something else involved?

Thought creates reality, and even those individuals who are mad as hatters contain, embedded deep within their psyches, the same set of "rules" or parameters that all others of your species share. Yet somewhere along the line perceptions are distorted, so that by the time the senses perceive the immediate physical surroundings, they present a picture so far from the common reality that they are considered "insane."

There are great variations among such persons, so it is difficult to generalize and declare ourselves the Great Cosmic Shrink and solve the world's problems. But, for the most part, what occurs in mental illness is not that they perceive the world as most do and then scramble that perception into their own private madness, but that their fundamental disagreement with the world so frays the lines of communication between subconscious and conscious that the conscious mind has no clear idea of how physically perceivable data is to be organized; and as a result, the picture presented to the psyche of the insane is, at its source— the interplay between inner reality and the physical senses, the root exchange taking place at the invisible membrane—scrambled and distorted.

It is not that they refuse to see things as their brethren do but that their inability to share the common reality distorts that given set of parameters to the extent that they literally do not see what others see, do not hear what others hear; but they do see what others don't and do hear what others cannot. Their experience is therefore no less valid, no less accurate a representation of their inner reality than anyone else's; but it is that inner reality which is so estranged from the species that the physical reality perceived is distorted beyond common understanding.

The root of such estrangement from the species is fear. Psychology will teach you that an early childhood which is abusive enough, frightening enough, unstable and insecure enough can produce lifelong trauma and withdrawal. The child's great task is to learn to trust itself and its world, to see the world as a safe place buoying its creative explorations; from this beginning do all your great achievements spring. A child deprived of such a sense of trust, of safety, of security, can become so frightened of the world, so distrustful, that the inner psychic bonds connecting it to the others of its species and the world are severed or frayed.

Again, the natural state of the universe, of your earth, of your psyche, is one of grace and natural leanings toward your best fulfillment. It takes an extraordinarily brutal early childhood to rob a child of this natural grace. Once so damaged, however, and depending on whether conditions about it improve, the child may decide that one's own fulfillment, one's natural grace, which even in its trauma and confusion it feels as yearnings within, can never find expression in the world. It feels that the world will never understand or appreciate the products of that grace. And this is where the inner psychic bonds are cut or damaged, when the child feels that all such exploration, all expressions of grace, must be directed inward or forever lost. The result of belief that one's natural grace can never find expression, inside or out, is death. For the impetus sustaining all life is not marking off day after day on the calendar of a meaningless and tenuous existence, but is instead the yearning to ride that grace to ever greater heights of fulfillment.

And the child who finds the world unreceptive, or actively destructive, toward any expression of its natural grace faces a choice: death or turning inward. Those whose purposes would not be best fulfilled by leaving the physical body at that time then choose the second option.

Over time, if the psychic bonds between the child and the species as a whole are not repaired or strengthened, they can atrophy, as any other unused talent or limb. This is why the "withdrawn" child becomes the full-blown psychotic adult. And this is why treatment of adulthood mental illness seems such a perpetually overwhelming and impossible task; for indeed, it is the psychic equivalent of trying to regrow a severed limb.

This was not meant as an exploration of mental illness and all of its ramifications as much as it was to point out that the perceptions of the mentally ill, appearing to be so outrageously distorted to the common view of reality, are in fact simply a different way of organizing the same basic information. An ant sees the world differently from you; so does the psychotic. Their perceptions are not less valid, but they spring from an inner structure of perception that varies so greatly from yours that there is virtually no common ground.

Let us now turn our attention to another example. You have, as part of your planet's bounty, a variety of substances that when ingested can produce a variety of altered states of consciousness—hallucinations, if you will. Before you pass stern judgment on those who use such substances, understand that if you follow our discussion so far, you realize that even reading these words is in itself a hallucination; that the room about you is a hallucination; that your very body is a hallucination. So do not be the first to cast stones at the hallucinators!

Let us take a look at what happens to a person "tripping" on LSD. In the first place, because this is a man-made substance, it differs in quality from those that the earth provides and with which your native peoples were familiar. Those substances were more easily assimilated by the body; the body knew how to process them. LSD, on the other hand, being a laboratory creation, is not instinctively recognized by the body and thus can have more unpredictable effects. It is rare for anyone to experience a "bad trip" on mushrooms or peyote, for example, but instances of such experiences on LSD are legion. This is the reason.

A person on LSD begins to experience the world in a markedly different fashion. Some claim to "hear" objects, to "see" music; it is as if the inner receptors and synapses of the brain assigned to the various senses are playing leap-frog, taking over each other's posts, processing sight as sound and so forth.

As with the mentally ill, the question is: are such people perceiving the same reality as all others and distorting the interpretation in the brain, or is the initial perception itself different? Again, the latter answer is correct. Understand that everything you perceive is a gridwork of intent manifesting in your perception in a certain way. That same gridwork of intent, when perceived by a differently tuned consciousness, will appear altogether different, and yet both perceptions are equally valid.

Remember that everything you perceive is just the tip of the iceberg; that the physical world itself is the icing on a far vaster nonphysical cake; that you perceive the outer expression of events, not their origin. Given that understanding, you can see that a person on LSD may well gaze across the invisible membrane, perceive a given gridwork of intent and declare, "Ah ha! A pink elephant!" Whereas that person's grandmother would more likely perceive a chair. Or, to her chagrin, she would be the object perceived as a pink elephant by the adventuresome grandchild. When is a grandmother a pink elephant? Don't we draw the line somewhere? Don't we ever declare that someone's perception of an event or reality is simply wrong, misguided?

No, we do not. Perception is dependent upon the neurological structure of the brain, which is in turn dependent upon an inner "blueprint" determining how it will perceive the world. So the brain is unaffected by LSD, contrary to your perceptions and those of your hallucinating scientists who misperceive it so regularly.

What happens, in fact, is that the existence of LSD in the body, circulating through the blood to every cell, loosens the normally solid bonds the psyche maintains with the "world consciousness"; once those bonds are relaxed, the brain is no longer instructed to perceive the world by its standard "blueprint," and the grid of intent formerly perceived as grandmother is now interpreted as a pink elephant. The brain is following orders, not disobeying them. But like every cell of your body, it is couched, buoyed, in the invisible framework of intent and desire easing across the membrane with a consistent "blueprint" for all members of the species. LSD circulating through the body actually rips through that membrane, pokes itself a hole and rips it open for a larger view. And the poor brain, flooded by information that it is not innately equipped to handle, much of it inexpressible in physical terms, nonetheless does its duty to the best of its ability by insisting on translating nonphysical data into material that it convinces itself it is receiving through the senses.

The exact same thing occurs in the dream state. There, you travel to planes of existence far beyond the physical, to realms where the notion of physical universe construction has never been tried or desired; and as you return to your body and its human consciousness, your brain again attempts to make sense of the data collected by squeezing it into physically perceived events. Dreams can appear so nonsensical, so convoluted and fragmented, precisely because of the brain's efforts to make sense, physical sense, of nonphysical data.

An LSD trip, then, is simply a way of loosening the body's rigidly held parameters of perception, allowing you to perceive the great invisible gridworks opposite the membrane, while the poor brain struggles to dutifully translate it all into physical material.

One final point about perception. Your literature has enough material on auras and their perception as to make their existence, if not a scientific fact, certainly a commonly held belief or assumption.

What the aura represents is an extension of the body's energy field beyond that perceived by most. Remember that your body is the result of an impossibly complex organization of building blocks of intent, each performing a specific function. This inner blueprint for your body does not end neatly at the limbs and skin you perceive. It is simply that such a physically perceivable area represents the site of greatest focus of intent, where the urge and desire are most powerful, virtually shoving their way across the membrane into physical existence. This you perceive as the body.

But the body is forever supported, cushioned, by a greater energy field that acts as a sensor, for the most part. This is no great shock to anyone; observe what happens when you walk past a television. You scramble the reception. Why? Your energy field extending beyond your body contains highly charged energy. You cannot see it or feel it, but the "inanimate" television certainly can!

So each body's physical manifestation extends beyond that which you normally perceive. Again we return to our understanding of the parameters of percep-

tion as they are given to the human species; you are able, under most circumstances, to perceive only a portion of the body's energy field, the most intense area which you perceive as the body itself. You do not normally see the
energy field extending beyond it. Some psychics can perceive this, of course, and
it offers many clues as to the health and mental well-being of its owner. Our point
is not to make a long discussion of auras but to encourage you to begin to understand that what you see, hear, touch, taste and smell is but a minute fraction
of all the information available; that your senses are programmed to perceive
within a given set of limits; that for all the pleasure and beauty the senses can
bring you, they are but one tiny slice of all that is available for perception, by
your species and all others, on your beloved physical plane.

And it is beloved, to those of us who have lived upon it; we do not wish to
deride or demean it in any way. If there was not a purpose in limiting your perception to a given range, All That Is would never have done so! The point is to allow
your brain, your conscious mind, to handle only as much information as it can
easily assimilate and still manipulate effectively in "space" and "time." The
neurological structure of the brain simply is unequipped to handle a far broader
range of perception. Indeed, many "bad" LSD trips are the result of unfaced fears
charging through the invisible membrane, seeking to find expression in realms
not normally available, and sending back to the brain a horrifying picture indeed!
Your brain thus perceives your physical world in an exquisite and miraculous manner, providing you a wondrous fiction in which to couch your explorations into
the meaning and purpose of existence.

It is not just that the human species is given a preprogrammed package of
perception with which to view the physical world, but also that human society
places its own restrictions, varying from culture to culture, which further restrict
the available data. Children perceive the world in ways far richer than adults can;
that freedom is lost as they grow into the harness of adulthood. Your society
grants no recognition of ESP or any "sixth sense"; thus much data, all quite
available, is never focused upon or brought to consciousness. Do not bemoan
your limited human perception, then, when you do not utilize half of what is
readily available to you!

We on the nonphysical realm have our own set of parameters, our own limitations of perception and our own frameworks for exploration.

So cherish your senses for what they are, lovable liars who faithfully and
miraculously present to you a living, full-color picture of your own inner world,
private and shared. It is the universe's gift to you, given freely and without restriction. Cherish these precious physical "moments," knowing that at each you stand
at the source of all creation, **creating yourself.**

It is not that the gridworks of intention we have been speaking of exist in order
to create physical reality. They are not designed solely to ease across that membrane. In fact, that is one of their minor functions. For **every thought, desire and
belief you hold** forms its own gridwork of intention, becomes its own energy struc-

ture. The very universe, then, all of creation, is composed of gridworks of intention, some manifesting physically, most never doing so. You cannot see love or hate or hope or fear; you can see their reflections under certain circumstances, but not the inner events themselves. Yet these are the grids of intent or desire that form the basis for your world.

When you plan something as simple as a trip to the store, for instance, you set into motion all kinds of moving, swirling energy, which must sort itself out into certain patterns, provide certain instructions to the neurological structure of the brain in order to carry out into physical expression what you desire. You think you will go to the store, and then you go. You do not suddenly find yourself in the store, wondering how you got there. The intent and the desire come first, followed by a "gap" of time as you think of it, and then the physical expression of that intent and desire.

Perhaps put in these terms it is easier to follow. Every act you commit is first a desire or plan that, on levels hidden from you and imperceptible, organizes blocks of energy, grids of intention, which shoot out into your physical space, affecting *you* primarily but also others who might be involved in a given "event". If there are no belief impediments in the way and it is to the best fulfillment of all involved for an event to take place, it will.

Perhaps this idea is now not so esoteric, for every day, every minute, you plan, decide, organize and then follow through. What you do, on your scale, is simply magnified, multiplied in an equation impossible for you to grasp, to then create the manifestation known as your world, your universe, which is in itself the equivalent to All That Is of your stooping to pick up a pencil.

You know the expression "like attracts like." It has validity in the terms of which we speak now. A grid of intent or desire, originating in your mind, will automatically seek out similarly contoured blocks of energy, joining with them as a means of strengthening and energizing that original intent. Again, for a physical example, consider a war in which one side consists of a lone soldier. Some war. Yet if that one soldier is joined by ten million others, buttressed with tank and air support, chances are you have a fair skirmish on your hands.

So it is with grids of intent. As they combine, their unified strength gives far greater impetus or thrust to the desire they represent, making passage across the membrane into physical reality that much easier.

Now this brings us to the subject of visualization. It is a topic bandied about with great vigor these days, not only in the New Age community but also in professional athletics, for example—anywhere that a certain performance is desired, one that requires strong effort and even then carries no guarantee of success.

How does visualization work? What does it accomplish?

First, you must consider the various levels of your mind and how they work together. As we have explained, the conscious mind, that which "perceives" physical reality, is dependent upon a given set of parameters or instructions from the subconscious mind, wherein lies what Jung termed the "collective unconscious," what we have explained as being the common "ground rules" each species brings with it to physical birth. All normal humans possess five physical senses which all operate within a standard set of parameters.

This division between the conscious and subconscious is to some extent necessary. The conscious mind, busy as it is sorting the infinite signals it receives every second, has enough of a job on its hands interpreting physical reality for you. It does not have time left over to go examining the great collective unconscious of the species. It leaves that up to the subconscious, so to speak, taking from it whatever knowledge it needs, much as you turn to a specific page in an encyclopedia for the knowledge you require, not needing to read the entire encyclopedia in the process!

The divisions between conscious and subconscious are stronger than they need be. For optimum functioning, in fact, a far more "permeable" barrier would be desirable. As it stands now, you do not know what to make of your own dreams. In dreams you come into contact with the deeper, "truer" aspects of yourselves; yet the conscious mind, so divorced from even the concept of such a journey, can only lamely attempt to manifest the journey in physical terms, and you end up with a jumbled movie that appears to have been spliced together by an alcoholic film editor.

A more natural state of being is one in which knowledge derived in dreams is intuitively understood, without the necessity for squashing their meaning down into physical terms. And this is quite possible. You need not suffer such a brick wall between the levels of your mind; it is only your culture, teaching you to pay heed only to the physically perceivable, that leads you to distrust and fear products of the subconscious. Our point is that though there must be some separation between the conscious and subconscious minds, and each has its specific function, they are capable of working in much closer harmony and unity.

The subconscious, as you think of it, is the gray zone where your physically tuned consciousness, and the great invisible source of your world, meet. You might view the invisible membrane of which we speak as passing through the back of your head, the intent of All That Is thrusting into conscious awareness at the point of the subconscious.

Now, this is not a one-way street. It can just as easily go the other way, if your beliefs do not impede the flow. In other words, you can begin with a conscious idea, and then shove it back across the membrane, into the nonphysical realm of intent and desire, where it will automatically join with similar blocks of intent and, duly strengthened and empowered, then thrust its way back across the membrane into what you perceive as a physical "event."

As long as you believe in, and therefore maintain, the strong division between conscious and subconscious, this will be very difficult for you to achieve. If you do not trust the subconscious, if you consider it to be Freud's conception of the id, a dank cellar rank and crawling with repressed and rotting leftover neuroses, then that mistrust automatically strengthens the barrier. Why should the conscious mind, doing its best to maintain a clear and safe picture of physical life, open itself up to such a Pandora's box of base desires and influences?

If you understand instead that the subconscious is a realm of greater beauty, harmony and power than the conscious mind can physically handle, then you more willingly toss into it your desires and intent. That trust, itself an energized block of motion, thrusts your desire back into the nonphysical source of life, where it can pop back into physical life with much greater facility.

So when you visualize something and really concentrate on it until it seems as if the picture is sizzling in your brain, you set up a frantic swirl of energy that consolidates or crystallizes on that idea, and as all energy is motion, that energy structure then carries the intent through the subconscious and into the factory where all physical reality is created.

First, then, there must be a belief that visualization will bring physical results, an understanding of the innate goodness of the subconscious, and then let energy do the rest. You do this every day, in so many ways, that it is difficult for us to believe this concept will be met with the least resistance, yet we know it will. How can thinking about something make it appear before my eyes? Yet this immutable law of the universe governs your every act, from feeling a thirst and seeking out a cool drink, to someone who yearns for children years later giving birth. The "time" lapse as you experience it is far greater in those two examples, but the fundamental reality is the same: Your desire and intent ride the grace and motion of your thoughts into physical expression.

CHAPTER THREE

Time

Now that we have broadened your conception of "space," let us turn our attention to "time." For these two, hand in hand, form the very root of your physical life. They are the base assumptions of your plane. And, in deepest terms, they are both nonexistent.

So. If space and the physical world is but a deception played on you by the senses, what is time? How is it created? How is it that you experience life as a series of moments?

Once again your scientists have an inkling of the deeper reality. A Mr. Einstein, particularly, was responsible for exploding the notions held until he postulated his theory of relativity. In simple terms, Einstein explained that time is relative, that the passing of the moments is not a fixed and immutable progression but is instead dependent on the observer and the observer's condition, particularly in terms of speed. According to Einstein's theory, the closer one approaches the speed of light, the slower time would appear to pass. An astronaut in a ship zooming to the stars and back would return, perhaps a year older, to find everyone he knew long dead and buried.

Now, step back from your earth and just play this out in your mind. A rocket ship blasts off from earth, launches into a furious trajectory beyond your solar system, returns and finds the earth far more "aged" than the astronaut inside the capsule. Another way of looking at this, hinting at the deeper reality, is to say that the earth is farther into the future than the astronaut. Instead of viewing the astronaut as having aged less, see that each unit of time has been stretched out like taffy, a moment of earth time stretching into a week of space travel time.

But what does the astronaut experience while this takes place? If you could view him from earth, would he be moving in slow motion? Would he move a moment's progress, then suddenly freeze for sixty of your seconds, then move again another second? How is it that the difference in the passage of time is experienced?

As with the physical world itself, if you limit yourself to the strictly physically observable, you will find yourself bogged down with a giant question mark around your shoulders and no answers to ease the burden. A true comprehension of time, then, requires an entirely new approach.

Understand that in deepest terms, just as there is no physical reality, neither is there time. It is a **construct**, a **parameter** of your existence, a reflection of inner events, not an ultimate reality.

We have explained how grids of intent and desire combine to form what you then perceive as physical events. You make a plan and carry it through to physical expression. You yearn for some distant success or accomplishment and if you work hard enough, you find it materialized before your eyes someday.

Once again we point the accusing finger at the conscious mind. Just as it is restricted to a given field of perception, so also is it limited in the amount of data it can assimilate and process in the world of events. Your conscious mind simply cannot conceive of everything that a single life's work can contain all at once. It must break it down into minute fragments or particles, each one then experienced as an "event" in "time."

You see, the gridworks of intent that are set up in order to propel you into physical life at birth contain in them all potential paths for you to take within that life. We will go into probabilities later, but know now that at birth you have before you a limitless road map with infinite paths from which you choose. Your beliefs, desires and intent, formed in the conscious mind, are sifted through the filter of your subconscious, where they join up with similar blocks of energy. Let us say at birth you carry the potential to be a dancer. You may find no encouragement for such a path, though you feel the yearnings, and abandon the hope in early childhood. That block of intent, which could have manifested as you as a dancer, then remains latent, unrealized in the physical, though of course it retains its full vitality in the nonphysical realm. It is simply untapped.

If, on the other hand, you are actively encouraged in your desire to be a dancer, then that desire propels itself across the membrane, links up with the grid of intent waiting there to manifest as you the dancer, and when conditions are right, that energy block will be inserted into the time continuum. It was always there—words fail us, really, for "always" implies the existence of time—waiting to be activated, and if energized by the force of your intent and desire, it will manifest physically.

But your brain cannot handle all the possible avenues open to you, not all at once. You can sit and dream about being a cowboy, a baker, a politician, a singer, but what would happen to your precious concept of reality if all of a sudden you were all those persons, simultaneously, in one room? You would pick up the phone and call the mental health hotline. For your conscious mind exists to teach you how thought creates reality; and no purpose would be served by its automatically creating every single thought or desire you hold. It learns by **directing** itself along certain lines, carefully and thoughtfully choosing among the various possibilities open to it, selecting those that seem ripe for great learning and fulfillment, and bringing those into actualization.

For if every little whim—the desire to be President, for example—was instantly materialized, you would never learn your innate **power** to create or manipulate reality to your best fulfillment. For all "negative" thoughts would also be instantly materialized, so that if you even once considered the possibility of death, off you would go to the morgue. Thus ends your little experiment in physical reality.

Such a talent, instant materialization of every thought or desire, would then be self-defeating. You learn by deliberately narrowing your choices, focusing your energies into specific paths and then seeing how the physical reality measures up to your expectations and desires.

So the conscious mind, again, is not some poor second cousin of the psyche, saddled with a nominal IQ and stumbling blindly along. Its limits are precisely those required to permit you to experience physical reality in a way most beneficial to your greatest fulfillment. It sifts, sorts and chooses. It discards some thoughts as unhealthy or leading to dead ends, and discards them. Those possibilities, while equally as valid in deeper realms as any other, are then not **materialized** on the physical plane, are not pulled into the time continuum as an "event" because they have not been energized; there has been no linking with the desires of the conscious mind.

From an infinite swirl of paths open to you, then, your desires, thoughts and beliefs will energize those whose physical expression will be of greatest benefit. Once so energized, those events will fall into place, seamlessly stepping into the fabric of your life, at the "time" of optimum opportunity.

You see now the power of thoughts. Anything that you want, anything you can dream, is a possibility—not just a possibility, but a **reality**. It is only a question of which reality you will pull down into the span of time as it weaves the pattern of your life, faithfully mirroring your intent. Good health, wealth, love. . .they exist as **possibilities** within each "package" of consciousness that the newborn brings with him/her into physical life.

Now. That is easy for you to say, you tell me, but what about those born into destitute poverty? Haven't they a tougher time of creating a reality of "wealth" than those born rolling in it? Of course. The parameters of a life are chosen at birth; poverty will be chosen for a **reason.** And it may well be, given the intent of the greater entity to experience poverty, that such an intent forms a powerful energy block, resistant to any meager interfering in the form of daydreams of fast cars and gourmet food. This does not mean such a growth into wealth is not possible but that it will require that much more **energy** to achieve it, that much more **intent** and **desire** to overrule the initial intent of the greater entity in setting up a life.

You see daily examples of those who break the bonds of poverty. Perhaps, just perhaps, though we do not wish to suggest that suffering ennobles or is "good" for the soul in your usual terms, perhaps such a person arising from a life of poverty has a greater appreciation for money and what it represents than one who is born into it. Perhaps the sheer force of will required to lift one out of the ghetto provides a clear and stark example to the psyche of the power of intent and desire, when held as a beacon burning through the years of struggle, until it is finally achieved, until the possibility of "wealth" has been so energized by intent that it steps into the time sequence of your life.

All is learning. There are no "negative" experiences from our perspective, only opportunities for growth.

Time is a plastic medium, then, one that can be manipulated and altered. You know this. You know that when you so concentrate on a task, perhaps painting a picture or reading a book, you become so engrossed that you are shocked to see how much time has passed when you finally break your concentration. What happens, in deepest terms, in such a situation is that your very concentration, itself composed of grids of intent, is so highly charged that it must "stretch" time in order to reach its full expression, must splash out across a wider span of "time" than would the experience of painting or reading if done absentmindedly. Once charged, an event must be expended, released, dissipated.

When you concentrate so strongly on the task at hand that you lose track of "time," what occurs is that that event must be broken down into a series of moments or seconds; and the more you concentrate, the more highly charged that event becomes, and therefore a greater number of units of time are required in order to give it full expression.

You can paint a picture while talking to a neighbor, for instance, and the energy and intent required to sustain the painting activity is slight; your conscious mind is also sifting much other data, like engaging in conversation with your neighbor. Once you shut out all such distractions, however, and lose yourself completely in a task, your intent energizes it, forms a tighter, stronger grid of intent which, as it squeezes into a series of moments, requires a greater number of "moments" to be fully released and dissipated.

Just as your perception of physical space begins at the membrane with the formation of an electron, so does your experience of time unfold as a series of "moments." You label these moments, given their duration, as being milliseconds,

seconds, minutes, hours, days, etc. These are all measures of duration that you assign to events. They are your way of keeping track of the importance of various concepts and realms of exploration.

For instance, contrast the duration in time of World War II with trimming your toenails. Consider for a moment the vast gridworks of intent, sweeping the globe and all its inhabitants, composed of great philosophical issues, that found their physical expression in World War II. Untold millions were affected in one way or another—some dying, some crippled and some widowed at home. Concepts of tyranny, freedom, dignity, life's worth and meaning, were all played out on a vast scale. Such an incomprehensibly complex grid of intent as powered World War II required much "time" to find its full expression and release in your physical world.

Contrast that with trimming your toenails. They look too long. This is no cause for worry or concern. You just grab the clippers and snip them off. It does not take decades. Your neighbors are not affected. It is precisely because it is such a mundane task, virtually uncharged with energy or intent, unrelated to any of the great sweeping issues of your day, that the event is played out and released in such a brief period of "time."

Time, then, is a root parameter of your plane; space is the other. Both are constructs of the mind, ingenious filtering devices allowing you to sort and sift through the infinite possibilities of life, bringing into physical focus and endurance in time those events that are most beneficial for you to experience.

Okay, Alex the friendly ghost, we've got you trapped now. If you say that time does not exist, that it is an illusion, then why is that chair right where I left it yesterday? Why is my car where I parked it last week? And what about these fossils dating back billions of years?

Again, every species contains embedded in its psyche the great collective unconscious, the root assumptions and parameters through which they will experience physical life. An object has consistency when viewed by a variety of people because they all share common ground rules of perception as to how the gridwork of intent hidden behind the object is to be interpreted.

The same holds true for time. You and I can meet for the first time, as perfect strangers, yet both look at our watches and agree that we are meeting at a certain "time" on a certain day. There is a great invisible "clock," then, underlying your physical earth, to which all species are connected in their own fashion. All individuals of your species are ticking away in an unconsciously agreed-upon rate of progression, perceiving the passage of "time" at a consistent pace.

When you come upon a fossil, claim it to be three billion years old, and subject it to scientific tests that supposedly establish it to be so, understand that you are once again facing a gridwork of intent—manifesting as that fossil—that carries with it encoded in its molecular structure a certain "history" or "age." Again we are dealing with the plasticity of time and the manner in which differing grids of intent manifest themselves in the medium of time. Some objects have virtually no permanence in "time"—a newspaper, for example, can be left out in the rain and disintegrate overnight. The intent behind the newspaper's manifestation did not carry the need for permanence in time; the newspaper is a human creation, designed to bring you the day's events and then to pass from your life. The idea of a newspaper is not imbued with the need for permanence; it splashes out into "time" quickly, impulsively, and then the energy behind it quickly evaporates.

The physical structure of your earth is of a far deeper significance. For one thing, you share it with all other species. Again, they all contribute in their way to the earth consciousness. They are just as dependent upon a series of "moments" as you are, though they experience them far differently. Precisely because they cannot consciously manipulate the earth as you can, the other species are even more dependent on the appearance of a "bedrock" reality, a consistency, a permanence. If conditions become inhospitable to life, man can pack up and move; animals, while mobile to some extent, are limited in that regard. In a much larger sense, then, the animals require a stability to the earth in order to survive; they reproduce in the **faith** that the earth will persist to sustain their young.

Thus the intent behind the physical world is of a far more tightly compacted, crystalline structure, intricately interlocked in a pattern that renders it virtually impervious to dissipation over "time." Your mountains exist for countless millennia before being washed to the sea. The seas themselves are structures present since the beginning of your earth, as you understand its history. The great "givens" of the planet, then, being expressions of a far more intricate latticework than the products of human civilization, therefore endure longer in the experience of time.

Thus your fossil. What you perceive as being three billion years old is instead the outer manifestation of a grid of intent so tightly woven that even existence over the virtually infinite series of "moments" that you count as three billion years cannot unravel it. The intent, the desire to be, the necessity for stability, for permanence, which all species require of the world, empower the rock holding the fossil to last virtually unchanged, undiminished, over such a huge chunk of "time."

Consider, for example, the relative permanence of your human creations over time. At this point in your history you can look to the crumbling ruins of ancient Greece or Rome, or excavate the sites of Indian villages. Yet you are acutely aware of the relative impermanence of your human products. Why? Because they exist solely as a medium of expression for the human race to use as guideposts with which to mark its progress. At times we become hopelessly entangled in linguistics and its shortcomings, for we speak of the "progress" of human evolution at the same time we tell you evolution is a fiction. At deepest terms there is no contradiction, but we acknowledge that you may not see it so.

So, from your perspective, the relative impermanence of your human creations reflects the great thrusting desire of your species to ever grow, expand and develop—mirroring All That Is in Its desire to do so through you. The structures of your civilizations, however grand, are simply the by-products of your perpetual joyous exploration of physical life; and as soon as you have fully experienced a given physical phenomenon, you discard it, moving on to the next invention, the next fad or craze.

Therefore, you do not vest your creations with much intent; they are means, not ends. Of course there are differences; it is far more important to you to know that the roof over your head will last through the rainy season than it is to consider the fate of your newspaper once you finish with it. You do not charge the newspaper with enough importance to sustain the energy behind it, and so it disintegrates rapidly. You do need a roof over your head, however, and that desire for safe shelter is a constant, albeit normally a subconscious one, and therefore empowers the grid of intent manifesting as "roof" with a greater charge, which then must be dissipated over a greater number of "moments." No roof lasts forever, as too many of you can sadly attest!

Understand that time is a medium through which you can see and experience the results of your own mind, its beliefs, thoughts and desires, laid before your eyes one by one in a series of "moments." It is a parameter of your existence, then, a loving gift from All That Is through which you come to know yourself, feel the power of your imprint upon the universe as you energize the invisible universe with your intent, seed it with desire and watch the miraculous unfolding of events in time.

We have been casting about for analogies, metaphors, visual pictures with which to illustrate our discussion of time. Consider an hourglass. A more evocative illustration cannot be found. For it is a device, literally, with which you count time. You flip it over and, given your knowledge of how long the sand takes to travel from top to bottom, can accurately gauge time's passage without using a clock. And, of course, it evokes your phrase about the "sands of time." So we are quite pleased with this analogy and let us explore it fully.

Again, time is a parameter of your existence, one of the root parameters through which you experience physical life. At its very essence, time is simply energy, expressed through the medium of time, just as space is energy expressed as physically perceivable objects.

When you consider an hourglass, think of the sand in the top portion as a gridwork of intent, locked together to form a given concept or idea. Your thoughts, beliefs and desires may give sufficient charge or vitality to that gridwork of intent that you thrust that intent into the medium of time. When you do, that intent must be unraveled in a way, pulled apart, and translated or miraculously transformed, as at the hands of an alchemist, into a series of "moments," or units of time as you perceive it. A gridwork of intent, then, cannot shove itself into expression all at once but must be broken down and released into a span of "time" as you experience it.

Consider a rock. If you set it in the top of an hourglass, you would be waiting a good long "time" until it ended up on the bottom half! Why? Because its structure is so tightly compacted, so intricately woven, that it holds its shape, and only over a period of millennia can it be broken down into—you guessed it—sand, which can then ease through the tiny opening connecting the portions of the hourglass.

So it is with events being manifested in time. Consider that tiny opening or passageway between portions of the hourglass as another invisible membrane, similar to that which creates physical objects; but in this case, as a given grid-work of intent is unraveled and thrust across it, it manifests as a series of "moments" or units of time. We will not assign a specific duration to our term "moments," then, leaving it deliberately ambiguous. It is you who break time down into specific blocks of duration.

If you think of time as a long line, marching from past to future, then consider our hourglass now cut in half, with only the upper chamber and the narrow neck hovering over the time continuum, dropping its "intent" in a steady progression, moving at a deliberate and even pace along your continuum of time.

Each "event" that you experience can be seen as just such an hourglass, dissipating its intent across a span of time. The event's importance to you, as expressed in the charge you impart to it on the basis of your beliefs and desires, will determine how "big" a structure is created, how tightly interwoven are its particles, and therefore how "long" it will take for that grid of intent to be fully "released" or dissipated over "time."

Consider your life, then, with its span of years, stretched out along the horizon. And just think of the uncountable myriad of grids of intent that manifest over its course—as you grow from childhood to adulthood to old age, interacting with scores of others, planning, scheming, dreaming and loving. All this is played out over that span of time, hourglasses combining, overlapping to create a seamless whole in which you perceive a steady progress of moments and events as the experiences you pull into physical reality play themselves out.

You are not alone in the world, of course, and your grids of intent will then intertwine with those of others, to the extent that mutual learning will benefit you and others, so that you will then share a given experience, each interpreting it in his/her own fashion but agreeing that it has occurred in a given span of "time." And of course your entire world has certain events that underlie it; each time period in history represents the playing out and exploration of grand themes as a background against which you each play out the drama of your individual lives, unique and yet inextricably connected with the race en masse and with all other species upon the planet in the time period you choose to experience.

From an even greater perspective, your greater entity gazes down upon the entire history of the earth, picking and choosing those historical time periods that will most benefit its desire to learn and grow, given its particular stamp of personality and leanings toward certain paths. It then creates a series of smaller entities—of which you are one—each one of whom may be considered to be an hourglass chamber in its own right, spilling its desire to be and learn across a span of, say, eighty years. And because of its free will, it then creates its own sequence of life experiences, not chosen by the greater entity for it, but communicated back to that entity, much as a young soldier might write a letter home, sharing his experiences with his family while they remain comfortably ensconced in an entirely different reality.

Let us examine further how it is that certain events take more "time" than others for expression.

Consider a marshmallow and a brick. Which would you rather build a house out of? Which would you rather float in your hot chocolate? Now, you think that you choose to build houses with bricks and eat marshmallows because of their inherent properties. Instead, you are seeing the **effect** and proclaiming it the **cause**.

Again, everything you can perceive is the outer manifestation of an inner reality. You do not build houses out of bricks because **they are solid; they are solid because you require their permanence and stability through time.** For you, the idea of a house, of a structure in which to dwell, carries with it a great charge of **permanence**, a need for **stability**. The bird builds his nest to last, and so must you or be washed away with the first rain. And it is this intent, this necessity for permanence in your structures, that manifests in a gridwork of intent that is tightly interwoven, highly compacted, so to speak. The structure of the grid of intent behind a brick is a very dense one with few "gaps" between the points of intention that compose it.

When such a grid of intention manifests in physical space and time, it requires that much more time to be dissipated. It drops its moment points along the time continuum over a far greater period of time than does the intent behind the marshmallow.

All energy is motion, movement, a flow. Grids of intent exist to be broken down, to form given structures, express them, and then unravel, their particles then free to recombine in a myriad of possible combinations. Life itself is movement; stasis is death. So a grid of intent, an idea, a belief, seeks **expression** through **dissipation over time**. Once dissipated, once experienced by you, that grid of intent is released.

Where is the summer of your eighth year? Where is your last birthday party? Where is your first love? Where is any event you have experienced? **Where do they go?** They don't go anywhere; they are released, dissipated, expressed, and then they **no longer exist** except as memories, which are in themselves gridworks of intent, but of an entirely different nature. They are more like those soldier's letters home, a record of an event, not the event itself, which the greater entity absorbs into the overall meaning and outcome of a given life.

Let us return to our marshmallow. What is the intent behind a marshmallow? It exists or, rather, you created it, for the simple purpose of a moment's gooey pleasure; one bite and it's gone. The event lasts perhaps ten seconds; a burst of glucose and it is swallowed, absorbed, forgotten.

Now if you follow our analogy so far, you could see that the intent behind an object whose entire life span of interest to you is ten seconds would not be great, would not be tightly compacted or intricately woven. It would appear as a slapdash agglomeration of molecules barely hanging together in a cohesive whole. And it is this intent that creates the marshmallow's softness, sponginess, malleability. You do not need marshmallows to last. They are food. And it is because the intent behind them, your relative need for them to endure in time, is so slight that they manifest as so soft and squishy. Remember, it is the intent that comes first, and the physical materialization that follows. Your marshmallow is the way it is because you do not need it to endure any longer.

And, of course, if you keep it around too long it solidifies into a fossil very rapidly. A fine analogy indeed for those who cling to ideas, blocks of intent, long past their day of proper expression! There are indeed many on your plane walking around with heads full of stale marshmallows!

To sum up, then, your need for permanence and stability in time of a given object will weave the grid of intent behind it in such a fashion that when it dissipates over time, drop by "moment point" drop from the hourglass, its endurance will be determined by that initial intent.

Let us now try to wrap up our discussion of time. At its very core, or root, time is simply energy. This energy is molded, given a particular cast or structure that permits its expression as a series of moments in time. All That Is grants your greater entity the power and freedom to create as many grids of intent—each manifesting as an individual in a given historical time period—as it needs or desires in order to fully experience physical life, given its leanings and interests. You then, in turn, are set free to actualize or pull into your life span those events that will be of greatest benefit for you to experience as your thoughts, beliefs and desires energize certain paths or possibilities, interlock with them to pull them into your experience, to be dissipated or released as a series of "moment points" over time.

You see, you literally create your reality. You are given the most wondrous power of all, to **create yourself**. You do so in every moment, whether consciously or not.

At its very root, or core, "space" is also energy. This is perhaps easier to grasp, for you understand atomic structure well enough to see it is a swirling dance of electrons, protons and neutrons, endlessly combining, interlocking, interweaving, breaking down and moving. And with the lovely fiction of your physical senses, you **perceive** that energy as objects in a physical world.

Together, then, space and time are the base roots of your existence. They are givens for every species on your planet, though each has its own highly individual manner of experiencing them. In the unquenchable desire of All That Is to manifest, expand and grow, It creates the physical universe as but one of many such media for exploration, infuses it with root parameters—space and time—grants each species a unique focus, or set of senses, with which to experience life within those root parameters, and then sets it free to create its own reality.

CHAPTER FOUR

Relationships and Karma

Now let us further examine time and how it specifically relates to human experience. Remember our analogy of time represented as an infinite line, with infinite severed hourglasses jockeying for position, joining forces, opposing each other, combining in a vast swirl of intent, dropping their "moment points" into your reality, seeding it with events.

We have also seen how the intent behind an object determines its endurance in time. Your need for an object to last determines its duration, then.

Now let us turn our attention away from the world of "inanimate" objects to that of human relationships. For such relationships also differ greatly in their duration or span of existence, do they not? You may be married to someone for fifty years and yet share a brief encounter with another, never seeing him again. What underlies this difference in duration of relationships?

Return now to our grids of intent; imagine them floating about a dark universe like so many glowing nebulae, each nebula representing the swirl of possibilities that is your life, a small fraction of which you will actually experience.

Like attracts like, as we have said. Therefore, a nebula recognizing a similar bent or leaning or talent in a particular field of exploration may link up, so to speak, forging a common experience that will manifest as a joint reality on your plane, as a relationship. It serves the greater purpose of both such nebulae, or greater entities, for them to marshal their energies in creating this joint reality.

A perfect analogy would be your act of procreation. Two people join together (literally, one inside the other), each contributes his/her very essence, and the result is a child, a creation containing elements from both sources, yet stamped with its own uniqueness, individuality. It carries the intent of both parents, then, but rides that intent to a new creation, an entirely new being.

So can you conceive (so to speak) of the way any human relationship is formed on the vast plain where all human experience is created before being materialized? Two greater entities, searching about the time-space continuum for those historical periods and parts of the world most suited to their mutual fulfillment, may find a common meeting ground and thus create a bond between them that will manifest itself as two human beings sharing a relationship. The intent of the greater entities determines how intricately or tightly woven will be the block of intent that manifests as "relationship" and will therefore determine the relationship's duration in time as well as its meaning to the individuals involved during that time.

It is fair to say that a fifty-year marriage represents a grid of intent about as strong as can be manifested in your human experience. The same might hold true between a parent and child, if the parent maintains a strong connection to the child throughout life, not releasing it upon reaching adulthood.

When we speak of the grid of intent behind a fifty-year marriage being the strongest, generally speaking, that two humans can share, we are of course limiting our scope to one relationship between two people. From a broader perspective, that of the greater entities involved, one historical time period shared by two individuals may not be sufficient to fully dissipate the grid of intent they have established. This is no problem to the greater entities; they simply search out another historical time period, and another and another, until they have created enough individuals who share enough experiences together that the grid of intent can be fully released.

It is also fair to say that any person with whom you share an intense relationship in this life has also joined with you in other reincarnational lives. This is because the intent of the greater entities for you to be together is also strengthened by you, and your other reincarnational selves, through those experiences. Your greater entity sets you free, but you then go about creating your own reality; and whenever you choose to tighten or intensify a bond with a given individual, that bond will therefore be strengthened in every other manifestation in time that you share. A happy fifty-year marriage in this time span, then, may well serve to strengthen the bond manifesting as master-slave, brother-sister, father-daughter in the other incarnations you share.

You have all experienced meeting someone for the first time and feeling something "click" between you, feeling an immediate ease or, perhaps, an immediate tension and loathing. Why? Because you are always unconsciously connected with every other historical manifestation, and you are recognizing the intent behind that person's coming into your life, recognizing the work to be shared, the lessons to be learned together. Since at deepest terms there is no "time" as you think of it, you are tapping directly into the grid of intent that your greater entities have established, recognizing that intent; how you choose to express that intent is your free choice. You pull into physical actualization those experiences with this other person that reflect your own individual beliefs, intents and desires.

Not all relationships last a lifetime, as you know. What happens in a relationship that was born in a feeling of intense closeness—say, young schoolmates, who as they age see each other less and less frequently, perhaps dropping each other a Christmas card once a year?

In this case, the grid of intent behind such a relationship was virtually exhausted, or entirely expressed, within the span of time you shared as schoolmates. Beyond that, there is no need for you to stay together, and since you are always infusing your life with fresh energy and avenues of exploration, it would be of no benefit to maintain, in constant and intense consciousness, a relationship that has served its purpose.

And yet you feel a fondness for that person and those days, and that fondness can itself create a grid of intent—not a very powerful or tightly woven one, since it does not represent what vitality you will share (in your time terms) but is instead a reflection, a ghost of that experience you did share. Such a grid of intent, lacking vitality and hanging together loosely, can infuse your experience with only enough energy that once a year, come the holiday season, you take a few moments to jot a note. And in so doing, the time you spend thinking of each other serves to strengthen or refresh the intent behind your relationship, and that revitalized intent then hangs there, undissipated and untapped, for the cycle of another year, when it will both be dissipated in your act of writing the note and refreshed and revitalized by your learning what your companion has been up to for the last year.

All too often you see people clinging to relationships that have served their purpose and can only lead to stasis or, worse, harm to the individuals involved if they try to pretend that what once existed still exists. It is the great fallacy of your plane (well, one of many!) that a romantic love relationship must last forever—till death do us part—or that somehow those involved have failed if it does not.

Nothing could be further from the truth, or sillier. Life is not meant as a straitjacket, where you are strapped into a given set of relationships at an early age, never to freely explore the bounty of human relationships with freedom again. It may well be that the intent behind a relationship is so strong, the opportunities for mutual growth and learning so great, that a marriage can last a lifetime. But it is unnatural to expect all such relationships to endure until death. It is a violation of the great flow and flux of your being to consider that all romantic relationships must last forever or be considered failures.

You live many lifetimes within a given human span of years. Are you the same person you were at three weeks? At ten years? Do you expect to be the same person at eighty? We hope not. The energy that powers your life is a vast swirl, a constant dance, its overriding characteristic being the randomness evidenced in the electrons' spin. You construct infinite grids of intent to experience over the span of your life, some lasting its length, most not. Every relationship has a given "span" after which it can serve no benefit to maintain. You do not try to force the sun to stay up beyond its natural cycle, to insist that the moon remain forever full, to order the daffodils to bloom all winter. They all ebb and flow through their own cycles, and so do you. Human relationships, being a bank of incredible richness from which you draw those individuals with whom you share your life's work, have their own cycles as well. Allow them their ebb and flow.

Let us turn our attention to the experience of time in a different realm of human activity. You perceive an event as lasting a specific length of time, then disappearing from your physical senses. Does that mean the event has been entirely dissipated, the energy behind it released?

Consider what happens when you are attacked, raped, beaten, in some way thoroughly brutalized, your integrity viciously violated by another. Of course, on deeper terms you draw all such events to yourself, but this is not our point of discussion here. The issue here is, once the event has occurred in your experience of time, once it "ends" from your perspective, is it entirely over?

The attacker leaves you, then, at some point. You are free to go home and resume your life as it was before. Do you just stand up, brush off your clothes and waltz away, letting the incident slip from your mind?

Hardly. It can stay with you for days, weeks, years, haunting your every spare moment. It can play out over and over again in your dreams; it can affect your relationships with everyone else in your life; it can instill fears and phobias you had not known before.

You can see that such an event is not "over" at the point where it stops in your time continuum. It remains alive in your mind long after. In such a case, the grid of intent behind the event is so intense, contains so much "stuff" that must be expressed, that no single experience of it in time can fully release it. Yes, you draw all such experiences to yourself; that you would do so, submit your dignity to such brazen and horrifying attack, means you have so denied certain portions of your experience that you have created and activated a highly charged grid of intent, and, as always, the greater the charge you imbue to a grid of intent, the more likely that it will work its way through the space-time membrane and become an event in your life.

In almost all such cases, what you have energized is a fear, or, more specifically, the fear has acted as a lightning rod, charging a probable path. Remember that at birth all possibilities lie open before you, all paths. Thus there is a "you" that experiences the attack and a "you" that does not. If you fear such an attack, if you organize your life around a fear of crime, for example, you then give your energy to the "you" that experiences the attack. And that event then falls into place in the time span of your life with greater facility than the "you" that never lives the attack.

We can expand this concept into all areas of life, and will do so later. For now, though, consider the subject of insurance. When you buy medical insurance, you are literally wagering that you will get sick. When you buy car insurance, you are laying bets that your car will be stolen or damaged. When you buy liability insurance, you are empowering the possibility of being sued. And so on, in every area of your life.

Let us return to our discussion of human relationships. While there is little charge behind a brief encounter with another, in all relationships that are long-lasting and intense, you may be certain that there is a purpose behind it, that you and your companion are working through the intent of your greater entities to experience certain themes in the physical medium.

You may know couples who do nothing but scream and throw the furniture, and you wonder why in the world they stay together. If they hate each other so much, why don't they just split?

You should sense by now that far more is involved. For whatever reason, their greater entities have set up an explosive situation, an intense one, which, until fully dissipated, will bind the couple together. Of course free will always operates, and either could choose to pack up and leave whenever he/she wished, but chances are they will never even feel the urge! For the bond underlying the relationship is so strong and enduring, and the day-to-day squabbles just a surface patina. It is that great undergirding such a couple feels binding them together, and until it is fully dissipated and the relationship drawn to a satisfactory close, the themes involved fully explored, they most likely will not desire to split apart.

And, of course, if one lifetime isn't enough, there will be others! You would do well to treat your fellows kindly, for if you do not and manage to escape their wrath in this life, you would be well advised to sleep lightly in the next!

Now that we have expanded our view from a single lifetime and its various relationships to one involving the greater entity, and its use of the reincarnational medium in which to express the themes of interest, let us turn our attention to the topic of karma.

All religions are magnificent constructs of myth and belief, hinting and probing at far deeper realities, wrestling into spoken form the great source of your planet and your place upon it. Some religions place a strong emphasis on karma; others do not acknowledge reincarnation at all. We will turn our attention, then, to the subject of karma as it is commonly understood by those religions that acknowledge its existence.

To some, karma is seen as a divine balancing act in which every action is met with an equal and opposite reaction in another life. Perhaps we find an omniscient God, keeping scorecards on his earthly minions, duly noting their every transgression and forcing them into a subsequent lifetime of sufficient degradation and pain that the unworthy deeds of the past are exonerated.

Such a concept, while certainly creative, and hinting at the deeper reality, is nonetheless fairly wide off the mark. For there is no great Being ensconced on a cosmic throne, recording your every act in a ledger of debits and credits. All That Is created you, yes, but then **set you free** to explore physical reality, in your multiple lifetimes, following the lines of intent and desire you create.

Let us look at the intermediate point between your single physical life as you know it now and that greater intent of All That Is. In between is your greater entity that, with a given set of leanings and interests it desires to explore in physical life, sends out grids of intent that splash across the space-time continuum in a variety of guises, birthplaces, professions and so on.

Your greater entity, reflecting the playful exuberance of All That Is, wants to explore every facet of the themes that interest it. On that level, you see, there are no judgments as to "good" and "bad" experiences; there is only growth. There is only learning, at the deepest levels, for all experiences, whatever your temporal interpretation, contribute to the overall development of the greater entity.

Thus you find that the greater entity may infuse one physical lifetime with experiencing one side of a coin, then flip that coin over in the next lifetime. The man of great wealth becomes the pauper. The king becomes the slave. The oppressed becomes the oppressor.

Now you see that there are no judgments involved here; there is no concept of punishment or retribution implied. It is instead simply a manifestation of the great exuberance of life that a given theme will be explored from all possible angles.

This holds true whenever two greater entities join forces to explore a theme of common interest by manifesting two individuals in a variety of historical periods and guises. It is a game! In one historical period one entity's expression gets to play the part of the king, while the other entity manifests as the king's slave. At the end of those lifetimes the entities "take stock," so to speak, evaluating and sifting the results of the common experience; and then, for fun, they agree to switch the roles, so the slave becomes the king and vice versa.

Now, where do you see any concept of punishment or retribution in such a situation? There is none. It is not that the oppressor is ordered, by a stern and angry God, to experience the role of the oppressed, but that the entity gladly accepts the role reversal for the sheer pleasure of it!

We are exquisitely sensitive to how this may strike many of you: Poverty fun? Slavery a pleasure? Surely your comments are directed at another galaxy, Alex, and were accidentally rerouted. No, they were not. Pain, poverty, deprivation and suffering are all part and parcel of the earthly experience, you will grant, and therefore they are one more medium or avenue of expression, growth and learning that your greater entities can employ in order to explore all the ramifications of earthly life.

Once again, you are never tied to a given set of circumstances for life, except those congenital defects not within your creaturehood's power to change. But the outer parameters of your experience—wealth or poverty, sickness or health— are always open to change.

Remember that at birth all possibilities lie before you. Your greater entity may have set up your life with a given grid of intent through which it expects your life to filter—but you can, with sufficient force of will, override that initial intent if you wish. Depending on how determined the greater entity is to experience a given facet of earthly life, your task in overriding the intent may be that much more difficult. It is not that your greater entity is blocking you from changing the circumstances of your life—it has set you free—but that the grid of intent that powers your every moment will be configured in such a way that certain avenues or possibilities will be manifested with much greater ease, and therefore require far stronger intent on your part to override.

This holds true of relationships, then, returning to our discussion of karma. If you murder someone in this life, for instance, you have automatically inserted the concept of "murder" into your greater entity's grid of intent. Like all grids of intent, it must be played out, dissipated, somewhere along the line. It could be in this life; it could be in another. Whenever you commit a certain act from one perspective, you set yourself up to experience it from every other angle, not out of punishment but because of your greater entity's exuberant passion to experience all facets of existence.

When you murder someone, not only do you charge your greater entity with the concept of "murder," but you necessarily intertwine your life with the one you murdered. The rules of physical life are that once a person is murdered, that physical life is terminated. This seems an obvious statement, but our point is that the concept of "murder," intertwined with the entity of the one you murdered, must necessarily be carried over to another life, since it cannot possibly be played out in this one. You will face the issue on another day, so to speak.

Does this mean that the murdered must become the murderer, that the desire of the greater entity to experience all facets of life must automatically and mechanically translate into a rigid role reversal? Of course not. One of the great lessons of your plane is the absolving, healing power of love. Violence need not beget violence. Murder need not give birth to murder. That grid of intent joining two entities in the concept of "murder" can be dissipated in ways other than a second such act. If the feelings welling up inside those involved can be expressed in ways other than murder, expressed fully and completely, then the energy will be dissipated without another heinous act. And what a lesson this provides for the greater entity!

Such patterns are rarely conscious. You do not meet someone and say, "Oh yes, remember when you murdered me back in 1674? Well, I forgive you. Let's have a drink." Instead, a situation may be created that, if allowed to play itself out, could well lead to such an outcome. But your free will always allows you the option of not following such a path. You can recognize the desire to kill someone, understand what the person is doing to cause such a motive, and then make the choice not to follow it through to the final act. You have heard the expression: I was so mad I wanted to kill him. You wanted to but you did not. You exercised your free will and turned away from the lethal outcome.

That lethal outcome, the second murder, always exists in the nonphysical realm as a possibility, as does the outcome in which the second murder does not physically occur. You pull into actuality, then, which outcome will occur by the power of your beliefs and desires. You may feel a murderous impulse toward another and, while acknowledging the impulse, also appreciate the profound violation—the ultimate violation, on your level—it represents. You choose not to give in to such an impulse.

And your decision, to leave the second murder forever on the nonphysical plane, is a great lesson to your entity, as it learns yet another twist on the game of life, that one's appreciation for the sanctity of all creatures must be forever respected, the integrity of your fellows never violated. You can turn the other cheek, not out of weakness but out of the strength that you have the choice to break the cycle of violence.

This holds true on a global scale as well, of course. Time and time again in your human history have you seen a series of little skirmishes escalating into full-blown warfare, all because those involved confused violence with strength, pride with integrity. You do not surrender your integrity or strength by refusing to return violence; you enhance them.

To sum up our discussion of karma, then. It is a valid concept, one that does hold sway over a series of incarnations, as you think of them. But rather than being an immutable law established by a balance-toting cosmic Judge, it instead reflects both the **exuberance** and **free will** of your greater entity, and of you, to dive into the medium of physical life and gleefully explore its infinite facets. And while you can choose to explore all aspects of a given theme or idea, you can also choose not to, after understanding why you have created a given situation for yourself and deliberately seeking to turn the direction of your life in a more life-affirming path.

You are at the mercy of nothing and no one, but stand always as the sentinel at the gates of your existence, allowing entry to those events that you choose to experience. Such is life, such is karma.

CHAPTER FIVE

Probabilities

Now we shall turn our attention to the topic of probabilities. We have hinted all along about them, mentioned them by name, but not fully explored their definition. We will do so now.

First we must confess we do not care for the term. To say something is "probable" is to say that it is likely to occur or has a better than even chance of taking place. Instead, we hope we have convinced you by now that your life is a series of infinite paths or **possibilities**, all of them valid, which are then actualized based on your intent and beliefs, dropping into your physical space and time.

Perhaps we feel more comfortable using the word probabilities to describe those events that are poised for insertion into your time continuum once activated by your intent and desire. Once so charged, they do indeed become **probable**, or more likely to occur than the other paths open to you.

So on deepest terms, consider that all paths are **possible**; as you live your life and send psychic charges to specific possibilities, thus rendering them likely to occur, they become **probabilities**. Now enough of the Webster's and let's begin our discussion.

You stand as the eye of a hurricane while all around you swirl and rage the infinite directions your life can take. At the deepest levels they are all equally valid. Your beliefs and thoughts, themselves being grids of intent, then interlock with certain possibilities and ignore others, empowering the interlocked paths and pulling them closer to physical expression.

When we say an event or path is probable, therefore, we are saying that you have charged it with your stamp of intent and desire, made its physical expression more than likely, and you will probably experience it at some point in your "future." Let us continue this discussion with a further examination of time and how it is expressed in your physical plane.

It is not enough to charge a possible path into a probable path and then find it instantly materialized. Probabilities must "wait their turn," so to speak, for insertion into the time continuum at the point of maximum benefit.

You know that your physical senses perceive waves. Light waves you perceive as colors along a spectrum, most of which is hidden from you, but some of which can be translated by your eyes into the experience of color. You all know that sound is also waves, a few basic structures like the sine wave or sawtooth wave being modified by a host of factors; then upon reaching your ear, they are translated by your ear's mechanism into sound.

When someone speaks to you, they are not saying what you hear. They are setting off a series of sound waves that are then translated by your ears into an interpretation of that person's voice. The color of the shirt your companion wears is not a bedrock reality but is interpreted by your eye based upon the type of light bouncing off it and into the pupil. Your scientists are all nodding their heads in agreement with us on these points; understand, then, that what you experience in physical reality is your physical senses' interpretation of various wave forms.

Now we shall leave your scientists in the dust. For time also rides on waves, on cycles, which are then interpreted by you in your distinct and individual fashion.

A probable event does not simply fall into your lap at random. It rides a wave or cycle that buoys it and sustains its charge as it waits for insertion into your time continuum at the time of optimal benefit to you.

You may have a yearning at age five to be a composer. Are you then a composer at age six? Not likely. Chances are you will need to grow up (and we will discuss the stages of growth later) and establish a certain gridwork of intent that manifests as "you the adult," at which "time" it will be far easier for the "event" of your role as a composer to slide into place; the "event" rides along, then, carried by a cycle that holds its charge until it can be dissipated at the point of optimal benefit.

The concept of time cycles should not be esoteric to you at all. Every day of your life is a 24-hour cycle, is it not? Within that daily cycle you alternate periods of rest and wakefulness; you eat along a certain familiar pattern; you may alternate speaking with others and watching a television program, then follow a period of inactivity with the refreshment of moving about. So every day contains within it a set of cycles that you have established for your life, and that you follow as ritual.

Taking a longer perspective, you find the earth moves to its own cycle; depending on where you live, you may experience a brilliant change in seasons or simply a difference in the smog cover! In any case, you are aware that the earth holds a pattern of seasons that buoys, supports, your own daily cycle.

You have annual cycles of your own: given holidays, birthdays, anniversaries, all of which occur once within every annual cycle.

And you have longer cycles. Every twenty or twenty-five years is a generational cycle, in which the children become young parents. The parents become grandparents. The grandparents become ghosts and hang out with us! And those tired of hanging out with us reincarnate and become the babies! Quite incestuous, this whole earth-cosmos connection.

Taking an even broader view, you can gaze back upon your history, the one you agree upon, and remark that certain ages were marked by upheavals of a particular flavor. You classify them as the Industrial Age, the Renaissance, the Middle Ages, etc. You are now nearing the end of the second millennia of the religion of Christianity, in itself an enormous cycle that again couches all the "shorter" cycles within their common experience in time.

Thus you see that time itself travels on waves or cycles. Events do not simply drop into your existence; they occur when they have reached the point in their cycle where they most easily interlock with your own grids of intent and enter your physical reality.

Thus, excuse us if we create another invisible membrane; but as an analogy, you might conceive of the possible events of your life bouncing on waves that approach and then draw back from physical actualization. Your grids of intent, being your beliefs and desires, approach that membrane from the side of physical reality. When those two grids of intent, the nonphysical "event" riding its time cycle and your physically oriented grid of intent seeking physical expression, meet at the membrane, that "event" will be pulled into your life at that point.

From the greater entity's perspective, such cycles can be set up ahead of time for a given lifetime. For instance, as part of the lessons you set for yourself, you may choose to experience the death of a child. Obviously, you cannot experience this at age ten. It must wait its turn, so to speak, until your physical life has progressed to the point where such an event is possible: namely, that you are of childbearing age and have a child. So the "event" of losing a child will be set on a cycle that cannot even be activated for the first twenty years of your life. At that point, the cycle will begin approaching the invisible membrane, closer and closer with each bounce, searching for the grid of intent sent up by your physically oriented consciousness to experience that event.

Free will always operates, and if you have in some way been able to experience this event in another fashion—say, the death of a younger sibling—then the grid of intent manifesting as "death of young family member" will have been dissipated, released. Therefore, the "event" of losing your child will bounce unmet, unrecognized on its side of the invisible membrane, never interlocking with a grid of intent created by your experiences on the physical plane. Such an event, then, will not occur on your physical plane.

Of course it **does** occur on deepest levels. It is simply not **physically actualized** because you have not pulled it into being. You have no need to experience it in this life and it will remain forever latent.

You might well be asking, if all these experiences are occurring on deepest levels, then exactly who is experiencing them? I'm down here and they sure aren't happening to me. Now we introduce a new concept, that of parallel selves.

CHAPTER SIX

Parallel Selves

What are parallel selves? They are infinite variations on the theme of you. They are a pack of invisible companions traveling with you along every moment point of your life.

When your greater entity decides to create you so as to experience its themes and interests in a given historical time period, it is not that it simply creates and energizes a grid of intent that you perceive as your physical body. It creates a swirl of infinite possibilities, all possible manifestations of you, that ride the greater entity's intent along the time continuum. What you experience as you in the physical world is an assortment of experiences pulled into your physical lifetime from an infinite swirl of yous. Those experiences you choose not to pull into physical expression will then be played out, experienced, dissipated by non-physical yous. These experiences are just as valid, just as real and contribute just as much as those you experience physically.

All such parallel selves are bumping up against our assorted membranes, and as your physically oriented consciousness goes through life, its experiences, but more importantly what it *thinks* about those experiences, will then call back across the membranes to the parallel selves, each riding on its own wave or cycle, and join forces with those selves who offer experiences most beneficial to you. These are then pulled into physical actuality.

A fine analogy for this would be when you go grocery shopping. You walk down the aisles, pausing to examine the multitude of possibilities open to you. You decide if you need tea at all, for instance. If you don't, you push on. If you do, there come the further decisions of which flavor, brand, size and price to buy. Once you sift all these factors, you make a decision to your optimal benefit, drop the tea in the cart and move on.

So it is with how your life is constructed. You might consider your physically oriented consciousness to be pushing a grocery cart through the aisles of time and space, shopping for experiences designed to bring it greatest benefit. At every moment, you are examining the lives of all your parallel selves, seeing what they're up to, and when something is of interest, you grab it, pull it into your cart and live the experience.

Somewhere, for instance, you have a parallel self who commits suicide. That is always an option available to you; thus a greater entity always creates such a possibility. As you shop your way through life, you may find yourself quite content, reveling in the beloved pleasures of earthly life, finding enrichment and satisfaction in your relationships with friends and family. In that case, you would not even notice the suicidal parallel self sitting on the shelf; its value to you is nil. It would serve no purpose for you to end such a contented existence. The possibility, then, is not even brought into consciousness.

But let us say you have had a harder time of it. You have lost your job; your wife has left you; your children do not respect or understand you; your money runs out. As you push your forlorn cart full of unhappy experiences through the cosmos, you might well take a good, hard look at the suicidal parallel self. You might stop the cart and examine this parallel self thoroughly. And you allow the scenario to play out in your mind at this point: What would happen if I followed this through? You see, when you imagine such a possibility, it is not just your own imagination at work; you are literally commanding a performance from a parallel self, bringing it into your mind's eye and watching it play out the considered experience in rich detail. From this you then draw a conclusion as to whether or not you wish to actualize such an experience.

You may decide, after thorough review, that it would not serve your best interest to commit suicide. If so, having acknowledged the impulse and seen the scenario played out in your mind courtesy of your poor suicidal parallel self, you can push on, buoyed by the acknowledgment that your life, however miserable it appears at the moment, can indeed bounce back to one of achievement and fulfillment.

On the other hand, once the parallel self plays itself out for you, you may find the blessed peace awaiting you on the other side of the veil, as you perceive and interpret it, to be so attractive that you make the choice to end your life. At that point you will find that you have not only one suicidal parallel self but a variety from which to choose. Do you wish to make a heroic statement with your death by wrapping yourself in the flag and hurling yourself from the top of a tall building? Do you wish revenge by blowing your brains out in front of your wife and children? Do you prefer the satisfaction of slitting your wrists and watching your very life's essence gush out upon the floor? Or how about the subtle model, the one who takes sleeping pills and lies down in the woods?

Again you will make your choice, and that choice is itself a grid of intent that rises to the invisible membrane, interlocking with the parallel self it most closely resembles, and together empowered they push into the time sequence of your life at the point where the statement you wish to make in killing yourself will have the maximum impact upon others and upon your own learning, as well.

By now you are beginning to wonder, if I am simply the slapdash creation of infinite parallel selves, then **who am I?** Have I no individual integrity?

As before, when setting up your life, your greater entity will create an infinite series of paths that you can follow, **precisely as a way of ensuring your free will.** You literally pick and choose from the infinite paths before you which you will bring into physical life.

Although each parallel self will live out its own version of your existence, they do not all carry the same weight, so to speak, with the greater entity. They are all valid but not equal in their contribution to the greater entity's development.

Specifically, the life that you know, the series of physical moments, automatically carries a deeper charge precisely for having been physically materialized. For in crossing the invisible membranes of time and space into your life, all events are thereby coated with a "polish" not found on events never physically materialized. The greater entity recognizes that "polish," then, as evidence of contributing deeper meaning to such physically experienced events.

Another way of expressing it is that physically experienced events are charged by the process of being pulled into physical space and time. Your life is then a series of such charged events. When your greater entity wishes to review your life, it focuses upon those charged events as carrying the greatest weight, since they were physically experienced, and your greater entity's very intent in existing is to experience physical life in a variety of historical guises. The you that you know, then, is indeed a unique and inviolate entity.

Upon physical death, you see, you imprint the universe with the sum of your physical experiences by means of those charges. Each charge is a unit of learning and carries with it a conclusion which can be "read" by your greater entity, or by others. For all of physical life is learning, and each experience teaches you something. The result of each such lesson is codified in a way, charged by virtue of having been physically experienced, and combined with all other experiences to create the sum total of your life.

What you now know as you, after physical death will remain forever immortalized or recorded in the journal of the universe by means of that burst of energy, that imprint which carries with it the sum of all your experiences and their meanings to you. If you live a miserable life, incapable of loving others and therefore finding no one loving you, then the imprint upon death will be of great value to the greater entity, for from it that entity can learn that certain paths do not lead to optimal development. To choose physical possessions over human company will not lead to happiness.

The greater entity then absorbs the imprint of each physical life, files away the conclusions drawn therefrom and can proceed, duly enriched by your experience, to venture forth in a new direction.

All of your parallel selves, trailing you like ghosts throughout your days, also leave imprints. But because their unmaterialized experiences do not carry the coating or charge created by insertion into time and space, they will serve more as background to the main event, the physically lived life. Their experiences are just as valid, in deepest terms, but do not imprint the universe with the force that the life you know does. These parallel selves, then, are the basis for free will.

They are more than that, though. Each individual reaches a point in life where he or she embarks upon certain paths or directions, consciously choosing not to follow others. In your society this occurs most acutely during late adolescence and early adulthood, during the time of career choice. At that point you can feel an inexplicable panic at the thought of making such a choice. You do not want to choose. This is because those parallel selves are all beloved; unconsciously you recognize them and their great potential, each of them. And once you pull into physical expression one given path, you automatically cut off from expression many others. It is this that you feel, the ineffable sadness at losing these invisible companions who up to now have accompanied you through life, latent, but eager for physical expression. But you must make your choice.

Having done so, it is not as if those paths you chose not to follow are forever lost to you. For instance, at the cusp of adulthood you may find yourself with leanings toward music, botany and teaching. All three paths, all three parallel selves, have followed you with equal strength up to the point of your decision. You must pull each path into your mind, creatively play it out and determine which appears likely to bring you the greatest happiness. Then you make your choice and cut off the other two from full actualization.

Note we did not say you cut them off from any actualization. For, despite not being selected as your primary focus, they do not run off and sulk in the far corners of the universe. They travel with you still, looking for openings, opportunities to dip into your physical life.

In the example above, you could choose to combine music and teaching, or botany and teaching, and thus create a hybrid self—you—who draws upon the strengths of two strong parallel selves. Even if you don't choose the outer title or mantle of "teacher," and decide to restrict yourself to research, still you might find yourself spending inordinate amounts of time with young research assistants, helping them along in ways far more comprehensive than are necessary for the advancement of your own research. The same holds true for music.

Finally, you could combine all three and teach plants to sing. We suggest you consult your greater entity as to whether commitment to a mental hospital would serve its purpose before so proceeding.

The you that you know, then, is one selected moment by moment from all the possibilities open to it. Again you see, more clearly than ever, how you literally create your own reality. Your thoughts, beliefs and desires float up to the membranes of space and time, latching onto those possibilities they recognize as sharing a common intent, and then pull those events into physical life, the life that you know. Knowing this, the truth sets you free, free to ride your natural grace to a life of fulfillment and limitless potential for growth.

You understand that what you know so far about parallel selves is magnified on every level of your existence. You alone have many parallel selves accompanying you through your days like a pack of rowdy schoolmates, jockeying for physical expression. When you join with another in a relationship, any sort of relationship, your combined intent forms its own pack of such "relationships," allowing you freedom to travel infinite paths together.

Your town, city, state and country all have infinite possible variations, too, as the combined beliefs, thoughts and desires of all their citizens swell en masse to the invisible membrane, interlocking with those communal grids of intent that most closely resemble them, pulling into physical expression the mass events of your world.

And finally, there are parallel earths following infinite potential avenues of learning and growth. In your terms, they all exist in the same "space" at once. You share your planet, its physical space, with civilizations you cannot conceive of presently, so radically have they departed from the paths on which you have embarked. Just as you chose to follow a certain line of concentration or focus, other parallel earths have picked up the strands you did not choose to grasp.

There are parallel earths on which nuclear weapons were never created. There are parallel earths that have already been incinerated by nuclear fire. Unconsciously you are aware of all such paths and, we hope, you will adjust your own path accordingly.

At every level of existence, what you perceive as physical, whether it be rock, plant, animal or human, family, neighborhood, society or world, is but one of infinite possible variations being played out on levels hidden from you. These parallel identities swarm together, each holding a latent development or path; it is the force and power of your beliefs that determine which of these infinite paths will be materialized, individually and en masse.

Thus is ensured your free will. Thus are you empowered to create your own reality. Thus are you unable to avoid the consequences of your actions.

Much of this is accomplished in the dream state. In the dream state, freed from the narrow confines of the conscious mind, you have access to all parallel phenomena, whether of your own life or that of the planet. You are able to command a performance, to watch it played out and determine if it suits your purposes to have it physically materialized. If so, you send up a grid of intent to meet that parallel entity at the invisible membrane.

If it is contrary to your best development to experience such a physical event—like nuclear war—after reviewing the consequences of your choice, you might well find yourself suddenly infused with urgings or leanings in new directions, discarding old, limiting beliefs in favor of more life-affirming ones. What happens in this case is that, having played out the potential outcome if your course continued unchanged, you realize that such an outcome, although faithfully reflecting your beliefs, is so harsh that you draw back from it. And in order to prevent that parallel phenomenon from becoming physical, all you have to do is change your beliefs. If that parallel entity never meets a similarly contoured grid of intent from your physical side of the membrane, it can never be activated and pulled into your physical existence.

Sometimes this process is so overt, the break so sudden, that you have what is called illumination. A person may be proceeding along a path of wicked recklessness, callous disregard for the earth and its creatures, lusting only for personal gain and possessions. In the dream state, the likely outcome of such a path will become brilliantly apparent as the greater entity asks, do you really want this? For you shall have it in spades if you continue along this path. And I shall learn from your experience, although you may consider the lesson to carry too high a price! And thus, upon awaking, such a person may find him/herself infused with a new-found compassion as the old conscious constructs and motivations are literally wrenched from their moorings in the mind, to be replaced with those following such a person's natural grace, always latent but long ignored.

You feel such swellings on your planet at this time. You see what the mad pursuit of profit and possessions has brought you. You see the earth being laid bare, its bounty plundered beyond all need. You possess the power to annihilate your own species. You are choking with overpopulation.

We will explore all these topics in much greater detail later. For now, understand that there are parallel earths on which the outcomes of these paths, if unchanged, are brilliantly realized. And All That Is is asking you, the earth consciousness, is this really what you want? And the rise of consciousness, of grassroots movements opposing the blind follies of science and "progress," is the first swelling into mass consciousness of a determination not to bring into physical expression such wretched outcomes.

You have far to go—far to go before you can turn the tide of your beliefs and thoughts, as they pull into physical expression with faithful accuracy the grids of intent you create as a species. But the most intuitive among you are already feeling the first tracings of a new consciousness, which must become conscious and global for your planet to change its course. You see the manifestation of this new consciousness in the environmental movement, the holistic health movement and the crumbling of the dogmas of religion and science as traditionally practiced.

Our speaking to you, directly rather than through hunches or intuition, is a result of channels being opened up between your plane and ours, as holes are ripped through the artificial barriers that have long cut you off from the source of your being. There is no time to be delicate about it; the cries go up from your plane, both en masse and privately through our host, and we make direct contact. This is happening more and more, and the proliferation of those able to directly channel entities from our plane will blossom and multiply in the years ahead.

For you stand now at the dawn of a new age. You have the freedom to continue along the paths on which your world has long been running, and to see the results realized in horrifying detail. You also have the freedom to turn away from those beliefs and structures that lead to such devastation.

Which parallel earth, then, shall it be? The choice is yours.

CHAPTER SEVEN

Divine Grace

Now let us turn our attention to the area we have been hinting at all along but never addressed directly. All we have discussed to this point is background, prologue to what we now consider.

What is the source of your world? What is the source of all worlds? What is the point of all these parallel selves and earths? What is the meaning behind reincarnation? **Why are you here?**

We struggle to express ourselves in your terms, for with your root parameter of time you force us to speak in terms of beginnings when, in fact, there are no beginnings or endings, no time at all, on deepest terms. Still, given those constraints, let us proceed.

We have seen how All That Is created your physical universe, and all others, as part of Its unquenchable thirst for experience and exploration. The physical universe that couches your existence is a construct, one given the root parameters of space and time within which to operate. There are other physical universes besides your own, also given space and time as the basis of their existence, but employing and interpreting them in far different fashions.

And there are dimensions of activity, far too vast for you to catch more than a glimmer of, in which physical universe construction plays no part. There are realms beyond the physical, exploring dimensions of activity of which you cannot conceive.

To say that All That Is "created" all such avenues of exploration is once again to fall into the trap of time, implying a beginning at some point in "time." We will simply have to settle for understanding that at your level it may appear contradictory to claim that on deepest terms there is no time while also stating that All That Is "created" your world. Your conscious mind is not equipped to reconcile the seeming contradiction, so just leave it at the doorstep of your subconscious, where no such contradictions exist.

What is it that powers your universe, all universes, all avenues of experience and exploration? What is the motivating force, the fuel, the source of all energy?

Once again we have been casting about for a choice of words most likely to resonate within you their deeper meaning. We will call that source of all life, all universes, that motivating power which buoys you in every moment, Divine Grace. Now let us examine what we mean by this phrase.

The word "divine" we use not without some hesitation, as it carries with it the stamp of religion, encrusting it like barnacles, masking its natural sheen. Yet the word "divine," despite its marred reputation, carries still the force of a pure and unearthly source of your being, your world. In traditional religious terms it referred to the characteristics of your traditional God. Now, we avoid the word "God" in our discussions because it also is so barnacled with the distortions of religion as to sink to the bottom of the sea. Instead we use the term "All That Is," precisely because your conscious mind has no ingrained connotations of the phrase, no connective memories or associations that would saddle it with distortion.

You have a saying, God is love. Note: you do not say that God provides love or grants love or offers love. **God is love.** The two are indistinguishable; they are one and the same.

We say that **All That Is is divine.** It is not the source of divinity; It is divinity. By divinity, again, we refer to that supernatural source of power, energy and intent that forms your world and all worlds. This we call All That Is; this we call divine.

Now, "grace." The word most likely carries pleasant, uplifting connotations for you. When you say someone is gracious, you mean they are considerate, thoughtful, sensitive to others. When you say grace before a meal, you offer thanks to the divine source that provides it. In religious terms, although meanings differ, it is perceived as peace, love, a gentle spiritual warmth enveloping you.

When we put the two together to form **Divine Grace,** we speak of the **motivating power of your life and universe.** Divine means the source is beyond your physical universe; grace means that the divinity rides on a loving, buoyant intent that seeks always to carry you to your greatest fulfillment. Divine Grace, then, is the natural order of things. It is the blessed bed of love and intent of All That Is on which your existence rests.

All worlds ride on Divine Grace, then. So does every society, every social group, every individual. You live because All That Is wants you to experience physical life as a unique contribution to Its exploration and growth; and It does not cut you loose in a cold, dark universe but forever cushions your life with the eternal flow of Divine Grace.

Again, it is the nature of Divine Grace to allow you your freedom. Divine Grace will never impose its will on you; it has no will, other than the intent to carry you along the paths you choose, miraculously reflecting your thoughts in the physical reality you create.

On an individual basis, you may conceive of Divine Grace as a gleaming railroad track of the purest gold, sparkling in the sun, stretching infinitely toward the distant horizon. On this Divine Grace you ride, propelled by its desire to carry you to your greatest fulfillment.

Now, remember our parallel selves. Perceive them as tracks leading off the main line of Divine Grace, affording infinite excursions into all realms of physical expression. Some will provide a pleasant journey of new experience and lead directly back into the main track, enriching you and sending you on your way. Some tracks quit in dead ends, forcing you to stop, turn around and work your way back to the main track. And some end in brick walls or bottomless pits, leading you so far astray of the Divine Grace you have turned away from that your path's outcome must necessarily be sufficiently traumatic as to force you to realize the error of your choice and to urge a return to the Divine Grace you have betrayed.

As is true on an individual level, so also holds for a given society or world. Riding Divine Grace to realms of untold beauty and harmony is the easiest route to take; but if you insist on side excursions into dark forests and perilous swamps, you shall be free to follow such paths, the better to learn the power of your thoughts and beliefs in creating your reality.

All paths, however, lead back to Divine Grace.

Divine Grace is raucous, exuberant, vital, active and inquisitive. It charges headlong into physical expression with joy and abandon.

When you visit the mountains in the springtime, do you report that the flowers were timidly displaying a few muted colors? That they reluctantly offered soft pastels to your eyes? No! You who know the mountains in springtime describe the riot of color, the orgy of beauty, that greeted you. Thus does Divine Grace manifest itself in your world.

Divine Grace allows everything its own time and place. It does not force you to tread an imperiously constructed, narrow path; it begs you to create your own! It does not favor one expression of creation over any other, nor sacrifice one to another. It seeks not to impose its values on you but to set you free to learn, through your experience, that you are happiest when you live by its values. You ride unknowing on its silent and hidden thrust, bursting into physical life like a pack of playful children running, laughing and free, through a meadow.

Divine Grace is the source and sustenance of your life, your world, ever cushioning it in a loving framework of limitless bounty and freedom, liberating you to explore this wondrous creation, this rich and fertile world, bouncing you upon its loving intent, creating infinite opportunities for growth, expression and fulfillment.

To say that All That Is "created" Divine Grace is once again to fall into a hopeless linguistic trap. All That Is is Divine Grace, and vice versa. You ride forever on the loving intent, the Divine Grace, which is the source of all worlds, all universes, all dimensions of existence and activity.

Knowing this, understanding the intent of All That Is, through Divine Grace, to allow you your place and time, to set you free without hindrance or restriction, can you begin to see how that Divine Grace is translated into your physical world and human society?

Consider the world's oppressed peoples, of this time and all others. You observe their struggles, their toiling under the lash of those who use them as dumb beasts, and something wells up inside you, some furious resentment. Why? Because it is a violation of Divine Grace to force another into a position of subservience, to strip away the freedom that is Divine Grace's gift to you, forcing some to subjugate their freedom to the whims of another.

You hear of abused children, abused animals, and something cries out inside. Why? Because the young of any species, especially, are possessed of a natural sense of the Divine Grace that cushions them; they have yet to saddle it with the cynicism of their elders. It is their purity that evokes deep intuitive connections, suppressed but not forgotten, linking you and all creatures to the divine source of your being.

Your beliefs make war a necessity, yet still you gaze upon the images of death and dismemberment, and a profound revulsion wells up inside you. Why? Because despite your species' straying so far from the path of Divine Grace as to have almost forgotten it entirely, still the thought of snuffing out the lives of your fellows over—what?—territory? prestige? ego? money?—cuts through the suffocating layers of belief right to the quick of your being, to the Divine Grace that gasps, astonished at the atrocities of the creatures it created. Despite the layers upon layers of suffocating belief, despite all the efforts of science and religion to rob you of your divinity and natural grace, despite a world rushing headlong into oblivion from your mistakes, still you feel rousing within you the stirrings of indignation, of outrage, when confronted with such a profound violation of Divine Grace as is a war, an abused child or slavery.

Let us turn from the realm of the ideal to that of the practical. How is Divine Grace manifested in your daily life and world? How do you recognize its power?

You are at a party. Someone enters, someone everyone knows as The Life Of The Party. His entry will be greeted with cheers and smiles. People will cluster about him, eager to bask in his special glow.

Listen to and watch carefully Mr. Life Of The Party. What does he say? How does he act toward others?

First, he is humorous. If he does not have a ready store of jokes to spring, he has a quick wit ready to insert in the conversation where it is most needed, never cutting or insulting, often self-deprecating.

He does not complain about his physical problems. Indeed, most likely he has none; if he does suffer from a condition, he will use it again as a source of humor, putting the others at ease about it, minimizing its importance.

He will have a cache of stories about his latest exploits and adventures. Even if he works a routine job, still he manages to search out the new, the unexpected, the adventuresome, to pursue novel experiences, and he relishes relating his exploits to the others, who equally relish hearing of them.

He treats all others with respect and deference. He does not kowtow to the self-important nor condescend to the low in station. He treats all others as his equal, according them the respect he naturally expects from the world.

Now, what is operating here? How exactly is Mr. Life Of The Party manifesting Divine Grace simply by standing in a circle of friends, making small talk?

First, he is humorous. Why? Because humor, as we shall explore later, is the great liberator of energy, puncturing inflated and self-important values or beliefs, releasing their energy, creating an atmosphere about him of swirling, undammed energy, **exactly replicating the flow of Divine Grace** as it powers and supports your world.

He does not mention ailments, except in a humorous vein. Intuitively, he understands that he creates his own reality, and to burden others with a catalog of his physical symptoms is to confess possession of beliefs so detrimental to one's fulfillment that they manifest as illness in the body. He who rides Divine Grace through life is rarely ill; when he is, he intuitively understands that he drew the illness to himself and privately cures it himself.

Mr. Life Of The Party also has a new exploit or adventure to relate. Why? Because Divine Grace, that great thrusting, rambunctious power behind all creation, created you as one exploration of physical existence; riding that, he always seeks to enrich his own life, to whatever extent possible, by seeking out the unknown, the untested, the unexplored.

It would not occur to Mr. Life Of The Party that he is better than anyone else at the party—his hosts, the other guests, the bartender or maid. He sees through the superficial disguises and masks, cuts through to the heart and soul of everyone he meets, instinctively linking with the Divine Grace carried within the heart of all life, not seeing the outer trappings or guises.

And as the other partygoers flock to him, surrounding him, basking in his humor and warmth, they too do so out of unconscious recognition of the unfettered Divine Grace he expresses in every moment, like huddling around a campfire for warmth. He makes them laugh; he makes them feel worthy and important; he allows them their uniqueness while acknowledging his own.

Now let us expand our view from the human species alone to the broader picture. Every object, every form that life takes, is a physical expression of Divine Grace. As radically and profoundly varied are the forms of life on earth, they all share in common their source; they all ride its warm and loving support in every moment.

We will take an example from the experience of our host, with his permission.

As a boy he lived in a house given to embracing many manifestations of Divine Grace, from fish to rodents to dogs and cats. One such creature was his dog Captain, who shortly after arriving in the household selected our host as his master for life and never wavered from the choice.

Years later, one morning our host's mother returned to the house carrying the stiffened corpse of another dog, a smaller one, whose allegiance was to his sister. The dog had been hit by a car while running free at night.

He loved the little dog too, and our host, not one given to suppression of emotion, sat down on the sofa to cry and release his grief. To his astonishment, his sobbing set off a frantic reaction in his beloved Captain. The dog paced furiously, rubbing up against the boy, licking his face, desperate to succor. He matched the boy's sad whine with his own; together their voices carried the very sorrow of the ages.

Your evolutionists would have you believe that this dog, this mere dumb beast, would be incapable of any act other than those self-serving actions required for survival. Yet here his master was in no physical danger. He was sitting on a sofa in a house. Why, then, the frantic reaction to his master's grief?

We will dispose of the theory of evolution later, but you can see that its fundamental flaw is that it allows no place to Divine Grace. And it is this Divine Grace that came to the fore in this situation; as profoundly different as are a human boy and a dog, still they carry in common the great hidden source of both their beings, the source of life itself. Recognizing that Divine Grace in each other, they formed a connective bond of love, which at its base is simply that: a recognition of the Divine Grace in another.

And this connective bond exists on levels far deeper than even the enormous contrasts in form and consciousness that a boy and a dog can take. The underlying Divine Grace rose to the fore, as it often does in times of great emotion, and dog and boy suffered together, the dog's love compelling it to offer every act that its doghood would permit: wailing in synchrony with the boy, licking his face, resting his head on the boy's leg. All as a way of saying, I am here and I suffer with you, and the gulf between us be damned!

Now we have seen, in two examples, how Divine Grace can manifest itself in your world, in your daily life. We present these examples because too often discussions of the source of the world can remain on such a lofty level that you feel degraded just pondering them! Instead, you should feel revitalized as you feel the surges within, that Divine Grace struggling to force its way into consciousness, asking to be allowed to guide you toward your own best fulfillment.

CHAPTER EIGHT

Divine Grace in the Physical World

How does one recognize Divine Grace? How does one know its face? And how does one know when Divine Grace has been shunted aside, betrayed, in pursuit of some less worthy goal?

Again, Divine Grace is the source of your world, the great limitless fuel that powers your every moment, from the smallest atomic building block to your mass civilizations. Always, always, it seeks to bring into actuality those events that will be of greatest benefit to those involved.

Divine Grace manifests most clearly on your plane as **respect**. What is respect? Respect is when you allow all others the right to ride their own Divine Grace as they see fit, understanding that you each live in a cocoon of your own creation, a highly private yet publicly shared existence in which each individual, pursuing his/her own greatest fulfillment, automatically and unconsciously contributes to the advancement of the species and planet as a whole.

Respect, then, is when you allow all others of your species, and all others of all species, their private place, time and path. Respect allows no place to coercion, force or violence against another. Respect is an intuitive acknowledgment of the **uniqueness** of each individual, each species, each form physical matter can take, a deep understanding of the greater cooperation that underlies your world, as each species and individual contributes its unique perspective, its private experience, to the shared venture on which you have embarked.

Respect is how Divine Grace manifests itself in your world. When you respect another, you recognize and acknowledge the Divine Grace within the other, understanding that it is not necessary for him or her to follow your footsteps in order to reach greatest fulfillment.

Notice we do not use the word "love." It is not necessary that you run around flinging your arms about every other person and four-legged manifestation of Divine Grace you stumble upon. There will be those whose paths differ so markedly from yours, whose inner awareness of Divine Grace has been so blunted by fear, that you are unable to connect. You need not love such individuals. You must, however, **respect** their right to pursue their path as they see fit, regardless of how obvious the deleterious outcome is to you.

You need not love all you meet. Understanding that they share the same source as you, All That Is pouring Itself into the physical world through the fluid medium of Divine Grace, you grant them your respect.

The rule of thumb to follow, then, when considering a choice or decision, whether individually or en masse, is to ask: Does this course of action respect my integrity and that of all others who may be affected? Will this action be only of benefit to others, or do some stand to be harmed by it? Am I, or are we, acknowledging the Divine Grace manifest in every aspect of creation?

Now let us turn from the theoretical to the practical. Let us apply this principle to one area of your shared reality: the generation of electricity. You have various methods of creating the electricity your society requires. As we will see, they differ in their effect on the world. We will examine why.

Remember, first, that your thoughts and beliefs are grids of intent, floating up to the membrane between your world and its nonphysical source, linking with those "events" bouncing on their time cycles that most closely resemble the contours of your thoughts. With that reminder, let us examine how you generate electricity.

One method is hydroelectric power. You build a dam and, as the water rushes through your turbines, it releases energy, which is transformed by you into electricity. The water is then allowed to flow free, unharmed and unchanged. We do not wish to condone the wasteful and unnecessary building of dams, but given that caveat, let us examine what grid of intent you might be generating by creating electricity in such a fashion.

To some extent you do violate Divine Grace by building a dam in the first place, forcing a river to back up, drowning all life along its banks. If you respect all manifestations of life, you would know you have no right to do this. Still, this is a minor quibble as the violation is localized in one area, one river's banks. The loss to you, then, is the fertile soil lining the river's path and the company of the wildlife and plants that brought richness to your existence. This you lose when building a dam.

But the water itself is unaffected, unsullied by your using it to power the turbines. Thus the overall violation is a small one, with the minimal localized effects just described.

Another method of generating electricity is by burning coal. You extract the coal from the ground and, as it burns, you capture the released energy (in most basic terms, the sudden unraveling of the grids of intent holding the rock together). This released energy you convert into electricity.

Let us examine this process. In the first place, while coal extraction methods vary, some of them are profoundly destructive of the earth. Strip mining, for example, leaves hideous scars upon the earth, seeping acids and other harmful elements into your water supplies. Any time you vigorously destroy an element of the earth, you also commit a violation.

Now, burning coal to create electricity may not seem like such a grand violation. Again, all form, all matter, contains consciousness, and it exists for its own purpose, not for yours. When you build a small fire out of dead wood, you are hastening the decay of the wood into the basic building blocks of the earth and providing yourself with warmth; the violation there is negligible. When you dig deep into the earth, however, and yank out its very undergirding without regard for anything but your own needs, the violation is greater. And when you do so on a mass scale, over a long period of time, you guarantee that the violation, itself translating into a grid of intent, will manifest itself on your plane in deleterious ways.

Observe what occurs in the neighborhoods of your coal-burning plants, and in those who work within them. You are familiar with black lung disease. You know that those living around coal-burning plants suffer a variety of ailments, ostensibly linked to the continuous burning of coal. The very health and lives of a great many people seem to be affected.

In greatest terms, where there is no time, cause and effect cannot exist. It cannot be said that extracting coal causes black lung disease, or that burning coal causes any of the ailments affecting those living nearby.

Instead, to the extent that extracting and burning coal is a violation of the earth's Divine Grace, that disregard for the earth, that lack of respect, manifests as a grid of intent that rises to the membrane and then attracts to it whatever events exist on parallel earths in which you will find reflected in your daily lives the same disrespect you show the earth. Again, there is no thought of punishment here; it is simply Divine Grace's determination that you shall find your thoughts and beliefs reflected faithfully in your lives. When you disregard the earth and its Divine Grace, you will find that disrespect manifested in your own lives.

Thus, to the extent that extracting and burning coal is a violation of Divine Grace, you find yourselves suffering as a result. You contract black lung disease, respiratory ailments, cancer—not as punishment, but as a reflection of the thoughts and beliefs of those who work in the mines and earn their living at the plant. For when you disregard or ignore the Divine Grace in any of the earth's forms, you necessarily disregard it in yourself. And when you demonstrate disregard for yourself, that thought will automatically bring into your experience a "negative" result (like health problems) as a way of guiding you away from such attitudes.

Let us turn to a far more serious violation and observe its outcome.

Another method of generating electricity is through nuclear fission. You are all too familiar with the hazards of such a process, generating as it does poisons that will last hundreds of years; your most enduring legacy to the generations of the earth is one of constant danger from your explorations into avenues you should not explore.

Why does nuclear fission create such toxic products? Scientists would have their own answer, of course, full of equations and diagrams. But as science knows nothing of Divine Grace, it can also know nothing of the true reason for the enduring toxicity of nuclear fission's products.

What is nuclear fission, then? What does the process involve?

YOU SPLIT THE ATOM!

Remember how physical matter is formed. Remember that first hesitant step into physical creation that is the electron's birth, joining joyously with its brethren particles to form the building blocks of every expression of physical form you know.

And you, in your search for electricity, **rip asunder the very basis of physical matter!** Note that it is not just life you exhibit contempt for in this instance, but all physical matter, including what you perceive as inanimate objects.

You have no right to wrench apart that joyful dance which is the atom. And in doing so, you demonstrate such incalculable arrogance, such total and bottomless contempt for the world that sustains you, that you find faithfully reflected as the end-product of such contempt substances **that will destroy all matter they contact.** Release of the radioactive end-products of nuclear fission will devastate all forms of matter, living and inanimate, in the area affected.

Why? You are simply seeing faithfully reflected in your world that grid of intent, that unspeakable arrogance and contempt you exhibit by creating such a process. You demonstrate **utter contempt for physical life** and you find faithfully manifested the most lethal substance ever known to this planet—pure, distilled, 200-proof death.

Again, the endurance in time of any substance is determined by the grid of intent of which it is a physical reflection. When you demonstrate such profound disregard for the world that sustains you, you create a grid of intent of such power and compactness that its physical expression, radioactive material, will endure far longer than any of the other creations of man.

If you think we are speaking idly here, observe your recent history.

Remember that "events," being grids of intent, travel in cycles or waves, first approaching the membrane of physical expression and, if not meeting a similarly contoured grid of intent from your plane, bouncing away from the membrane, to return another "day." There is a progression in which a given event may find the first hesitant intent on your plane with which it can link; such an event will then approach your plane at an oblique angle, not finding full expression, leaving only a trace of itself in your awareness. If you ignore that trace and do not change your course, then the next time that event's cycle approaches your plane, it will find your grid of intent duly strengthened over time and will be able to manifest more clearly, with less static and distortion. This ensures your free will, you see, in that you may observe an event as it first makes a hesitant appearance on your plane, and if you find it not to your liking, determine to change your course. Once you do so, the grid of intent on your plane evaporates, and the event will bounce forever latent on its cycle, never linking with your plane to create a physically experienced event.

For the purposes of this discussion, know that a seven-year cycle is highly significant to human life. You have heard of the "seven-year itch" that affects many relationships; after seven years, they seem to come up for intense scrutiny and examination. Many relationships end at this point, others being strengthened for the examination. You know that the physical molecules and organs of your body are entirely replaced every seven years. That cycle of seven years is highly significant to the human species.

Now let us turn our attention, given this understanding, to the recent history of nuclear fission on your plane. It was not until several decades after the process was first created that a full-scale effort to harness nuclear fission as a means of generating domestic electricity supplies was implemented. The widespread installation of nuclear reactors about the country meant that the grid of intent of arrogance and contempt, which had previously been the exclusive domain of science, became dispersed among the general populace. People living in communities where nuclear reactors were being constructed had to face the conscious knowledge that this process was to be utilized to generate the electricity by which the community would be powered. Many felt uneasy stirrings within, unconscious cries from the source of their beings, unrecognized as such, that this profound violation of life itself would surely lead only to disaster.

There were many small incidents at the plants—accidents, leaks of radioactive gas, etc.—many of them hidden from the public by the government. But as the use of nuclear power became more widespread, and the voices opposing it unfocused and weak, the communal grid of intent that permitted its use inevitably rose to the membrane and, meeting an "event" of similar contour, pulled it into physical expression. This you experienced as the accident at Three Mile Island in Pennsylvania.* Close, very close, to a meltdown, though averted at the last minute. A release of some radioactive gas, but not enough to kill. A community up in arms at the appalling sloppiness of the operation.

This was the first hesitant expression in your physical reality of the "event" of nuclear fiasco. As the first such event, diving into your world at an oblique angle, it manifested in highly attenuated form, a little radioactive gas and a few billion dollars in clean-up bills.

Did you heed the warning? No.

So the "event" of nuclear fiasco continued to ride its cycle, its wave, along the significant seven-year human cycle. When it again approached your plane, it found the grid of intent allowing nuclear fission strengthened, the intervening years bringing more plants worldwide. Faithfully reflecting that strengthened grid of arrogance and contempt, the "event" again slid into your time continuum.

This was the explosion at Chernobyl, in Russia.† Observe what occurred there. The entire plant, or a large part of it, blew up. People died this time. Many were severely injured. A huge area around the plant was devastated. All of Europe was affected to some degree or another, in the food and water. The event found much clearer and undistorted expression on your plane.

Now that "event," nuclear fiasco, has again bounced back on its cycle. When it returns at the end of its next seven-year cycle, what grid of intent will it find waiting for it at the membrane? **You choose.**

Will it find that grid of arrogance and contempt so strengthened by the continued folly of your species that it finds its expression virtually unhindered? What will it be this time? Colorado? Western Europe? Central America? **You choose.**

Will you begin to see the connection between your continued arrogance and its inevitable result when your children and grandchildren mutate into hideous caricatures of human form? **You choose.**

Will that event return to the membrane, only to find that you have changed your ways, abandoned the thought of splintering the atom to power your television sets? Will it then bounce away, latent, unexpressed, leaving you safe? **You choose.**

Now, examine this from another angle. Remember that all possible worlds exist in the great nonphysical realms from which you select, by way of your beliefs and thoughts, those events you will bring into physical actuality. Every problem has a solution. Whenever you experience one facet of a situation or theme, understand that its **opposite** also must exist; it is by altering your **beliefs** that you can pull in the opposing facet of a situation.

---

*The accident at Three Mile Island occurred on March 28, 1979.
†The Chernobyl explosion occurred on April 26, 1986.

In this case, you now face hundreds of years of radioactive end-products seeping into your air, your oceans, your land. No container can hold them safely. Yet, understand that there exists, on a parallel earth, the solution to this problem, a means of eliminating the toxicity of such end-products. That solution exists now, in your terms, as all events do, and is **there for the taking**. And to bring it into your world, you need only **alter your beliefs**. You need only decide that you will turn away from any process that is based upon such utter contempt for physical matter, however convenient it may be for your life. When you do so, if you change your beliefs to embrace respect for physical life, the solution to the toxicity of radioactive materials will fall into place as surely and easily as did Three Mile Island and Chernobyl. **You choose.**

By examining one minor facet of your global reality, the generation of electricity, we are able to see how miraculously and perfectly you find your beliefs and thoughts manifested in your physical reality. A process that uses the power of a rushing river without altering the water has little effect. To strip coal from the earth and burn it is a greater violation, resulting in adverse health effects. And the most profound violation of which you are capable, splitting the atom, results in pure, unadulterated death.

This process exists in every facet of your lives, from the most private decision to the grand sweeping themes of your historical periods. In every case, you find manifested the physical expression of your beliefs and thoughts.

This returns us to our original discussion, that of Divine Grace. As you can now see, to the extent that you demonstrate your recognition of Divine Grace in all the earth, you will find yourself with a bountiful, healthy, joyful reality. To the extent that you deny Divine Grace in yourself, others or the physical world, you will find that contempt mirrored in your physical world.

You are not cast adrift in a neutral universe, ekeing out a lonely existence, divorced from your creator. Instead, you are in every moment buoyed and supported by Divine Grace as it rides the contours of your thoughts into physical expression; it is therefore far easier to create a positive reality than a negative one. All That Is far prefers that you experience a joyful reality, but if you insist on so denying the Divine Grace in yourself and others, then you indeed shall find that disrespect manifested in your world.

Your religions intuitively understand this when they speak of an eye for an eye, a tooth for a tooth. Karma is another creative construct expressing this idea on a reincarnational scale: what you do to others, you will surely experience yourself, if not in this life, then in another. This concept, that what you do to others you will necessarily experience yourself, is so intuitively obvious that even science has a version: every action has an equal and opposite reaction. In every field of human activity, then, this principle is understood.

We might turn briefly to a corollary issue, that of revenge.

In your society, when someone commits a violation against another, he or she will be brought to trial and, if found guilty, punished by a jail term or a fine.

The justice system, which all human societies share in one form or another, is a reflection of the deep and basic understanding that one must experience personally the results of one's actions toward others. Violate another's Divine Grace and yours shall be similarly violated, through loss of freedom or money.

Your justice system is a reflection of the deeper reality, not its actual manifestation. For the process by which one's thoughts and beliefs manifest in one's life occurs automatically and unconsciously. You do not sit around consciously creating grids of intent and floating them up to an invisible membrane; they do it for you! You need give it no thought. The process is automatic.

You see, now, that the notion of anyone "escaping justice" is impossible. It may well be that a criminal escapes the reach of the law until his physical death, but that is only one life of many! And once you commit a violation against another in the physical realm, remember that such an event retains a "polish," alerting the greater entity that it carries special weight and should therefore be explored from all possible angles and facets. So if a person murders another and escapes justice during one lifetime, the greater entity will most assuredly set up a situation where that event is experienced on the victim's part in another life. Again there is no idea of punishment here, simply the unquenchable desire of All That Is to experience every facet of physical life. Once one facet of an event is pulled into physical expression, so will be all others, if not in this life, then in another.

Any time you bring an event into physical expression, therefore, you are recharging, energizing, the grid of intent of which it is a reflection. You see now the danger of revenge. For one thing, it is not necessary. Revenge is a distorted expression of the intuitive understanding that what one does to others will necessarily be experienced against oneself. But, as this process is automatic, it is superfluous for you to step in and commit a second violation against the violator.

It is more than just superfluous. If, in a blind, vengeful rage against a murderer, you commit a second murder, you have energized the concept of murder, strengthened its force, such that it remains a more vital and active force on your plane. This is true not only on an individual level—if you murder a murderer, you will certainly experience the flip side of the event—but also on a mass level, as there are no closed systems, and the beliefs of a single individual will combine with those of similarly contoured beliefs in others, pulling into physical expression your mass reality.

There is a battle raging now on your plane between opponents and proponents of capital punishment. When you read of the heinous violations of which some are capable—unspeakably vicious mutilations and murders—you find welling up inside a profound revulsion, a determination that the violator shall indeed meet an equal fate. Understand that what you feel in such a case is your intuitive understanding that such a murderer **will** experience a similar fate, and with no help from you! The process is automatic. But your divorce from the Divine Grace that supports your world, your society's refusal to consider the reincarnational checks and balances that smooth things out over time, leads you to misinterpret your instinctive understanding, to force it into the one life of which you allow conscious awareness, this one, and to insist that the process of karma work itself out now, in this life.

When someone strays so far from his native Divine Grace as to commit murder, you are well justified in incarcerating him, perhaps for life. You need do no more. Such a person's greater entity will do the rest! And by insisting on putting the individual to death, shortening this one physical life, you do nothing but recharge the perversion of Divine Grace that led to the murder in the first place. Thus does capital punishment not deter murderers; it encourages them, on levels hidden from your conscious awareness. A society that condones capital punishment is one that tells its citizens it is acceptable to murder under some circumstances; and those circumstances are not absolutes but eminently mutable, depending on the mores of a particular time. Thus do you grant permission to those twisted souls who are so deadened to their innate Divine Grace that they take the lives of others. Society approves of such conduct by maintaining a system of arbitrary and capricious murder.

Christianity teaches you to turn the other cheek. You see now that this is not weakness but **strength**, a determination not to capitulate to the perversions of others, to further energize the poisonous grids of intent that lead some to violate others. You will not participate on their level. You will turn away, refuse to strengthen the beliefs that allow such violations to occur in the first place. Revenge is weakness, a surrender to ignorance, ignorance of the workings of Divine Grace.

We have examined the ways in which Divine Grace manifests in your world and the results of violating it, both on a personal and a global scale.

Turning to you, an individual, how does Divine Grace make itself known to you in your everyday life? Understanding that it **always** urges you on in the path of your greatest fulfillment, how can you discern its quiet signals and hints?

CHAPTER NINE

Impulses

Impulses are the means Divine Grace employs to contact you on a daily, conscious basis. Where do impulses come from?

Remember that the "you" you know is but one possible manifestation of all the infinite yous your greater entity set into motion. Your beliefs and thoughts energize or charge those probable yous most similar to them, pulling into physical expression the events of your life.

These probable yous are no shy wallflowers, hiding in the shadows, hoping for your call but making no demand on your attention. Instead, they are like a pack of unruly children, slamming their fists on the door of your conscious mind, demanding entrance. These insistent voices you know as impulses.

We must remind you of several items already covered. First, the basis for your space and time illusion is **energy**, and energy is constant motion, never static. Second, all events exist at "once," and you pull into expression those matching your beliefs. Third, events must unravel over "time," their duration determined by the power behind the grid of intent of which they are a reflection.

Now, impulses have a bad name on your plane. To call someone impulsive is to deride him, accuse him of surrendering to a spur-of-the-moment existence, incapable of charting a clear course and following it with single-minded determination.

Religion also has few kind words to say about impulses. In the past you believed any "bad" thoughts or ideas in your head came straight from the depths of Hell. As religion lost its influence, psychology stepped in: Freud invented the "id," that repository of salivating repressed demons, forever taunting you to give them voice, against which your superego struggles mightily to maintain your civility.

No wonder impulses have such a bad name in your time. You have been taught that they are untrustworthy urgings from Hell or the id, to be ignored, repressed, stomped out of consciousness lest you accede to them and commit unspeakable atrocities.

Now, let us examine the reality.

You have swirling about you now an infinite number of possible yous, all of whom you can choose to pull into physical expression. They present themselves to you in the form of impulses.

You would not choose a spouse without first submitting the prospective sweetheart to a thorough examination, would you? If you rejected all such suitors, you might well lose the one best suited to your temperament.

The same holds true for impulses. We do not mean to suggest that you instantaneously surrender to every thought that pops into your head but that you consider them, examine them, with a critical eye toward determining whether following them would lead you on a path to fulfillment.

The danger in repressing impulses, in refusing to examine them, is that you therefore charge the intent behind them. And, of course, whenever you charge an idea, you strengthen the grid of intent behind it, guaranteeing its continued existence and also that a greater period of "time" will be required for you to dissipate that event.

If we may turn your religions on their head for a moment, we submit that it is a far more **spiritual** act to allow full conscious expression to impulses than to deny them. Our definition of a spiritual act would be one that furthers the intent of one's Divine Grace. In your terms, Divine Grace rides the intent of your greater entity into countless probable yous, which then clamor for your conscious mind's attention, asking for physical expression. The conscious mind, then, properly functioning, sifts and sorts all such choices, granting physical manifestation to those paths it deems most healthy.

Again, we are not suggesting you grant physical expression to every impulse that enters your head, but that you allow them the **respect** to plead their case before your conscious mind. Thus do you acknowledge your own Divine Grace; thus do you allow it to ride freely and undammed through your days.

Let us look at an example. You may feel an impulse to murder your boss, rev up the chain saw and reduce him to ground round.

If you think to yourself, "Oh, what a terrible thought!" and shove it from consciousness, you have done nothing to dissipate the charge behind such a thought, and it will surely reappear, strengthened and more insistent.

If, on the other hand, you allow that thought to play itself out in your mind, in full, gory detail, you allow the grid of intent behind it to dissipate without ever being physically expressed. What you are doing, quite literally, is allowing a parallel self to experience the event; if you allow it to do so fully and completely, the intent behind the impulse will be unraveled, liberated, free to move on.

For, in allowing that event to play out in your mind, allowing a parallel self to put on a performance, and observing the outcome, you may well come to the realization that it would not be in your best interest to bring such an event into physical expression. You understand that murder is a profound violation. You understand that your own freedom will be taken away for the rest of your life, or most of it. You therefore choose not to pull such an event into physical expression; but you do so consciously, having played the event out, and then it is gone.

You have heard stories of meek and mild individuals, men usually, taught as they are to suppress all emotion, who one fine day pull a gun and slaughter their families, their neighbors or a band of strangers. And those who knew such men are shocked, for, after all, he was such a good person! Such a model of decorum!

What occurs in such situations is that the impulses that can spring up in response to life's daily petty insults are suppressed, never granted conscious awareness. "Good little boys" don't entertain thoughts of dismembering their families. And because those impulses are denied, they are therefore energized, given greater strength. And each time the strengthened impulse presents itself, it is again denied, thus multiplying the charge behind the impulse.

Ultimately, something has to give. There is literally a psychic explosion in which that dammed energy is suddenly released in an uncontrollable rage, beyond all reason, and friends and family are slaughtered physically because the murderer could never even allow himself the thought of anger toward them.

Instead, by playing out such an event in your mind, you release it and ensure that it need never be experienced physically. And if not physically experienced, the greater entity will see it only vaguely, as background to the meaning of your life, not a major theme.

The process, then, is this: Possible or probable yous present themselves to your conscious mind as impulses. Your conscious mind plays out the event carried on an impulse, exploring its ramifications and results. Then it decides whether bringing that event into physical life would help or hinder your fulfillment. If it would help, that event is brought into physical expression. If it would hinder you, it is simply released, having been acknowledged and played out.

This is how your Divine Grace manifests itself to you in every moment of your lives. This is how your free will is ensured.

Those who view themselves as infinitesimally tiny portions of God's creation, who fear themselves cast adrift in an infinite and often unfriendly universe, can begin to feel cut off from the source of their being. If they can allow the notion of Divine Grace at all, they see it as somehow "out there," a province of divine and sublime beauty and harmony cruelly hidden from human experience.

Understand, now, that **in every moment** of your life, Divine Grace is riding into your conscious mind by way of your impulses. In the infinite swirl of possibilities from which you can choose, some paths will lead to fulfillment, others to harm. Know that there are no "bad" thoughts or impulses, only "bad" actions. You can safely and with impunity allow full expression to any idea, thought or impulse; carry them to any extreme in the security of your mind, and you are guilty of nothing. Far from guilty—you are blessed for having granted recognition to Divine Grace as it seeks always to guide you along the path of your greatest fulfillment.

Impulses, then, are the constant telegrams from the depths of your very being, your Divine Grace, asking for respect and consideration. Grant them that; and those whose outcome you perceive as beneficial, grant them physical life.

Such is Divine Grace made manifest in your daily life.

CHAPTER TEN

Events Revisited

Let us return briefly to the topic of "events" and how they manifest in your reality. Remember that the grid of intent behind an event, its size and compactness, determines how long such an event will play itself out over a series of "moment points." The stronger the intent, the greater the importance you impart to it, the longer it will take for that grid of intent to play itself out over time.

A grid of intent does not simply unravel, insert itself into your time continuum at a steady and unvarying rate and intensity, and then drift out of your awareness. Instead, what can happen is that as an event approaches the end of its expression in "time," it can send off a highly charged "spark" that manifests as a concentrated expression of that event. It is like that event's last, dying gasp, rousing itself from its deathbed to make one last solemn pronouncement before succumbing. A fish out of water does not resign itself to its fate and lie still, awaiting the inevitable, but flips and flops furiously against the prospect of death. So it is with events in many cases. They trail off, then send off a final "burst" of themselves as a way of ensuring you are consciously aware of them, and of their passing.

Much of this occurs hidden from your conscious awareness, despite the final spark a given event will throw off. But you know the satisfaction of finishing a book, watching a film come to a successful conclusion or hearing the final thundering chords of a symphony. At the end of such events, you pause for a moment and let their meaning sink in fully before turning your attention to the next task at hand. That pause, that moment of reflection, is your awareness of a given event's final spark, its imprinting itself in your memory and awareness before disappearing from your life.

On a larger scale, such is also true of the great creative constructs you know as the world's religions, political philosophies, scientific advancements, etc. You will often find, as an idea or philosophy plays itself out, that some people will be left tenaciously holding onto the beliefs intrinsic to a philosophy, vigorously and sometimes violently opposing its natural demise. Such people do so out of fear, which we will explore later, but they also serve to bring to the greater society's attention a given idea or construct, so it can be finally and forever dismissed.

An example in your society now would be racism. After all the upheavals of the Sixties, the legally codified prohibitions against racism's expression in the Seventies, you find in the Eighties an ugly upsurge of racist incidents. Know that these represent racism's dying gasp, its deathbed cry, before being dismissed from your awareness; it is a way of ensuring that racism is brought once again to your eyes for review and utterly repudiated by every decent member of your society. Racism is a profound violation of Divine Grace, a refuge for twisted souls so blunted to their own Divine Grace that they can feel important only when clinging to their most superficial characteristic—skin color—and ignoring the enormous similarities among all of your species. And as such a concept plays itself out, it throws off one final spark, one last series of white-robed atrocities, before being dismissed from your consciousness, except as a measure of how far you have come.

Why is it that some concepts and philosophies play themselves out, only to disappear, while others remain? Why, for instance, has Christianity lasted almost two thousand years, while thousands of religious cults spring up almost daily, to be washed away in the first rain?

Again, an idea or belief's endurance in time is determined by the grid of intent that stands hidden behind it. The more powerful the idea, the greater the charge behind it, the longer it will last in "time."

More is involved, however, as we expand our earlier simplified model. For a grid of intent will be recharged, re-energized to the extent that it supports Divine Grace.

Any idea or philosophy that recognizes, cherishes and upholds Divine Grace will find itself constantly refreshed as it finds expression in physical life. For just as you constantly seek out sources of pleasure and satisfaction, returning to them again and again, so too do you energize or recharge those ideas and thoughts that work to ease the path of Divine Grace in your life. Any idea or philosophy inimical to your best fulfillment will find itself played out without any recharge from your plane and will thus disappear from your awareness.

Let us look at a few examples.

Look at maternal love. There is an instinctive bond between a mother and the child she has carried, a tie of inexhaustible love, protection, warmth, food, concern and security. Now, is such a bond of benefit to the child? It is not only of benefit—it is necessary for the child's very survival. The infant is utterly helpless, dependent, and its mother, recognizing the Divine Grace within the child, ceaselessly and thanklessly assumes burdens and disruptions for the child's sake that she would never offer anyone else—even her husband!

Thus, maternal love is necessary for the very survival of the child; it also provides the child with a source of security, a comfort that the world is a safe place and can be trusted. You all know what happens to children of unloving mothers, those incapable of putting their own needs after those of the child. Maternal love, then, in its true form, is one that recognizes the child's Divine Grace and will bear any burden to protect and support it.

Thus, every time a mother cuddles her child, the concept of "maternal love" is strengthened. The child, too, feeling itself warm and safe, finding its Divine Grace buoyed, sends back to the greater entity the message that this "maternal love" business is highly beneficial to the species. Although you each live private lives, there are no closed systems, and a world full of mothers and children sending the message that they find maternal love to be a handmaiden of Divine Grace will surely re-energize, recharge, the idea such that every new mother, tapping into the experience of motherhood for the first time, will find welling up inside her an inexpressible love for her child, the gift of all mothers who have gone before her. Maternal love, then, is a creative construct that finds itself replenished over time because it recognizes and respects the Divine Grace in all it touches.

To return briefly to racism, then. What is racism's relation to Divine Grace? They are antagonists. Divine Grace recognizes the intrinsic worth of every form of consciousness, human or otherwise. Racism denies that intrinsic divinity to certain members or classes of a society. As such, it is antithetical to Divine Grace's work in your world. And however vicious its manifestation, know that over "time," a construct or idea that does not aid Divine Grace will fizzle out. It must, for it will not be replenished by the happy cries of delight of those who find it deepens and enriches their lives. No racist is a truly happy person; only the deeply insecure would seek to bolster his own self-image by projecting his own feelings of worthlessness onto others—another class, another race.

In broader terms, a greater entity reviews the life of a racist and finds that using racism as a means of boosting self-worth does not work. It does not lead to happiness. And having duly filed away such information, the entity will not employ racism again in such a capacity, although it may well set up a life where one of its offshoots experiences the brunt of racism, as a way of bringing balance to the entity's experience of the issue.

The world's great religions are magnificent creative constructs, ripe with myth and truth and yearnings. And as they play themselves out over time, they will either reveal themselves to uphold Divine Grace, in which case they will endure longer in "time," or they will be dismissed by a populace that finds they cannot lead to fulfillment. You are in an age when your great religions are in a crisis, losing members, losing priests and ministers, wondering if they can hold on into the next century.

Divine Grace seeks always to expand your field of experience, to embrace as much of the earth's bounty of adventure as it can squeeze into a lifetime.

Religions that prohibit your enjoyment of earthly life, that deprive you of dance and music and laughter, that restrict the food and drink you may enjoy, that condemn sensual sharing with others, that prescribe the cut of your hair and clothes and political affiliations—

Religions that posit an endless reincarnational cycle to which you are forever bound by your past sins, helpless to escape—

Religions that promise a nirvana, in which your unique selfhood is extinguished, snuffed out as the final step of your spiritual journey—

Religions that teach that it is ever morally justifiable to conduct warfare against others—

—all such are religions alienated from the Divine Grace that gave them birth in bursts of fire, truth and power.

You see that you approach an age when the world's great institutional religions, whatever their benefits and positive contributions over the millennia, will draw to a close; in doing so, they may well shoot off "sparks" of belief, and those too fearful to release the worn-out beliefs can be expected to put up quite a fuss, giving voice to the dying gasp of these magnificent constructs as they ease themselves out of your world.

CHAPTER ELEVEN

Fear

We have been discussing Divine Grace and the manner in which it rides into your daily life by means of impulses.

Again we emphasize that we do not advocate permitting physical expression to every impulse that presents itself for inspection, but merely that you acknowledge them. Few on your plane currently do so.

What stops them? What dams up that easy, natural flow of Divine Grace into your existence? What is therefore responsible for all the misery, confusion and anguish on your plane at present?

You have but one enemy, an ingenious one who cloaks itself in an infinite variety of disguises and subterfuges, the better to avoid detection and wreak its havoc. That enemy?

Fear.

The great conflict of your age is fear versus understanding. You are at a unique juncture in human history in which all of your formerly strong and proud institutions, from religion to science to politics, are fraying at the seams, revealing themselves morally bankrupt. And what are you left with? What does this signify?

Remember that any idea aiding Divine Grace will be strengthened and replenished over time. Any idea antithetical to Divine Grace will play itself out, to be dismissed from your awareness. It now seems that such is the case with your great institutions. What, then, are those institutions based on, that they should be unraveling before your eyes, disintegrating as you realize they do not aid or comfort you?

The answer is fear. We are not suggesting that such institutions were originally based on fear but that they have become so entangled in fear that they have lost all sight of their initial intent; and those who cling tenaciously to their precepts do so out of fear of losing the security such institutions provide, even while they cheapen the lives of those who support them.

Let us take a good, hard look at fear. How can you recognize it in your society?

First, remember that you assumed human form in order to learn to manipulate physical reality through your conscious, reasoning mind. This reasoning mind is your unique gift among all the creatures of creation. When finely tuned and clear of distractions, it allows you to chart an undistorted course toward your best fulfillment. It can be blunted, however, when crippled by fears that sap it of its logic and reason. Fear, being irrational, is the enemy of your conscious, rational, reasoning mind. It can only serve to thwart your attempts at living a life of Divine Grace.

Fear is no open enemy, swaggering about the streets loudly proclaiɾ presence. For it knows all too well that one piercing glance from a reasoninₒ ......ᴵ◌ can reduce it to rubble.

One key characteristic of fear is its ingenious ability to seek legitimacy by latching onto what appear to be rational ideas, thus cloaking its true, bare essence. By hiding itself behind a seemingly rational idea, fear is able to play itself out without ever being submitted to logical analysis.

As we shall see, fear is a chameleon, ever changing its color to disguise itself or, like the demons in your fairy tales, assuming human or animal form as the situation requires, the better to work their evil. Know, then, that you will rarely meet fear face to face. It is too clever to be caught in the open, where one rational mind could render it impotent.

How, then, can you distinguish between a legitimate idea or philosophy and one based on fear? Fear provides two giveaway clues for the discerning mind to detect.

First, it will cause its host to latch onto what appear to be contradictory beliefs. A logically considered philosophy is one that can be reasonably applied to every situation and found to be consistent. A philosophy based on fear, however, latches onto a host of different ideas, some of them opposing, in its desperate attempt to camouflage its true reality. When you speak with someone whose beliefs seem to cancel each other out in a contradictory shambles, know that you are speaking not to reason but to fear.

The second clue fear provides is that if a philosophy based upon it is allowed full expression and played out, it will invariably bring about precisely the opposite result of that which it claims to promote. Why? Because, as we have seen, an impulse that is denied out of fear is energized by the denial, the grid of intent behind it empowered to a much greater degree than the superficially desired goal. Thus, with all the probable yous swirling about, when it comes time for an "event" to slip into your time continuum, the probable you who experiences the "negative" version of that event will find a far stronger grid of intent awaiting it at the membrane than that which lives the "positive" version of an event. Thus, inevitably, a policy based on fear will result in the precise opposite of what it claims to desire.

Fear is a crafty adversary indeed, as you can see, but one that is unable to cloak itself forever behind a veil of seemingly rational ideas. Played out, it will always reveal itself.

Let us look at some examples in your society.

You have among you now a fervent group calling themselves pro-lifers, who campaign tirelessly against abortion. They claim that their revulsion against abortion is based upon their belief in the sanctity of life, which must be protected above all else. Seeing the fetus as helpless and unable to speak or act for itself, they therefore take it upon themselves to defend the fetuses of the world from violation and destruction.

Let us examine such pro-lifers. First of all, how many of them have within their families the products of unwanted pregnancies? How many have adopted racially undesirable infants? If the compassion they evidence for the fetus is genuine, it should follow through to concern for the entire life span of those fetuses in question. Curiously, this seems not to be the case.

Secondly, you are now living on a planet in which overpopulation threatens to suffocate you and every other species. How do the self-appointed pro-lifers justify bringing into existence unwanted children when the world cannot sustain those already here? We hear silence in answer.

Now we come to the clincher. Many pro-lifers, being of a conservative nature, are also proponents of capital punishment. Now, this is curious indeed. Is life sacred or is it not? If it is, as they claim, then it is never morally justified to snuff it out, even against one who has perpetrated such violations against others. If society grants itself the right to destroy such individuals, then it acknowledges that life is not sacred at all but eminently disposable once it becomes a threat or bother to others.

While many who oppose abortion speak out from a spiritual base of reverence for all forms of life, there are pro-lifers who hold what appear to be both pro- and anti-life positions. On deepest levels, there is no contradiction—because the motive power behind their rallying cries is not one based on reason, but on fear. What do they fear?

They fear for their own worth and security. Their religions have convinced them that they are sinful creatures existing at the whim of a capricious and vengeful God, Who can "take them" into Heaven at any moment or cast them into eternal hellfire if He so chooses. Their science teaches them they are but a mere agglomeration of chemicals slapped together, ekeing out meaningless lives in an unfriendly universe. These philosophies hold sway in almost all of your society, to some degree, but in some they can provoke a terror that one's life is without meaning, apt to be snatched away at a moment's notice by an arbitrary God or snuffed out into a decomposing heap of chemicals.

This fear of unworthiness and insecurity is then projected outward, into the world. Whom does it find is the most helpless of all creatures on earth, reflecting their own helplessness? The fetus, existing at the whim of the mother, subjected to swift and cold termination by the abortionist.

This fear also explains the puzzling advocacy of capital punishment. Fearing for their own worth and security, they seek to bolster what little security they have left by eliminating from society those whom they see as endangering their lives and security. Snuff them out! Fear is desperate, and if only all those who threaten one's security could be eliminated, the world just might become the secure place they inwardly feel it is not.

Looking beneath the surface contradictions, then, subjecting our subjects to reason and logic, we find that the unifying concept behind their beliefs is fear. We do not mean to imply that such is always the case among pro-lifers; certainly many deeply and profoundly believe that all life is sacred and that any society that permits its unborn to be flushed out of existence due to their mere inconvenience is one that cheapens all life in the process. Our point here is that a large segment of the pro-lifers are masking their fear behind the legitimacy of that genuine indignation, revealing themselves by their advocacy of anti-life positions like capital punishment.

Those who calmly explain their opposition to abortion when asked, couched in a logically cohesive framework, hold their beliefs out of genuine moral concern. Those taking to the streets, shrilly claiming to agitate for the rights of the unborn while ignoring the effects of overpopulation on the born and advocating societal murder, are shrieking with fright, not reason.

Before we proceed with further examples, let us examine one more aspect of fear's expression.

By now you should intuitively understand that the end can never justify the means, no matter how legitimate the cause; a second violation, perpetrated in response to an initial denial of Divine Grace, serves only to strengthen the thought or belief that led to the first violation. In deepest terms there is no time; thus when you respond to a violation with a second violation, you solve nothing. Instead you merely energize the concept that led to the initial violation.

Let us suppose you are at bat in a championship softball game, with two outs and the bases loaded. The pitcher sends strike three whizzing past you into the catcher's mitt. When the umpire yells, "You're out!" and the game seems lost, you, determined that your team shall clinch the pennant, pull a gun, aim it at the umpire and demand one more pitch.

Most likely you will have it. And let us suppose you nail that fourth pitch right over the outfield wall, round the bases, grab the trophy, hug your team-mates and waltz off, the supposed "victor" of the game.

What have you done? You have "won" not by playing according to the established rules of the game but by violating them with force, the threat of death. And your "victory," as manifested in the trophy you cart off, is an empty one indeed, born as it is of the illegitimacy of defying the rules of the game.

This ties in with our discussion of fear. One further characteristic of fear is that it will always seek to justify the use of any means to obtain the desired end. If the rules of the game do not suit it, it does not seek to change them but to violate them, in its determination to mask itself and to win final victory over the imagined threat. Such a victory, as we have seen, is always hollow and empty, resulting ultimately in the precise opposite of the proclaimed goal.

Knowing that fear will justify the use of any means to achieve its end, let us proceed to examine fear in your society with further examples.

We are exquisitely sensitive to the privacy of the individuals on your plane. We keep our discussions general, not pointing cosmic fingers at specific individuals—for we understand that all of you are on the same path, toward Divine Grace, however perverted that initial good intent may be by fear.

In this case we shall make an exception to include in our discussion a man who has chosen to be a public figure and is therefore, perhaps, fair game. We shall examine the philosophy of the man who is currently your president. We choose to examine this man and his administration because they provide such a crystal-clear example of the workings of fear and how it reveals itself in the end.

What were the elements of this man's platform that he presented to the electorate? First, he promised security. Proclaiming Russia an "evil empire," he swore to protect your society from its evil influence. He saw Russia making insidious inroads all over the globe and promised to stamp out all such excursions. Thus, he pledged to make the world a safer place. Has he?

We have seen that strength is not manifested in weaponry but in reason. The man who has no fear for his safety doesn't bother carrying a gun; the timid and fearful soul who feels powerless packs the most lethal weapon he can find, imagining it will save him where his reason has failed.

On a global level, then, under this president your country has amassed the most extraordinary collection of weaponry ever assembled in the history of mankind. And now this president has advocated extending such weaponry into outer space, fantasizing about some floating shield that would render incoming missiles harmless while providing lethal counterattacks.*

No rational person believes this is possible. Yet billions of dollars have been sunk into this project, the very best minds science can offer have signed up, and Congress has compliantly funded the project while sending up an occasional whimper of protest.

How can such a project possibly lead to safety? A weapon cannot be used unless it exists; and once a weapon exists, happy trigger fingers are going to want to try it out; failing that, human error or mechanical failure can lead to "accidental" displays of the lethal power.

The outer space fantasy is but one part of this man's weaponry agenda. In all areas he has bolstered the armed forces with gadgets and toys far beyond any rational need.

And is the world safer? Of course not. Because any nation philosophically opposed to yours must watch with concern at your military build-up, wondering if there must not be some secret agenda, and such nations must inevitably play catch-up, bolstering their own forces. Thus does your clamoring for safety ensure the continued and mindless expansion of your ability to destroy yourselves.

The irrationality of this can be seen in your current involvement in Central America. There, you find to your horror what you perceive as a Russian satellite, a beachhead of communism threatening your stability, a mere two days' drive from the Texan border! It is like an elephant quaking at the approach of an ant.

Take your fears to their logical extreme. Let us presume this nation you so fear decided to attack the United States. Might the Mexicans perhaps not notice the caravan of tanks rolling their way through Mexico City on to the border? Might not your satellites detect such movement? We do not mean to ridicule those who

---

*In 1983, President Reagan proposed development of the Strategic Defense Initiative commonly known as 'Star Wars,' which theoretically would destroy incoming enemy warheads during a nuclear attack.

fear communist presence in Central America but to point out how irrational the fear is. You may not like their presence there, but they cannot possibly do you any harm.

As your military budget has increased each year, a few voices have been raised in protest, inquiring as to the meaning and purpose when, after all, yours is a nation officially at peace with the world.

Realizing this, fear once again cloaks itself behind the banner of "strength" and finds to its dismay that the world is not interested in providing venues for you to demonstrate your military prowess, to justify the continued military expansion. Fear, clutching onto weaponry for security, then goes out and manufactures incidents for your country's military involvement. You have been the perpetrator of several ugly military excursions that had no basis as far as the country's security was concerned. It was fear, pure and unvarnished, riding the bullets and missiles in a display calculated to make the continued build-up seem necessary.

Your president claimed he would make your country walk tall again. Yet you are not walking tall but crawling belly down in slime, when you betray your country's ideals with bullying displays of firepower.

And the rest of the world, allies and enemies alike, is aghast at the abandonment of the principles that made your country great, those of reason and fair play. Your stature in the world, far from being enhanced by fear's miserable little military excursions, is diminished.

Another promise of this president was to "get government off the backs of the people." Curiously, his administration seems more intent than any other in digging government's talons deeper into the backs of the people, particularly those whose ideas it disagrees with. Again, when surface contradictions appear, you know fear is at work.

The threat of attack is perceived as coming not only from the world outside your borders but from inside as well. Dissidents, those who dare to submit the administration's philosophy and practices to logical analysis, are to be silenced. Your great Constitution forbids the more blatantly obvious forms of repression, but there are others: classifying government documents far beyond national security needs, preventing former government officials from writing about or discussing the inner workings of government, and using the tax collectors to harass those whose views are opposed by the administration. The tools may be more subtle than in an overt dictatorship, but the desire is the same: to stifle dissent. This from the administration promising to get the government off your backs.

What lies behind these contradictions—the "walking tall" president leaving your world reputation in a shambles, the "off your backs" administration stifling free speech?

Fear of attack from within and without.

Underlying this president's policies, and those advisers he draws to him, is a profound distrust of the world, one that sees it as a hostile and dangerous place, populated with peoples and nations hell-bent on destroying your lives and freedom. The attack is from without—Russia and Central America, primarily—and within (internal dissidents).

Any philosophy an individual holds will be faithfully reflected both in his/her interpretation of world and society events and also internally, in one's body. Your body is your most miraculous and personal creation, and it faithfully reflects those beliefs you hold about it and, further, about the world at large.

Let us further examine our president. What clues are there in his health and bodily experiences about his world view?

We find a continuous series of little tumors cropping up—a steady stream of attacks from within, manifesting as cancers in various parts of the body.

This president also experienced an attempt on his life, an attack from without on his very existence. It was not in his interest to leave physical life at that point, so the attack left him grazed but not deeply wounded. And while we in no way excuse the actions of his assailant, the fact remains that the president creates his own reality just as you all do, and to face a hail of bullets is a faithful representation of one's fear of attack from without.

Tumors and an assassination attempt. An "evil empire" and internal dissidents. They all reflect the same root fear: attack from within and without.

If you think we hold your president up to ridicule, you are mistaken. The beauty of your democratic system is that it so faithfully reflects that you **create your own reality** by consciously choosing your leaders. This president did not storm the palace gates in a bloody coup. He presented his policies to the populace fairly and honestly, and met with such agreement that he was elected, then resoundingly re-elected.

And it is no accident that this president rose not from the ranks of politics, academia, industry or science, but from Hollywood. For he is **literally playing the part of fear** for you and for the world, the better for you to examine it in all its manifestations, to watch it unravel before your eyes and determine if you find it leading to a happy, healthy, sane society.

In the final days of his presidency, you are finding his administration unraveling indeed, undone by its use of any means to justify its ends, fear cloaking itself in self-righteous bleatings about national security. The president who swore never to negotiate with terrorists ultimately paid them to release hostages; the result was further abductions as terrorists worldwide found fresh encouragement in the use of kidnaping to achieve their ends.

You have seen, then, a stunningly brilliant performance from this actor president, in which he has played the part of fear to perfection. And you now must examine the results with your conscious, logical, rational minds. Has he kept his promises? Is the world safer? Do you stand taller? Is the government off your backs?

You see that fear is a crafty and creative adversary, but one whose true nature will always be revealed upon critical, rational examination. For fear is a creation of your conscious minds, a creative tool with which you explore physical reality. Yours is the age when fear must come up for final scrutiny, either to be embraced and lead to world collapse in all reaches of life, or to be repudiated in favor of a world based on reason and logic, the very essence of the conscious mind which is your unique possession in all of creation.

Again, **you choose.**

Now we have completed the introductory material in this work. You understand how you create your own reality through your beliefs and thoughts, finding them manifested through the fiction of your physical senses.

You understand that the universe is powered by Divine Grace, which seeks always to lead you to your greatest fulfillment, while always allowing you the freedom to choose other less beneficial paths as a way of creatively exploring the results, noting them and altering your beliefs accordingly.

And you have come to understand that fear is your only enemy, that yours is the age of struggle between fear and reason, fear and understanding. The outcome of this struggle, which is **in no way predetermined**, will lead to your world's entering a new age of peace and harmony, or to its destruction.

PART TWO
THE UNHOLY TRINITY
Politics, Religion and Science

CHAPTER TWELVE

Introduction

Let us now turn our attention to the great constructs of your day, your religious, scientific and political philosophies, and hold them up to the light of Divine Grace.

Much of the resistance of the general populace to the expanding volume of metaphysical writings is due to their divorce from the everyday workings of your world. Tracts dripping with flowery prose about realms of beauty, light, peace and harmony are all well and good, but they can also serve to alienate you even further from such realms, when you compare them to the physical reality that faces you daily.

You have seen that we have attempted to avoid such a style by proposing a new concept and then immediately following it with examples on your plane with which you are familiar. By doing this, we help to expose the inner workings of the universe as made manifest in your reality, joining every phenomenon of which you are aware in the framework of Divine Grace.

Some of our concepts are difficult, if not impossible, for your rationally focused mind to fully grasp. You cannot conceive of the power of All That Is which gives your universe, and all others, birth. Your conscious mind cannot consciously understand simultaneous time, while you must take a certain number of "moments" to consider the concept! And your precious senses resist our claim that they are but a lovely fiction.

For the remainder of this work, when we introduce a concept, we will try to point out those areas of your experience where you can see the workings of Divine Grace already made manifest, before your eyes. You have two such areas in which you will find a relatively unfettered, undistorted expression of All That Is.

First are your partners on your earth, the animals. Because they lack your conscious, reasoning mind—which is yours alone to explore—they therefore do not clutter their experience of physical life with all the baggage of beliefs and fears that those of the human species often do. They experience physical reality in a far different fashion—not that theirs is diminished when compared to yours, but different. Again and again we will turn to the animal kingdom, with which you are familiar, for evidence of how All That Is and Its agent, Divine Grace, manifest when allowed clear expression.

Closer to home for you is the second group to whom you can turn: very young children of your species. We will explore the stages of life later, but for now, know that young human children are your truest link to Divine Grace as it couches and supports your world, hidden from sight. It is the job of young children to learn to manipulate physical reality within the given parameters of the culture or society in which they grow; before those connections are fully made, the young child's mind is afire with the promise of Divine Grace.

When considering a course of action, then, you might ask yourself these questions: Does it matter in the woods? Does it matter to a three-year-old?

Before we begin examining political philosophies in your society one by one, a little introductory material is in order. First, we need to further examine the nature of fear. While we have seen that fear is a clever and ingenious chameleon, wearing countless disguises, still it is not the very root expression of the problem. For in order to fear something, you must believe that it exists, or that it can. You do not fear what does not or cannot exist. Fear is the varnish on a belief that your life or security or happiness is threatened from without.

These beliefs are even more undetectable to the casual eye than the fear, as they hide undetected behind fear's facade. And fear, of course, latches onto a host of legitimate concepts as a way of masking its presence.

Now. Political philosophy.

First understand that in any given age of your history, certain themes will be chosen for exploration in all possible aspects and manifestations. An advancement in science or religion or art is never an isolated event but always occurs within the context of the larger themes with which a given era concerns itself. Certainly the power of Christianity, its march through the ages, has left a trail of artworks in all media of expression in its wake, art that never would have been created were it not for Christianity's existence. So as we begin to examine the great constructs of human life, understand that there are no closed systems and that the grand themes of an era will be reflected in every aspect of your existence.

Given that understanding, let us turn our attention to your age, your day, and examine the political philosophies extant, the better to determine which among them, if any, are powered by Divine Grace, and those that blunt its expression.

CHAPTER THIRTEEN

The Left

Let us begin by looking at the left side of the spectrum, from liberals in your democratic society to full-blown communist states.

A communist state based on the classic Marxist model finds its best expression in your day in the country of Russia. Although it is a relatively closed society, you know enough about its inner workings and challenges to state with some confidence that this is not a society in which Divine Grace finds its greatest expression.

Looking back in Russian history, when Stalin sought to consolidate and tighten Bolshevik power over the country, he literally slaughtered millions of his own people. One slaughters the public for the sake of the public good. **Any political philosophy that allows the slaughter of its citizens for any reason has revealed its intrinsic immorality.** Murder is always a violation of Divine Grace; to murder the public for the sake of the public throws in hypocrisy and arrogance, as well.

In Russia today, you know there is a long waiting list of people trying to get out of the country, with the government granting egress to only a trickle. You need look no further; any time the populace of a given social system is begging to get out, you know that Divine Grace is being denied, blunted.

And it is only a question of degree, whether discussing hard-core communist states like Russia or the liberal element in your own society. If a philosophy, in its clearest expression (like Russia) is shown to hinder Divine Grace, then you cannot claim that a milder dose of that philosophy is likely to aid Divine Grace's expression. And when Divine Grace is thwarted, fear is at work, not reason.

What are the battle cries of the liberals in your society? One, that people, the unfortunate especially, must be helped. Two, that social policy must be based on what results in the greatest good for the greatest number.

Let us jump right to the source of the liberal's philosophy and compare it with the reputed goals. If, as we have seen, the philosophy of the left, whether as a liberal in your society or as a Marxist state, leads to the blunting of Divine Grace, then what fear is at work? **The liberal fears annihilation.**

Now, precious few people who pride themselves on their concern for the poor walk around worrying about annihilation. Remember that fear, any fear, will disguise itself by latching onto a legitimate idea, ultimately bringing about the precise opposite of the concept to which it clings.

Annihilation? Where would such a fear come from?

Remember that there are no closed systems. You can chart the rise of your present-day liberalism to the latter part of the last century, when Marx wrote *Das Kapital*. It was in the early part of this century that your country instituted an income tax as a means of rectifying what were perceived as inequities in distribution of wealth. And in the 1930s, the country plowed ahead into full-scale liberalism with the New Deal.

What other concepts were gaining prominence at the same time?

It was toward the end of the last century that Darwin's *Origin of Species* gained wide dissemination. In it, he postulated a theory of evolution in which only the fittest would survive; that the species of the earth were engaged in constant life-or-death warfare; that "natural selection" determined who would survive and who would die. This theory of evolution began to cut loose the previously unshakable tenets of religion, which held, whatever their stripe, that the world was created from without, by an omniscient God.

In the early part of this century your society, and much of European culture, was influenced by the work of Freud. Postulating the division of the psyche into id, ego and superego, he saw the human mind as a constant battle within, a swarm of malevolent impulses desperately fought by the superego while the ego played referee and tried to maintain some degree of civility.

The twin theories of Darwin and Freud cut man loose from his self-image as a creature of God (whether benign or capricious); convinced him that his every impulse was the croak of a repressed childhood neurosis; and that the constant battle within was matched by a battle without, against every member of his species and with all other species of the earth.

Science, of course, also began its rise in prominence in your century, building on Darwin's theory to create a system of thought in which only the physically perceivable could be considered valid, that nothing invisible—thoughts, emotions, dreams, love itself—had any place in understanding the workings of the world. And science therefore rewrote the dawn of your universe, tossing God and his miraculous seven days out the window and postulating a Big Bang in which all the matter of the universe suddenly appeared out of nowhere.

Freud, Darwin and science, then, all combined to convince man that the physical world was the totality of his reality, that nothing lay beyond, no power or energy source outside the perceptions of his physical senses, and that he was condemned to battle his fellows and all other species for his share of an accidental universe, while simultaneously suffering a constant pitched battle between savage repressed neuroses and a frantic superego.

Liberals, as a rule, disdain the more traditional forms of religion. You may search long and hard in a Southern Baptist church for a liberal—check under the pews, but chances are you will come up empty-handed. If liberals profess any religious leanings at all, they claim to be "cultural" rather than "religious." Religion, being outside the province of science and the physically perceivable, is dismissed as the pathetic graspings of the ignorant masses for meaning in their lives.

What provides the meaning to a liberal's life, then? Perhaps nothing. If he thinks he floats aimlessly in a dark and accidental universe, his body the haphazard result of eons of evolution, battling the world for survival, then where is the meaning in such a life? For what can he strive, if his every shout dies unheard in the empty reaches of space? Why should he struggle or dream or build at all if all leads only to the black void of death?

The liberal, then, must clutch to the physical for meaning. His most intimate physical creation, of course, is his body. He believes that the universe is forever out to destroy him, as both his fellows and other species seek to naturally select him out of existence. And with no concept of a source of divinity from beyond the physical plane, he must therefore **live in terror at the thought of annihilation.** For he must limit his values to the physically perceivable, stake his claim on its intimate expression, his body, and seek to protect it and prolong its life at all costs—never stopping to ask himself why, if death brings the blessed relief of nonexistence, he should not prefer it to the daily struggle he believes earthly life presents.

Now, no fear is going to parade about openly. For, as we hinted in just the one tiny question in our last sentence, the notion that each individual is cast adrift in an unfriendly universe, ever at the mercy of his fellows, would fall to pieces if examined critically. What is the source of love? friendship? achievement? pride? The accidental results of chemicals slamming into each other in hopes of outwitting one's neighbors?

This fear of annihilation latches onto one of man's highest attributes, his instinctive empathy and compassion for all others with whom he shares his planet. It manifests in the slogans of "helping others" and "the greatest good for the greatest number." Let us examine the final outcome of these policies on your plane and see if we can reveal fear, not reason, at work.

As we said, fear works by latching onto legitimate ideas, those whose natures lead to smooth expression of Divine Grace. Whatever the distortions of science, religion and politics, you carry within you an **instinctive urge** to assist those in trouble. Observe your species in a crisis: Divine Grace fairly bursts at the seams in such incidents, as strangers flock to aid a victim of crime or someone struck by a car.

It is when fear disguises itself behind such instinctive altruism that the trouble sets in. Such is the case in the liberally oriented policies of your society. Let us see how.

What would you think of a parent who always made excuses for her children's misbehavior, bought their way out of trouble, shielded them from the results of their misdeeds and sought always to blame the outside world for her children's transgressions? You would not think highly of such a mother, for you know that such defective parenting can only lead to children devoid of any sense of **responsibility**, who find **action** divorced from **consequence** and feel that the world exists solely for their pleasure, to do as they wish without regard to the effects on others.

In your society you permit a teen-age girl who gets pregnant to drop out of school, sign up for welfare and live the rest of her life off the earnings of others. In justifying this you claim that she comes from a "disadvantaged background," that "society failed her," that "you have a duty to the poor and helpless," that her children will suffer without government aid.

Remember the very reason for your existence in the physical universe: to creatively explore physical reality by experiencing the **results** of your thoughts, beliefs and actions. **Any time you relieve another of the responsibility for the consequence of his/her actions, you betray Divine Grace.** In greater terms there are no "good" or "bad" experiences, only opportunities for learning and growth.

By supporting a girl who chooses not to support herself while she brings into the world children she cannot feed, you betray her Divine Grace, you deprive her of the consequences of her actions. It is not natural to live without making an effort to care for oneself.

This initial betrayal is then compounded. Who, after all, is footing the bill for this girl? The taxpayer. Someone who works, who instinctively understands that he may make no claim upon the efforts of another, is then robbed of the results of his labor, the stolen wages then handed gratis, no strings attached, to the girl who wishes not to support herself. Thus is the violation compounded: First you deprive the girl of the consequences of her actions, blunting her experience of Divine Grace; then you rob another of the consequences of his actions, his labor's expression in wages.

The fundamental violation, then, is to deprive both parties of the full effects of their actions. It is a **denial of responsibility**, of finding one's beliefs and actions faithfully manifested in results. This is in line with the belief behind the fear: that life is without meaning. If life has no meaning, then thought, desire and purposeful action are also without meaning; thus there can be no room for **personal responsibility** for one's life in such a philosophy.

You see as this denial of responsibility plays itself out, what the results are. **Nobody is responsible for anything.** You find the service at stores and government agencies to be lackadaisical and lethargic. You find the President and Congress pointing accusing fingers at each other for the fiscal mess for which neither will shoulder responsibility.

The clearest expression of this denial of responsibility is in your liability crisis. Here, it has almost become a running joke to see what lunacy people will sue each other for, and particularly the government. People hurl themselves before subways and off piers, then sue the government for their damages and win! People sue tobacco companies for the harmful effects they can appear to produce in those who choose to smoke. The absurdity has now expanded its range beyond human society to the ludicrous extreme of people suing the government for attacks by wild animals, as if the government itself has replaced God as the master manipulator of the universe!

And what is the result of this litigious nonsense? **You don't dare help each other.** You are warned in no uncertain terms that when you come upon a sick or injured person, whether lying on the street or in an automobile accident, that you must not aid them because to do so will expose you to ruinous liability. You must thus repress your every instinct to aid your fellows in time of crisis.

Thus is fear revealed. For the philosophy that holds as its aim the desire to "help people" plays itself out to its extreme expression and you dare not help anyone, no matter how grave the consequences of your inaction. You will watch people die before you can lift a finger to help.

To "help others," in the right circumstances, is a human instinct. When the fear of annihilation latches itself onto that instinct and builds up a network of social programs and laws that deprive society of the consequences of its actions, you end up with fear revealed: you must not help others.

How is genuine compassion manifested in your society, then, if not through social programs? Genuine compassion, or feeling for others, necessarily reflects an understanding that each person is unique, that you must allow all others the right to seek fulfillment in the manner of their choosing, and that there be no coercion or force involved at any level in your society.

You may well gape in horror at the situations some people create for themselves. You may aid them, if you believe that the temporary aid will enable them to get back on their feet. You may not deprive them of living the consequences of their actions by assuming responsibility for them. And you may not put a gun to the heads of others, as your taxation system currently does, to support you or anyone else.

Genuine compassion, then, is an expression of your instinctive connection with all others of your species, while allowing them the freedom to choose and to experience the results of their choices, with no thought given to force, however noble the goal.

Our discussion may leave you a bit dazed if you have grown up believing that a panoply of social programs was healthy and desirable for society, that you had a responsibility to the less fortunate and so on. If we now pull the rug out from under those ingrained beliefs, with what will you be left? A society of anarchists, each battling for his own good with no thought given to others?

Is there no model for a society based on Divine Grace, in which each individual is granted its freedom while at the same time contributing to the welfare of the group, without force or coercion? Of course there is. Observe the animals.

How is the welter of social programs and regulations ostensibly designed to "help others" related to the fear of annihilation? Remember that the liberal who fears annihilation feels himself ever at the mercy of an unfriendly universe, his only meaning being the continued existence of his body. To surround oneself with a cushion of social programs, beginning at birth with day care programs, right on up to Social Security in old age, relieves the anxiety over being at the mercy of an unfriendly universe. When liberals agitate for such programs, it is not the "poor" or "helpless" they plead for; it is themselves they seek to comfort, surrounding themselves with what they imagine to be a cradle-to-grave cocoon ensuring the sheltered, continued existence of their highest value: their bodies.

The liberal's standard is the "greatest good for the greatest number." The liability crisis has resulted in a steadily diminishing number of options and choices available to your society. Many firms are going out of business or closing down lines of products that expose them to too great a risk: birth control products, airplane manufacturers, many government services, etc. Divine Grace seeks always to **expand** its avenues of exploration in its search for new experience; the result of the liability crisis is to ensure the least good for the greatest number. Thus does fear again reveal itself in opposites.

We are not suggesting that capitalism, as practiced in your country, is necessarily the highest and greatest of all possible economic systems. But it is the one you have chosen to explore; it is the root parameter of your economic system. The rules of the capitalist game are that whatever you achieve in the way of wealth resulting from your own effort, you are entitled to keep. This faithfully mirrors what we explored earlier, the concept embodied in science and religion, that your efforts will result in consequences commensurate with your initial actions.

The tax collector, then, is like the softball player with the gun, forcing a new outcome to the game instead of changing its rules. When you deprive a person of his/her wages because "someone else needs them more," you are betraying the very foundation of your system. As long as capitalism is the game you play, it is a violation to rob anyone of the fruits of their labors.

Nowhere in our discussion of Divine Grace did you hear the words "responsibility" or "sacrifice." You are not responsible for others to the extent that you must sacrifice yourself for them. Remember the key word, the manner in which you manifest your recognition of Divine Grace in all others: **respect.** You respect their right to pursue their own paths, to make their own choices and to bear the consequences of their actions. If they choose not to work, they may well starve. It is not your responsibility to save them from doing so, however horrified you are that anyone would make such a choice.

For responsibility carries with it a host of eviscerating drains on your natural vitality—you "should" and "ought to" and "owe" and "feel guilty"—until your great, natural exuberance is so drained that you lose sight of your Divine Grace entirely. Divine Grace knows nothing of sacrifice. It never requires others to sacrifice themselves for you; nor must you ever sacrifice yourself for others. Divine Grace seeks to expand, grow and rush headlong into all the avenues of exploration open in your physical system; the notion of self-sacrifice is thus a contradiction in terms to the Divine Grace that finds itself blunted, thwarted, because its easy flow through your life is suddenly diverted into concern for others at the expense of one's self.

Nowhere does this manifest more clearly than in the communist state. Are you under the impression that the citizens there are happy, vigorous, hearty, active, exuberant and free to experience whatever they wish?

Your picture of a bleak and miserable existence, which is the lot of the vast majority of the citizenry of such "classless" states while their leaders speed to their dachas in limousines, is an unmistakable sign that Divine Grace has been mangled beyond all recognition or hope of expression. For when one is required to work and yet not receive the fruits of one's labors, but instead finds one's efforts expended only to benefit the "people," then one never finds the consequences of one's actions accruing to personal benefit. If one works harder at a job, is one paid more? If not, then why work harder? Why work at all?

This fundamental betrayal of Divine Grace, that one should not enjoy the fruits of one's labors, is the reason for the condition of communist countries, and the harbinger of their eventual collapse. You have nothing to fear from such states; they will implode under the sheer weight of their own idiocy.

Let us examine how these policies manifest in your society.

You are burdened now with spiraling deficits that no one is willing to attack seriously for fear of upsetting the powerful voting blocs, jockeying for position at the great feeding trough of social programs.

Your politicians are elected not by appealing to reason but to your fear.

The person who feels secure, who feels the world supports and buoys him, has no need or desire for social programs. He does not wish to benefit from the labor of others; he will take care of himself. When he falls, he stands up and scrapes off his knees; he does not sue the inventor of staircases. He does not expect to be supported for life by others.

Your fear of annihilation, then, your fear that the world is a hostile place against which you must cushion yourself with a blanket of social programs, hides itself under the banner of the "greatest good for the greatest number."

The time is soon approaching when your fiscal irresponsibility will awaken and present itself in full, fire-breathing glory for you to see. What kind of voodoo economics is this, that you spend more than you take in? Where do you expect those dollars to come from?

You live now at the top of a precarious house of cards, swaying in the growing breeze of reality. All that sustains you now is the continued faith of foreigners in the stability of your system. And when they lose confidence or interest, and stop snapping up Treasury bills?

Then you shall see the inevitable result: **the greatest misery for the greatest number**. No one will escape the results of economic collapse. No one will be immune from the panic and collapse in standard of living that will result.

Like all your other great constructs, then, as the fallacies of your social and economic programs play themselves out, driven not by reason but by fear, you will face a clear, stark, unavoidable choice. If all the world has been looking to you for stability, and you collapse, to whom do you turn as a scapegoat to maintain the fiction?

You see the first hints of the answer in your Social Security system, a system that pays people simply for being old, without regard to need or their contributions to the system. And who pays for this? The young. You have thus institutionalized a system in which grandparents are subsidized by their struggling grandchildren.

This is, as we observe, the first expression of what can occur if you do not unmask the fear driving your social policies and turn instead to policies riding on Divine Grace.

The liberal's professed goals of compassion, altruism, concern for others, and the greatest good for the greatest number will ultimately lead you to one stark choice: change your ways or devour your children. As in all the areas of life in this age of fear versus understanding, such need not come to pass if you but strip away the disguises the liberal's fear of annihilation assumes, and reveal it for its true nature.

Again: **you choose.**

Any philosophy or world view is a creation of the collective mind, and those subscribing to a given philosophy will also find it manifested in their most private and unique creations, their bodies. What happens to a body that consistently expends more energy than it takes in? It starves. The body, in its desperate attempt to maintain life under such circumstances, first sacrifices the most expendable organs and muscles. Gradually, if the output exceeds intake, organs of increasing importance are sacrificed, until one is left with heart and brain embraced in a frantic symbiotic duet—the brain keeping the heart's beat while the heart nourishes the brain's cells. Ultimately, without food, this partnership must collapse and the body cannibalizes its very life source, the heart and brain.

As in the private body, so in the society at large. As these words are written, newspapers carry the story of homeless persons freezing to death in your cities. The most expendable members of society are the first to go. Far from representing the failure of liberal policies, such deaths serve as warnings of their triumph.

Ever-growing deficits and the economic havoc they wreak must ultimately devour the body politic, if unchecked. The heart and brain of your society—its intellect, talent and productive capacity—will be the last to go, will fight furiously to keep the whole alive. Yet finally even this symbiotic duet will sound its last note, the final coda to a culture devouring itself with fear.

Your country, your society, shines like a beacon to those who suffer in foreign lands under the dictatorships of Left and Right, blunting their people's Divine Grace in all areas of life. That the list of those desiring to immigrate to your country is so long, as the poor, oppressed and hungry yearn for the freedom and bounty of your land, is an indication that your system is more conducive to the natural flow of Divine Grace.

As immigrants arrive and pursue the American Dream, they find to their delight that this is indeed a society in which hard work, ambition and intelligence can be rewarded with the outer trappings of success in financial terms.

It is to such people liberals often turn to embrace into the fold. To the liberal's astonishment and bafflement, a large percentage of these immigrants are of a conservative bent, not returning the liberal's embrace. The betrayed liberal cries, "What's the matter with these people? These are the ones I want to help!"

They do not want or need help. Any immigrant who arrives with just the shirt on his/her back, with only drive, integrity and intellect as resources, who then climbs to the top of the ladder, is intrinsically aware that **life has meaning**, that action leads to commensurate consequence, and that one who takes **personal responsibility** for oneself will find one's ambition duly rewarded.

The liberal loves to proclaim that the American Dream is a sham, a thing of the past, an anachronistic hoax. This attitude is born of the core belief that life has no meaning, that action and responsibility fall unrewarded in the depths of an accidental universe. Meanwhile, determined Asian and Latino immigrants, barely speaking English, struggle through years of effort and find themselves well off, pillars of the community, sending their children off to Harvard. What do such people need of the liberals and their philosophy? They know that it is the sham, the bogus hoax perpetrated by those who refuse to admit that one creates one's own reality. They know that the universe is an ordered and logical place where action meets consequence in due measure, where work begets reward. What use have such people for a philosophy that views their achievements as accidents, coincidence, the roll of the dice?

All of the great constructs of human life can be viewed as toys and tools, with which you explore your reality. Those leading to deeper truths will be duly strengthened by their acknowledgment of Divine Grace. Those inimical to Divine Grace will inevitably lead to unhappiness as a means of showing the fallacy underlying the belief.

A system of thought that claims to profess concern for "the people" and their "greatest good," but results in a litigious nightmare in which the colors and variety of life are bled from society while racking up a deficit that will devour your children, cannot be considered a philosophy riding on Divine Grace, but one blunting it.

CHAPTER FOURTEEN

The Right

Let us now turn our attention to the right side of the philosophical spectrum. From those who call themselves "conservatives" in your society to the right-wing dictatorships, one can find a common theme. A common fear.

While dictatorships of the Left manage to cloak themselves in a mantle of respectability by claiming their concern for the welfare of the people, what do dictatorships of the Right proclaim as their philosophical goal? Precious little. Almost inevitably such dictatorships are military governments; and as we know, those who surround themselves with weaponry and imagine themselves strong and protected are desperately fighting a truth they can't face. Rather than promulgating a logically considered philosophy, such dictatorships can only mumble about "public order"; indeed, they often spring up in reaction against a society's perceived lawlessness.

Here is our clue. The conservative fears anarchy. Where would such a fear come from?

Again, there are no closed systems. We find among conservatives a strong religious commitment, a dedication to the more traditional forms of religion, Christianity in particular. And what does traditional Christianity teach?

That you are born in sin. That you are flawed creatures, fallen from grace, wallowing in the sinful pleasures of your tainted flesh, condemned to Hell by a capricious and vengeful God unless you renounce your flesh and throw your unworthy selves at His feet, begging redemption.

In such a system of thought, impulses are seen as literal messages from Hell, demons perched on your shoulders squawking in your ears, urging you to pursue sinful, earthly pleasures while your soul struggles to carve a path of righteousness and ensure you a place in Heaven.

This, then, is the system of belief hiding behind the fear: you are born in sin, the flesh is weak and vile, life is a pitched battle between good and evil, and impulses are urgings from Hell. And if those impulses were to be given full, unfettered expression? **Anarchy.** Thus the only hope for salvation, for an ordered, safe world, is to repress, deny and wish out of existence the dark mutterings from Hell that plague you at every moment.

Knowing the true nature of impulses as you do now, you know that allowing them full conscious expression, the better to evaluate and choose among them, is the manner in which you express Divine Grace on a daily basis. So any system or philosophy based upon denial of impulses will necessarily lead to blunting of Divine Grace.

Let us observe this in action.

The great rallying cry among conservatives is the call for "law and order." They see liberals as soft on crime; they see the world as a dangerous place, festering as it is with all those demonic impulses, full of tainted individuals who dare to give them expression. The call for "law and order" is thus a wish to project one's own fear of impulses onto the world at large.

You might observe the careers of those who enter public service waving the banner of law and order. In the late Sixties, for example, you elected a presidential ticket promising just such a commitment to law and order. Observe the outcome of these two gentlemen vis-à-vis respect for the law.*

You feel betrayed when elected officials campaign on a platform of law and order and then fall from grace, exposed as criminals. Yet any time opposites or surface contradictions appear, you know fear is at work.

Fear will employ any means to stamp out the perceived threat. Fear knows nothing of law and order! The use of force, of illegal activities, is always justified in the eyes of fear, when a greater issue, the repression of impulses, is concerned.

Thus the puzzling demise of those elected to office proclaiming a commitment to law and order—not in all cases, of course, but in enough to give you pause.

Just as the physical world is a reflection, a projection, of inner realities, so can the psyche project onto others those unsavory elements it is unable or unwilling to face in itself. This is a basic psychological truth. In the case of the conservative, the belief in one's inherent sinfulness is too overwhelming to be con-

*Vice President Spiro Agnew, under investigation into alleged payoffs while Governor of Maryland, resigned on October 10, 1973 and pleaded "no contest" to one count of tax evasion. President Richard Nixon resigned on August 8, 1974 after the House Judiciary Committee recommended impeachment for his role in the Watergate cover-up, among other counts.

sciously faced—for who can live believing one's every act is motivated by sin? The sensed sinfulness is therefore projected onto the world at large, rendering it a swarming pool of debauchery, against which the conservative rails and cries. For none is so self-righteous as those who project onto others their own unfaced inner battles.

What is the agenda in the extreme example of a right-wing dictatorship?

First, repression of free speech. This occurs in communist states also, but for a different reason. On the Right, free speech is seen as unfettered expression of impulses, blurting out without censure one's thoughts and opinions, and such cannot be tolerated among those who tremble at the open expression of impulses. Speech must be ordered, controlled, officially approved along the narrow line of thought permitted by such governments. Jailings, tortures, beatings and murders of the populace result from the frantic need to mutilate and destroy any expression outside rigidly defined boundaries.

A society ruled by the Right will also be highly repressed sexually. As we shall explore later, sexuality is indeed a most uninhibited expression of impulses and represents such a break from control, order and law that it profoundly threatens a society fearful of its own impulses. Sex is then narrowly channeled into "acceptable" expression: an adult man and adult woman, married to each other, eternally monogamous, engaging in sex solely for the purpose of procreation. Anything else—anything outside the socially beneficial outcome of childbirth—is furiously repressed. For any other avenue of sexual expression—homosexuality, recreational enjoyment and so on—has no purpose but the sheer, uninhibited expression of impulses, the desire for pleasure. Flawed and sinful creatures that you are, such expression strikes terror in the heart of the conservative. The church locks hands with government in this area, of course, both condemning the enjoyment of sex as the base pleasure of tainted flesh; only an act that includes God, in the possibility of conception, can be considered worthy. Thus does the church assert that the only acceptable sex is a divine ménage à trois, with God hopping in under the sheets.

Another area of repression in a right-wing society is the world of art. For art, genuine art, is born of impulse, of a desire to reshape the world, give it fresh expression, through the medium of sound or color or language. Reasonable people can only puzzle at the repression of art, for how can a mere poem threaten the security of the state? It is not the words of the poem that pose the threat but the manner in which a poem is constructed: free and open expression of an idea along unofficial lines, constructed in fragments, not sentences, unruly, undisciplined, splashing out across the page with not structure but feeling determining its construction and impact. Again, such unfettered expression of impulse deeply threatens the right-wing society, and the offending unarmed poet faces a row of muzzles, the conservative's perverted symbol of strength.

This leads us to the fascination with firepower and weaponry which is the conservative's hallmark. Again, most right-wing dictatorships don't even bother with a cohesive philosophy as justification for their assuming command; they proclaim the need for law and order and hide behind battalions of firepower in answer to their critics.

We have seen that weaponry is a substitute for strength, not its true expression. Violence is not strength but a cry of weakness. As humans, your contribution to the world is to manipulate physical reality through the filter of your reasoning, conscious mind. Violence against another represents the abject failure of reason, the surrender to chaos and rage. The conservative's fetish for weaponry is thus an **admission of failure of reason.**

"Security" is the word so often heard when discussing the need to build bigger, better, more lethal weapons. The outside world, that festering cesspool of uninhibited impulse, must be guarded against with a perpetually escalating race to arms.

But fear knows no reason and thus can never be satisfied, quenched. Has there ever been a conservative government that proclaimed, "Okay, we have enough weapons now; we can protect ourselves"? There can never be enough as long as fear is at the wheel; it is beyond reason and logic, grasping at weapons for security that will never be found.

We have examined the results of such fear in your current administration and its proposal to extend the madness into outer space. For fear knows no reason; and although no rational person believes such a defense can work, fear is uninterested in reason, seeking only to placate its terror with an ever-expanding field of defense. Planet earth is not good enough, not big enough. If we could just fill the very skies with weapons, perhaps we could finally feel safe!

Of course if you proceed with such a plan, you will inevitably find that it does not work, and fear will furiously search out new avenues of expression: the moon? a Minuteman in every pot? mine the world's oceans? move the entire society one hundred feet underground? The point is that fear can never be placated or satisfied; no amount of weaponry will ever make you feel safe as long as it is impulses you fear. And whatever the supposed sources of your fear, whatever your leaders rail against, know that at base they are trembling not out of a reasonably considered evaluation of the world but at themselves, their own impulses which they must repress in themselves and in the world at large.

Conservative governments have a more difficult time providing a cohesive framework for their policies than do communist societies, built on the Marxist model. So conservatives cast about for slogans, to justify their policies.

"Security" is a major theme, as we have seen, representing the fear of one's impulses projected onto others, viewing the world as the dark and threatening manifestation of one's own impulses, if given free rein.

Another common slogan of conservatives is to justify their policies through concern for the "family." This is curious, as families would presumably be the first to go in the nuclear holocaust for which conservatives so ardently prepare. Nonetheless, words are symbols, always carrying deeper meaning, and what can we discern about conservatives from their defense of the family?

It is an ache to return to early childhood, to that magical time when the world was secure, when Daddy was omniscient strength, when Mommy was unqualified love. The world was safe. As the child grew older and learned in Sunday school of his/her essentially flawed and base nature, confirmed at home with a thousand restrictions on innocent avenues of inquiry and expression, that natural sense of security was lost, replaced with a view of oneself and the world as dangerous and chaotic repositories of malignant impulse. So the conservative's concern for family is an unconscious wish to return to the only security he/she has ever known: early childhood.

For this reason, conservatives are the most vociferous opponents of sex education in the schools. They do not want to believe their children are sexual creatures, for such acknowledgment necessarily means the end of innocence for which they yearn. To acknowledge sexual urges in one's children is to admit their passing from the world of innocent security to a dangerous age of impulse. Conservatives claim they desire to teach children about sex at home, but as the children of conservatives can attest, such education rarely takes place. The subject is never mentioned. It is too painful an acknowledgment for the conservative, that these beloved children are forever lost to the innocence and security of childhood.

To sum up, conservatives in your society, and in all governments of a rightist slant, fear anarchy, believing anarchy the inevitable result if impulses are given their full expression. This is why rightist ideology seems so narrow, so rigid, so bland. Only one line of thought, the official one, can be permitted.

Since conservatives lack a cohesive philosophical framework for their beliefs, it is not so readily apparent when the results contradict the stated goals, brilliantly betraying the fear driving them. But you can see, in your society, where your present administration's concern for "security" is leading you. True security is not protection from attack by others but **freedom from fear of attack by others.** The truly secure person feels no need to study self-defense or carry a gun. It is the truly insecure who do so. As you by now know, whatever you fear will be duly charged, energized, rising to the membrane where it will pull into your existence the truest expression of what you most fear. If you fear attack, you most likely will be attacked.

To claim that policies are designed to protect your security, while you stockpile ever more lethal megatonnage and construct a multibillion-dollar celestial sieve, is to demonstrate the principle of opposites in all its deadly glory.

Nuclear weapons will not be eliminated by chanting, demonstrations, prayers, laws or treaties. They will be eliminated when you simply **walk away from them,** shaking your heads in wonder that you ever thought them necessary. Such a world, and only such a world, can provide you with genuine security.

CHAPTER FIFTEEN

Democracy

Democracy is so powerful a political construct precisely because it very nearly replicates what we have been drilling into you all along: **you create your own reality.** In this case, you go to the polls and select your leaders. They are not born into the position; they are not appointed by the church or anyone else; you select them. The problem can arise, as it has in your present-day society, when this reflection of Divine Grace is perverted into the **tyranny of the majority over the minority.**

Remember that you are each a unique, inviolate expression of All That Is, set upon your own deeply private path. While there are certain societal parameters that you best follow because they promote everyone's best interest, at some point the mass "good" must surrender to the primacy of the individual. This was the triumph of the American Constitution. The founding fathers established a system in which government's only role was to protect and serve the citizens. The government itself had no rights.

You hear echoes of this in your terminology, politicians calling themselves "public servants," government workers called "civil servants." Yet the entire initial intent of the founding fathers has been stood on its head, to the point where you now exist to serve the government. While on the one hand the government provides a host of programs that allegedly inure to your benefit, at the same time you are choked and suffocated under a crush of regulations and restrictions on your freedom.

Your Supreme Court recently decided a case in which it declared that there was nothing in the Constitution that guaranteed homosexual conduct, and that states had a right to pass and enforce laws against it. The court was partially correct: there is no such provision in the Constitution. Where the court fell flat on its face is in its apparent ignorance of the fact that if the founding fathers' intent had been followed through, there would be no need for such a provision, for it would never occur to any state to pass such a law.

The founding fathers were vociferous about prying apart the alliance of church and state, forcing a division which they codified into law. They knew only too well that once the church got its hands on the machinery of government, there would be no end to the legislating of morality. A state has no business deciding issues of morality except where the rights of one citizen have been violated by another, and a determination as to the severity of the transgression and appropriate punishment meted out. Activities between consenting adults, however distasteful to the general public, are entirely outside the reach of the state. This was the intent of the founding fathers, yet your present-day society appears to have forgotten it.

It is the church that is the arbiter of morality, for those who choose to have their reality created by others. As soon as you codify morality through legislation, church and state have once again joined hands to impose the church's code of morals onto the populace.

This is the tyranny of the majority over the minority, and it is an illegitimate use of democracy. No state, no majority, however large, can hold itself so omniscient as to legislate the morality of the minority.

Looking back in history, you can see the progress of political systems, see the careful steps toward the New Dawn, beginning centuries ago.

Up to a certain point, church and state were inseparable, one. With the signing of the Magna Charta, church and state began to go their separate ways—church to continue the religious life of the people, the state to protect and defend. The lines were often blurred as, for instance, kings ruling by divine right claimed to be the mouthpieces of God, as did the Pope. Thus, "morality" remained still in the province of government.

It was against this suffocating blanket of religiously coated law that your colonists rebelled. They were bound and determined, when drafting the Constitution, that such would not occur in this country.

Yet somewhere along the line, it has. Legislatures, state and federal, take it upon themselves to proscribe the activities they deem "immoral." Thus is the initial intent of the Constitution, as divinely gracious a document as ever written, blunted and perverted. And whenever Divine Grace is so blunted, the system of thought it hampers must necessarily play itself out, reveal its fallacies and be discarded.

What? Democracy discarded?

You are coming upon an age when you will again reassert the primacy of the individual. You will do so this time out of a conscious realization and acknowledgment of the workings of Divine Grace in your world. In such a world, there is no need for strong government. No one would even consider imposing his morality on another. Government will shrink to the bare rudiments necessary to process the essential legal transactions of your society and no more. This can only come about when you feel **secure** (no more fear of anarchy) and **full of meaning** (no more fear of annihilation).

For what has your electorate had served up to it in your recent decades? Intuitively you recognize the fallacies of the far Right and far Left, but you are then left with an unappetizing choice between Fear X and Fear Y, both of them determined to impose their morality upon you, both of them bleeding the society of respect for the primacy of the individual, both of them blunting Divine Grace. So the poor voting populace careens madly from one of your great parties to the other, tossing one set of scoundrels out, only to find them replaced with another. And you realize it doesn't matter who is in office; the regulations and restrictions multiply, the deficit balloons and the society weakens. Such a system cannot persist.

Now, if you think we advocate running through the halls of Congress wielding machetes, or even engaging in a bloodless taxpayer revolt, you have not been paying attention. When you perceive the government as separate, outside yourselves, you fall into the trap of blaming others for the reality you have created.

As a people, as a society, you have embarked in certain directions, one of which is to project your feelings of weakness onto government, which duly enforces that feeling by shoving you around at every opportunity. When you realize that government, like all your other great institutions and constructs, is but a reflection of your inner life, then you will realize you can change the government simply by **altering your beliefs.**

When it would not occur to a teen-age girl to expect others to support her procreational activities...

When it would not occur to any legislature that they were in business to proscribe sexual conduct that they found distasteful...

When it would not occur to you that you are weak and vulnerable and therefore must protect yourselves with the hardware of death...

When it would not occur to you that a minority of one should ever be subjected to the morality of millions...

...**Then** shall government assume its proper place in your lives: as a means of settling those disputes that arise, carrying on relations with other nations on issues of common interest, and holding always the primacy of the individual above the mass.

Then shall your elections simply become a matter of the majority selecting those individuals best qualified to carry out these minimal duties, without regard for the candidates' personal opinions or morality. It would not occur to the populace that these private beliefs are of public importance; it would not occur to the public servant to violate his oath of office by imposing his morality on those he serves.

You see the evolution of political systems, from the church *as* state, to church *and* state, to majority rule over the state. And the next step...the individual, riding Divine Grace at full throttle in the comfort of the state's blessing on his/her unique path.

The choice, again, always, is yours: fear versus understanding. You may persist in basing your politics and policies on fears and insecurities, and live out their inevitable horrors—economic collapse, ecological catastrophe, nuclear holocaust—or you can change the beliefs driving you toward those ends and affirm, instead, your desire for a world of peace, prosperity and harmony with the natural world.

You choose.

CHAPTER SIXTEEN

Religion

Throughout the history of your race, you have always sought to bring into symbolic expression the source of your world, its miraculous play of tide and sun and rain, to capture in stories and myths the deep intuitive wellsprings of your lives. No man has ever walked the earth without wondering where he came from and what the purpose of his life was. En masse, such yearnings for meaning have resulted in the creation of rich constructs of symbol and myth known as religion.

Religion is universal, present in all times and cultures. Intuitively, whatever the emphasis of the culture, mankind understands that he springs from a source greater than sperm and egg, that such are only the seeds planted by a greater reality to give him physical life.

In some cultures the religious beliefs infuse every aspect of existence, inform every decision and desire. In others, yours particularly, religion is seen as a task, relegated to observance once a week, then largely passing from conscious attention during the week's remainder.

Always, always, man seeks to explain and understand the source of his existence. In that sense, life without religion, without intuitive recognition of life's source, is impossible.

In your evolutionary terms, primitive man felt the sway and reach of the divine in all the workings of the earth. The wind brushing against his cheek was the gentle caress of God; fire was the twinkle in a spirit's eye; the babbling brook, rustle of windswept trees and the call of distant animals were all echoes of divine spirits. In such a world, finding the divine in every impression of his senses, man intuitively felt himself divine, as part of the physical world. He felt safe. Of course he sought refuge in caves, security in fire, as the world was a stage on which man and animal played roles of both predator and prey. Yet on deep biological levels, man understood that this dangerous dance among the species ensured the continued survival of both man and animal, and was thus of benefit to the workings of Divine Grace as it splashed into physical expression. There was no thought that death was annihilation, that life was battle, that the spirit of the divine riding on the wind and water watched man's struggle with disinterest. Feeling the earth suffused with divinity, knowing himself a part of that earth, he knew without conscious knowing that he was divine, cushioned by Divine Grace.

In later times, when civilization flourished into the bustle of Athens and Rome, the intuitive knowledge of earth's divinity was anthropomorphically projected into a hierarchy of gods, each assigned a specific natural function, ruled over by the master of all, Zeus. Not only the workings of the physical world were so projected, but the inner reaches of the psyche as well: love became Eros, Venus, Aphrodite.

Such civilizations thus assigned different personalities to the elements and natural forces of the earth. The gods were given to human frailties and weaknesses, and exasperated Zeus frequently had to consign them to eternally pushing boulders up hills or having their livers eaten by eagles just to maintain order among his unruly messengers of the divine.

In time such gods became too human, lost their divine edge. The myths detailing their adventures fell from stories of the divine, spoken in tones of reverence, to crude barnyard yarns, frequently of lascivious nature, in which the sense of the divine was lost; rather than gods descending to earth from a higher spiritual plane, they were seen as invisible humans. Religion thus became spectacle, comedy, coarse and cheap.

Against this backdrop rose a new myth, the all-knowing, all-powerful God, no longer parceling out the elements of the earth but keeping firm rein over all dominions in His firm and unsparing hand. Jehovah.

For in the decline of the Roman and Greek empires, as gods lost their divinity, so was lost the moral compass governing human life. If gods were human, humans became as animals. The civilizations collapsed in an amoral, unprincipled rubble, as must any society that loses sight of Divine Grace, whatever its mythical expression.

It was against this perceived decline of civilization, and the intuitive understanding that a debasement of a society's religion leads to moral collapse, that this new god, God, arose from the ashes. No longer a frustrated den mother presiding over unruly assistants, this God ruled all, and He ruled by fear. If man had lost his moral compass and his intuitive sense of right and wrong, then he would be forced back into the path of righteousness by a God willing to fling him aside, into the bowels of Hell if necessary. Thus was born your omniscient God; thus was born guilt; thus was born fear.

The Jehovah myth sustained its believers, the Jews, through years of deprivation and slavery; no godless culture could have survived such degradation; it would have collapsed in chaos. But the quietly carried secret of having been "chosen," of knowing that one's life mattered, however appalling its conditions, bound this culture in a cohesive embrace of meaning. Moses' return from Sinai with ten inviolable commandments, sizzled into stone by the finger of God, provided both the moral backbone that earlier cultures had lost and a promise of reward to those living according to their dictates.

In time, any philosophy or religion based on fear will fray at the edges, as fear blunts the easy flow of Divine Grace. Fear of God became fear of man, of one's fellows, one's neighbors, even one's family. The heart yearned for a new breath of enlightenment, a break from fear into grace.

Thus entered the Christ entity into your world, manifesting as a Jew, Jesus of Nazareth. Your myth tells of him communing in the woods with God for days; upon emerging, Jesus pronounced a new image and intent of God: love.

Where once you dared not commit adultery, and by inference avoided all unseemly sexual contact, now Jesus consorted with prostitutes. Where once you were forbidden from coveting your neighbor's property, you now offered him your own. The fear and wrath of Jehovah, then, gave way to an image of a beneficent and loving God, still omniscient and all-powerful, but working now with paternal love, not strict obedience, as his motive.

In your myth Jesus was crucified on the cross—by the Jews—as a means of driving home the lengths to which God would go on behalf of His beloved people: "For God so loved the world that He gave His only begotten son." The myth's distortions since are deplorable, infecting it with notions of sacrifice and guilt. At the time, the crucifixion myth was a demonstration of God's love; God did not sacrifice Jesus but through the crucifixion demonstrated that despite your world's murder of His earthly representative, still He loved you. It was the parable of Jesus' prodigal son played out in literal, excruciating detail: despite your murder of His only son, still God loves you. Thus was the world wrenched away from viewing God as a hard and unforgiving source of uncompromising justice, led by the Christ entity into a path of unqualified, eternal love: Divine Grace.

It is impossible for you to sort out the physical events of your religious myths from later invention and interpretation. In your terms, Jesus walked the earth 2,000 years ago. Do you imagine his words, his story, have come down to you in undistorted veracity?

In your own time, you have seen the Bible progress from the King James version to the Revised Standard version and many "popular" versions following that. Now there is a push, for example, to eliminate the sexual bias of your language in which God is projected as Father, a He. We are not passing judgment on the evolution of your Bible but showing you how in your own time the meaning of the original passages must necessarily be altered, however slightly, with each new expression.

For centuries the Bible was laboriously copied by hand in the cloisters where only the few literate priests could perform such work. Do you imagine that the words of Jesus emerged from such reproductions entirely unchanged?

Just as you now may work to eliminate what you perceive to be a sexist bias from the Bible, and do so with the best of intent, so as the church grew were there passages in the original Scriptures that were deemed offensive. These were eliminated.

Jesus led an earthy life; frequently his parables and moral guidance contained situations his listeners could relate to, including exploration of sensual pleasure. All this has been lost to you.

Moreover, reading Jesus' words can leave you with an image of a dour, stern preacher of the hellfire and brimstone variety. In your own day, the majority of society flees from the sight of any such self-appointed interpreter of God's word. Do you imagine society was different in Jesus' day? And knowing from your stories of his reception wherever he went, the palm branches lining his path, what can you conclude?

Jesus was a stand-up comic, in the very best sense of the term. The comic knows that by coating a truth with humor, it is swallowed much more easily. A sideswipe at authority is overlooked when delivered on a breath of laughter, while the same truth delivered in harsh, unvarnished anger warrants arrest. Knowing this, ever mindful of his precarious liberty under the watchful eye of Caesar, Jesus laced his sermons with humor, slipping his message of love and liberation in between the guffaws. All this is lost to you now.

We could go on ad infinitum with such examples, but the point is made. What actually, physically occurred to the man, Jesus of Nazareth, cannot be discerned from reading your present-day Bible. And though his message has been stripped of much of its poetry, still the essential truth of the Christ entity comes through. Knowing what you do about the endurance of things over time, looking upon your own time and those preceding it—where ideas and trends are picked up, played out and discarded in so brief a time—imagine the **power** behind the Christ myth, and that of the Jehovah myth which preceded it. In your terms, the Christ myth has been playing itself out for two thousand years, the antecedent Jehovah at least twice as long.

The longer a philosophy endures in time, the greater its alliance with Divine Grace. Thus does Christianity endure through the millennia while cults and fads sprout, blossom and die in the wink of an eye. The power and the truth behind your great religions have caused their endurance over so long a stretch of your history.

Incidentally, we do not mean to appear to slight the great Eastern religions in our discussion. But because we address a Western audience, and any truly comprehensive study of Christianity alone would require volumes, we must restrict our scope of inquiry, or risk writing an encyclopedia.

You must remember that a religion's birth is its truest expression, because the eternal truths of Divine Grace are always channeled through the mores of the society and the time in which they are first expressed. Not only were many of Jesus' teachings eliminated from the Bible as more "time" passed from their original expression, but what remains intact is often misinterpreted out of ignorance of the context in which the words were spoken. Jesus spoke to his time; the truth behind his words was of a depth such that he continues to speak to you today, however distorted, and to suffuse many lives with meaning.

The more "time" that passes from a religion's birth, therefore, the greater the distortions and misinterpretations can arise, and the greater the blunting of the Divine Grace that empowered the religion's birth. As each new era reinterprets the original words in its own fashion, according to its own dictates, it must necessarily distort the initial intent. The further from the initial creation of a religion, therefore, the further you are from the truths expressed.

You can see, in both Judaism and Christianity, how fissures have appeared in the previously monolithic, cohesive philosophy. Judaism has broken into three sects of varying adherence to original Hebrew law, as those called Reform wish to.retain a cultural sense of their precious heritage while throwing off the outdated restrictions on diet, dress and behavior.

Christianity has fractured even further. After the Reformation, the Roman Catholic church retained the tightest adherence to traditional principles and observances, while the flourishing Protestant branches scattered in a multitude of directions, some entirely abandoning the church's strictures regarding behavior and issues of sin, guilt and punishment.

Over time, those philosophies enhancing Divine Grace's flow into your world will find themselves duly energized, replenished. While much of the population has given up on religion altogether, finding its restrictions incompatible with the intuitive, liberating quality of Divine Grace, still there are branches of Protestantism that insist on plurality of belief, encouraging their followers to find their own interpretations of Biblical teachings. Meanwhile, even devout Catholics cannot help but question the wisdom of the church's exhortation to be fruitful and multiply in a world choking with overpopulation. The rigid insistence on unquestioning obedience grates against each soul's uniqueness, and some celibate clergy secretly yearn for the touch and comfort of a spouse.

Despite these appearances of pockets of fresh liberal thought, it is the tradition of placing religion and its values in an institution that must give way in the time to come. As seen in politics, yours is an age that will come to celebrate the **individual**, come to understand that Divine Grace, though manifest in all of creation, must necessarily be filtered through each individual's **highly private experience of reality**, and that no body of thought, however liberal and well-intentioned, can truly grant expression to Divine Grace in the life of all members of society.

Man has always had religion, and always will, in the sense of shaping inner truths into outer myths and beliefs; as gregarious a species as yours must also constantly share your private truths, working to fashion them into a cohesive philosophy that can embrace and enhance private experience. In this sense, religion will never be lost. But as you feel the swellings of Divine Grace inside you and begin to recognize it in all others, you will feel less of a need to construct churches and temples—externalized truth—and to vest some of your fellows with quasi-omniscience—priests, ministers and rabbis—with you as the ignorant supplicant. As Divine Grace makes itself manifest to you in every moment of every day, you will retreat from the channeling of "religion" into an hour or two on Saturday or Sunday; **every day, every moment, will be a celebration of the divinity you feel within yourself and find reflected in all others.**

When we speak of the waning of religion, then, we do so with the utmost respect for your present state, understanding that the loss of any institution that was of consistency and comfort must be traumatic. Again, there is no need to fear. You will simply walk away from your houses of worship, carrying with you always the fond memory of their hymns and stirring ceremony, yet knowing that the new age upon you will celebrate the individual above all else, above all creed, dogma, tradition and scripture.

You will worship yourselves.

CHAPTER SEVENTEEN

The Early Church

Before we explore some of the distortions of your present-day Bible, both in the words as they come down to you and in the church's misinterpretation, we need to explore a corollary subject.

In your own time, you watch with wonder at the political progression in countries about you; it seems odd that so many times, a group proclaiming itself the liberator of the people, when finally installed in power, becomes just as despotic in its repression as the leaders thrown out. How does this happen?

It is always easier to oppose than to maintain. Knowing the nature of energy, knowing that it is flow, motion, you can see there will be little energy behind a government that is simply trying to maintain the status quo. On the other hand, an organized resistance, which by definition is butting up against something, will find itself duly strengthened by the battle.

Once installed, once success has been achieved, how is that energy to be sustained? Against what can it throw itself, searching for new avenues of expression?

Related to this is what any government official anywhere in the world can tell you: people are just too damn independent! Why must they hold opinions and beliefs different from those of their perspicacious leaders? Why must they take to the streets protesting against the infallible wisdom of their betters?

There is a great fallacy in such thinking, and it is one of the major battles of your era to finally learn that there can be no "public good" without the primacy of the individual assured first. You have all embarked on your highly private journeys; the notion of consolidating you into one monolithic block betrays the very essence of the Divine Grace that gives you life.

So a government in such a situation, feeling that it must sustain the flow of energy or be tossed aside, has two choices: start a war or repress the populace.

Wartime is heaven for government leaders: opposition can be silenced, those refusing to serve tossed into prison, the newspapers censured out of "public security," and even the most idiotic of actions are hailed by the people.

Your present administration has been frustrated in its attempts to find venues of warfare to silence its critics and justify the military buildup. It has had to settle for a few minor skirmishes around the globe, and to pretend that events in Central America represent a threat to your security. The population yawns. This time, as your sophistication grows, you cannot be fooled.

The other route a government can take, then, to keep the energy flow moving, is to repress its populace. If the people are too stupid to realize how good their leaders are, they will be arrested, beaten, tortured or murdered, the more random the repression the better, to keep the entire population in terror. All this will, of course, be justified in the name of national security. They might even stage a sham election to keep the population happy while the international news media record soldiers stuffing ballot boxes.

It appears that any government has only two choices to maintain power, both of them "negative": find a war or repress the people. This is an unconscious recognition of the fact that stasis is death, that energy must always search out new avenues of expression. Another option, as you see played out in your country, is for the government to simply keep on growing far beyond any need or reason, channeling its energy into devouring more and more of the nation's wealth, gorging itself on the life blood of the people until there is nothing left to devour.

There is one more option available to government. It can recognize the intelligence and decency of its citizens and deliberately wither away. Unfortunately, we can offer no examples of this during your recorded history.

How does this tie in with the early evolution of the church? We will see how both the progress of language and the early church's need to consolidate its power resulted in distortions of the Christ myth.

Jesus' mother, Mary, was a woman of fair hair and complexion. She was an anomaly in a race of dark-haired, olive-skinned people.

As in your own time, the words used to describe contrasting shades of skin color also carried subconscious evaluations of the different races. In your culture, black is the color of evil and destruction; white is pure godliness. This use of language subliminally reinforces your view of black people in your culture.

The same held true in the times of which we speak. Although the vast majority of the population was of dark complexion and therefore was not slandered en masse by words connoting darkness, still the language describing persons such as Mary, her fair skin and hair, carried a charge of purity, godliness. There are no accidents or coincidences, ever, and of course it was part of the overall Christ myth that Jesus' mother should indeed be special, pure and godly in appearance.

So the dual meaning of the words used to describe such physical attributes was used both to describe Mary physically and to confirm her special divinity.

This was the intent of the early Scriptures, then, to capture both meanings in a phrase that could now best translate as "the fair one."

After Christ's crucifixion, in your myth, the early church consisted of ragtag bands of followers, hiding in catacombs, drawing the sign of the fish in the dirt to surreptitiously determine if a stranger was a fellow in Christ. The early church was thus the opposition and, as such, as we have seen, the energy of opposing was sufficient to keep it cohesive and directed.

As time passed, and those who knew Jesus and Mary were buried, the dual charge behind her description in the Scriptures began to fade. Who had known her, to verify that she was in fact of fair skin? So, "the fair one" gradually became interpreted strictly as "the pure one." The dual connotation was thus lost.

By the time several centuries had passed, the church had sufficient followers that it needed an organization, a hierarchy, a bureaucracy. It was becoming an institution of the society rather than fighting the institutions of society.

As such, lest it wither and die, it had to rechannel its energy into new avenues. Initially this was not difficult as it had enough on its hands trying to consolidate itself; there was still political opposition. A sense of urgency arose over the church's future—would it survive at all?—and the early churchmen cast about, searching for a way to make their church, their religion, stand apart from the Judaism from which it sprang.

At the same time, as we have seen, the distance from the events of Jesus' life had stripped the description of Mary of dual meaning and left her solely as "the pure one." Now, language never ceases its evolution; words will appear and die, or change meanings over time so that they completely alter the charge behind the symbols of language.

These two concurrent flows, Mary's description in the early Scriptures and the church's need to set itself apart from Judaism, then converged into a brilliant construction. Mary ceased being "the pure one." Now she became a virgin. There was no need to erase all the passages referring to her in the Scriptures; the word then meaning "pure one" could also be interpreted as "virgin." So no deliberate altering of manuscripts was necessary; it was simply interpretation that changed.

You see what a windfall this was for the early church. For if Jesus had been born of a virgin, from a seed planted by God, not man, then he had to be divine. There could be no question, no argument. Jesus' words were no longer the wise teachings of greatness but instead became the word of God on earth. This carried with it the implicit threat that if one chose to ignore the word of God, one would certainly have plenty of time to regret it in the bowels of eternal Hell!

Thus you see, in this one small example, how little, incremental steps in the evolution of language and the need of a fledgling church to consolidate its power resulted in a distortion of the original Scriptures.

In the centuries since, you have lost much of the beauty of Jesus' story. For the point was precisely that he was an ordinary man, a carpenter, who heard the word of God and sought to disseminate it. He was no Caesar, no Pilate, no high priest in gold-hemmed robes. Again there are no coincidences: **the Christ**

entity appeared in such a man precisely as a way of demonstrating the divinity inside each of you. He was a common man, bringing hope of salvation to everyone. In your time, having lost this sense, elevating Jesus to the right hand of God, flinging yourself at his feet for forgiveness and hope of redemption, you completely contradict the initial intent of the Christ entity. You know the incident of Jesus being surrounded by the sick and crippled; in exasperation he cries: Heal yourselves! Jesus was not lazy. He was ordering you to find the source of the world's divinity **within**, not **without**.

If we may update the Scriptures, as your church has done throughout its history, we would paraphrase Jesus' message as this: **You create your own reality. Look within for the divine source of life. Worship none other but yourself.**

You can see that there was no malicious intent anywhere in the gradual evolution of Mary from fair-skinned to pure to virgin. Her status evolved as language evolved; and it aided the early church in consolidating its tenuous grasp on its followers, torn still between this new sect and traditional Judaism.

But the public relations gold mine of restoring Mary's virginity three centuries after her death was not without aftereffects, as you know only too well in your own day. For by equating virginity with divinity, what is the inescapable conclusion? That **sex is sinful**, the sordid urge of tainted flesh. And this provided the church with an unexpected and incalculable boon, for as we have also seen in your own day, that institution which can regulate sex successfully need not worry about regulating any other aspect of life. Thus the confluence of language's evolution and the church's desire to inject magic into its origin converged with the need to regulate and control into the brilliant construct of Mary's virginity and thus the inevitable falling from grace of the previously unhampered sexual urge.

To further drive the wedge between spirit and flesh, the church then decreed that all of its messengers, priests and nuns must remain virgins for life! This served both to elevate the priesthood to the status of the divine while further debasing sexual expression. You have seen the result: century after century of untold, unspoken, unnecessary guilt, fear, shame, suffering and murder in the name of a God Who desires nothing more for you than that you appreciate and exult in your bodies, revel in their every sensation without restriction or shame.

The only permissible sexual expression now becomes heterosexual intercourse without birth control, thus allowing God to jump in, if He so desires, and create a child. As if the sperm and egg are not divine on their own! As if God must chase about the globe, wrestling gametes into zygotes while the rest of the universe suffers from neglect! As if the ultimate pleasure of which you are capable does not provide God with exultant joy as He hears the cries of ecstasy and smiles in knowing that you so enjoy the bodies He provided you!

You recall what we said about how the distance from the birth of a religion must necessarily impair the truths initially imparted. You see now how this has occurred in the church. The evolution of language flows through the need of a struggling religion to tighten its grip and infuse its origins with divine magic; this leads, centuries upon centuries later, to a church in tatters. Jesus' voice boomed from the seas to the skies with its message of unqualified love, forgiveness and acceptance; now those who claim to carry his legacy croak hoarsely about sin, intolerance and the need for violence. Where truth once was spoken by a carpenter in humble clothes, now rigid, weary dogma spills from those in gilded frocks and costumes. Outer opulence replaces inner truth and divinity. A religion that holds as its earliest myth the fall from grace has now fallen from Divine Grace.

You must worship yourselves.

We do not mean to slight Judaism in our discussion of the decline of institutionalized religion! You have seen how its initial cohesiveness, which sustained it through centuries of oppression, has fractured into three distinct sects, with plenty of quarrels among each division!

Further, compare the initial Ten Commandments with the current homeland of the Jews. Search those stone tablets as you will, you will find no footnotes, asterisks or appendices delineating any exceptions to those ten inviolable rules.

Thou shalt not kill. No exceptions. The present State of Israel is armed to the teeth and, if not violating that commandment, is prepared to do so on a moment's notice.

Thou shalt not kill—no exceptions, not even in self-defense. For if you find yourself attacked, you know that reason has failed on both sides. Delicately now, the Jews have long held themselves to be victims of the world, and as **you create your own reality through your beliefs**, so you have found that belief manifested in pogrom after pogrom, culminating in the horror of the Holocaust. While in no way diminishing the suffering of those who died there, such an event was meant to force an examination of the beliefs that permitted it, not to result in creation of a state whose swaggering gun-toting in the face of its Arab neighbors is possible only with the implicit consent of another nation that confuses armaments with strength—your country.

Thou shalt not kill. No exceptions. A state that claims the Ten Commandments as its heritage, and violates them daily, is playing out for all to see the betrayal of that heritage, not its fulfillment.

CHAPTER EIGHTEEN

The Christ Entity, the Second Coming and the Antichrist

Let us turn now to an examination of the Christ entity to which we have referred throughout. You have noticed a distinction between the Christ entity and Jesus, the man. Let us examine this in more detail.

You know that "events" travel in cycles, on waves of varying size, approaching the linear time continuum, manifesting to the extent that they find a grid of belief arising from the people alive at a given "time," then bouncing back to return another day.

What is the Christ entity?

In all areas of existence you see automatic self-regulation. Your body burns whatever fuel is necessary to sustain itself, its constant temperature, its chemical balances, etc. Nature itself is a wondrous self-balancing dance, as you shall see when we dispose of the theory of evolution, shortly. In your experiments you observe that a population of rodents, if it exceeds the number allowable for quality of life to be sustained, will resort to cannibalism and infanticide until the optimum population is restored.

In all of nature, in every organism, from the single-celled amoeba to the entire reach of the globe, constant self-regulating balance is sustained to allow for the greatest quality of life that supports the fulfillment of all those upon the earth's surface and beneath its seas at any given time. You can see this readily from a physiological and biological standpoint. But such also holds true in the spiritual realm.

All That Is has not cut you loose in a cold universe but has infused your earth, its experiences over "time," with a source of self-regulation devoted to your spiritual well-being. This source is of such power and intent that it can approach your linear time continuum once every two millennia or so; as it approaches, it becomes aware of the condition of the planet, its spiritual condition, and thus infuses your world with whatever knowledge and insight, which you know as sparks of divine intuition, are necessary to correct spiritual imbalance.

You may call this self-regulating spiritual intent the Christ entity, as we have chosen to do, because the Christ myth represents the last appearance on your earth of its intersection with the time continuum. As the Christ entity approached the earth two thousand years ago, searching for areas in which Divine Grace had become blunted, it found that the great Jehovah had played itself out, evolved into a God of fear, guilt, shame and punishment. Divine Grace betrayed. And so this loving intent of All That Is, that you should live lives of spiritual fulfillment, began its search for the place, the time and the individuals who could best give fresh expression to the spiritual source of your world.

You know the story of Jesus, at age twelve, astounding the religious leaders of the temple with his knowledge, and also probing and questioning them with precision and insight unheard of in such a lad. This story represents your understanding of the workings of the Christ entity as it approaches your plane, examines the spiritual conditions there and works to comprehend every detail of how the extant philosophy helps and hinders the expression of Divine Grace.

No one individual can possibly contain the power and intent of the Christ entity. It is a construct of such force and depth that it must splash out among a number of individuals who then work together to play out a drama that will awaken the Divine Grace slumbering within a people, arousing their intuitive insight which has been blunted by the era's religion.

Thus you had played out on your earth the great drama of the life of Jesus of Nazareth. All those close to the drama were infused with the Christ entity's intent: Jesus to the greatest extent, of course, but also Mary, John the Baptist, his disciples, and to a lesser extent the other players in the drama, Jesus' retinue and followers. The political structure of the time played its part, of course, demonstrating the intrinsic anti-authoritarian quality of Divine Grace that knows only the worth of the individual and nothing of bureaucracy. Judas played an especially significant part in the drama, representing the germ or seed of betrayal—which has now sprouted in your culture's wholesale betrayal of divinity.

Jesus' message, again, was to wrest God's image away from that of a capricious dictator to one of unqualified love. **Unqualified.** Nail His earthly representative to the cross; **God loves you still.** In its time, this represented an enormous leap forward in thinking, celebrating the **divinity of the individual** over that of any temple, infusing all who heard the message with hope instead of fear, with promise instead of resignation.

Such is the power of the Christ entity, such was the power of Jesus' words, that it has taken two thousand years to fully play out; and even now it is only the institution, the bureaucracy, that is crumbling. The words of Jesus still bring fresh hope and liberation to multitudes. Imagine the power!

Just as the prophets foretold the birth of Jesus, revealing their intuitive under-standing of the cyclical appearance of the Christ entity in your reality, so did Jesus predict his own return. The second coming of Christ.

It will not be only the second time! Nor will you find Jesus descending from a cloud to reclaim his place on earth.

You are now at the cusp of the New Dawn; and if the collapse of institutions, government and science leaves you bereft as they reveal their incompatibility with and betrayal of Divine Grace, remember that All That Is did not cut you loose to wallow in eternal despair.

The cycle on which the Christ entity rides is one of two thousands years' dura-tion. Two thousands years have almost passed since the birth of Jesus. Do you follow?

If you scan the earth for a warrior on horseback, or a king or president who will right the wrongs of the world, you will be disappointed. For as the Christ entity approaches your plane this time, it sees that the intent of Jesus' life, that you view God as love, has become common knowledge, codified in your church, despite its distortions. This concept is now thoroughly ingrained in your culture.

The Christ entity sees also the crumblings of your institutionalized religions, their failure to speak to the needs and hopes of the people. These also served their purpose.

You are at the cusp now. You see the dim glimmer on the horizon of the New Dawn. You have learned that God created the world and watches over it. You have learned that God is love. Now you will learn that **you are God.**

Again we prefer to avoid the word "God" for all its negative connotations with which the church has saddled it. The new age upon you is one in which you will finally meet All That Is face to face, without distortion, and realize that you look in a mirror.

Every atom, every molecule, every creature upon your earth is infused with divinity. Its source is not outside your world. You are its source. There is no divi-sion. You see, now, the underlying basis for our emphasis always on the primacy of the individual; the individual is the source of the divinity in your world, all its great institutions merely reflections of that source.

You have been given a wondrous creation, the fiction of a physical world, through which to learn lessons available nowhere else in all the realms of ex-istence. **You create the world. You create your life. You are the creator of your own existence, your senses perceiving only the reflection of your divine inner life.**

This is the lesson of this age. You create your own reality. It is the final lesson of the earth plane.

We do not presage the world's destruction with such a statement, but its evolu-tion into a realm of peace and harmony inconceivable to you now, trapped as you are in the quicksands of ego, pride and institution. You see where your politics, your science, your religions have brought you. You may now exercise your free will and follow them blindly into the oblivion of nuclear holocaust or ecological disaster, or you may instead choose to usher in the New Dawn.

Again, the Christ entity is of far too great a power to manifest in a single individual. Given the message it hopes to impart in its present return to your earth, it is therefore deliberately spreading itself out among a multitude of individuals, in all nations, among all races, as a way of ensuring that no one individual may rise to claim the crown. There will be no Jesus this time. Those who claim to speak God's truth exclusively should be discarded with yesterday's newspaper.

For if the intent of the Christ entity in this manifestation is to convince you of the divinity within all creatures, then you must **each** begin to feel the swell of long-repressed Divine Grace inside. You **each** must celebrate yourselves, the individual supreme above all structures of society.

The Christ entity will thus manifest not in a single man but **in every person alive on earth.**

Again, there will be differences; variety is the signature of Divine Grace. Some will emerge as teachers, as bearers of undistorted truth, to a degree not found in the general population. Some of these have already been born.

For what you find in the upsurge of contact between spirit and earthly planes is the initial ray peeking over the horizon—the palm branches lining the road to Jerusalem. However wondrous it may seem, this explosion of unfiltered contact between the planes, it is but the tiniest fraction of what lies ahead.

Now. Your Biblical predictions about the time upon you now, the return of the Christ entity, include dire warnings about the rise of an entity called the Antichrist. This element of the myth is partially a result of your love of duality, of opposites. If God exists, we must have a Satan. If Christ is to return, we must have an Antichrist.

There is some truth behind this element of the myth, but not in the traditionally understood sense. As we have said throughout, yours is the age of fear versus understanding. Either you relinquish your fears, wondering how they ever could have gripped you and your institutions, or you follow them down the path to oblivion. In the time to come, what has been termed the Antichrist will simply be increasingly pure, undistorted and potentially dangerous expressions of fear.

Remember that no idea plays itself out over time and then withers away. Always, at the end of its cycle, it will send off a super-charged spark as a way of bringing to your awareness the intent behind it, whereby you finally and forever discard it as blunting Divine Grace.

Yours is a very fearful world, and as your various fears clamor for your attention, forcing a choice between your affirming or denying them, there can be some unpleasantness. Always, always, reason is on your side. For one characteristic of the nature of events we have not yet mentioned is that, as they play themselves out over time, infused with less and less Divine Grace, they necessarily become more and more ludicrous to the rational mind, ridiculous caricatures of the intent behind their initial appearance in your world.

As an example, one of the constructs you must dispense with is that of war. There can be no place for it in the New Dawn. As the idea of war plays itself out in your society, you see to what ludicrous extremes it must go to grab your attention. Again we pick on the present administration. Installed during peacetime, battling a deficit, it immediately proposed a huge increase in military spending!

Where was the reason, the logic, in such a proposal? Reason was on vacation. The populace, finding their fears duly represented by this administration, cheered the proposal while Congress rolled over and played brain-dead. So you increased the military budget. So this notion, of strength through armaments and war, tooled along, grasping at ever more ludicrous concepts and policies to give itself expression.

Thus your president's beloved cosmic colander, the Strategic Defense Initiative. In overwhelming numbers your scientists affirm that such a space defense can never work. Common sense tells you it can't; even a layman with no scientific training can dismiss such a plan after only a cursory review, so inherently unworkable and ludicrous is the idea. But still Congress happily mortgaged your children's future to underwrite such nonsense.

So now this concept becomes truly desperate, as you find a Soviet beachhead in Central America before which you, the greatest nation on earth, quake in unmitigated terror. What is this? Nicaragua? Where's the fly swatter? But no: a deadly, deadly threat is this, and again we mortgage the children's future to subsidize drug runners and mercenaries, and while hailing them as the moral equivalent of your founding fathers, you spit on the graves of those who gave your country birth.

Where will it end? When will you finally, forever abandon the notion that weaponry is strength, that arms provide security, that war will keep you safe?
You choose.

The digression into politics was necessary just as an illustration of how a concept, devoid of Divine Grace, will manifest in ever more ludicrous grotesqueness until you once and for all toss it on the trash heap of history.

Observe now what is occurring in the Christian religion.

There are no closed systems, and you now find a marriage of technology, art and religion: the television evangelist! The miracle of television brings into your living rooms the beaming beneficent faces of God's personal messengers, here to spread the word of the Lord. In smooth, sincere tones you are told that the preacher loves you, cares for you, prays for you.

Consider what is happening here. Place yourself in the television studio with the man of God. What do you see? He announces, "I love you, I care for you, I pray for you," to a television camera! Where before, whatever the distortions of religion, as priests and ministers railed against your sins, at least they looked you in the eye! Now, as Christianity plays itself out in anticipation of the Christ entity's return, you find the utterly ridiculous spectacle of preachers talking to inanimate television cameras, the faithful receiving benediction from a picture tube and shipping off their money to keep the spectacle rolling!

The entire intent of religion, that of a direct connection between God, pulpit and worshipers, has been disemboweled, the opportunity for personal contact rendered impossible by electronic gadgetry. The beauty, poignancy and poetry of religion have been completely stripped away, leaving you with the sham spectacle of religion reduced to the sputter of alternating current and high-frequency waves, while the millionaire preachers need never budge from their chairs as donations pour in. In a sane culture, one who swore love and devotion to inanimate cameras would be committed; in yours, they become rich.

Such preachers are fond of seeing evidence of the work of the Antichrist everywhere they turn. The rise of the fundamentalist Right in your culture is a reaction against the perceived sinfulness of your society and the certain wrath of God to be brought upon your heads.

We have seen that the only genuine expression of the Antichrist is fear. And who are the most fearful members of your society? The fundamentalist Right. Perhaps you see the irony—those who wail the loudest before the imagined approach of the Antichrist **are** the Antichrist! And you thought them without humor!

By being facetious we hope to take some of the fear out of any discussion exploring the nature of the Antichrist, for fear is what you must discard, not strengthen. Know that there is no Antichrist as a separate, conscious entity; there is only fear that must be fought and defeated.

The process can be as painful or painless as you wish.

You choose.

CHAPTER NINETEEN

Science

Man is distinguished from the animals by one feature: his rational, conscious, reasoning mind. With it he can consider past, present and future in a way unknown to the animals; he can allow his imagination to soar without restraint; he can dream, scheme, plan, hope and meditate.

His conscious mind also allows man the unique ability to learn to manipulate his environment in ways inconceivable to the animals. Like the animals, you always learn from experience; unlike them, you are able to deliberately manipulate your environment in order to **consciously** fashion your experience. This, your unique and precious gift, to learn and then manipulate on the basis of your learning, is the basis for science.

The first taming of fire was science. The first fashioning of an animal skin into a warm garment was science. Learning to map the stars and their movement through the seasons was science. The first crude dwelling was science. The first weapon was science. The first spoken word was science. Identifying the animal cries in the night was science. Digging the first well was science. Placing moccasins on the feet was science. Grinding food was science. Building paths to follow game was science. The pyramids, the catacombs, the monasteries, the castles, the rocket ship—all these were science.

Life without science is impossible.

Given that illustrious beginning, comparing it to the potshots we have been taking at science throughout our work, what has happened to the natural, innate inquisitiveness that it should have reached the condition of modern-day science? Can we find nothing positive to say about it?

Let us put the matter into perspective.

As we have seen, in early man the sense of divinity was felt in every moment, every aspect of life. There was no separate god or God; there was only the universal, unifying **spirit** that infused every rock, tree and animal. "Science," then, man's manipulation of his environment, was one more expression of his divinity.

In your recorded western civilization, for many centuries the church was not only the source of religious life but also of political structure; it was the state. Those alive in those times thus had no doubts whatever about the existence of divinity in the world; perhaps God was a bit cranky at times, but there was no question He was there. In those days, science was also seen as a natural expression of man's divinity.

After the Protestant Reformation split the church asunder, you embarked on the long, slow march away from an intuitive sense of divinity infusing every corner of creation. The traditional church, the Catholic church, as it lost its former power and connection to Divine Grace, relied more and more upon costume, pageantry, ritual and hierarchies of angels and saints to ensure its survival. The Protestant branches split and divided like an embryo, following a multitude of philosophical paths.

The result was that for the first time, you had a choice. You could choose the Catholic church; you could choose a Protestant sect; and, most importantly, you could choose none at all. Any time you are faced with a choice, you are therefore given the option of saying no.

Believing the church an anachronism out of touch with present-day reality, many individuals chose just such a path, of declining to participate in any religion at all. They thus sealed themselves off from any intuitive understanding of the divine source of your world. As liberating as it was, then, to be freed from the shackles of religion, such a development also allowed for the first time in your history that one could choose not to allow the possibility of the divine to enter one's consciousness or decision making.

As we approach the time of your era, we see the church in increasing decline.

As we have seen, an institution in decline, losing more and more touch with Divine Grace, becomes more and more ludicrous, an increasingly ridiculous caricature of its prior self. To any rational person, the church held no meaning; it was full of spooks and saints and cherubs, devoid of any practical application to life.

As we have seen, the rise of the philosophies of Darwin and Freud drove the final wedge between the divine—religion—and the practical or rational—science. Since that time, as you can see in your own day, the gulf between them seems unbridgeable; their paths diverge further and further every day.

As the church plays itself out, gasping and wheezing about sin and hellfire, it can offer nothing to those determined to live in a practical world in which their reasoning minds are held supreme as the final arbiter of reality. To the religious, science can be an appalling violation of the divine, poking about creation in an arrogant and contemptuous way, ripping asunder the divine fabric of existence, declaring the entire universe an accident and human life the lucky roll of the dice after eons of natural selection.

We have seen what has happened to religion, insisting as it has upon abandonment of reason and logic in its followers. Now let us observe what has happened to science, divorced from any sense of the mystery and divinity of life.

There are those who claim that scientific exploration and investigation should be unhindered, unfettered, that the mind must not be limited in any avenue of inquiry.

Consider what science is: It is like a two-year-old, excitedly stomping about on its newly sturdy legs, poking into everything, leaving nothing unturned, unexamined, in its exuberant quest for knowledge. The wise parent will allow such exploration to proceed with as little interference as possible, knowing that it is the young child's job to learn to manipulate and explore its environment. But there are limits to what such a parent will allow.

If the young child, enthralled by the dance of flame on a stove top, reaches to touch the fire, what does the wise parent do? Stand back and allow the child to burn its hand?—and as the crippled hand is bandaged, to cheerfully declare, "See? You learn something new every day!"

If the parent is walking along the sidewalk with the child when a car pulls up and a strange man offers the child a ride, would the wise parent bundle the child into the passenger seat, plant a kiss on its cheek and wave the car goodbye, calling, "Have a nice day!"

In both these examples, learning would occur. The child would learn never to touch flame. The child would learn never to take rides from strangers. But a parent who allows such learning is severely deficient. Why? **There are some avenues of exploration that must not be permitted.** Yes, learning will take place, but are the permanently disfigured hand, the deep psychological scars, worth the knowledge? Of course not. And how does the wise parent know which experiences not to allow; what is the criterion for making that decision?

The parent loves the child. Love is a recognition of and respect for the Divine Grace in another. Mere "learning" is not an adequate rationale for permitting a child to suffer such experiences, because in both instances the child's **Divine Grace has been violated.** The child's hand is meant to grasp and explore, not be crippled. The child's body exists for its own pleasure, not that of strangers. So the distinction, the point at which any loving parent decides whether or not to allow a given experience, is love: Does the event portend enhancement of the child's Divine Grace or its violation?

Now we return to our grown-up two-year-old, the scientist. The same principle applies here. **There are avenues of exploration that must not be permitted,** whether or not learning will take place as a result. What is the criterion? How does one decide which course to take?

The answer, again, is love. This time, it is **love for the earth** that is the criterion. Will a given scientific exploration or invention lead to **enhancement** of the world's Divine Grace, or its violation?

The end can never justify the means. If the means to an end, however worthy, violates the earth's Divine Grace, then that path best not be followed.

Here is what science in your age lacks. Having divorced itself from religious influence, insisting on restricting its scope of inquiry to the physically perceivable, it has no sense of the divine in the world. It is therefore unable to make determinations as to which paths should not be followed. It has no respect, no love, for the planet, believing it the mere roll of the dice in a cosmic crap shoot.

Herein lies the source of your trouble. We have already seen what occurs when you split the atom to generate electricity. No culture with a respect for the earth's integrity would dream of using such a process, no matter how worthy the goal. You may not tamper with the very building blocks of physical matter.

Again, there is no punishment, no angry God hurling lightning bolts of retribution. But as your physical reality always faithfully reflects your beliefs and attitudes, when you exhibit such bottomless contempt for the world that gives you life, you find your world poisoned with a substance whose toxicity will plague you for centuries.

Science has brought you a highly technological society that has provided you with comfort and ease unknown to any other era in your history. The all-consuming tasks of food gathering, shelter building and so on have been eliminated from your daily concern. Science, when its exuberant investigation does not violate Divine Grace, can provide you with unprecedented freedom to explore whatever path you choose, freed from the everyday cares of your less advanced brethren.

We speak now through a young man and his computer. There is no violation of Divine Grace in building a computer; the end—freeing you from performing complex calculations, reducing them to bits and bytes—and the means— microchips—are both either beneficial or neutral in aiding Divine Grace's expression in your world. With both ends and means clear of any violation, the end result—computers—can only be of benefit to your society.

Again, you acknowledge the Divine Grace in another by granting him/her your **respect**. Science, not allowing itself conscious knowledge of the divine source of your world, must thus careen about like a bull in a petri dish, its granting respect to the earth simply a matter of chance, not evaluation.

We have seen what your wrenching apart the atom has brought you. Now let us examine a few more examples of how science, ignorant of Divine Grace, has or can bring your society face to face with disaster.

You are now on the threshold of a new field of inquiry, that of genetic engineering. By splitting apart the genetic structure of the animate species of the world, you are able to create entirely new species, to rearrange chromosomes like shuffling playing cards. You may **not** demonstrate such profound disrespect for life as to scramble its very blueprint.

Recently there was an incident in which a genetic engineering firm was upbraided by the government for conducting unauthorized tests of a new strain it had created. And what was the vaunted social benefit behind this genetic engineering? Frost-free strawberries.

Admittedly, those involved in genetic engineering can claim far loftier goals, such as curing genetic diseases. But the idea, the notion, that your society permits the willful destruction of its very genetic blueprint over the hope of frost-free strawberries demonstrates in ludicrous glory just how far science has fallen from any comprehension of Divine Grace.

You have seen, with nuclear fission, what has occurred as the event of "nuclear fiasco" has twice ridden its seven-year cycle into your time continuum: Three Mile Island and Chernobyl.

Genetic engineering is too new, too small in scope, to yet provide you with an equivalent biological disaster. But know that there exist on parallel earths an infinite range of genetic disasters from which you may select, depending on how far you pursue this avenue of inquiry. We will not describe them to you. For if you continue in your present path, you will see them with your own eyes; and if you abandon such nefarious research, it should be out of conscious choice, not fear.

Again, notice how perfectly and miraculously your thoughts and beliefs are manifested in your reality. When you split the atom, thereby exhibiting contempt for all matter, both animate and inanimate, the result is a substance that will destroy all matter with which it comes in contact.

If you continue on your path of genetic manipulation and suffer the inescapable result of biological disaster and mutations too horrible to describe, only animate life will be affected, as it is the blueprint of life you have betrayed. The rocks and mountains will be unaffected, as they carry no DNA blueprint.

Which shall it be? A recognition of the profound violation that genetic manipulation represents, sparing yourselves biological disaster; or an unrestrained plunge into this brave new world, to watch your children eaten alive from the inside out by microscopic life forms of which you cannot conceive?

You choose.

Your society is currently thrashing about in the quagmire created by science's exploration into another field of inquiry that it may pursue only in violation of Divine Grace. It is poking about in the very creation of your species, in the processes of conception, test tube babies and all manner of illegitimate manipulation of the conception process.

This has reached its nightmare apex in the battle over surrogate motherhood. If you take a sperm cell from a man, plant it in another woman's womb for a fee, your society must then ask: Whose baby is it? Who owns the baby?

Who owns the baby? Who **OWNS** the baby?

We were under the impression your society had decided the morality of owning human beings at Appomattox.

The dilemma is unsolvable; science, religion, ethics, morality, law and parents all have their say, with consensus impossible. Why? Because the fundamental process itself violates Divine Grace so profoundly, infecting it not only with science's customary disrespect but then further fouling it with issues of money and baby ownership, that no reasonable, rational solution can ever be found. There simply is none.

And in an appalling display of science's utter divorce from any moral sense, you are left with the spectacle of high-priced lawyers bickering over movie rights to the sperm's life story and whether the womb rental rate includes utilities, while literally hundreds of millions of children bed down hungry every night in your world. Hundreds of millions of hearts aching to be touched, cheeks yearning for a kiss, eyes waiting to reflect the ineffable love and devotion of a parent.

All of life is chosen. If you are infertile, the choice has been made to steer you toward new growth and experience. You may well find that a child born to parents unknown to you can still fill your home with joy and laughter, and the unutterable, rich reward of imprinting a young soul with the indelible mark of your love.

And science? Fooling around with the very essence of your species' existence, while children starve? Are your resources infinite? If not, perhaps you could direct them into fields of inquiry designed to enhance the lives of those already born, instead of squandering them on research that can bring benefit to so very few, at such great cost, with so terrible a violation.

A final example of the misery science can produce, having lost its moral compass. In this example, you find in clear, stark detail the result of disrespect and contempt for life: Seven astronauts had their lives cut short when the Challenger exploded shortly after lift-off. The subsequent investigation revealed that, despite the engineers' warnings not to permit the launch to proceed, these warnings were overruled by those higher in the chain of command.

For what exalted purpose? The space agency was becoming impatient. It was bad for public relations, these interminable delays. And a company's prestige was on the line. What is this? Impatience? Prestige? What is this noise when compared with the sanctity of human life? Overruled.

You know that Divine Grace always seeks the most "positive" outcome of an event, and the negative can slide into physical expression only as a result of a profound violation of that Divine Grace.

There are parallel earths on which those astronauts returned home to the welcoming arms of friends and family. Such was the most natural outcome of the space flight. But the profound contempt displayed by those deciding to proceed with the launch over the objections of the engineers created a grid of intent so powerful, of such force, that it blocked from physical expression that happy outcome, instead pulling into expression the tragic result that your country experienced. It was not necessary. But when you display contempt for life, destruction of life is what you shall have.

Of course the circumstances of one's death are always chosen, though most often subconsciously, and those who died had their own private reasons for choosing to leave physical life at that point. It was precisely their **love of life**, which compelled them to the ultimate thrill of a ride in a spaceship, that enhances the sense of tragedy over their deaths; they united in sending a communal message: **Learn to love and respect life as much as we loved and respected ours!!!!**

A tangential cause of the explosion was not so immediately apparent. Until recently, space has been seen as a wondrous medium of exploration, of dreams, of imagination unlimited. It was always seen as either neutral or beneficial; and it responded in kind, your trips to the moon and back without tragedy being an example.

With the advent of the present administration's Strategic Defense Initiative, this changed. Planet earth is simply not big enough to hold all the weapons we need to feel secure; now we must junk up outer space with them also. So the concept of space, previously neutral or benign, became "polluted," in a way. As a species you, for the first time, exhibited contempt for outer space by presuming to use it as a battlefield. This allowed the Challenger explosion easier passage into your physical reality, though this is a secondary cause against the contempt displayed by those who held ego and prestige as higher values than human life.

There is another area in which science is illegitimately engaged, and in this instance the violation is so profound that there is now organized resistance within your society, one more battleground between the old and the new at the cusp of the New Dawn.

You find animal rights groups springing up in appalled horror at the atrocities science commits in its alleged desire to benefit human life. Once again, animals are seen as playthings, as toys to be bashed about and mutilated, all with an eye toward finding out what makes them tick. Building on the erroneous belief in evolution, science holds mankind as the supreme victor of mutational battle and justifies its butchery and torture of other species as the prerogative of the victorious breed.

You may not justify any means by the end. You may **not** regard the animal kingdom as your personal menagerie, to be tortured, slaughtered and maimed in your claimed reverence for human life.

How can one claim reverence for human life when one grants no divine source to the world? In such a framework, man is the product of accidental chemical reactions in a primordial soup, just as is every other animal on earth. By that reasoning, none could be any more worthy than another. You may not deny the divinity of the world and then claim your research aims to benefit the "value" of human life. Either we are divine or we are not. Either we are accidents or we are not. If the latter holds true, there can be no legitimate discussion of values, ethics or morals.

This is one arena of scientific inquiry so blatantly in violation of the most rudimentary morality that as the world swells with the intuitive rush of Divine Grace, there is vocal and organized opposition displaying in horrific detail for the previously cloistered public precisely what our "compassionate" and "life-loving" scientists have been up to. Do you embrace and cherish the species of the earth as sparks of divinity, or do you mutilate, torture and murder them as raw materials in your quest for knowledge?

You choose.

The present state of science in your society parallels what we have seen in the political and religious arenas: As it strays further and further from Divine Grace, it displays increasingly ludicrous behavior until finally an aroused populace is forced to examine it. For the birth of science, which is that great exuberant exploration of the small child, has resulted in your time in a discipline so divorced from any understanding of the world's divinity that it now holds the power to destroy life itself. No child would ever seek to destroy the world it explores; the child rides always on Divine Grace. Science, insisting on limiting itself to the fiction of the physical senses, plays itself out as the very antithesis of the inquisitive, loving delight that was its birth.

If our words have been harsh, perhaps we can now demonstrate some compassion for our modern-day scientist.

Consider the plight of the intellectually honest scientist, steeped as he is in the theories of an accidental universe spawning an accidental globe on which mammals descended from fish in a furious battle of natural selection.

And when this scientist returns home at night from his day at the lab, repressing the thought that all his efforts are without meaning, as the universe itself is without meaning, at least he can take some small joy in the comfort of his family. But the true scientist, determined that he lives in an accidental universe that never transcends the five physical senses, can take no real comfort in the company of family.

For as he tucks his children into bed at night, and their accidental eyes glisten with the unverifiable impossibility of emotion, as he presses his accidental lips to the naturally selected forehead, if he is true to his science he must hear the child's gentle words, "I love you," and know they represent the random guttural sputters of an accidental larynx forcing neutral sound waves through his ears to a brain that exists solely to sustain the life of his limbs, the child's words then decaying as random firing of synapses, dropping into the empty nothingness from which the universe sprang.

Oh, for the day our poor scientist can gaze upon his child and appreciate the divine miracle resting in his arms.

CHAPTER TWENTY

Evolution

We have maintained throughout that the theory of evolution is a fallacy, have promised to address ourselves to the theory and will do so now.

In a nutshell, evolutionary theory as proposed by Darwin is based upon the principle of natural selection, in which those mutational strands of a given species that best adapt themselves to their environment will survive, seeding the gene pool with their victorious adaptations, thus perpetuating the species. In addition, the species of the earth are cast in a constant battle for space and resources, competition determining the "survival of the fittest."

Think for a moment what would happen if the world's species were genuinely engaged in competition to the death. Think for a moment what would happen if your own species truly acted, at all times, from a motive of competition and the desire for survival.

Why do you aid victims of a car accident? Will they not survive to compete with you for precious resources?

Why does a grizzly sow adopt an orphaned cub, ensuring that her own offspring will suffer increased competition for space and food?

Why does your country respond with instantaneous, instinctive generosity any time disaster strikes in the far reaches of the globe? Why do you not instead rejoice at the loss of those who make demands upon the earth, reducing your own share?

Why does the whale remain at the side of a mate harpooned by your species, risking its own life?

Why do you flee from your cities—eminently human constructions, symbols of your superior intellect—to revel in the wilderness? Why would you "step down" into the natural world you evolved from so long ago?

Why will your loyal dog die for you?

The belief in a world running on competition, of every species and animal battling for itself, dissolves in an instant once the evolutionary blinders fall off and you truly see the world as it is. Such a world could not survive for a fraction of a second.

Your world is a divine crucible of **harmony** and **cooperation**. Every species **contributes to** the existence of all others. Every person contributes to the growth and learning of the human race. All That Is seeks fulfillment through the unique focus of every individual entity upon the earth—and each individual's fulfillment cannot help but contribute to the fulfillment of the earth as a whole.

In deepest terms there is no time. Hence, evolution is an impossibility. You may indeed find certain species appearing and vanishing over the span of the earth's history—as you perceive and record it. Know that each such species is a "probable" line of development, appearing on your particular earth, at a particular "time," because its presence will contribute both to its own growth and to the earth's. When that purpose has been fulfilled—when the species no longer finds the earth conducive or receptive to its intent and purpose—it vanishes—from your earth—to seek greener pastures, greener probabilities, elsewhere.

There is no extinction, no death. Species may dip into the time-space continuum of your earth when it suits their purpose and remain as long as paths to fulfillment lie open.

Humankind bears a burden of collective guilt for the disappearance of an extraordinary richness of flora and fauna. You look about the world, at the march of destruction you have conducted, and find yourselves forever lost to the company of species never to reappear.

Remember how you acknowledge the Divine Grace in others: respect. In your self-image as the ultimate victor of evolutionary battle, the premier species of all history, you look upon the earth's other species as your inferiors; you look upon them with disrespect.

Very well. They will seek their fulfillment elsewhere. The loss is yours.

There is no time. The energy pulsing behind your universe bursts into fresh expression in every moment. It seeds a world of divine harmony, cooperation and respect, urging you toward your highest fulfillment, buoying you in a sea of species to share your journey.

Cast off the blood and battle and terror of a world swarming with competing species at each other's throats. Embrace instead the real world, the true world: a divine family of infinite variety sharing a blue-and-green sphere of a bed, interlocked in a cohesive embrace of purpose, growth and love.

CHAPTER TWENTY-ONE

Summary

We have now completed the second section of our work, in which the principles learned in the first section are applied to the three great institutions of your day: politics, religion and science.

In each case, we find these institutions born afire with Divine Grace. Democracy was, at its time, the highest celebration of the worth of the individual. Religion unites man with his spiritual origin. Science is the exuberant curiosity of the young child.

In all three cases, we have seen how far your institutions have fallen from their initial partnership with Divine Grace.

Your government has become a voracious glutton and tyrant, demanding you work half the year to feed its insatiable appetite and subsidize the paranoid fantasies of your leaders with your labor and the lives of your children. The drain on the economy is so severe that you now rush headlong into second-rate status, flushing your country's productive life blood down the sewer of the Pentagon, while mendaciously pointing accusing fingers at your foreign trading partners, blaming them for the inability of your economy to compete in the world marketplace. The divine notion of participatory government has been reduced to a porcine feeding frenzy, each narrow-minded special interest biting off all it can chew of the body politic, mortgaging the future, the very lives of your children.

Religion, that great crucible of myth and wonder, staggers to collapse as your traditional Christian religion exhorts a world choked with overpopulation to reproduce without restraint, soothing your fears with mutterings that God will provide. Perhaps God is due for a wake-up call. Half the planet is starving. Untold misery, unspeakable atrocities are the result of religion's divorce of spirit from flesh, as if the body is some poor second cousin of the spirit, a base and untrustworthy nest of festering impulse and desire, besmirching the spirit's purity. Judaism finds its institutional apex in the State of Israel, whose status as a major arms supplier to the Pretoria regime manages to betray both the heritage of the Ten Commandments and the lesson of the Holocaust in one contemptible display of apostate greed.

Science, born of the wonder of the world and the urge to understand its workings, distanced itself from the excesses of religion and lost all sense of the divine. As it staggers from disaster to disaster, poisoning your water and air, fidgeting with the genetic structure of life, the process of conception, torturing animals, reducing you to mere ciphers in a worldwide battle for existence, science indeed confirms that there need be no supernatural order to the universe, for whatever good is inherent in mankind stands in stark contrast to the malignant evil of modern science, as vicious a voodoo as any culture ever devised.

We have seen how the institutions embodying the three great constructs of human civilization have failed you. Yet on the individual level, you can no more dispense with government, religion and science—in their pure, original form—than you can survive by refusing to eat and drink.

Municipalities, cities, counties and states chafe under the onerous burdens of federal restrictions and regulations, knowing that only at the local level can government truly be participatory, democratic and fair.

The committed Christian, stirred and inspired to a life of righteousness by the words of Jesus, looks on appalled at the hypocrisy and avarice of the television preachers, spitting out electronic venom and raking in millions. Many Catholics yearn to heed the divine urgings within, rather than submit to those uttered in St. Peter's Square.

The scientist peers into the microscope, and as one more mystery of life reveals its secret to his eyes, exclaims, "My God, a miracle!", his words unconsciously sweeping away the decades of training and dogma that would strip the world of its divine source.

For what are you, you men and women of the late twentieth century? Do you not feel the world crumbling about you? Do you not feel yourselves hurtling headlong into an abyss as your economy, your religions and your science all collapse in a heap of puerile rhetoric and mendacity? You know life has meaning, but who can provide it? Where can it be found?

Consider what it is to grow up in your society. Every child is born riding full tilt on Divine Grace; the process of socialization in your culture is one in which science robs you of your divinity while religion stuffs your head with fairy-tale nonsense; then government steps in, demanding that you spend your life as a slave to its voracious appetite and show proper gratitude for the privilege.

You are divine creatures. You assumed human form in order to experience physical life through your conscious, reasoning minds. Such is Divine Grace manifested through you, unique, inviolate, precious and divine creature that you are.

Reclaim your mind. Reclaim your senses. Reclaim your divinity.
Enter the New Dawn.

PART THREE
THE WORLD
AT LARGE

INTRODUCTION

Let us now take a desultory look at sundry areas of your society, your world, the workings of your bodies and so on. Applying what we know about Divine Grace, ignoring what you've been taught by science and religion, let us take a fresh look at a number of issues, knowing that the physically perceivable is always but a reflection of deeper, inner activity and truth.

CHAPTER TWENTY-TWO

Geography

Let us first look at geography.

Your world appears to your eyes to be a palette of infinite color, form, climate, vegetation and animal life, an extraordinary gift of limitless variety. Remember that variety is the signature of Divine Grace. Remember that all is, at base, energy, energy's intrinsic quality being motion.

Thus your world, as you perceive it, is a reflection of the inconceivable swirling clouds of energy that seed its mountains, rivers, deserts, seas and plains. Each such area of the planet has its unique purpose, a highly specialized field of exploration inextricably intertwined with the grand cooperative drama of the earth.

When this notion is combined with the nature and purpose of humankind, we find that people also specialize, those in a given geographical area most likely sharing certain personality characteristics, intents, desires and aptitudes. You create your own reality, including the world in which you live. Every geological structure of which you are aware is therefore a projection of your minds, a representation of one aspect of the infinite banks of energy and design that power your world. As such, you will find the inhabitants of a particular region faithfully reflecting the geographical features of the locale.

In your country, where are the regions of greatest innovation, artistic achievement, social progress and prescient thought? On the coasts, east and west. For a beach represents a bridge between realities, in your terms, between land and the mystery of the sea. In deeper terms, beaches reflect the membrane we spoke of much earlier where all "events" you experience are pulled into physical expression—onto land, so to speak. Thus you find the areas of greatest innovation and artistic expression located on the coasts.

There are differences, of course! California, being one such center, is also riddled with earthquake faults. Knowing that such a geological feature is a reflection of a hidden reality, what masked truths lie behind an earthquake zone?

An earthquake zone is one in which tremendous energy is stored, not easing itself into reality slowly and gently but in sudden, violent bursts. Vast changes occur in the earth's physiognomy overnight. Such land is highly unstable. Thus we see that an earthquake line represents an area of highly unstable energy, manifesting in sudden bursts, instantly altering the contours of the land.

It is thus no accident that the center of your film industry, film being the premier twentieth-century art form, is located smack on top of an earthquake zone! For genuine art is no shy debutante but a boisterous, raucous rowdy, pulling society forward in great bursts of energy, instantly changing the contours of society.

It is also no accident that you find such an accumulation of highly creative, highly unstable people inhabiting the coastal areas of California! For their states of mind perfectly mirror the geological structure on which they live, which in turn mirrors the desire of Divine Grace to maintain a balance, a counterpoint of highly unstable, creative activity against a nation of otherwise bedrock stability.

By the same token, that bedrock stability, geologically speaking, of the Midwest is reflected in those who live there. Traditional, conservative, solid and dependable folks are these, the keepers of the nation's breadbasket. Their comfortable traditions in the ebb and flow of society mirror the immutable cycle of seasons that provides their livelihood. Lives of tradition, of deeply rooted values, reflect the tradition of deeply rooted forest and stream, susceptible to no sudden grind of the earth's plates but couched in a secure and familiar framework.

If you can imagine a membrane covering the globe, the membrane through which all events you experience must pass, see it now as varying in thickness, allowing events smoother and faster passage in some areas than others. It is easier for wishes and dreams to come true in some places than others; in some spots memories last longer, as events play themselves out more slowly through the thickened membrane.

Again, California may be viewed as having the thinnest membrane of any section of your country, for not just in the entertainment field but also in the Silicon Valley are dreams and fortunes made with remarkable facility and ease. It is literally easier to consciously create one's own reality in such a locale, despite the physical membrane of the smog cover!

This again reflects the intent of All That Is to provide a world of infinite variety. In some locales, events fall into place more easily than others. There is no sense of hindrance in those areas of thicker membrane but a means of playing up contrasts among areas of the country, keeping the society and world always in a state of tension among differing qualities.

An example of how events take longer in some parts of the country to dissipate would be your Civil War. To the northern child, the war is dead and buried, a chapter in a history book, its essential dates and figures dutifully memorized and then forgotten come summer. In the South, the Civil War is still very much alive and kicking! The resentment of defeat lingers there, imbues the area's consciousness with a communal solidarity, as the "event" of the Civil War has yet to fully dissipate itself.

Again, in deepest terms there are no judgments, and the South is as much a part of the divine intent of All That Is as any other region, a means for your society to literally hold in its sight the past, present and future—South, Midwest and West Coast—the better to mark your progress, to try out the cutting-edge innovations of California while retaining the stability of the South and Midwest to scamper back to for cover! For some can dance a fine soft shoe on the cutting edge while others merely lacerate themselves; those in the traditional areas of the country can observe the process, pick and choose based on the results, and gradually ease into your society those innovations most beneficial and salubrious.

Today, as you know, your earth holds pockets of Stone Age tribes, as an even deeper reflection of the intent of All That Is to hold before your eyes the past, present and future—all time is simultaneous—with which to evaluate your society's progress. Until now you referred to such tribes as primitive, savages, the same way you dismissed your own Native American peoples. But as your soulless science wreaks death and destruction in every corner of your globe, you will return to those native cultures, humbling yourselves before them and seeking to relearn what you once knew but discarded in your blind rush to "progress."

Past, present and future; they all exist at once on your earth. From Stone Age tribesman to astronaut. From the bored northern schoolchild to the flag-waving Confederate drummer boy. From the heartland's chorus of "Onward Christian Soldiers" to the redwood-scented chants of Om.

All time is simultaneous. Variety is the signature of Divine Grace. States of mind are reflected in the states of the union.

Before your eyes, your geography displays in unfiltered truth the fundamental laws of the universe: the world you know is a reflection of your thoughts, beliefs and desires. You create your own reality.

CHAPTER TWENTY-THREE

Race

Have you ever wondered why there should be different races within the human species? Especially if evolution is but a fiction in the minds of the sons of Darwin, why should the human race be divided into different shades of skin color, varieties of physiognomy?

Did All That Is stop making flowers after the daffodil's creation?

Was the poodle sufficient to populate the world with dogs?

Why not stop at trout and keep all the world's fish supply in one, uniform strain?

Remember, variety is the hallmark of Divine Grace as it seeks always to explore every facet of physical existence.

With your love of divisions, you count four great races: white, black, yellow and red. Of course there are infinite gradations and combinations; your metaphor for your society is a melting pot, not a beaker with liquids of differing density jealously staking out their territory.

Again, always, any physical reality you experience is a reflection of deeper inner truths. What purpose might there be behind the variety of human races?

If mankind's unique and precious quality is its conscious, reasoning mind, that characteristic will be splintered into an infinite variety of human consciousness, the better to explore the planet through an infinite spread of reasoning filters. The different races, then, reflect both the quality of diversity within unity and also a diversity of purposes to which the rational mind can be put to use.

Your European civilization, manifesting principally in the white culture, is one of highly verbal and technological culture in which language is reduced to symbol, and the species' innate urge to manipulate its environs is put to service of practical ends—inventions, machines, designed to ease the drudgery of everyday life. Reflecting the white culture's predominant religion of Christianity, whose central theme is the divorce between spirit and flesh, white culture set up divisions, wedges, throughout all aspects of its existence: free-flowing language was harnessed into symbol, and inspiration channeled only into practical fields of endeavor. The fundamental quality of the white race, as you see in your society today, is **divorce from the natural order**. It is European culture, with its science and technology, that leads the march to doomsday. Thus, in this culture, mankind's conscious, reasoning mind was used to split asunder: speech from alphabet, body from soul, mankind from animal, God from peasant and feet from earth.

Contrast this with the cultures native to your country, your Native American peoples. Here were cultures of great sophistication and organization, hierarchies of tribal leadership, elaborate ceremonies and rituals, but all couched in a framework allowing no division between mankind and the natural world. As with early primitive man, Native Americans felt the divine's touch in every corner of creation. They too were inventors, innovators, their technology manifesting in weapons for the hunt, pottery to aid with food preparation, and a tradition of using every part of a downed beast for some practical purpose: the hide became clothing, the meat became food and the bones became tools. And always leaving little trace of their passing on the earth, knowing it to be the divine bed on which they and all other creatures rested. So in the red culture, man's conscious, reasoning mind was used to manipulate, build, create and invent, always in harmony with the natural order.

The black race is similar to the red in its instinctive harmony with the natural order but with the additional quality of gregariousness, of social contact with others. The vast area of the early American continent allowed most red tribes to exist with little contact from other tribes; but on the plains of Africa, numerous tribes coexisted in varying degrees of harmony, thus flavoring their culture with the exploration of social organization, cooperation, warfare, tribal loyalty and so on. African tribes were not nearly as distinct genetically from each other as were Native American tribes, thus allowing issues of loyalty and group cohesion to be played out without genetic basis. To this day, you know of tribal warfare among the clans of Africa, of truces made and broken, as this great exuberant theme of social intercourse is explored in rich, multifaceted drama.

No mention of the black race is complete without an exploration of their presence in your present culture. For, one hundred years after emancipation, the issue of race remains one of the most divisive and intractable of all you face.

Remember that all persons living in a given historical period are born with a preprogrammed package of information about the mores, traditions, customs and so on of the time and locale in which they are born. To some extent, the choice of race before birth also carries with it the history of that particular race, as heritage material. Thus blacks in your society, though descended from slaves brought over three hundred years ago, still carry vestigial memories of tribal origins.

This sets the stage for the conflict in your society. The white culture, its fundamental quality being divorce from the natural order, leaves by the wayside any individual or culture that holds cooperation higher than competition, that insists on a sense of community above personal achievement at the expense of others. When this brew is spiced with the economics of capitalism, the result is a fallout of haves and have-nots, the fissure invariably cutting a swath along racial lines. Other factors are involved, of course, as both on a personal and global scale one will experience both facets of an issue; if you enslave a race, forcing them to work not for their benefit but for yours, then centuries later you shall inevitably find many of that race not working at all, ground down by poverty and despair, draining your wallets as you now work for them.

Within your recent past, some researchers attempted to prove that blacks were genetically inferior to whites in terms of intelligence, as if cultural differences could somehow be eliminated in intelligence testing and faulty genes used to justify the second–class education in black schools.

And what would happen to our distinguished professor if he were suddenly dropped in the Kenyan bush with only his wits for protection? When we returned thirty days later, would we find him cataloging the flora and fauna of the plains? If we found him at all, it would only be as the carrion eaters polished the last scrap off his bones. For our beloved researcher reflects his own culture, the European line of development in which book learning and technological achievement are held supreme. But what of the razor-sharp intellect required to last even a day in a jungle full of carnivores? What of the cunning, the stealth, the deep instinctive knowledge of the animals' behavior that any jungle dweller knows without conscious thought? How can such be examined on a test written on a piece of paper, by definition a divorce, a symbolic retreat from firsthand reality?

We do not suggest that there is validity to the researchers' findings that black children are not the intellectual equals of their white counterparts. Instead, perhaps you can see that those choosing birth as black Americans in your time would carry not only the requisite intellectual skills to survive in European culture, but also carry the heritage of the jungle, of social organization and cooperation, and of intuitive connection with the earth.

And notice how the notion of genetic foundations of intelligence fell out of favor with the wave of Asian immigrants almost invariably outperforming their white friends! So much for genetics! What of the yellow race, then?

At base, this is also a culture with a strong bond between the spiritual and temporal, as you find in the religious philosophies of the East, their martial arts which emphasize inner discipline over outer violence, the mind–body synthesis of yoga, and the law of karma codified in their religions.

And yet, rising from that base, Eastern culture specialized in abstract reasoning. Where white culture leaned toward verbal expression, devising alphabets, Eastern culture concentrated on grand philosophy, looking for physical evidence of the deeply felt unity of creation, finding the patterns of that unity miraculously reflected in the workings of mathematics.

It is no accident that white culture invented the alphabet, in which a few symbols are rearranged in an infinity of meaning, while the Eastern culture devised more ponderous symbols of verbal expression, but also the abacus, a means of manipulating vast amounts of mathematical data centuries before white culture's invention of calculators. By contrast, observe the tortured calculations of early white culture, working out mathematical equations with his beloved paper and pen!

Thus did Eastern culture develop the ability to manipulate, rearrange and consider concepts and relationships reducible to mathematical equations, to order and understand the world as a series of such relationships.

In your time, with the history of that culture implanted before birth in all choosing birth as Orientals, we find such individuals excelling in the fields of mathematics, science and technology. For while white culture may justifiably claim itself the instigator for much of your history of scientific, technological advancement, such a line of development, when blended with Eastern culture's facility for manipulating symbolic relationships and patterns, results in those of Asian heritage succeeding brilliantly in technological fields in your culture and in the synthesis of East and West, Japan.

The notion of reducing the great racial heritage of the earth to a few paragraphs is so ludicrous we almost forewent the attempt. But as race is a key issue in your culture, it would be remiss of us not to mention it, at least in passing.

As you can see, the various races reflect various specializations of man's conscious, reasoning mind, following lines of development into verbal emphasis, synthesis of body with spirit, social organization, and manipulation of patterns and relationships. As such, each line of development is equally valid, of as much importance to the experiences of All That Is on your plane as any other. **No judgments of any kind** are implied or to be inferred by this discussion. Indeed, it is the white culture that comes out looking sorriest, its fundamental quality being divorce from the natural order, and yet such a path is just as creative as any other, provides just as much learning, in deepest terms, as the others.

And you have seen the extraordinary results when these unique strands of development combine, blend and interweave to form entirely new strains of consciousness. Such is the meaning of race.

Thus you can see what a sorry creature the racist is. For a true understanding of the role of race would bring an ever greater appreciation of the diversity of color. To turn that diversity into a liability, to proclaim any line of development as "inferior" to another, reflects a messy and bruising divorce indeed from the Divine Grace that granted you racial diversity!

Any divorce from Divine Grace leaves one floating helpless, unanchored, insecure, floundering about in an accidental world or one condemned to Hell. Against this backdrop, what is one measly human being? The racist who cries, "Nigger!" is shouting in hopes of drowning out his own inner cry of "I am nothing!" For only from an inner vacuum of despair and fear could one convince oneself that skin color, this most superficial of your attributes, reflecting the diversity that enriches your entire globe, shall be the mark and weight of a person's worth.

In the New Dawn upon you, those clinging to the disease of racism will be swept aside. You will celebrate your diversity, recognize the fundamental unity behind the rainbow of white, black, red and yellow, and join your varied strands of consciousness in a new intellect of unimaginable power and creativity, building a society that celebrates the diversity of consciousness while holding forever in mind that beneath your multihued skin there beats one heart, flows one blood and sings one divine, eternal song.

CHAPTER TWENTY-FOUR

Money

Remember that whenever faced with a question of importance, one need apply a two-pronged test: Does it matter in the woods? Does it matter to a three-year-old?

Does money matter in the woods? If you are lost in the forest, starving, and come upon a grizzly devouring a fine cut of tenderloin, would you pull out your wallet, offer it a fifty with a little extra for the wife and kids? Would the grizzly be impressed? Would you care to be dessert? Does it matter in the woods?

In the world of young children, has money any significance? If you want a child to do something and hand it a $50 bill, is it impressed? No; it wants reasons for your request, which it will then happily perform for free. A young child certainly understands barter and exchanging value for value, but in a direct fashion, not one reduced to scraps of green paper. Does it matter to a three-year-old?

With this background, we can see that money is made necessary by divorce from the natural order, by the specializations of an industrial society where one is paid for performing services for others and turns around to pay others to do the same.

There is no judgment implied here; we are simply stating a few basic facts. We do not mean to suggest that money is to be regarded with scorn, that poverty is spiritual, that the rich are any less worthy than the poor, or that the desire for comfort is a violation. These ideas are all perversions of the concept of money, as we shall see.

The need for money arose as individuals specialized in the sundry tasks necessary for sustaining an increasingly complex society. The farmer, the priest, the shopkeeper, the candle maker and the blacksmith all concentrated in the fields of their talent rather than each trying to grow his own food, shoe his horses, bake his bread and absolve himself of sin.

Money became an expression of value, then, based upon a society's judgment of the worth of the contributions of its members. What good is a horseshoe in a region without horses? Who needs a Catholic priest in a Buddhist society? What value has the candle maker in a world powered by electricity? The worth of an individual's contribution is thus relative to the time and place in which he/she lives, a consensus of the importance a society places on his/her efforts.

Money is thus an entirely metaphysical concept, one divorced from the workings of the natural world—does it matter in the woods?—and aligned only to the trained reason of adulthood—does it matter to a three-year-old?

There are those in your society who decry the loss of the gold standard, by which every note of your currency was backed by an equivalent value of gold in the nation's treasury. But what is gold, and how is its value determined? Does it not fluctuate up and down in value like the stock market? It has no intrinsic worth—can gold sustain the starving?—but is instead, like paper money, simply the reflection of the value assigned it by your society. Is gold valuable because it is rare? So is plutonium. We do not observe a rush to the plutonium standard, though your government certainly has more stockpiled than it has gold in Fort Knox!

Money, thus, is a metaphysical concept of value, agreed upon by mutual consensus. Let us observe a few facets of its presence in your society.

Your society is one that holds a panoply of paradoxical views of money. On the one hand, everybody wants it. On the other, you hate those who have it. On the one hand, the poor are spiritually pure. On the other hand, everybody would rather go to Hell in a gold-weaved handbasket. Your economic system proclaims wealth your just reward for hard work, while the church admonishes you about squeezing camels through the eyes of needles. You are told that money cannot buy happiness, yet many are miserable for want of it.

There are no closed systems, and thus we find the concept of money colored by the multiple contradictions and paradoxes inherent in your society with its divergent economic, philosophical, religious and social schools of thought.

Remember that the fundamental quality of European culture is divorce from the natural order. As such, divorced from a sense of one's innate divinity and an understanding of the great cooperation that sustains your world, you turn to a concept entirely foreign to the natural order—money—as a means of trying to regain the value that your divorce from nature created. You value a person on the basis of his or her wealth.

What other criterion have you? You see, in the last century, as the twin theories of Darwin and Freud conspired to rob you of divinity and reason, you nevertheless felt stirrings inside—as all creatures do—to strive for your greatest fulfillment. If such could no longer be found in a framework of divinity and natural order, you were left floundering, with only the essentially meaningless concept of money as your standard of value, your mark of a person's worth, your cushion of security.

Thus, it was no accident that at the early part of the century you saw the great rise of the industrialist giants of oil, railroad and automobile, poised in brilliant and stark contrast to the suffering multitudes whose labor made such fortunes possible. (There are no judgments implied in that sentence.) The point is that your society had embarked in a new direction, one divorced from a divine sense of the world, and in the scramble for meaning which you—like all creatures—must find or die, God was replaced with the industrialist, the cross with the dollar sign. The great industrialists were the high priests of their day, were they not—worshipped, revered and despised as surely as the leaders of any religion ever were.

The contrast between the wealthy few and the impoverished multitudes was so profound, so violated your innate sense of justice, that your country embarked on a path of correcting the perceived imbalances. You instituted an income tax. With the arrival of the New Deal, you marched to the tune of justice, fairness and equal opportunity for all. We are able to return now to our earlier discussion of the liberal philosophy, brilliantly realized in the New Deal, and examine once again the fallacious underpinnings.

Although your country was capitalist from the very beginning, and Freud and Darwin appeared much later, there are indeed themes and paths that require centuries to be fully played out. This is the case with the intertwining strands of capitalism, the fall of religion, the rise of science and so on.

We must now mention a few principles we have not offered before. First, know that every creature upon the face of the earth has embarked on a search for its greatest fulfillment. Nothing simply exists. Everything has a **purpose**. If you are unable to find the meaning in the life of a slug, the loss accrues to you, not the slug. Life is always **a search for meaning**. You see in your time how the economic system of capitalism—which permits vast contrast in wealth—intertwines with the theory of Darwin—life is constant battle—and science—you are accidents floating through empty space—to the inevitable result: a mad scramble for cash as the only medium of worth, the only societally recognized judge of a person's character.

And yet, on deep levels, you know such is not the case. Our point is that, try as you might, you can never fully mask the innate knowledge that life both has intrinsic meaning and is a search for greater meaning. Are you not touched by stories of heroism, of those who take great personal risk to aid others? What is the value of such a person against the soulless entrepreneur? You thrill to the laughter and bright eyes of your children. Do such bring you wealth? Your heart swells with joy as you watch a rainbow. Can you exchange the sight for cash? If you could, which would you rather have?

Again, you ride always on Divine Grace, and try as you might to deny the fact, construct grand theories of natural selection and Big Bangs and festering ids, Divine Grace always has the last laugh, for it is only when couched in its secure framework that you can turn around and deny its existence! You can never fully lose sight of it.

Divine Grace's one and only philosophy is that you create your own reality. This is the lesson of the earth plane, the reason you assumed human form, to learn to manipulate physical reality through your reasoning mind. Now, having denied Divine Grace, yet being unable to completely shut it out of consciousness, you then create an economic system that precisely replicates the philosophy that you create your own reality! This is the system of capitalism. The effort you expend will be rewarded in due measure by the society's measure of value, wealth. Those who do not work will starve. Years of concentrated effort will bring wealth. **You create your own reality,** and if you choose a path in which you refuse to acknowledge this consciously, you therefore construct a system in which this immutable law is played out every day, in every corner of your society.

The law that you create your own reality is thus reflected in your economic system of capitalism. Since this is the way you have chosen to manifest that law, the ground rules of the game are that what one works for, one is entitled to keep. No one shall be sacrificed for the sake of those who choose not to sustain themselves.

Remember our analogy of the softball player pulling a gun to walk off with the trophy, as shallow a prize as was ever won. Perhaps you can see more clearly the maze of contradictions and illegitimacy that is the liberal's philosophy. It begins with an outrage against a society displaying such great disparity of wealth—some eat off gold plates; others starve. You are offended by this contrast precisely because you ride always on Divine Grace, and in the natural order such a system would never come about. But it is precisely the abandonment of Divine Grace that led to the establishment of capitalism. Even still, denying Divine Grace as you are, the capitalist system nonetheless is the best you can come up with to reflect the universal law that one creates one's own reality. Capitalism thus reflects the mechanics of the universe while divorced from its divine source.

Whatever the ground rules of a society, whatever expression, however blunted, you grant to Divine Grace, it is illegitimate to betray the rules of the game, like our softball player, in order to force one's way back to the sensed but abandoned natural order. In this case, capitalism is the game and you know the rules. When you find the results so horrifyingly unjust, you are meant to examine the nature of the philosophy itself. Instead, you commit the violation of attempting to correct the imbalance that is a result of abandoning Divine Grace; and in doing so, you commit a further violation.

If the rules are that what one earns one keeps, you may not violate the rules by requiring those who achieve success at that game to relinquish their winnings at the point of a gun. Do you think we speak idly?

What happens if you refuse to pay your taxes, sensing the violation they are? A series of legal proceedings is instituted against you, culminating in foreclosure upon your property and the arrival of the sheriff to remove you from the premises. And if you meet the sheriff's firepower with your own, defending what you have earned? You will die. No tax protestor has yet to win a shootout with the government!

Any political philosophy that permits the slaughter of its citizens for any reason has revealed its intrinsic immorality. You who nodded in smug satisfaction when we dismissed communism with that sentence, are you smirking now?

The idea that you can be murdered by the state in order to liquidate your house in order to underwrite the beliefs and whims of others can only hold in a society gone mad.

On top of the denial of Divine Grace which is capitalism in pure form, you commit the further violation of then punishing those who play by the game you set up and succeed. Thus, you are prevented from finding the fruits of your labors accruing to you, prevented from creating your own reality.

We now tie this in with our discussion of money. Remember that it is a concept unique to mankind, and then only to those societies divorced from the natural order. (Bartering and trading are common among native peoples, of course, as value for value; they do not beat the symbolic retreat of printing money.) In a society that has lost its sense of the divine, of the natural order, drifting about in your accidental universe, the only value left you is money. It is your only security. It is your only standard of worth. It is your only mark of a person.

The liberal thus attempts to force at the point of a gun the rearranging of society's wealth precisely as a way of ensuring security for all, him/herself therefore included. One's body, being the liberal's sole value, must be swathed in an array of cradle-to-grave social programs, as nothing else has meaning. The liberal can offer nothing else, can he? No hope of salvation. No promise of an afterlife floating on wings and playing the harp. No sense that poverty and wealth are not absolutes of your existence but the result of your thoughts and beliefs.

In a religious world, you create your own reality by behaving yourself and going to Heaven, or by betraying God's word and going to Hell. The liberal, his life reduced to a paltry spread of a few years, must struggle for meaning—though he may deny that life holds any—and create his reality—though he refuses to see that he does so—by wrapping himself in a cocoon of social programs that will at least make the passing of accidental years bearable.

The great violation lies in the liberal's claim of altruism, his cornering the market on righteousness and compassion. Where is the compassion for the industrialist, who slaves for years to achieve his status? Where is the righteousness in a system that punishes those who struggle to create their own reality?

Your society is thus based on a crazy patchwork of misguided, misdirected and ultimately self-defeating philosophies. First you deny Divine Grace, robbing yourself of a sense of the natural order. Still feeling the intrinsic meaning of life, you establish an economic system mirroring the law that you create your own reality. When this plays itself out in vivid detail and contrast, revealing the fallacy of its secular underpinnings, you further the insult by punishing those who succeed by the rules you have established. With a host of fears fueling your social policies, rather than reason and divinity working in tandem as in the natural order, you rush headlong into economic Armageddon.

Remember that money's impetus, its reason for being, was as a medium of exchange of value. It always represented a deeper meaning. Now, with your society's divorce from divinity, money becomes meaning, the sole measure of a person's life. Your loss of the gold standard is instructive here. For as long as paper money was backed by gold, you understood in literal terms that money was the reflection of a more solid reality. This falls neatly into the original intent of money, being a reflection of deeper meaning. Abandoning the gold standard, you find that paper money is not a reflection of meaning, but the meaning itself. Divorced from divinity and the natural order, you view money as meaning itself, an end instead of a means.

After six decades of New Deal liberalism, you look about you and what do you find? Has poverty been eliminated? Have all wrongs been righted? Does everyone live in peace and contentment? Finding yourself shouting a resounding "no" to these questions, you have come to learn that "throwing money at problems," as you phrase it, cannot solve those problems.

Of course it can't! Money is not meaning in itself, but a reflection of meaning. How can it possibly solve a problem, by definition a challenge involving issues of deep meaning? You must tackle the source of a problem, not paper it over with the reflection of an entirely unrelated concept.

Lack of money is not the cause of poverty. Lack of money is one characteristic of poverty, but the true root lies elsewhere. In your society, it lies in your economic system, capitalism, coupled with social Darwinism, all built upon the quicksand of divorce from the natural order, from your divine source. When you throw money at the poor, you do not address the fundamental cause of poverty.

And here is another grand conceit of the liberal. While the liberal professes to engineer social policies out of compassion and responsibility for others, to simply throw money at others—other people's money to boot!—is to refuse compassion, to abandon responsibility. If you are truly responsible for others, you take care of them yourself; you do not pay others to express the compassion you are too busy to display. By constructing a panoply of social programs, then, by insisting that the government be responsible for the world's problems, the liberal wriggles out of any responsibility or direct involvement with others. It is hypocrisy, apostasy and mendacity rolled into one self-righteous bleat of concern for others.

Genuine compassion for others is not manifested by hiring surrogate caretakers for those for whom you profess concern. Would you give birth to a child, pay someone else to raise it and then proclaim your self-righteousness for being a responsible parent and taking care of your children? In this situation you have abandoned your responsibility as a parent, papered over the violation with a patina of cash and now consider yourself absolved.

Consider the state of your society. You have spent hundreds of billions to eliminate poverty. Are there any fewer poor among you? You have spent hundreds of billions, trillions on defense. Are you more secure than before? You have spent hundreds of billions, trillions on health care. Are you a healthier people?

The use of money to further a social goal is **always a refusal to face the root cause of that problem.** Spend yourselves into economic collapse, as you are doing, and still you will find nothing changed, no problems solved.

Even in a case like cleaning up toxic wastes, to simply paper over the problem with taxpayers' money again evades the fundamental issue. **Who created these toxic materials in the first place?** What is this imperial monster you have created, this bastion of science, that you allow to plunder and rape your world? This is the issue you must face, for otherwise as soon as you clean up one spill, another is certain to occur.

You must begin to attack the roots of your problems, not their effects.

Money, being simply a medium of exchange, is incompetent to do the job.

You must use your conscious mind, and do so with an understanding of the divine source of your world.

It may appear from time to time that you have indeed "conquered" a given problem through expenditure of money. In all such cases, what you have instead done is to eliminate one reflection of the problem, leaving the root cause unexamined and therefore unexorcised.

This occurs because money is an expression of value to you. When your society expends vast sums on a given facet of a problem, that "value" imparted by such a sum stirs things up in the great unseen cauldron where your physical reality is created, such that the intent behind the expenditure of money will indeed produce the desired effect, i.e., eliminating that specific problem.

But remember that any fear or philosophy given birth by your divorce from Divine Grace will manifest in increasingly obvious, ludicrous or lethal expressions, as a way of drawing your attention to the root source. You are never given insolvable problems, dropping from the sky to crush you without warning. Always, first comes a slap on the wrist, then a slap on the cheek, then a blow to the kidneys, and finally, if you have not faced the root issue, you will be beaten black and blue.

Such is the case, for instance, as we have seen, with nuclear power. Three Mile Island was the slap on the wrist. Chernobyl was the smack in the face. Must you be beaten black and blue?

To return to the involvement of money in this process, you have, for instance, "cured" certain diseases by expending vast sums on research and developing a vaccine that prevents its expression. Thus, you feel you have "solved" the problem, "cured" the disease.

You have done no such thing. What you have done is to eliminate one facet, one expression, of the root problem, the root being **disease itself.** There is no need for disease; it is not an intrinsic part of the natural order. It is a result of your beliefs, especially those of science, in which the miracles of your bodies are reduced to machines, spring-powered toys wound up at birth and set off careening through life, forever prey to any germ or virus that happens your way. Further, of course, science and medicine scoff at the notion that you create your own reality, that your body is your most intimate creation and is therefore **forever under your control.**

In the issue of disease, then, observe your recent history. Polio was a scourge a generation ago. How did it operate? It crippled. It left you impaired but alive. After expending vast sums on research, you indeed created a vaccine that rendered the disease impotent. But you did not face the root issue, that of disease itself.

Now you find yourselves with the AIDS virus. You created this virus—yes, you created it—as a faithful reflection of the nonsense of science and medicine; and what is the virus's effect this time around? It is an automatic death sentence. None of this "wheelchair for life" business anymore! Now you die.

So again you gear up to expend hundreds of millions, billions, trillions of dollars on research; and perhaps in a decade you will have a vaccine and eliminate this scourge. And what then? The AIDS virus is a weakling, dead on contact with oxygen. What of a virus combining AIDS's lethal certainty with transmission through casual contact, by mere presence in the same room with an infected person?

Let us hope you need not be beaten black and blue over the issue of disease.

We are getting somewhat off the track here. But you understand now that even when you appear to have solved a problem by spending money, you have only eliminated **one facet** of the problem and will be faced with increasingly harmful reflections of the root issue until you face it squarely and dismiss it from your reality.

Money, poor little innocent, neutral money, has a bad name in your society, after decades of being branded the root of your problems, when instead it merely reflects them. Those with money are expected to feel guilty, to do penance by setting up philanthropies and demonstrating their compassion; one must never actually allow oneself to enjoy it, at least not in the sight of others!

You are here on this earth to enjoy it, to explore its richness and variety in as many areas as you can. If your system be one in which money is your reward for effort and the medium through which you can enjoy life, then enjoy it! What is your crime—that you have worked hard to support yourself and your family? That you choose not to wallow in listless poverty? As long as you play by the rules you have established, you had best enjoy your success, as an exuberant and joyful celebration that **you have created your own reality.** For that is the fundamental law of the universe; if you know it and act on it, do not deny yourself the pleasure of success, as your system is currently established.

And enjoy it while you can, for as the world moves toward renewal with Divine Grace, no system will survive that allows such contrasts in wealth, nor one that doubles the violation through taxation and social engineering. The times ahead can be as difficult or painless as you wish, but however you choose to experience it, you must at long last begin to face your problems at their roots, not throw money at their reflections. You must cast aside those philosophies and fields of endeavor inimical to the expression of Divine Grace in your world. You must return money to its proper place, as a medium of value, not as your highest value itself.

This will come about when you reclaim your soul from science and your mind from religion. The time of challenge can be as traumatic or effortless as you wish.
You choose.

CHAPTER TWENTY-FIVE

Good Intent

efore we proceed, it seems important that we pause to examine a few issues that may have arisen by this point.

After our last chapter, those of you of liberal persuasion may well feel yourselves humiliated and angered. But you **are** compassionate, you say; you **do** want to help others live lives of happiness and fulfillment.

Of course you do. It is human nature to assist others of your species, to wish to help them when they stray from life's sure path. You, like every other member of your species, act always out of good intent. Always. Perhaps we have not stressed this before.

You see the world shortchanging some of your brethren, and in your instinctive desire to help, you fashion a political system that will alleviate the suffering of those worst off.

The problem arises, as it always does, in that the system used to effect such concern is one divorced from Divine Grace. As such, it must necessarily play itself out as a betrayal of the very goal you hope to achieve. It must. It is the universe's way of gently demonstrating to you whether your actions and beliefs are in your best interest or not. If they are not, if they are divorced from the sure beacon of Divine Grace, they will always ultimately collapse upon themselves, the better to bring to your attention the fallacy of basing any system of thought on anything other than Divine Grace.

You act always out of good intent. You who dutifully lip sync the Evolution Rag of Darwin, why do you then turn around and help the most downtrodden of your species? Are they not clearly defective strains, better left out of the gene pool? While chanting the anthem of evolution, you demonstrate daily your unconscious recognition of its falsity by your instinctive demonstrations of compassion.

Remember that all paths, all avenues of exploration, are **creative**. That includes paths resulting in the most horrific cruelty and degradation. For from them, you **learn**, do you not? And that is what you are on the planet for, in human form: to learn to manipulate physical reality through your conscious mind. On deepest terms there are no judgments, ever—simply an unquenchable thirst to learn, grow and expand.

The further a philosophy or system of thought is from being based on Divine Grace, the sooner it will collapse in a heap of contradiction, violence or absurdity. In your time, you still bear the searing scars of Hitler's Holocaust, do you not? For such a philosophy—that Germany's loss in World War I was attributable to the Jews and they therefore deserved extinction—is the vilest betrayal of Divine Grace known in this century, and it therefore collapsed within several decades, while pulling the entire world into the process, the better to awaken the entire earth consciousness.

There is an instructive note here, so let us digress a moment. The choice of the Jews as the focus of the blame is a key to why Hitler failed so horribly and completely. We have seen that European culture's primary quality is divorce from the natural order, the natural order's only law being that one creates one's own reality. Observe the Jews through the centuries. Wherever they go, they prosper, despite the prejudice and hostility of the host culture. No matter how beaten down, how circumscribed their avenues of activity, they survive to build anew, to prosper, to triumph. They stand as an example, therefore, of the immutable law that you create your own reality. Have you known of a time or place where the Jews simply gave up, threw up their hands, resorted to crime and welfare? Never. We cannot go into detail now, but the Jews are a manifestation of a certain family of consciousness that weaves its way throughout your history, throughout the globe, ensuring that "you create your own reality" is always held before your eyes as the fundamental law of the universe.

You see now why they are persecuted: The last thing the miserable of the world want to hear is that they are responsible for their lot! And the Jews, proud, industrious, thriving, are a slap in the face to those self-pitying souls who prefer to blame fate, God, racism, poverty, what have you, for their lot in life. Thus are Jews singled out over and over again, as if by snuffing out the carriers of the universe's immutable law you can eliminate the law itself!

So for Hitler to blame the Jews for Germany's loss in World War I is a perfect illustration of projection of one's failures upon others, as well as a desire to eliminate the supposed source of what are in fact one's own shortcomings. By turning upon the people who best exemplify the universal law, he guaranteed that his system would crumble sooner rather than later. Divine Grace was flailed alive along with the Jews, and thus the system that pursued such a course was doomed to collapse.

And the final lesson of the Holocaust, of World War II, of all the millions of lives lost, of all the blood spilled, is to bring before your eyes in horrifying detail the results of a philosophy based upon a betrayal of Divine Grace. It did not work, did it? It did not bring Germany renewed pride, did it? It did not restore the economy, did it? It failed utterly on all such counts, and do take heed! Betray Divine Grace and you will find your philosophies turning inside out, presenting their very opposites to your eyes, the better for you to see the fallacies underneath.

In our chapter on politics and liberals, then, we examined how fear of annihilation drives the liberal and his policies, and the end result is precisely the **opposite** of "greatest good for the greatest number." Do take heed!

The philosophy of the modern-day liberal is far less of a betrayal of Divine Grace than Hitler's Third Reich, and therefore it takes much more "time" to play itself out and reveal its fallacies. But they are present, and you see in the unmistakable signs of impending economic collapse that such a philosophy has failed.

Any philosophy based on **fear** is automatically a betrayal of Divine Grace, for in the natural order of things **there is absolutely nothing to fear!!!** Fears are always the result of a misinterpretation of reality, the conscious mind cut off from its divine source and left to flounder, seeing goblins and hoodlums where there is only divine harmony.

The ghetto mother reading these words may well wonder what planet we think we are addressing. Despite all evidence to the contrary, we do affirm that there is **nothing to fear** and that the **universe is safe.** If you experience it otherwise, **examine your beliefs,** both individually and as a society. The ghetto is a literal representation of the state of your society, for on its mean asphalt streets one is literally cut off from the natural source of the world, from the company of tree and flower and bird song. Thus you find such seemingly intractable conditions of poverty and despair, of cheap, disposable lives struggling for mere existence against impossible odds. The ghetto is the very quintessence of your society as a whole in its divorce from Divine Grace. Do take heed!

We have been rambling about for a bit here, so let us sew up this discussion. First, we do not mean to imply that any of your philosophies are deliberately calculated to lead to harm. Instead, we affirm that every person acts always out of his/her **best intent.** This is true of the priest warning against premarital sex, of the parent beating the errant child, of a society fractured by racism. Always, you strive toward that greater meaning you sense your life holds, but you do so crippled as long as you relinquish your understanding of the divine source of the world and of the importance of using your conscious mind to manipulate it. The "negative" experiences you encounter, individually and en masse, are always meant to demonstrate that a fallacy is at work, that Divine Grace has somewhere along the line been betrayed. If you understood the workings of Divine Grace, you would then critically examine the philosophy leading to the "negative" outcome and change accordingly.

So. You ride always on Divine Grace. You act always out of the best intent. Your universe is safe. If you experience it otherwise, examine your philosophies and beliefs under the divine, reasoning eye of Divine Grace, for the fallacies behind such beliefs will always lay themselves bare under your scrutiny.

You create your own reality.

CHAPTER TWENTY-SIX

Sexuality

Let us examine one curious facet of human sexuality, as distinct from that of the animals. You have no doubt noted that in the natural world, the world of animals, sexual activity is almost exclusively limited to a specific "mating period" when the females are in estrus and the males in the mood for love. Following the mating season, depending upon the nature of the species, the two sexes can either go their ways or remain together; but the sexual activity ceases. It is thus an instinct in the animals, one leading solely to procreate the species, rather than as a source of continuous pleasure.

Why should you be different? Does it not seem a contradiction that you, whose distinguishing feature is your conscious mind, should know no seasonal ebb and flow of sexual energy, but a fairly steady stream of desire? Is this not a paradox? From an evolutionary standpoint such an attribute makes no sense either, for the female of your species is ripe for implantation only several days out of the month.

Your time terms make a "beginning" to your world a linguistic and chronological necessity, though in deepest terms there was no "beginning" and will be no "end." Still, accepting the limitations of your perceptions, there was no gradual evolution of life forms upon your planet; each species you are now aware of was thrust into physical existence **all at once**, in your terms. You may consider the intent of All That Is to be, on a massive scale, what you now know about how you create your own reality: thought creates physical reality. All That Is therefore "seeded" your world with an infinite variety of consciousness, form and purpose, all set in motion in one grand self-balancing mechanism working ever toward the greatest fulfillment of all its members.

Humankind's distinguishing feature is its conscious, reasoning mind. Precisely out of concern that such could lead to divorce from the natural order, your species was "set up" to seek and enjoy sexual experience at all times, regardless of the female's menstrual condition. You were thus kept always in touch with the natural order, for sex is the most impulsive, irrational act of which you are capable, in the sense that it is an abandonment of reason to pure joy and sensation. It is meant to be enjoyed, then, on a regular basis, precisely as a way of ensuring that you do not lose contact with the divine source of the world and its natural order.

The animals, you can now see, have no such need for constant sexual experience, as they are by nature living in harmony with the natural order and its divine source. They have no conscious minds that can fabricate nonsense about natural selection and Big Bangs. They know better, without conscious knowing.

And so there is no need for them to experience sexuality beyond the simple pro-creative act. They indeed had better concentrate on storing up food for the winter!

So what sets you apart from the animals in your sexual experience is that you are able and urged to experience it at all times and in all seasons. It is your gift from All That Is and your constant reminder of your divine source.

Built upon this foundation is the further feature of sexuality: Both the sex act and the birth process so closely and beautifully parallel the very creation of your physical world. You call it your act of procreation, do you not, and your words again betray your deep, unconscious knowledge.

Remember that the fundamental quality of All That Is is an exuberant energy thrusting across the membrane of the physical world to create the earth and everything upon it. And the sex act? We do not mean to spoil the surprise for those yet to experience it, but one does not simply insert penis A into vagina B and go wash the dishes while the sperm and egg lethargically meet for drinks. The sex act is one of great thrusting energy, of exuberance. It thus **exactly replicates** the very creation of your world. The **motion**, the **energy**, the **intent**, the **ecstasy** of the sex act are all also fundamental qualities of Divine Grace made manifest in your world.

And birth? A human child is **thrust into physical existence across a membrane by the thrusting intent, love and desire** of the mother. Sound familiar? All our talk about thrusting intent across membranes into physical existence was not mere idle chatter, as you can now see. You **replicate the very process** by which the world is made every time a baby's head pokes out from the birth canal to face the physical world.

There is no more dynamic, powerful or aggressive act of which your species is capable, and it is the sole province of that fair, weak and gentle sex! Your male warriors with all their weaponry and implements of death can't even approach the strength, the power, the energy of this uniquely female act.

So we see that the sex act, and birth, precisely because they return you to a realm of impulse and irrational action, are your closest links with the divine natural order from which you spring, and replicate precisely the very creation of your world.

Given the above discussion, given the understanding that the intent of All That Is was precisely to ensure sexuality as a constant and pleasurable experience, how have you fallen so far from that initial intent? How have you managed to saddle and encrust it with so much contrary belief?

Alas, we must once again point the accusing finger at religion. In its birth, a religion's fiery exultant promise attracts and holds its followers; but as time goes on, and the initial energy of a religion's genesis wanes, new channels of energy must be found. All persons run always on impulse, so the repression of impulses is a job never finished, never complete. To circumscribe and repress the sexuali-ty of its followers—that most private and impulsive of acts—ensures both a perpetual source of canon fodder and that all other impulses will fall meekly into line.

We do not suggest that such strictures began with the Catholic church, for Moses' stone tablets carried the stern "thou shalt not commit adultery," did they not? Again, this has been so misinterpreted over the centuries as to have virtually no relation to the initial intent behind the proscription. At that time, it was common for men to pursue all women of interest, whether married to them or to others or not at all. The result was a cheapening of the special bond between a man and a woman committed to each other, particularly where the raising of children is involved.

Moving up to Christianity and its need to consolidate power early in its life, we saw how the mere interpretation of the Scriptures resulted in Mary's posthumous restoration to virginity, the determination that the men and women of the church should replicate her virginity by remaining chaste, and the resultant wedge driven between spirit and flesh. And here lies the source of your sorrow, shame, guilt and heartache.

The body is the **physical manifestation** of spirit. There is no divorce between them. Your greater entity assumes human form through you; it does not cast off human shapes into the earth plane, to watch with disinterest at the events of their lives. The only distinction between your body and your spirit is that your body is that physically recognizable portion of your spirit that has crossed the membrane into physical reality. There is no divorce, simply a **projection of intent** across the membrane, manifesting as your body. There is no divorce between spirit and flesh; the body is simply the reflection of the spirit. If you could understand and believe this, half the world's troubles would end tomorrow! As we have seen, the acts of sex and birth are reflections of divinity, not their betrayal.

The only acceptable sexual act in the eyes of the Catholic church is that which leads to the possibility of procreation: heterosexual intercourse without birth control. Yet, as we have seen, your capacity for continuous sexual enjoyment, irrespective of whether the act will lead to conception, is the distinguishing hallmark of humankind, as opposed to the animals. To thus accuse you of surrendering to "animal instincts" is to insult both you and the animals. If you had animal instincts, you would feel the need for intercourse only once a year!

Of all the philosophies based on the betrayal of Divine Grace, what has shown itself in more appalling and excruciating result than the church's condemnation of birth control and concomitant urging you to be fruitful and multiply, beyond all capacity of you, your society, your nation and your earth to sustain the resulting billions? In Latin America now, where the Catholic church's hold is strong, you find the populace drowning under a sea of children for whom it can never properly care. Is this God's plan? What sort of God is this, then? If He is to provide, in exchange for devotion and worship, has He not failed to keep His end of the bargain? If so, are not those who claim to be His earthly representatives guilty of deceit and hypocrisy? Should their philosophy not therefore be abandoned, as a betrayal of Divine Grace?

Pleasure, yes. Overpopulation, no. For too many centuries have you allowed your men of the collar to deprive you of your instinctive understanding of sex's role in your lives, to equate chastity with divinity when true divinity knows nothing of restraint and denial!

The great tragedy of your society is that not only is sex in general considered "dirty," but any expression outside adult heterosexual intercourse becomes therefore an outright sin, if you are meant to enjoy sex solely as a procreative act.

The guilt and shame are built upon hierarchies, then. Religion is the top of the heap, justifying its intrusion into this most private area of life by misinterpreting Scripture and, through their chaste clerics, driving a wedge between spirit and flesh. Society then joins in, to some extent basing its prohibitions upon religion's, but even those who are not devout frequently share the church's view of sex. On the family level, parents, having absorbed decades of negative programming about sex, induce shame and guilt in their children, their adolescent children particularly, perverting what should be an arena of joy and pleasure into repression, guilt, shame, fear and anger.

As we have seen, humankind was given the capacity for continuous sexual pleasure precisely as a way of balancing the influence of the conscious, reasoning mind. We do not mean to suggest, therefore, that one must always have a sexual partner or be considered abnormal or defective. Always, variety is the signature of Divine Grace, and there are indeed those whose preoccupations with career or artistic achievements are so all-encompassing that a relationship with another, long- or short-term, would be a distraction, a hindrance. There is no need for everyone to be involved in the frantic libidinal game of musical chairs that is the current state of your society.

For one thing, no partner is necessary for sexual pleasure. You have been taught that masturbation is a sin, for a variety of ridiculous reasons not worth mentioning. To determine what the intent of All That Is was vis-à-vis this issue, please perform the following exercise: Stand in front of a full-length mirror. Allow your arms to dangle freely at your sides. Observe what area of the body your hands naturally inhabit.

End of exercise. End of discussion.

Given that the vast majority of the species is heterosexual, and given the undeniable special quality to that bond between male and female, what can we determine about the intent of All That Is in setting up such an attribute of your species? What is the difference between men and women, and why the thrill when they combine their differing intent and energy?

Observe the natural world. Observe your own species, up until recently. You will find that the male is the physically stronger, the protector of the herd or brood. The female is frequently smaller, slighter in build and heft, and occupied much of the time with the process of bearing and raising young.

Now, in your society in recent decades, the rise of feminism has tended both to shatter some choking restrictions placed on women in your society but also to mask the real differences between the sexes.

The great problem in your society, based as it is on capitalism—no closed systems!—is that when a person's sole measure of worth is his/her financial status, then the homemaking mother is indeed the lowest on the totem pole, for she is dependent upon her husband's financial status for her own identity. There is no worth imparted to her by virtue of being a mother—anyone can do that!— and since it is not a paying position, it is therefore looked down upon as being without value.

What higher value could there be than the proper rearing of one's children?? There is none. There is nothing your society, any society, your generation, any generation, does that is of greater importance than the way it rears the next generation. Yet because of your economic system, that most crucial of responsibilities was viewed as the **lowest** of all possible aspirations, the title of "homemaker and mother" viewed as a pathetic grasping at worth and dignity by those who cannot do anything else.

Now, while you are part of the natural order, it is precisely your rational minds that set you apart from it. In a highly technological society, where you are free from constant physical danger, there is no **need** for men to remain the providers and protectors of the family. Women are blessed with the same intelligence, creativity and skills as men, and for those who wish to pursue avocations on their own, it is no violation for them to do so.

The unfortunate result of feminism in your society is that women are **assuming traditional male values** instead of liberating the society from them. Women are donning drab business suits, entering the sterile environment of the business world, abandoning their children as men have traditionally done in your culture, joining the competitive rat race and therefore **abandoning** the especial feminine qualities of nurturance, warmth and empathy. There is no **place** in the boardroom for such qualities; so rather than force a change in the boardroom, women are instead assuming the repressed demeanor of men in order to compete in that world.

Nowhere is this more evident in appalling shame than in women agitating to join the armed forces. For all your history, women have wisely kept out of the murderous squabbles of men over territory, pride and money, waiting at home with the children for the nonsense to end. For you now to claim liberation by abandoning the nurturance of children in order to learn to kill them is to stock your ovaries with grenades instead of eggs, transform your wombs into bloody fields of battle instead of bloody channels of birth, and to violate the purpose and intent of every fiber of your beings.

The fundamental flaw in the path of "women's liberation" in your society is in women accepting the traditional male qualities rather than **challenging** them.

There is no shame in being a mother! What contemptible betrayal of the natural order could lead you to believe that the bearer of children is lower in station than the stockbroker? the doctor? the lawyer? There is no higher calling than the parents—men and women, now—who actively involve themselves in the rearing of their children.

To return to our initial point, then, there are differences between men and women, as viewed in the natural world, but your technological society diminishes their importance. Still, the image of the strong, aggressive, explorer male and the warm and nurturing female do have basis in fact.

For it is precisely the **blending** of these qualities that creates the special synergy of the loving couple. One outward looking, one inward looking. One manipulating physical reality, the other nurturing the spirit. Together, their intrinsic qualities meet their complements, and the result is a symbiotic synthesis that no man or woman alone can achieve.

Remember that variety is the hallmark of Divine Grace, that the world is a great drama of cooperation leading to the fulfillment of all its members. Men and women are different precisely as a way of lending diversity and therefore strength to the world; their joining together in a bond of power and strength that no lone individual can achieve is a demonstration of the symbiotic cooperation that blesses all the world.

True liberation, of women and men, can only come when your society returns to an understanding of Divine Grace, recognizes the unique contributions of male and female, values the mother as highly as the scientist, affirms that every person has worth regardless of net worth and that nothing matches the importance of raising the next generation to be happy and sane.

The great danger in speaking as we have is that our words will be used as instruments of oppression, of proscription and limitation. **Divine Grace knows nothing of oppression.** If you think we advocate a return to a time when women were denied the expression of their intellectual abilities, and men were repressed automatons, we must return you to our remedial class! Our point is that while there are differences between men and women, they are meant to **complement** each other, to create a special bond when joined, that bond **strengthening and enriching** the society.

And while we have held the raising of children to be the highest calling to which you can aspire, we do not mean to suggest that everyone must bear children or be reduced to a bereft life of dreary emptiness. In the great span of time, with the infinity of times and places from which your greater entity can choose to project itself into physical reality, there will certainly be lifetimes of refreshing contrast, where the usual mantle of heterosexuality and parenthood will be left aside in favor of fresh experience.

This brings up another essential point: Nothing we say about the "normal" condition of your species is ever meant to imply that those who deviate from it are in any way betraying the natural order. The signature of Divine Grace is **variety**, and just as your society benefits from its infinity of colors, attitudes, lifestyles and beliefs, so too do you **enhance** the natural order by breaking out of the mold and experiencing life in fresh and uncharted waters. Nothing we say is ever intended to repress, to rob the individuality and uniqueness of each of you, or your importance in the overall scheme of things. To claim a special bond between men and women is not to degrade the homosexual; to claim that motherhood is a woman's natural calling does not cheapen the lives of those women who choose other fields of challenge; to claim there are natural differences between men and women does not justify using those differences as tools of repression.

No repression. No restrictions. No oppression. Divine Grace knows only exploration, challenge, growth and variety.

As an example of a path on which your society has embarked that moves toward greater expression of Divine Grace, rather than its betrayal, you find the computer revolution has allowed many persons to work part- or full-time at home. Thus, men and women can pursue their intellectual and avocational goals while remaining in constant proximity to their young children. Now we're talking liberation!

Since we have broached the subject, let us explore now why some would choose sexual attraction and intimacy with those of their own sex.

With your love of labels and divisions, you split the experience of sexuality into heterosexual and homosexual. You grant that there may be bisexuals as well, though they make you nervous, not fitting neatly into either category.

Sexuality is, at its base, a means of ensuring "intimate" contact between the members of your species. Remember that your sexual desire is a fairly constant drive, precisely as a means of reminding you of the natural order from which you spring. At its most basic, sexual energy is neither heterosexual nor homosexual but simply the intent of All That Is that you should share intimate experience with each other.

As it approaches your plane, there being two sexes, it necessarily divides into two main camps of heterosexual and homosexual. Particularly in your society, these divisions are unnaturally rigid. How do you define the individual who has mostly homosexual experience at a young age, later moving on to heterosexual expression? What of those able to maintain attraction to both sexes throughout life?

At your base, you are neither heterosexual nor homosexual, but simply **sexual**. You feel an urge to join with others of your species in pleasurable union; this basic and undifferentiated intent then specializes, such that most will indeed choose to experience that special synergy of man and woman and, incidentally, to procreate the species. Children are the icing on the cake (you harried parents, skip this sentence), not the purpose of sexuality at its core.

So while most choose heterosexual expression, others choose to concentrate on exploring the essence of male and female within their own sex. For just as heterosexual union has a special synergy, so too does homosexual experience. It is a way of experiencing "concentrated" masculinity or femininity. It thus always involves a more intensive exploration into the meaning of male and female than does heterosexual expression, just as the scholar who pursues a study of Shakespeare achieves a unique insight that his colleagues studying the range of English literature cannot match. The homosexual is thus, without exception, a scholar in the study of what it means to be female or male.

As such, with the unquenchable desire of your greater entity to experience life in all its dimensions, somewhere along the line you will **always** manifest as a homosexual, for at least one lifetime. Now! Knowing what you know about how your conduct in this life influences your experiences in all others, would you rather be marching in a gay pride parade or pelting them with stones? Those who rail the loudest and shrillest against homosexuality are setting themselves up for some fine peltings down the line! For the essential, universal quality of self-balance holds always within the greater entity's experience of physical life.

The choice of homosexual expression is thus selected by the greater entity as a refreshing break in a new dimension of activity, as a way of exploring the essence of one sex rather than the synergy of heterosexual union.

An additional factor may be that the planned achievements of the life involve such all-encompassing dedication throughout life that children would be a hindrance. Thus you find a preponderance of homosexuals in the arts. Not only is the artist by nature compelled to create, dance, sing, whatever, above all else—including family ties—but in the young years, the childbearing years, frequently much study, practice and sacrifice are required before achieving mastery of the craft. There can be no place for children in such a life. So while you condemn homosexuals both for not having children and posing a danger to those of others, in fact, homosexuality is an expression of how greatly children are cherished in the grand scheme of things, and the inability to create them an act of love toward little creatures better off not born than neglected.

Given this, why the revulsion toward the homosexual in the history of western civilization?

First of all, they don't "fit in." They are not "normal." With your love of divisions, labels, categories, sameness, the homosexual represents a troublesome spark of variety. They do not procreate. Thus, as a result of the church's evolution, they are condemned a priori, for they defy by their very nature the commandment that sexual activity shall always allow the possibility of conception. Thus have we found good Christian souls throughout your history doing God's work on earth by torturing, dismembering and murdering these abominations, these who know pleasure as an end in itself, not simply the means to conception.

Look where centuries upon centuries of these attitudes have brought you. Who are your heroes, in your day and age? Whom do you flock to see in your movie theaters? Men shouldering weapons the size of aircraft carriers, whose sole modus operandi is to kill and maim other men. Your heroes are those who destroy life.

And the homosexual? He who desires only to give pleasure to other men? He is the scourge of your society.

You cheer those who kill other men. You revile those who give pleasure to other men.

There is another aspect of homosexuality that deserves mentioning. Though your stereotypes exaggerate such qualities, you find with some frequency that lesbians tend to "act like men," while homosexual men act and appear feminine. What is occurring here? In one more expression of the variety and ingenuity of Divine Grace, the homosexual experiences heterosexual synergy within the confines of his or her own body. Male and female are combined under one roof, so to speak, as a means of intensively exploring what it means to be male or female. There is no need for a partner of the opposite sex; one carries it always within one's own psyche! It is one more expression of the intent of All That Is to explore physical life and all its attributes in as unlimited a variety as possible.

Let us turn our discussion of sexuality to an area of great concern and confusion: adolescent sexuality. What is the intelligent, rational and compassionate approach to it?

As we shall see later in our discussion of the stages of life, adolescence is a time in which the psyche literally unravels and reshapes itself. During the process, the psyche is diffused, unfocused. Unable to form the lasting commitments of adulthood, but feeling the rush of new hormones, adolescents feel strongly compelled toward sexual activity with a variety of partners. Early adolescence is the most likely time for homosexual exploration, as at this stage sex is entirely devoid of any sense of commitment, is experienced solely as a means of pleasure, and before those first hesitant approaches can be made to the opposite sex, it is natural to explore this brave new world with one's own sex.

The purpose and meaning of sex change as one ages. In adolescence, diffused and unfocused, sex is primarily to be experienced on the level of pure pleasure. Adult, life-long commitments are impossible.

Anyone at age forty who still approaches sex as an adolescent, as a means of gratification devoid of commitment, has missed some very important boats along the way. The purpose of sex at age forty is to cement an emotional commitment.

You see now the setup for the great trauma over sexuality between middle-aged parents and adolescent children. They are like creatures from different galaxies trying to communicate through crude sign language, each interpreting the signals in its own fashion, finding no common ground or understanding. The parent, naturally sensing within him/herself that sex is meant to express commitment, looks on aghast at the relative shallowness of the adolescent's commitment and therefore concludes that the adolescent should not engage in any sexual activity at all, until sex can be linked with love in an adult fashion.

The purpose of adolescence, as the psyche of the child unravels to re-form into that of the adult, is to try out everything life has to offer. Sex included. Thus the adolescent's peripatetic sexual explorations are most natural at that age, while from the filter of middle age they are simply perceived as unbridled licentiousness.

Compounding this conundrum in your society is that long centuries of repression and homophobia have blocked many normal avenues of seeking out the tenderness and affection that all must have or die. While you consider it "normal" for teen-age boys to pursue sexual activity with single-minded lust, this is not the most "natural" expression of adolescent sexual urges—you will not find such compulsion among the young of native societies, for instance.

Just as adult men in your society can find tenderness, warmth and affection only in the arms of women they love, so are teen-age boys taught that their quite natural urges for tenderness and touch—which exist apart from and in addition to the ascending sexual need—can be fulfilled only in the arms of girls. The dual layers of sexual urge and the need for affection are thus melded into one driving, urgent, insatiable hunger for sexual experience.

A culture that understood and encouraged the natural, spontaneous, easy flow of affection between members of the same sex, and among members of a family, would find a marked decrease in the **urgency** of the teen-age boy's urge.

This is not to say the urge would disappear! Nor that it should not be acknowledged and accepted. The loving and attentive parent will recognize it and offer guidance available from the wisdom of maturity: the importance of respect for one's partner in all aspects, not simply as the satisfier of one's sexual needs; information on sexually transmitted diseases and their prevention; and above all, about the necessity of using birth control!

Ultimately, the parent must allow the child to explore the world as he or she sees fit. This may well involve sexual experience. The groundwork for wise and intelligent exploration must have been set far back in earliest childhood, and the parent must trust that one's example of responsible and respectful living will guide the child along whatever path is chosen.

And you might consider wrapping yourself around your strapping teen-age son once in a while, however much he squirms in protest, so he need not seek the solace of touch solely in the arms of a classmate!

We have seen how the natural expression of sexuality in the human species is that of a fairly constant drive that compels you to intimacy with others as a means of reminding you both of your divine natural origin and of the great cooperation that sustains your species and world. As we also have seen, any time Divine Grace is blunted, it will find expression, but in avenues of increasing harm or absurdity, the better to bring to your attention that a betrayal is involved.

Given that understanding, let us now turn to two topics of interest in your society: pornography and sexual perversion.

Pornography is the pictorial or written depiction of sexual activity. Again, the attitude one brings to viewing it is the key to determining its effect. Is it viewed once in a great while, then only with some amusement, not investing it with much importance? Or is it slavishly collected and pored over, the sole venue of one's sexual expression, a nightmare of shame, guilt and forbidden lust?

Thus it is one's interpretation of pornography that determines its effect; and that interpretation will be based upon the beliefs and upbringing of the individual involved. Is sex an accepted, natural part of one's life? Or has its purest expression been so bludgeoned by guilt and shame that genuine contact with others is impossible, reducing one to a mere voyeur seeking release while viewing couples engaged in what one cannot allow oneself?

You can see that the need for pornography increases in a sexually repressed society. You who rail against its proliferation, kindly pay close attention. The rise of pornography in a society always reflects repression, not licentiousness. The truly healthy society has little need for pornography—other than for amusement or to see what the Joneses are up to—while the harshly repressive society will sprout a huge underworld of smut. For what is repressed is automatically attractive, as any parent knows! When society saddles sexuality with shame, guilt and fear, it therefore makes pornography that much more enticing.

Now, many are appalled at what appears to be a trend toward ever more horrendous depictions of sexual activity, in which physical suffering and mutilation are involved. Do you think you can eliminate the intent of those who produce and purchase such material just by eliminating the product? Once again, with your society's love of curing effects rather than problems, you never stop to question, why would anyone be attracted to such materials?

Again, the greater the betrayal of Divine Grace, the more extreme the outcome. When a society's pornography is filled with depictions of bondage, sadism and mutilation, it is a sure sign that the natural, easy expression of sexuality is being increasingly repressed. Is such not the case? Are you not experiencing a rise in the fundamentalist ranks of your society? As with any other group seeking to control and dominate the populace, repression of sexuality must be top of the list. Can you not see the fallacy at work here? If the simple viewing of the female body is to be prohibited, then that sexual energy, needing to turn somewhere, will seek a more extreme outlet—sadism, mutilation, child abuse and pornography.

If all visual depictions of sexual activity are banned, then those incapable of forming lasting adult relationships may therefore seek their pleasure with children. Thus you find the principle of opposites brilliantly realized once again; those who screech the loudest against pornography as dangerous to children end up endangering their children, as the rise of childhood sexual abuse must necessarily increase in a time of repression.

Sexual energy will be expressed. If society saddles normal heterosexual expression with shame and guilt, those affected will turn to magazines. If you take their magazines away, they will turn to children.

Which type of society would you prefer? One in which adult sexuality, in all its varieties, is acknowledged, respected, appreciated and condoned? Or one where repression forces a rise in the abuse of children?

You choose.

In an ironic display of how opposites come to the fore, precisely because your society is so repressed sexually, allegedly to protect children from harm, observe a recent phenomenon. Having encrusted sexual intimacy with the barnacles of the ages, having banned and repressed pictorial representations of sexual activity, what is the latest extreme to which sexual energy must go for expression? The telephone. Now you can call up a stranger, often a recorded stranger, to obtain the sexual experience you can have no other way.

Thus, any child with a determined index finger can dial him/herself an earful of lascivious lechery which even the most libertine of parents would hesitate to allow in the child's presence! Thus do your policies based on fear manifest themselves in the principle of opposites. Ban sex, ban sexual expression, ban pictures of sex, all in the name of sparing your children, and what is the result? Sex education in the home, indeed, with the toll charges accruing to the parent as the final insult!

Sexual expression is your most divine act, your closest link with the natural order, your greatest intimacy with those of your species. It is your gift, to be cherished, enjoyed, explored and celebrated.

CHAPTER TWENTY-SEVEN

Why Conservatives Hate the Natural World and Love War

You may have puzzled over the curious contradiction of those proudly wearing the label of "conservative"—and therefore, presumably, interested in conserving the present state of the world—betraying that label by almost always siding with those who seek destruction of the natural world. And it is the "liberals"—those who see themselves as progressive—who in fact try to apply the brakes to the wholesale decimation of the few remaining areas of wild land left.

Part of this is attributable to the conservative's love of finance, for in the world of business one finds an ordered, logical arena of obedient little ciphers lining up on quarterly statements. If the conservative's central fear is of impulses, then the world of finance, with its balance sheets, interest rates and promptly maturing CDs, is a welcome haven from the chaos of the rest of human society and of the natural world.

More is involved, however. For you see your present administration, a proudly self-proclaimed conservative one, claiming concern for the deficit while continuing to run a deforestation program for the benefit of the timber industry at a loss to the taxpayer, thereby betraying two fundamental tenets of conservatism: no government funds for private enterprise, and to maintain a "holding pattern" of the status quo. Further, the administration is determinedly pushing bulldozers through your last remaining stands of virgin forest, as a means of ensuring that they can never be declared wilderness areas and saved from the threat of the ax and condominium developer.

Why? Because the core motive of the conservative in your society is fear of impulses, and because the natural world is one of perfectly self-sustaining impulse, it represents a threat to the very heart of the conservative. The beauty and self-balancing harmony of the natural order is an insult to the conservative who believes deeply that impulses lead always to disorder, and that the only safe course is to repress and deny them, cementing rigid structure in their place lest chaos break loose.

It is thus a deep and unconscious resentment against the natural order, for its daily demonstration of the fallacy of the conservative's philosophy, that compels conservatives to betray their alleged ideals for the sake of destroying what little wild areas remain. It is not an issue of greed, as those fighting to preserve the wilderness perceive in their conservative adversaries. The drooling over the profit potential of a redwood forest is the surface patina on the deeper, unconscious determination to eliminate the daily insult the natural world presents.

Observe the natural world. Observe a meadow, a lake, a pond, any ecosystem. You can see each of these as a marvelous self-sustaining and self-balancing mechanism, whose **order is determined by impulse**. If man alone has the conscious, reasoning mind, then it follows that the rest of the natural world acts always out of impulse. It does. This does not mean the natural world conducts itself with the negative connotations you place on the word "impulse." It means that all creatures and plants in the natural world seek their greatest fulfillment without the possibility of rational thought.

This is what is so disturbing to the conservative. This is what is so insulting to the conservative. Here is this magnificent philosophy constructed on fear of impulse, and the natural world comes along and thumbs its impulsive, irrational nose at the whole construction.

Think for a moment what would happen if the conservatives could impose their sense of order on the natural world.

The tax collector, perhaps a raccoon, would threaten the flowers with uprooting if they did not hand over half their chlorophyll to underwrite construction of a gargantuan beaver dam to intercept those pesky little field mice and their threat to the existence of the meadow.

The primary carnivore of the area would ensure that all creatures great and small paused in their activities for a moment of silent prayer of gratitude to the Great Grizzly in the sky, Who curiously seemed to insist on such demonstrations of obeisance rather than deriving Its satisfaction from the purposeful lives of those It created.

A band of black-robed deer would post sentinels at the entrance of every lair and den, calling out the constitutionality of the various mating positions engaged in by the occupants.

You see we wax ludicrous. Our point is that the conservative's rigid need for order and structure would have no place in the natural order, for in the natural order **impulse and spontaneity are the handmaidens of Divine Grace** as it seeks always to create a harmonious, balancing order in which each creature is accorded dignity, respect and an invaluable role in the divine drama of life.

Of course it would be impossible to impose the conservative's sense of order on the natural world—other than running a bulldozer through it—but we cannot speak facetiously when viewing what the compulsion for "order" has meant when European culture meets the native peoples of the globe.

Remember that the fundamental quality of European culture is divorce from the natural order, a step back into second-hand existence of paper money, written language, blunted emotions and ideals. And when this culture meets a native people, surviving if not prospering in harmony with the natural world, it is again an insult to the European sensibilities. How can such savages possibly be content without *The Iliad*? How can they possibly avoid the fires of Hell without reading the Good Book?

And so the approach of the European culture, always, is to wrench native peoples from their instinctive harmony with nature. Always, this is the first priority, to drive a wedge between human and natural order, to impose the European value of humankind's superiority over the natural world, its alleged commandment to hold dominion over the beasts of the earth.

In Africa, in Latin America, in Australia, in Alaska, everywhere, the process is the same. Divorce the native people from their intuitive understanding of the natural order. Then teach them to read, to dress like westerners, to lust after second-hand experience like money and power instead of the deeper and truer satisfactions of life in harmony with the natural order.

An instructive example is occurring now in northern Canada. There, the Indian peoples have long been nomads, following game, ice flow and the sun in an instinctive harmony with the cycles of the earth. And what is occurring now?

The government is destroying the culture by insisting that the children be educated in western fashion; and since they must therefore attend year-round school, the tribes are forbidden from pursuing their nomadic instincts. They must stay put. The very connection with the earth and its natural rhythms is therefore cut off. For what? To learn the alphabet?

You know that the fundamental building block of the universe and your world is energy, and energy is motion. Now, what are the buzz words and phrases of your European-influenced culture? Children must learn to sit still. They are to be seen but not heard. When they go to school they are to keep quiet while the culture's values and history are imparted. After high school they are expected to settle down rather than travel about with the foolish notion of seeing the world before assuming responsibilities of parenthood and career.

Your language and phrases always reveal deep, unconscious truths. If energy is motion, and European culture's dictum is to "sit still" and "settle down," what can we conclude? We can conclude that when you meet a Masai tribesman, you might humble yourself, learn his language, study his culture and allow him to lead you back to the natural harmony you have forgotten existed.

When we speak of the New Dawn that awaits now below the horizon of your time, do not think it will sweep the globe, infusing every culture with new understanding. The Stone Age tribes among you need no New Dawn. They have been living in it all along.

Since the natural world is a miraculous mechanism forever couched in the security of impulse and spontaneity, the poor conservative is a threatened creature indeed! Surrounded by impulse every way one turns! Is there no escape from the smoldering swamp of spontaneous impulse that belies the conservative's fixation for rigid structure?

Of course there is: the conservative's beloved military and its hardware of death.

Why should it be the conservative who rails the loudest for an annual increase in the defense budget, peacetime notwithstanding and mildly annoying, piling up weaponry to the ludicrous extreme of possessing the megatonnage to destroy the globe dozens of times over?

Again, fear of impulse is the core of the conservative philosophy. Since the whole world runs on impulse, the only proper response is to subjugate it, control it, annihilate it, destroy it. While in no way is this motive consciously available to even the most ardent missile lover, the conservative delights in firepower precisely because every round or missile fired will end up killing something, and since that something is part of the natural order, the conservative will have gained a little victory over that swamp of impulse that is the natural order. People are the preferred targets, of course, since they refuse to obediently fall in step to the march of the conservative's drum, but if only a blade of grass is destroyed in an exchange of firepower, well, that's better than nothing. At least one element of the natural world has been obliterated.

Thus we see the conservative's fascination with firepower and the instruments of death. First, the world is seen as a festering cesspool of impulse: plants, animals, native peoples all coexisting in divine harmony and laughing in the face of the conservative who fears all impulse. So the conservative spins a cocoon of order by surrounding himself with weaponry that is both created and controlled by man's rational mind; and when utilized, these implements of death cannot help but destroy some part of the natural order, thereby chalking up one tiny victory against the threatening universe of impulse.

You may point out that warfare is not the creation of European culture. True enough; it has almost always existed among the peoples of the earth, native populations as well. But note the difference. A squabble over territory between two African tribes was, first, over a tangible, concrete, physical concern: a piece of territory. Second, the combat itself was hand-to-hand; it was necessary to face one's enemy in the eye and hurl the spear. In both purpose and execution, such warfare was a firsthand experience: hand-to-hand combat over territory.

Observe where the state of your scientific culture has brought you. Your technology now allows you to conduct warfare without ever meeting your enemy's eyes, as you sit in the comfort of your underground chambers and push a series of buttons, sending nuclear death across the ocean.

And what are you fighting for? The single battle of your time, in your country's eyes, is the battle against communism. Democracy versus communism. An entirely metaphysical battle that has no physical results: no land, no women, no animals to be divvied up when the smoke clears. Just a concept.

It was thus inevitable that the country would be fractured into stridently contrary factions in your conduct of the Vietnam War. What were you fighting over there? A metaphysical concept. Even had you won, and installed a government friendly to yours, no benefit in terms of land would have accrued to you. You were fighting over an idea. And the rising chorus swelled throughout the land: What are we doing over there? There was no danger to your country, no threat to its security whatsoever. And the boys sent over to fight—how were they to justify to themselves what they were doing there? Somebody in Washington doesn't like commies? For this I die?

Once again, the twin strands of your European divorce from the natural order and the march of technology combine to push warfare into a new stratum: one of second-hand reality. You fight without seeing the enemy. You fight over ideas, nothing tangible. You fight because someone fears impulses.

Since the military is the pride and joy of the conservative, let us examine its effects upon those who serve. What happens to the new recruit upon arrival?

First, every physical trace of individuality that can possibly be obliterated is obliterated. The hair—that unruly mass of impulsive beauty—is shorn off. Those who wear glasses are issued standard hideous black frames, lest they appear stylish or attractive.

More brutalizing is the process of boot camp, in which one's emotional and intellectual individuality are trampled. You march here, you march there, you say "Yes Sir," you never talk back, you never express an opinion, you make that bed perfectly, you forget you are human.

Why? Because the members of the armed forces are being trained to commit the ultimate violation against oneself, sacrifice for the sake of others, and in order to instill even the possibility of such a desire, every shard of individuality must be stomped out of consciousness, every last tenuous strand of connection with the natural order, with one's impulsive desire to live, must be obliterated.

The African tribesman fighting over territory understands that his tribe is under threat and that he must respond with violence if reason fails. What can the army recruit tell himself as to why he is fighting? He is told he is fighting for democracy. He is not. Democracy, or government by the will of the people, would allow the sovereign nations of the world to select their own leaders; and if a country's people permit themselves to be overrun by communists, let them live with the result. No, in almost all cases, your armed forces are employed to protect your business interests.

Now! What does business produce? Money. What is money? It is a reflection of meaning. So! You establish a technological system of death permitting second-hand slaughter of the enemy over a reflection of meaning, nothing tangible; and this process of second-hand killing over metaphysical concepts is so heinous a violation of Divine Grace that the only way you can ensure a ready and willing supply of troops is to divorce them from any intuitive connection with their own Divine Grace, reducing them to brainless automatons in the service of those whose core motivation is relief from the threatening harmony of the natural order.

Any volunteers?

Remember that any concept divorced from Divine Grace will play itself out in increasingly ludicrous steps until it finally grabs your attention. On the tribal level of Indian or African clan, occasional warfare to establish territory was a logical and necessary event that led to peace as the tribes then understood where the lines of demarcation were drawn.

In your time, your two World Wars were fought because European culture allowed madness to overrule reason and sanity. The first World War was caused by a single bullet, was it not, which resulted in an appalling bloodbath over territory and pride and who said what to whom. The second World War was the result of much of Europe's refusal to squarely face the rise of the madman Hitler, later to offer little protest as the Jews were carted off to the ovens, finally to drown in a sea of blood as a means of faithfully mirroring the thoughts and beliefs that made Hitler's rise possible. Abandon reason, abandon divinity, and human society will collapse in an orgy of death and unspeakable cruelty.

Hitler at least overran territorial boundaries in his desire to cushion himself with a buffer of land—deeply conservative and fearful man that he was—much as the deeply conservative men of the Kremlin do today. But your Vietnam War had no such squabble over territory; the boys sent there were fighting for nothing tangible, just someone's idea that communism was a threat to the rigid and therefore comfortable security of capitalism. And when the war ended, the boys came home asking, for what were we sent there? The bereft parents, siblings and children of the dead asked: What did our son/brother/father die for? The country asked: What were we over there for?

For nothing. As war plays itself out, you see, it will become an increasingly ludicrous caricature of itself, until you are left with the spectacle of conservatives in Washington and Moscow pushing red buttons and obliterating the planet. For what?

For **nothing.**

Why must warfare be dismissed from your society or destroy it?

In the times to come, you must reclaim your reasoning mind and your divinity. You must come to see how they work in unity to create a stable, happy and fruitful society.

War is the abandonment of reason, the ultimate violation of divinity.

If someone angers you, which is the more rational response? To point out how their actions upset you, or simply to furiously strike out? The rational response is the former, because it can lead to greater understanding on both sides. To merely strike out and assault the other would lead to both a violation of the other's bodily integrity and, most likely, prevent any true communication.

You equate weaponry with strength, yet the opposite is true. The truly secure and strong individual, who feels intuitively that he creates his own reality in a safe universe, has no need to carry a big stick. He carries his reason and divinity, and they will see him through any conflict life can offer up.

Violence is always a passive surrender, a surrender to feelings of anger so intense—having not been dissipated along the way—that they strike out in one furious blow, devoid of reason, beyond rational control.

Your movie heroes, with their portable cannons as weapons, are thus symbols not of strength but ultimate passivity. They abandon reason, violate divinity, by their scampering to the imagined safety of weaponry.

You want strength? Look at Gandhi. Look at Martin Luther King. Did they carry weapons? They had no need to; they were right, and the moral will always win over the wrong. What were the fire hoses and attack dogs of the cowards in police uniform when confronted with **I Have A Dream?**

And as part of the drama, made necessary by the fabric of your society at the time, King was felled by an assassin's bullet. And? Did you silence King? Do his words not **speak to you today?** Unleash the dogs, turn on the hoses, kill the bearer of the message, but you can no more stop the march of Divine Grace than you can order the sun not to rise tomorrow.

True strength, then, carries no weapon, commits no violence; true strength faces all adversity with the calm self-assurance that divine reason will always prevail.

You are at the crossroads now, ladies and gentlemen. The administration serving you now, as deeply conservative and fearful as any elected this century, is stockpiling weapons beyond any possible need, stomping on treaties, proposing to launch the arms race into outer space; there is no end to the frantic grasping of fear at any vestige of security, and as there are no closed systems, the military build-up will bankrupt your society, forcing it to collapse from within, without the "evil empire" ever firing a shot. You will have a fine, polished shield from border to border, sea to sea, land to ozone, all in the service of protecting...the rubble of your society.

Alternative number two. Understand that violence and weaponry represent the abandonment of reason and the violation of divinity. Decide that you wish to reclaim both reason and divinity, and with the understanding that you create your reality and that the universe is safe, you leave the bombers and tanks and nuclear warheads to the Smithsonian, to instruct future generations as to how your society once lived before emerging from the Dark Ages of passive surrender to fear.

You choose.

CHAPTER TWENTY-EIGHT

The Body and the Five Senses

Let us now turn our attention to your most unique, private and precious creation, your body.

Remember that everything physically perceivable is a reflection of deeper meaning. Remember that the physical body you perceive is simply your **spirit made flesh**. It is not a cast-off second cousin of the soul; it **is** your soul, in physical form. With that knowledge, you are able to learn much about the intent of both the human species and you, individually, as your greater entity seeks its fulfillment through your body.

Let us take a general look first.

Given that the miraculous workings of the body reflect the intent and design of your greater entity, let us consider several of your attributes.

First, your internal organs, while necessary for the maintenance of physical life, are also reflections, or clues, as to the purpose of the human species. At the very center of your body—ignoring for the moment your gangly appendages— is the heart. This you have inexplicably though quite accurately called the muscle of love. Love is a recognition of and respect for Divine Grace. Your heart, then, is the closest physical manifestation you know of Divine Grace in your world. And how does the heart operate? Does it slumber through the day, awaking from time to time to squeeze a lethargic chamber full of juice from ventricle to ventricle, only to lapse again into lethargy?

If you have ever seen films of open heart surgery, you know that the heart, though you can rarely feel its power in your chest, is a bundle of incredibly powerful impulse, set into constant motion and energy with the intent to sustain your life. All our favorite buzz words, right in a row. Your heart, then, in its pounding, its rhythm, its squeezing, its motion, most closely replicates the great unseen dimensions from which you and all physical creatures spring. It is your closest and most intimate link with Divine Grace as it meets your world. Without the heart's pumping action, you die. And for all its fury, energy and work on your behalf, you need never give it a moment's thought. So too does Divine Grace manifest in your world; though splashing exuberantly into your world, you never need consciously consider it, as long as you ride its impulsive energy to the nurturance of your soul.

Much of your insides are taken up with the organs of digestion and elimination. From an evolutionary standpoint, these are mere input and output devices in the machine that is your body. But you know better. Knowing that your source is a divine one, why should you need bother with all the trouble of eating, drinking and eliminating? Why can you not be self-sustaining, running on solar power?

Remember that the hallmark of Divine Grace is variety. Variety seeks always new experience, new growth, new opportunity. The intent behind your need to maintain a constant process of eating and elimination, as do all other creatures, is precisely to ensure a **constant contact with the physical world**. Every day you must ingest substances springing from the natural world or face starvation; and you do so precisely to acquaint the cells of your body with the bounteous variety the world has to offer, to daily confirm your place in that world by taking in a variety of foods from a variety of sources.

Here is another clue. Why did All That Is not create All-Purpose Manna, the total nutritional needs of your species all met in one widely available substance? Again, Divine Grace finds its greatest expression through variety, and it is by exposing your body to the unlimited offerings of the world that you acknowledge your body's secure foundation in that world, and you acknowledge the importance, indeed necessity, of variety, change or new experience.

The very process of eating, then, is one in which you unconsciously pay tribute to the bounty and variety of the world, acknowledge your body's rightful place in that world and expose the very cells of your body to a constant, refreshing variety.

You are amazed, for instance, at the ability of adolescents, boys particularly, to pack away boxcars of food at a time. You chalk it up to high metabolism or the body's work of building adult shapes from the material of children. This is partially valid, of course, but as we have briefly mentioned and will explore in more detail later, adolescence is a time of unraveling and re-forming the psyche, and it is not coincidence that just as the child emerges from its cocoon and begins exploring the world of adult society with a vengeance, so too will the body match that unquenchable hunger for new experience with a literal unquenchable hunger!

Here is one small example of how everything you observe physically reflects deeper unseen truth.

Your religions and science have conspired to rob you of any intuitive connection with the workings of your body. Your religious training may have taught you that the body is a repository of base instincts and desires that must be repressed, ignored and squelched, lest you accede to your craven desires and spend eternity regretting the decision!

If you are of scientific bent, you see the body only as the mechanism that serves to transport the consciousness from place to place—though where that consciousness came from and why it should want to go anywhere is never explained. Still, the body is viewed as a machine by those of science.

What we hope to inspire, instead, is an appreciation for how the miraculous workings of the body reflect both the intent of the species as a whole and, through your private experience, the intent of your greater entity in assuming human form.

Let us examine your five physical senses. As a species, particularly in your culture, your dominant sense is that of sight. You communicate through written language, sign contracts, write letters, watch television and movies, gasp at a rainbow and so on. Of all the senses, that which you utilize most often and depend on for an accurate assessment of your position and condition is sight.

We hate to once again interject that what your senses perceive is, in deepest terms, a fiction, but to do so will help illuminate our discussion. For it forces you to consider: Why should we interpret nonphysical reality in this fashion and not another?

Consider the workings of your eyes. They are your strongest and most crucial sense. Through them you interpret the bulk of your reality. Now, how do they function? Alone of all the senses, sight offers you the ability to consciously cut off your eyes' perceptions at any time. You can simply close your eyes and all sensation, as interpreted by your eyes, is lost. Now, you can also stick your fingers in your ears, hold your nose, spit out an offensive taste. But to shut off your eyesight, you need only drop your eyelids.

Why? **You create your own reality.** If eyesight is your strongest sense, your truest means of interpreting physical reality, then it follows that it should also be the sense most under the control of your conscious mind. You can choose whether or not to experience a given visual reality by simply opening or closing your eyes, with a rapidity and easy flow not possible with the other senses.

Consider what happens if you hear horrible news. You may close your eyes, as if to shut out all of physical reality, as if to refuse to allow passage into your psyche of that which you cannot bear to know.

What do you do when you lie down at night to sleep? You must close your eyes, while leaving all other senses alert; even if they do not allow passage into consciousness of their sensations, still the initial connections are made. But your eyesight is completely shut off. Why? Because in the dream state you are manipulating nonphysical reality in the same way that you do with physical reality during the day, eyes opened. You cannot consciously do both, not over a long period of time. So, by definition, when you sleep you must close off your truest and strongest pathway to physical reality as a means of deliberately letting go of the physical, the better to return to the nonphysical realms from which you and all your world spring.

This may sound so intuitively apparent as to be ridiculous. You see, the world is not out to fool you. It is not a big mystery, taunting you with a few clues but denying you the full reality. Nature does not design to deceive you. It is you who have convinced yourselves that life is full of traps, tricks, deceptions, illusions and trap doors.

Instead, everything you experience physically reflects deeper reality and will always do so in as plain and undistorted a way as possible. It sounds obvious to state that you close your eyes in order to dream; but have you ever asked yourself why? Now you know—sight is your strongest physical sense, and you are symbolically cutting yourself off from the physical, returning to the non-physical, when you dream. Simple, clear and plain as that.

Taste is an enhancement of the intent that you should ingest as great a variety of foods as possible; for not only do foods differ in texture and color but also in flavor. The differing tastes you experience are like one last triumphant shout of individuality of the foods you eat as they disappear down your gullet to become part of you. What would the world be with only one ice cream flavor? If it's ice cream you want, why should you care what flavor it is? You care because your tongue, being the portal through which the physical world enters to sustain and nourish you, has literally encoded on its surface a desire for variety, for fresh experience and growth. This is what taste buds represent. They are your experience of the variety of the physical world as it is literally absorbed into your body. This is why you taste.

Smell is the sense closest to taste, but notice how miraculously they have divvied up the chores of sampling physical reality as it enters your body. For the tongue to taste, a physical substance must be placed in the mouth. It is thus a direct encounter with physical reality.

Smell, on the other hand, specializes in interpreting nonphysical reality, or nonmaterial reality. With it, you sample the air, your food from a distance, a flowering meadow, a chocolate factory, a garbage dump or a cloud of smog. It thus alerts you to your surroundings in a way that taste, highly focused in your mouth, cannot.

Again, think now consciously about how different areas or objects smell, and then compare that with the expression of Divine Grace in your world. What do you think when you step into a home redolent of freshly baked bread? You feel good, warm. You unconsciously recognize that food is love, that a baker cooking for his or her family does so out of love, and you cannot help but feel welcome, secure, in such a household.

The alpine meadow in springtime keeps your nose in frantic delight as each flower's unique scent wafts to your nostrils. You bend down and shove your nose among the petals, precisely as a way of drinking up the very essence of the unique divinity that is each expression of flower. You see, then, in this example, that you are not passively limited to accepting whatever odors drift your way, but you can actively seek out those that bring you pleasure; and those that bring you pleasure—fresh bread and flowers—invariably are the truest expressions of Divine Grace in your world!

What offends and assaults your nose? Rotting garbage. Smog. Factories belching smoke. Almost always, an offensive smell will result from a creation of your species in its divorce from Divine Grace. Think! Use your conscious mind now! Is this not so?

A factory spewing poisons into the air offends your nose because it offends your soul. In a world in harmony with the natural order, no such construction would be built. Yet if a member of the same species bakes a loaf of bread out of love for one's family, the smell is irresistible, comforting. It is the intent behind what creates these smells, whether they betray or cushion Divine Grace, that determines whether you seek out the odor or flee from it.

It is all so plain, so simple, so obvious.

Touch is the one sense that is not localized or specialized anywhere in your body. Though some areas are more sensitive, every inch of your skin feels the world up against it.

Your skin and its nerve receptors of pain and pleasure serve always to feed your mind a constant and true stream of information about your body's condition. The young child learns to manipulate physical reality by exploring and probing, shrinking away from whatever causes pain as a way of exploring the contours of what is safe and what is not.

Again, your ability to feel pleasure and pain is, at base, a means of constantly steering you in the direction of Divine Grace's sure path. Which would you rather experience, torture with a cattle prod or an act of sex? Assuming you chose the latter, what led you to such a choice? It is your instinctive recognition that sex, being the most pleasurable act of which you are capable, is also the truest expression of Divine Grace as physically made manifest through your body. The reason you shrink away from torture with a cattle prod is that the intent of the sadist wielding the instrument is to cause you harm, and is therefore a blatant betrayal of Divine Grace. This you experience as physical pain, but always, a deeper meaning lies behind the physically experienced. When someone deliberately causes you pain, it means that person has abandoned reason and betrayed divinity; and in the most heinous example of this century, that leads to the wholesale incineration of the Jews in Hitler's Holocaust. The pain and suffering of such an event, on a scale too profound for any mind to grasp, reflect the deeper meaning of the violation expressed in the determination to eliminate from the face of the earth those people who best express in their lives the immutable law that you create your own reality.

Pain, then, always alerts you that Divine Grace is being betrayed, bludgeoned along with the physical body. Pleasure is your sure sign of harmony with Divine Grace and the natural order, as in sex, a warm bath or a massage.

We might consider for a moment the sense of touch as it relates to your relationships with others of your species.

For while you can see others, hear others and smell others, in all such cases you are passively receiving a given set of information about them. With touch, though, your volitional choice determines the extent of your contact: Should we touch at all? shake hands? embrace? make love?

Note, for instance, the differences in the world's peoples as to how much distance they keep from each other when engaged in conversation. Your European-influenced culture, not surprisingly, prefers to keep a far distance away, while other tribes and races come pressing in far too close for your comfort.

Remember that the body is the physical expression of your greater entity's intent to experience human form; remember that the physical field of that intent extends beyond the boundaries of your physically perceived body, and that the closer to the center of the body, the stronger and truer the intent. Thus, it is no accident that your heart, being the center of your body, is both the most active and rhythmic part of your body—being the truest expression of Divine Grace—while as you pull further back from the heart the body's features are of less importance to sustaining life, until you reach the skin, which is the mere wrapping on the precious internal organs.

Extending beyond the body, beyond the skin, is a field generally about six feet in all directions. Thus you begin to commingle your essence with that of others when they approach within six feet. This is why you back away from those you find disagreeable; you will not have them in your field. This is why you rush to the arms of loved ones; you wish to clutch them as close to the center of your being as possible.

For what is a hug? It is a means of bringing your two hearts, those two thrusting, dancing cores of your beings, in as close proximity as physically possible, the better to approach the very essence of the loved one. Why should hugs differ in duration? Why is the hug you give your spouse or child at the end of the day briefer and more casual than the one you offer a long-lost relative suddenly appearing after years of separation?

Because when you live with others on a daily basis, you naturally and unconsciously flow through their energy fields as a matter of course. In each such encounter you quite unconsciously exchange information with each other, like two gossipers hanging over the back fence, talking about their health, their mood, their hopes and dreams. All this is exchanged on levels hidden from you, whenever you enter the field of another. So a parent and a child, naturally coming into close contact regularly throughout the day, are thus kept constantly apprised of each other's condition, and need no rib-crushing hug.

Yet, after a long separation from a loved one, such a suffocating embrace is required because there is so much your bodies need to tell each other! Remember that all physically experienced events carry a certain polish or coating or charge; during an embrace, these charges, representing the events of one's life, are released, exchanged, as a way of mirroring on a cellular level the verbal exchange of information that always occurs during reunion with a loved one. You catch up on each other's lives. So do your bodies, unbeknownst to you. This is why you embrace so tightly, so long; the closer you are to the center of each other's energy fields, the easier the transmission of these long-held bursts or charges of information.

In moments of transcendent love with another, locked in a tight embrace, you may even have felt that your two bodies for a moment became one entity, one circuit, the bodies mere recyclers of current as it flowed one to the other. In such a case, you have experienced a virtually **unfiltered** exchange of information from heart to heart, cell to cell. The knowledge of one body becomes available to the other, absorbed, as a way of transmitting the experiences of one to the race as a whole.

Why do babies deprived of affection shrivel and die? Why do people living alone fall ill more often? Why do those remaining single throughout life die younger? Precisely because you depend on the constant exchange of information with others, on a cellular level, that only touch can provide. Touch is a source of undistorted truth; the bodies do not lie—and how often can you say that about the words you hear from others? Your body needs a constant, honest appraisal of the world situation, and it receives this through touch, through the exchange of information with others. You know how you are repulsed by someone you dislike approaching you with open arms or quivering lips. Why? Precisely because their conscious minds are forcing a replica of a nonexistent bond, invading your field with the subterfuge of feigned affection; and your body recoils from such disingenuous contact because it is such a profound violation of your body's determination to use the sense of touch to absorb and exchange honesty.

Many lonely men pay for the privilege of being held in a woman's arms. And are they therefore just as fulfilled as the loving husband? You know they are not. Because touch alone is not enough; it is meant as a vehicle to express honest and undistorted truth. To seek it in the arms of a stranger is to violate one's bodily integrity and leave it with only temporary relief, afterward sinking even lower into the depths of despair and loneliness.

You must have touch or die.

The ears, like the eyes, function by interpreting wave forms, the patterns of air pressure sent bouncing through your environment by the workings of the world. The ears work in tandem with the eyes to present you with an accurate "picture" of your immediate surroundings.

Light waves and sound waves are, at their base, energy patterns; and on deepest terms, all energy that creates and sustains the physical universe is the same. As it approaches your plane, it "specializes" into distinct patterns or forms, some of which can be perceived by the eyes, some by the ears.

Your sense of hearing, then, is like an auxiliary system of interpretation, aiding the eyes in their effort to keep you apprised of your situation. While the eyes can look only ahead, the ears can detect sound coming from all directions; they thus complement the eyes' precise focus with a generalized background of information that couches the eyes' perception in a broad framework.

Of all the senses, that of sound is in many ways the truest facilitator of Divine Grace that you can know. The range of sounds you can perceive is far greater than the range of objects you can perceive. Your sight is limited to a certain narrow spectrum, only that which is necessary for you to function in physical life. Sound, however, has a far greater range; and in addition, it is your truest arrow to the heart of Divine Grace, for it brings you music. You can close your eyes, shut off your primary physical sense, and let your mind soar free on the wings of a melody. Music, genuine music, serves to transport you out of physical reality by casting off the shackles of your rigidly ordered world, urging you into a realm of impulse and spontaneity. If the beat is infectious enough, you get up and dance, dance being motion, motion being energy, energy being life, all far beyond the reach of reason and order and logic.

Music thus restores you, more than any other creation of your world, to your source: the dancing, swirling clouds of energy that seek expression in the physical realm, carried like a song on a breeze by the loving intent of Divine Grace.

Taken as a whole, you can now view your body for what it is: the miraculous expression of spirit in the physical world, which is equipped with a variety of perceptors all working always toward one goal—keeping you on the sure and loving path of Divine Grace. When something smells good, tastes good, looks good, sounds good, feels good, it **is** good! Divine Grace surely smiles in approval when your senses register delight.

And again, in almost all cases, you will find that when your senses are offended, assaulted, it is because Divine Grace is being betrayed, blunted or denied. If your air smells bad, question why you have permitted its pollution and the violation such represents. If something in your mouth tastes bad, it cannot do you good to ingest it, and it would be a violation to do so. When you gaze upon the bombed-out tenements of your ghettos and mutter, "I can't stand to see this," you unconsciously acknowledge the betrayal of Divine Grace that leads to poverty.

What offends your ears? A scream of agony? a buzz saw ripping through a tree trunk? a freeway snarled with honking cars? an out-of-tune musical instrument? Such always represent, to one degree or another, the betrayal or casting aside of Divine Grace.

And what hurts you? When someone strikes you out of abandonment of reason, violation of divinity? burns you at the stake? stretches you on the rack? nails you to the cross? In all such cases your body is screaming in outrage at the violation being perpetrated against it, that outrage jumping from cell to cell in your body, sending stabs of pain through you, the physical reflection of injured Divine Grace.

Your body is not only your unique and private creation, but it also serves as the faithful arbiter of Divine Grace made manifest through you. Your five physical senses, deep fiction though they may be, serve always to maintain a sure and steady beacon toward Divine Grace, forcing recoil from any betrayal, urging you toward all reflections of the divine in your world.

CHAPTER TWENTY-NINE

Medicine

Now that we have examined the body in the stained-glass cathedral light of Divine Grace, let us descend the dank dungeon steps into that realm of ignorance and superstition known as twentieth-century medicine.

In our discussion of science, remember that the key source of the scientist's folly lies in his divorce from any sense of the divine in the natural order; he therefore cannot love and respect the planet and its creatures.

The same holds true when the world of science is applied to the human body. Divorced from any sense of the divine origin of the body, of its being a mere reflection of spirit, medicine is forever forced to deal with **reflections** instead of bedrock reality. You know that everything physically perceivable simply reflects a greater reality; divorced from any sense of that greater reality, the scientist and doctor are forever condemned to a second-hand, superficial comprehension of the true workings of the body. Worse, with their background in evolution and a secular origin of the world, they can only view the body as the result of a long string of accidents and mutations, culminating in this gangly creature known as the human body.

Medicine is concerned with the healing of the body precisely because you recognize that illness, all illness, is a reflection of deep-set, and to you invisible, conflicts and issues being played out in realms beyond your sight, reflected in your body's condition. You thus automatically and unconsciously recognize that a sick person is dealing with powerful conflicts, and you naturally seek to aid them in their time of need. Yet, because you limit yourselves to the physically perceivable, you are left assuaging the reflection, not the cause, of the problem.

Compounding this is the inevitable evolutionary belief that death is the end. The grand finale. End of the line. Given this, your medical personnel become frantic at the possibility of death, prolonging life far beyond its ability to grant free expression to Divine Grace, hooking up wires and tubes to keep alive a mere shell because they cannot see anything beyond death, considering it an irretrievable loss and the universe's cruelest joke. Work as hard as you might, live a life of beauty and riches, provide yourself and your family with security, but sooner or later, you are snatched away into the black emptiness from which you spring.

The combined evolutionary strands of reducing the body to a mere accidental machine while considering death a loss and insult compel your medical people, driven as they are by an urge to restore the body's inner balance, to heights of folly and barbarism. Your medical beliefs have caused far more unnecessary deaths than they have ever prevented. Let us see how.

You know that the fundamental quality of your European-based culture is divorce from the natural order. In the natural order, plants and animals live cushioned by the security of an instinctive harmony with the earth, an unconscious recognition of its rhythms and their inviolate place in the grand design. Illness does occur among animals, though to a far lesser extent in the wild than among your domesticated pets, picking up as they do all your negative beliefs! In the wild, as in your own body, any instance of disease is always a reflection of deeper meaning; the animal understands this and will seek to correct the imbalance to whatever extent it is able. There is an instinctive understanding that disease represents an imbalance of some sort and is a red flag waved by the hand of Divine Grace, alerting you to conditions that must be faced and remedied.

What is your perception of disease?

If you consider your accidental body to be floating through its meaningless days on a planet swarming with germs, viruses, bacteria and other pestilence whose sole purpose and intention is to strike you dead, to eliminate you from the gene pool, then the course of one's life thus becomes a constant microorganismic target–shooting game with you the frantic target, dodging projectiles of death by donning the armor of pills, vitamins, diet and so on.

Remember, above all, your beliefs create your reality. If you believe you are ever at the mercy of microscopic organisms that intend you harm, you shall indeed find yourself falling ill on a regular basis, pumping yourself full of antibiotics to kill the little buggers, and then enjoying a brief respite before the next onslaught. You live, therefore, in perpetual fear of disease.

Remember our old friend, fear? Does it ever lead to understanding? Does it ever lead to purposeful action? No, it always leads to paralysis and irrational action.

Thus your entire medical system is structured upon beliefs that guarantee that you will become ill on a regular basis; that you, an individual, can have no comprehension of how your body works and must not attempt to heal yourself in any situation, always depending on the advice of your schooled betters; and reducing your life to a game of chance, a roll of the dice, forever the prey of pernicious creatures you cannot even see.

Now let us state the reality.

The universe is safe. It is not out to deceive you, to deprive you, to batter you about. The state of health, of your body working in smooth unison with your mind, is the most natural course of events. When you do become ill, it is a sign that you have not faced certain issues; you are therefore urged to stop and consider the state of your life and what might have brought on the illness. And the illness itself, its expression in your body, will always carry a host of clues as to the genuine source. The world is not out to trick you! Any disease or illness will always represent, in plainest terms, the issues you have not faced that brought it on.

Let us turn for a moment, then, to some of your major health problems and see what reflections of meaning we can find in their expression.

Probably your most intractable and seemingly insoluble disease is cancer. What is cancer? The unrestrained growth of cells, interfering with the body's natural health and harmony.

What is the most pressing social issue of your day? Unrestrained growth, interfering with your society's natural health and harmony with the natural world.

What is another pressing health issue? Heart disease. What is the heart? It is that thrusting, exuberant, life-giving, motive power of Divine Grace made manifest in your body.

What is the source of your society's problems? Divorce from the thrusting, exuberant energy of Divine Grace made manifest in your world.

It seems so obvious as to be ludicrous, does it not? Yet this is how the universe works: plain, simple, clear and undistorted. No tricks, no deceptions.

Your society's most intractable and persistent disease states thus **precisely mirror the issues you have not faced as a culture.**

Now, we do not suggest that the universe is picking off members of your society one by one as a way of bringing attention to these issues. There will always be private reasons for disease, personal issues involved, but as there are no closed systems and you are a member of society as well, once the choice to experience illness is made, it will frequently serve as both a vehicle for your own conflict and to express a truth the society has forgotten.

Who has heart attacks most often in your society? Men, driven to obsession with pursuit of money and status—hollow reflections that they are—to the extreme that all else—family, hobbies, travel—is shunted aside. So severe is the divorce from Divine Grace that it has no choice but to simply quit the body in an abrupt and threatening manner; and the heart, its handmaiden in your body, ceases to function, or is gravely impaired.

And what occurs after a heart attack? Such driven men frequently find themselves thinking, my God, I have only so many years and my children are growing up and I don't know them and I haven't had a day alone with my wife in twenty years and what have I been doing all this time? And so Divine Grace is revived, the natural harmony restored, to a life that had strayed so far from the path of Divine Grace as to have entirely lost any sense of balance.

One of the most pernicious results of medicine's ignorance of the true natural order and design of the universe and your body is that it is limited to the physically perceivable. Knowing these to be mere reflections of deeper reality, you thus see the danger when medicine attempts to force causal connections between oftentimes related but not causal phenomena.

Coupled with the literal hypnosis that permeates your society, convincing you that you are forever the prey of viruses and germs, that you had best be always on guard with a shield of antibiotics and vitamins, you find that medicine causes far more disease than it cures.

In deepest terms, there is no time; therefore, there can be no cause-and-effect relationship between any two phenomena, though such is how you perceive the world, given your linear time perspective. You may say, if I drop a brick on my foot, does it not inevitably result that I will feel pain? In this case, in deepest terms, you couple the physical law of gravity, in which you believe without question, with the intent to cause yourself pain; and that intent is then mirrored in the physical pain you feel. You experience a time lapse between the intent to feel pain and the pain itself, but in deepest terms, they are simultaneous.

Perhaps you can begin to perceive a glimmer of the tragedy resulting from medicine's wrenching together unrelated phenomena into cause-and-effect relationships, announcing their "scientific" findings to the world, and effectively hypnotizing the population into disease.

Take cancer, for example. We have already seen that on a mass level it represents your society's greatest unfaced problem, uncontrolled growth destroying the natural order.

Science, blind science, can only find its cause in a virus.

Now, science is edging closer to the truth in its recent research which has revealed that everybody is host to incipient cancers all the time; and it is only when the body's immune system breaks down, fails to differentiate cancer cells from "self" cells, that a tumor can take root.

This reflects the deeper truth that you all carry latent potentials for every disease known to man. We do not wish to send you rushing to the medicine cabinet in panic! The point is precisely that such potentials remain forever latent unless they are triggered into activity by an unresolved conflict or issue in your life.

Science, while understanding that every body holds the "potential" for cancer, cannot explain why some immune systems should suddenly break down while others remain resistant to the attack. Now you know.

To return to our earlier point, as science grapples with the scourge of cancer, it studies the environment, diet, habits and lifestyles of those afflicted, all in an attempt to locate the source of the disease. But the true source of the disease is not available to you on physical terms; you will only find its reflection. Thus, science wrenches into causal relationships phenomena with no genuine cause-and-effect qualities.

Smoking cigarettes does not cause cancer.

Sodium nitrate does not cause cancer.

Radiation does not cause cancer.

The researchers among you, and those accustomed to digesting their findings without protest, are howling now. What? Smoking doesn't cause cancer? After all the billions of dollars we spent proving it? But there is a statistical correlation between lung cancer and those who smoke cigarettes!

It is illegitimate to transform a statistical correlation into a causal relationship. Most heroin addicts began by drinking mother's milk. Does mother's milk cause heroin addiction?

Your scientists have no choice but to draw the conclusions they do, given their self-imposed limitation to the physically perceivable. And while there is a relationship between cigarette smoking and lung cancer, it is not causal. Let us examine in detail precisely what the nature of that relationship is.

Remember that the way you acknowledge the Divine Grace in another is through respect. When you respect others, you allow them their freedom to be, do and say as they wish, disagree with them as you might. On the other end of the spectrum, in total, abject divorce from Divine Grace, is contempt. When you cannot find the Divine Grace in another, when you demonstrate contempt for the other's uniqueness either by physical harm or emotional abuse, you are demonstrating profound disrespect for the Divine Grace made manifest in the other. In the middle of the spectrum would be cavalier disregard or unconcern for another, neither acknowledging the divine potential nor seeking to destroy it.

A second point. Knowing now that the body is simply a reflection of your spirit, you find that the same principle holds. You can choose to acknowledge your body's Divine Grace by demonstrating respect for its miraculous workings, or you may blithely dismiss it from your attention, or you may actively seek to destroy it. In all cases, you are either acknowledging your own divinity, ignoring it or committing self-hatred.

Further, because you alone of all creatures have the quality of rational thought, there is a division between conscious mind and body that the animals do not share. This is not in itself an unhealthy divorce from Divine Grace; it simply represents the way you were "set up" as a species. The body therefore depends on your conscious mind for a constant, accurate assessment of your condition at all times, so that it can serve you always in light of your best interests. Remember that cellular communication takes place at all levels in the body, and the final source of information for the cells is your conscious thoughts. Your beliefs. Your attitudes.

Given this as background, let us proceed with our examination of the relationship between cigarette smoking and lung cancer.

What is the natural reaction of your body when you inhale a lungful of smoke? It recoils, coughs furiously to rid itself of the invasion. What is pain, again? The sure sign that your Divine Grace is being betrayed. Your lungs were not designed to inhale superheated carbons but to provide the body with a steady supply of clean oxygen. Any time your body instinctively recoils, you know you have endangered its natural harmony.

What does the cigarette smoker do?

First, the conscious mind, which is the source of all addictions and habits, overrides the natural reaction of the body. This is a violation on two counts. First, you demonstrate disrespect for your body when you force it to experience that from which it normally recoils. You are thus disregarding your body's messages, those messages delivered with only one intent: for your own good and that of your body.

The second violation is that your conscious overriding of the body's reaction throws the entire body into a state of confusion, because the normally clear and salubrious channel between conscious mind and body is not being used to assist the body in its comprehension but to muddle it. If the lungs could talk, what would they say the first time you smoked a cigarette? They would scream, "Hey brain, let's get out of here! We're in a forest fire!" To which your brain replies, "Aw shut up, we're just standing behind the junior high school trying to look cool." Thus the normally clear and symbiotic relationship between mind and body is clouded, rendered opaque, no longer serving its proper purpose.

Now. You can see how these twin lines of development—the disrespect of overriding your body's instinctive reactions and a deliberate clouding of the mind-body channel—can result in a setup for disease. It is not enough, however. For you know plenty of people who live to a ripe, old age smoking three packs a day.

There must be a trigger to allow disease to enter your existence and awareness—some unresolved conflict or, perhaps, the deliberate though unconscious desire to leave physical life at that point. In either case, that intent—the need to face an unresolved conflict, or to die—will then search for the most likely nexus in the body. And since disease always represents disrespect, where would the focal point likely be in a long-term smoker? In the lungs—in the site where the constant, daily insult to the body occurs as the conscious mind overrides the body's instinctive purpose. Since the lungs thus represent the area of most concentrated disrespect, they will naturally serve as host to any disease state that you have brought into your life as a result of deeper issues. Now you see the connection between cigarettes and lung cancer; though not causal, they are related.

Just as cancer represents the state of your society at large, just as heart disease reflects your cultural divorce from Divine Grace, so on an individual level will the focal point of disease serve as a clear clue to the nature of the unresolved conflict that brought on the disease state.

Now you can also see the danger in all the dire warnings and threats from your medical, scientific and governmental establishments about how the very world causes cancer. For as long as you abandon your own divine reason and allow others to create your reality for you, then you are indeed highly susceptible to the suggestions of causal relationships between substances in your world and cancer. In all such cases, you are literally being hypnotized, first into believing your body prey to cancer against which you have no defense, and then in identifying specific alleged causes of that cancer.

Every pack of cigarettes carries warnings about how their use leads to lung cancer. These warnings are required by the government, after scientific studies "proving" a causal link. Consider now what this means. No closed systems! The government commits a violation against you in the form of taxation, which it then hands over to the soulless field of science, which then erroneously claims a causal link between cigarettes and cancer, bouncing the mess back to government, which passes a law requiring the studies' findings be plastered on every pack of cigarettes; thus every time you reach for a cigarette, you are literally being hypnotized to death by the government. Then, of course, government robs you further to supply medical benefits to those who choose to violate their bodies and have fallen under the spell of the government's mass hypnosis! Isn't this fun?

If there never comes a time in your life when you would benefit from finding an unresolved conflict manifested as a tumor, you will never get cancer. Smoke if you like. Do so with the understanding, though, of what we mentioned above, the violation such entails.

Again, if you examine the reputed causes of cancer in your world, you will find that science at least has a glimmer of the truth in that all such substances invariably reflect a divorce from Divine Grace. You are not meant to stuff your lungs with smoke on a daily basis. Preservatives and additives to your food, while not causing cancer, nonetheless represent an intent on the part of the supplier to preserve the length of time during which the food can be sold—money being a mere reflection of meaning—and thus the relationship between food and love is sullied with avarice. Thus, there is a relationship, though not a causal one. And radiation, of course, represents a profound violation, the splitting asunder of the atom; and when you are even in the vicinity of such a profound violation, you may indeed be infected by the residue of belief that permitted such a violation to occur; and this may manifest in your body as both your unconscious protest against this violation of the world's order, and to add your voice to the cries of outrage swelling from the hospitals from sea to sea: Something is very sick in this culture of ours!

Medicine's blasphemy does not stop there. Divorced from any divine sense of order, limited to the mere reflections of meaning in the physical world, they then attack expressions of cancer by further violating the body. They add insult to injury by their treatment methods.

What are medicine's tools of attack? Radiation!! Our comprehension fails us. To submit a weakened body to a literal blast of malicious intent, which is radiation at its core, makes us wonder if you were not better off in the Dark Ages. For Dark Ages you are in now, but this time you have the tools to commit atrocities on a scale never contemplated by the most sadistic inquisitors!

Another tool is chemotherapy. Because cancer cells multiply so rapidly, chemotherapy works—you think—by killing off all rapidly growing cells. And what is the result? The hair falls out. Each session of chemotherapy is a veritable vomit festival, as the stomach, its lining insulted beyond all capacity, desperately seeks to rid itself of this liquid violation of the natural order being forced down the gullet. Again, another attack on the body's integrity, a profound display of disrespect, all in the name of healing, by your well-intentioned but utterly ignorant medical personnel.

And consider for a moment the result of these tools of evil. They render you sterile. Now, why? Science, of course, would have its answer, but we won't even grant it the respect of a single line! Observe animals in the zoo, how they refuse to reproduce because they would rather terminate the species than live divorced from the natural order. The same occurs to any human body that is subjected to the malicious violations of radiation and chemotherapy. So great an outrage is this, so profound and despicable an act of violence, that the body declares itself unwilling to bring young into this world. If this is the state of the world, of your society, that one's body should be trampled and plundered by those paid to heal, then this is not a world worth living in. And thus does the body simply shut off its capacity to reproduce. It will bring no young into such a world, not ever.

Finally, of course, medicine can resort to simply hacking off the offending portion of the body. Breasts, limbs and organs are routinely chopped off as a way of halting the spread of cancerous growth. You are thus left permanently disfigured, a very symbol of the failure of medicine in your society to perform its function of healing and restoring the body. It mutilates you because it sees the body as a machine, and if that machine breaks down in a certain area, remove it. **You are not a machine. You are the spirit in flesh.** If you could meet your soul, would you hack it into little pieces if it lacked perfection? Would you destroy its natural beauty? impair its natural function? prevent its true fulfillment?

And yet, always, our men and women of medicine act out of the best of intent. This is what makes the whole arena of medicine so pathetic in your society— that you are so divorced from any sense of harmony with the natural order that those you pay to keep you well often end up killing, maiming or disfiguring you.

Let us turn our attention now to a corollary issue, that of health insurance.

Now, as you may have noted, we have endeavored throughout our work to select our words with precision, to avoid ambiguities or distortions. Our concern for verbal veracity thus compels us to drop your phrase "health insurance" in favor of the concept's true meaning. We will hereafter refer to this issue as "illness insurance."

Given your understanding of money, what it represents and how it works, and the miraculous manner in which your beliefs are reflected in your body, what can you conclude about the ubiquitous use of illness insurance in your society?

Money is an expression of value to you. When you pay money for something, you charge or strengthen whatever concept lies behind your purchase.

You believe that your body is a machine, an untrustworthy one at that, prone to falling apart at any minute, forever prey to any microscopic organism that cares to take up residence.

Combined, the intent behind a purchase and your belief in your body's vulnerability result in illness insurance, which therefore **ensures that you will fall ill**. You have laid money on the possibility of illness, have you not? You have therefore strengthened the concept of illness in your life. Combining that with your belief in the body's fallibility, you thus literally make yourself sick by purchasing illness insurance.

Now, we do not advocate your running out and cancelling your policy! Remember that any concept or event, as it plays itself out, can throw off a super-charged spark or version of itself as a way of ensuring that you consciously evaluate it before dismissing it from your reality. Therefore, if you move toward a new appreciation of your body as the miraculous harmonic divinity that it is, and yet you retain residual beliefs about its vulnerability, you may well find yourself suffering an illness the likes of which you have not seen before! Precisely as a way of forcing you to examine the deeper issues involved, to consider them and make a conscious determination as to which beliefs you wish to hold, which seem to lead to your greatest fulfillment. Thus, while you work toward a new understanding of your body and its **natural state of health**, you would be wise to retain whatever illness insurance you hold for the time being.

But once freed from the beliefs that make illness insurance necessary, think what you can do with the money! Get a massage. Buy a hot tub. Lie on the beach. Learn to scuba dive. All these are activities that demonstrate respect for your body, that enhance its natural health and that bring you great fulfillment for the money spent. For your illness insurance premium—Where does it go? Does it bring you benefit?

This brings up another point. Knowing that money is a reflection of meaning, a second-hand reality, you are now able to realize that any time money is a major issue or component of a given area, Divine Grace is most likely being trampled.

Look at medicine. Your doctors are among the highest-paid professionals in your society. It costs more to stay a day in a noisy, drafty, miserable hospital room than in a fine hotel. You spend hundreds of billions of dollars every year on "health" but remain among the world's sickest people.

With money so intricately woven into the fabric of modern medicine, you know that the field has strayed far indeed from the natural order. You can see why; limiting itself to dealing with the physically perceivable, medicine is stuck interpreting and treating second-hand reality, not the root source of any illness. And money, representing second-hand meaning, necessarily plays a large part in the whole enterprise.

True health costs you nothing! The body will support you in fine and glorious health to your very last breath, if you would let it. There is no need for disease or illness; they are products of your culture. Why further the violation by wagering money that you will get sick? Why not trust your body, respect its integrity, and take a vacation instead of filling the coffers of those whose mangled compassion leads them to cut, burn and poison you?

The field of medicine is so blatantly a betrayal of Divine Grace that you now find a veritable revolution taking place in your society. Holistic health is rising in prominence and acceptance; hospice care seeks to usher the dying out of physical life in a more home-like setting; "birthing centers" replace the sterile and harsh environment of the hospital delivery room and on and on. Even medicine is beginning to make changes to respond to the upswelling revulsion against traditional medicine, but as long as it limits itself to the physically perceivable, it can never reach a true comprehension of the workings of the body, the meaning of disease or the treatment of the ill.

The danger can arise that a new philosophy bases itself on the same misguided notions of the old, simply changing the outer coating. You now have many schools of thought that proscribe the foods you can eat, insist that you eat certain others, take vitamins, perform certain exercise routines and so on.

This is the same old story under a new cover. A true revolution in the health field will bring about an empowerment of the individual in finding within him/herself the source of all knowledge necessary for the body's sustenance and good health. The danger in some of the newer philosophies is that the world is still broken into "bad" and "good" in terms of food, exercise, medicines, etc. Your body is a far more resilient, adaptable and self-sustaining organism than you give it credit for. And any time you plant a fence around it, forbidding contact with allegedly harmful influences, you are again confirming your belief in the body's inherent weakness and susceptibility.

CHAPTER THIRTY

Food

Y ou will observe that the different species upon the earth have different methods of feeding their young. The differences all relate to the extent to which "consciousness" is granted as part of the overall "package" of a species. Fish, for instance, operating almost entirely on instinct, finding their challenges in areas not physically discernible, are born carrying yolk sacs that sustain them until they can feed for themselves. There is no bond between mother and young; indeed, the mother often eats the young, quite unconsciously!

Birds, possessing the maternal instinct, patiently sit on the eggs until hatched and then devote their lives to chasing every insect in the neighborhood, taking great care to ensure a balanced diet among the four major bug groups! But, as you observe, in this instance the parents must hunt for food and bring it to their young; birds, while a step "up" from fish in terms of consciousness, still are strongly instinctually based.

Moving up to the mammals, we find a new development: the mother carries sustenance for the young inside her. The newborn suckles directly from the body of the mother. Why? Because mammals are possessed of a greater degree of "consciousness" than the other species of the earth; and this intimate contact, this literal life-giving sustenance passing from body to body, is—like sex in your species—a means of ensuring a constant unconscious bond with the earth and an intuitive understanding of the great cooperation that underlies and sustains it. You exist because All That Is feeds Its energy constantly into your plane, and you receive and utilize it quite unconsciously. As the mammal most possessed of consciousness, then, your suckling newborns is a means of ensuring, in the very first days of life, that the immutable laws of the universe are transmitted to the child, quite unconsciously, along with nourishment. You merely seek—cry!— and nourishment is given you, in an atmosphere of tenderness, body-to-body contact.

Notice also the position of the mammary glands in your species. Dogs and cats can stretch out on the floor and allow the hungry little ones to dive right in while the mother's conscious attention is elsewhere. In your species, the breasts are placed such that the child, while suckling, stares directly in its mother's face, precisely as a means of cementing, from the very first, **that life without touch and love is impossible**, that **genuine contact with others of your species is necessary for your life's sustenance**, that **the energy of the universe flows steadily and unconditionally—like mother's milk—whenever you require it**. All these parameters of your existence are thus passed on to the infant in its earliest days, when it still straddles the membrane between physical and nonphysical life, and are meant to introduce the beloved child to your species' highest qualities from the very first.

So, from the very start, the human child learns that food and love are inextricably connected; that the giving of food is the giving of life itself; that taking nourishment should be one of life's most special and cherished moments.

You observe this in your society by the importance placed on meals, on bringing the family together, saying grace as a way of acknowledging the greater source from which your lives spring, and taking nourishment together. At the holiday season, when you most celebrate the divine source of the world and your gratitude for your place upon it, meals are a central part of the occasion, are they not? What matches Thanksgiving or Christmas dinner for sheer symbolic evocation? And of those alone on those holidays, eating solitary meals? Instinctively your heart swells with pity, for you understand the bond between food, love, celebration of life and gratitude for the world given you.

With that as background, let us explore developments in your society vis-à-vis food.

One seemingly curious phenomenon is when grown children, out and about in the world, eating in the finest of restaurants, find themselves harking back to the good old days of Mom and her home cooking. Now, what are Mom's meat loaf and instant mashed potatoes when compared to the fine cuisine and variety available in your restaurants? Why would you ever choose the former?

Because Mom loves you. When she cooks for you, she does so out of love, replicating that long-ago relationship at your birth. Intuitively you know this; and each meal set before you by her loving hand brings you an inexplicable warmth that the finest of restaurant meals cannot approach.

Why? Again, **intent** is the key. Your mother cooks for you out of **love**, the desire to sustain you in good health. The restaurant feeds you, a stranger, out of a desire to make money. Uh oh! Red flag! Second-hand reality at two o'clock, captain!

Love is the very deepest firsthand reality you know, being the recognition of Divine Grace in another. The desire for money, a reflection of meaning, cannot approach the intent behind a home-cooked meal. Thus, because the intent between love and desire for profit differ so radically in their treatment of Divine Grace, a home-cooked meal is literally more nutritious than the identical fare served in a restaurant. Mom's intent is to sustain your body; the restaurateur's is to sustain his business. While restaurant food certainly will not harm you due to this, nevertheless Divine Grace will ride Mom's intent at full gallop and nourish and invigorate your very cells in a way that a purchased meal cannot.

Now you see the relationship—not causal!—between your society's emphasis on fast food, processed food, packaged food, and the host of health problems that you unconsciously understand are related to such a diet. And because medicine, the stepchild of science, restricts itself to the physically perceivable, it must therefore wrench a cause-and-effect relationship where none exists.

191

Again, a diet of fast food alone is insufficient to cause any damage to you whatsoever! There must be a trigger, an unresolved conflict, an issue not faced squarely, which will then manifest in the focal point of your body that has been subjected to the greatest disrespect—and thus your many ailments of the digestive and eliminative organs of your body.

Because sex roles are so rigid in your society, and only mothers can breast-feed their infants, you are intuitively taught that only women are qualified to provide love through food. Only women should cook. (Your great male chefs apparently belong to a nebulous third sex, along with your brilliant female scientists!) As a result, men are incapable of expressing love through the medium of food, either to others or to themselves. The classic and stereotypic bachelor meal consists of a TV dinner thrown in the microwave, washed down with beer. There is no intrinsic harm in such a meal, but neither has the instinctive connection between food and love been maintained. Remember the connection between mind and body, how the body depends on the mind for an accurate assessment of its condition. When the mind—full of nonsense about women being the sole caregivers—takes the cavalier step of tossing a TV dinner—food created by a stranger for profit—into the microwave—radiation!—and then eats it without thought of gratitude or its effect on the body, the body is left literally undernourished, because the intent behind food, love, is absent.

When you take the time to shop at the market for the freshest ingredients you can find, when you take the time to fashion those ingredients into a well-cooked meal, balanced for texture and color, pleasing to the eye and nose, you are employing the conscious mind in the service of the body. The mind has taken these steps; the body, sensing the love and intent motivating such a meal, is necessarily nourished to an extent not possible in an unconscious slapdash TV dinner and bottle of beer.

Thus it is the intent behind a meal that determines, in large part, its effect upon your body, how nourishing it will be.

You are so concerned with nutrition and your four beloved food groups, and this and that and everything else, and let us not forget the roughage, but look about the world and will you not find cultures whose diets simply appall you? And might you not find such cultures, locked away in isolated mountain settings, to produce far healthier people, of far greater longevity, than your society can provide?

Use your conscious minds! What does this mean?

It means you are far, far off the track. Once again, restricting yourselves to the physically perceivable, you are left floundering in a swamp of ignorance, forcing causal relationships where none exist and, worse, setting up the world as a dangerous place, full of dangerous foods out to destroy your very body.

Again, remember the fear of annihilation that powers the policies of the liberal and, to some extent, flavors your entire society. Since those who fear annihilation can hold their bodies as their only highest value, they must necessarily fret and worry constantly over the slightest danger to its health. But divorced from any sense of the divine origin of your world, as anyone fearing annihilation must be, you divide the world into black and white, good and bad, healthy and unhealthy.

Hear this. A meal composed of the finest "health food" ingredients, eaten out of fear of disease, is far more damaging than a fast-food cheeseburger eaten without a thought to its effect upon the body.

Much is made in your time of "natural foods." How is a tofu and avocado sandwich on 43-grain bread any more "natural" than a bag of greasy french fries? Are they not both products of the earth? Your society's concern for "natural" foods is a step in the right direction, a yearning for a return to the initial intent that food be understood in a sacred and loving light, but holding natural foods to be more "healthful" than others once again divides up the earth into a battlefield of good and bad. It is the **intent** behind a meal that determines its effect upon the body.

Fast food is the particular delight of adolescents, precisely because it represents a break from the bond between Mom and food, and that bond must be loosened for successful maturity to adulthood. Additionally, fast-food restaurants allow adolescents to cavort with others of their species, thus replacing the family group with the peer group, another essential component of healthy adolescent life. Thus, to the adolescent, the fast-food restaurant unconsciously symbolizes much of the work to be done, given the fabric of your society, to grow to successful adulthood.

And if you infect that process with dour warnings in health class about the dangers of fat, salt and sugar—funded by the government, of course, confirmed by science, of course—then you are literally hypnotizing your young people into ill health. The adolescent body is so resilient, so indifferent to the solemn sermons about its fallibility, that few health problems will appear in adolescence. But such beliefs, if accepted and unconscious, may well remain latent—like any other disease state—and, if a time arrives later in life when unresolved conflicts seek expression through the body, those unconscious beliefs will be triggered and produce the very result predicted by science. Thus, once again, science and government conspire to hypnotize you to death.

One historical note will be instructive here. One of the major prophets of your era, John Muir, spent most of his life traveling the wild reaches of the world, subjecting himself to severities of weather and hunger that would fell the hardiest down-mummified "mountaineers" among you. And did he carry freeze-dried food, carefully balancing the four food groups, counting out roughage by the gram, skimming the cream off the milk? Muir lived for years on end on only tea and bread. Yet his vigor, his endurance, his ability to withstand whatever the High Sierra could hurl down upon him, stand as a monument to the resilience of the human body, its extraordinary ability to produce whatever it needs within itself, if only the mind directing the body acknowledges the spirit binding the two.

Your body can literally create vitamins and minerals that you now believe must be ingested from outside, lest you perish. Remember, at the very base, you have no body; it is a gridwork of points of intention directed by your conscious mind; and if your intent is to respect the body, acknowledge its divine source, and to express your unflagging confidence in its capacity to sustain you in all your adventures, then indeed it will joyfully ride that intent to a life of unbroken health.

Muir was a prophet of your age for his voice rose in brilliant counterpoint to the nonsense of Darwin, Marx and Freud, his contemporaries. All was "divine harmony," in his words; and with that unshakable understanding, indeed he could travel the world wearing only an overcoat, carrying only tea and bread, his body joyfully and unflinchingly sustaining him, securely couched in recognition of its divinity and Muir's respect.

May we suggest that you clear out your bookshelves of all current medical, scientific and New Age tracts on the dangers of food and the body's frailty and replace them with the works of Muir.

Bon appetit.

CHAPTER THIRTY-ONE

Exercise

First consider that in a well-lived life, no thought need ever be given to "exercise." Native cultures are not known for their contributions to the field of calisthenics. Such were unknown to them. For in a life of vigorous and purposeful action, the body receives all the exercise it needs.

Because your society is one in which many lead sedentary lives parked behind desks, on the assembly line and in front of the television, you naturally find your bodies growing soggy. Your response is to introduce vigorous activity in one daily block, as "exercise." You see now how the field of exercise can be laced with land mines, for its very existence arises from your divorce from the natural order.

Above all else, you must ask yourself the purpose for your exercise regimen. Do you fear age and decay? Do you want to attain someone else's standard of perfection and beauty? Do you enjoy the tingling exhilaration that follows a workout? Are you afraid of having a heart attack if you don't exercise?

Remember that your body depends upon your conscious mind for a clear and accurate flow of information as to where you are, what you are doing and why. The "why" is particularly crucial, for if the activity involved does not make sense to the body's cells—and on the level of cellular communication, this matters—then they cannot contribute to the body's health and vitality as they are meant to.

There is a saying: no pain, no gain. Remember what pain is: the physical reflection of the body's reaction to a violation. Therefore, an exercise regimen that **encourages** pain as essential to progress is one that **clouds** the mind-body channel, in which the mind deliberately overrides the frantic signals of the body that it is suffering a violation. This is the same process involved in those who smoke, as we have seen. The normally clear mind-body channel is clouded.

You have all seen photographs of marathon runners being carted off on stretchers, collapsing in agony by the roadside, their bodies refusing to submit to such violence. You are not meant to run twenty-six miles at a stretch, on cement, for no purpose. The body will never fail you when it understands the conscious mind's intent and purpose behind the urge to action; but to run frantically down a city street in a pack of hundreds of others for no purpose other than a trophy is incomprehensible to the body. And it is a demonstration of the body's miraculous resilience that it will sustain you for twenty-six meaningless miles of wasted energy, though indeed it will collapse in a heap of confusion when your conscious mind has crossed the finish line.

Thus you find such a huge problem of injuries among runners. The intent behind their activity is so divorced from any need or purpose that the easy fraternal bond between mind and body is clouded; the body goes along with the mind's intent for the most part, but because it has no sense of purpose, its normal resilience is absent.

Your Native Americans could chase game all day long, in feet never knowing the harness of technologically designed footwear, and never know an injury. For to chase game is to engage in purposeful action, in which the mind is directed toward sustenance of the body; the body, receiving this intent through an undistorted channel, willingly sustains the activity for whatever duration is necessary. The intent makes the difference.

Another form of exercise popular in your culture in which the body is often violated is the field of aerobics. For one thing, your ears are frequently assaulted with loud music, something of a violation in itself. Further, you are miming the motions of a leader, thus following her natural rhythms, not your own. Respectful exercise encourages you to find the rhythms that come most naturally to you.

Remember that the body is a physical reflection of the psyche. An injury in the body reflects an injury to the psyche. The fact that both runners and aerobic practitioners have such high injury rates should alert you that both fields are ripe for abuse of the body and spirit.

Most important, again, will be your intent in approaching exercise. Do you perform your routine out of love and appreciation for your body, reveling in its suppleness, flexibility and the warmth of blood flowing from heart to limb? Or do you do it because others expect you to, you are disgusted with your ugly body or you fear death and decay?

Remember that what you fear, you energize. If your exercise regimen is fueled by fear of age and decay, you may well find increased brittleness and ill health as you age, whatever the temporary improvement in your body's condition.

So, exercise must respect the body, must be motivated by clear and salubrious intent, and find execution that keeps clear the mind-body channel.

There is now a surge of interest in "walking." Perhaps this seems too ordinary to qualify as "exercise"–which must be exotic, and requires special uniforms and health club dues! Instead, walking is highly beneficial as it is a natural function of the body and does not punish it in any way. Particularly helpful is to give yourself a task or chore to accomplish on your walk–going to the post office or work or the store. This way, the message from mind to body is clear–there is a task to be accomplished–and the body understands and responds with full energy and delight.

Another highly beneficial form of exercise is swimming. Like walking, it comes naturally to the human body. Your body revels in the aqueous standard of its very earliest days, before hopping into the physical world and abandoning the backstroke for the two-step! Swimming's all-around cardiovascular conditioning is well known; equally important is the sensation of swimming itself, one that thrills the body, thus strengthening the mind-body channel in a way that physically grueling and punishing regimens cannot.

An exercise regimen that is considered esoteric in most areas of your country is yoga. Perhaps this one also fails to pique your interest as it has existed for thousands of years–and you must have the newest fad! And again, the only equipment necessary is your body and a floor.

Behind the physical regimen of yoga stands a body of philosophical thought regarding body, mind and spirit; this profound understanding of the nature of reality informs the exercises performed. The body is treated respectfully, as the divine vessel it is. All the limbs and muscles are stretched and toned in a mood of gentle respect, never to the point of agony.

Remember that the closer a philosophy is to Divine Grace, the longer it will endure in time. Do you expect to be running marathons and performing aerobics thousands of years from now, as yoga has persisted into your age?

Whatever you choose, do so out of loving respect for the body that carries you from birth to death, cherishing its sensations, its vigor and its mastery. Your body will never fail you as long as you respect its messages and needs. Now, enough on the subject from a nonphysical lecturer–who has no body to toss into the pool or onto the mat!–and get off the sofa!

CHAPTER THIRTY-TWO

Aging

How do you age?

The scientists who gnashed their teeth when we inquired how they explain cell specialization in the growing fetus are now waxing apoplectic. For every cell carries the genetic blueprint for the entire body. How, then, does the liver know to be a liver and not an elbow?

And once the whole agglomeration of the body is set into motion, how does it age? There is no genetic encoding for a thirty-year-old liver as opposed to a fifty-year-old liver. How does the body know?

Further, you understand that the material forming your cells is constantly dying and being replenished and, indeed, that there is not a cell or atom in your body now that was there seven years ago. How, then, is the consistency maintained? How do fresh molecules know to lend their structure to the maintenance of a heart cell? a toenail? a hair follicle?

This process so flabbergasts science, limiting itself to the physically perceivable, that there are scant theories propounded as to how the body ages. Well, hormones, or wear and tear and...

Let us examine the reality.

Remember that your body is the physical reflection of spirit, that it is a gridwork of points of intention, a structure of organized energy patterns that, when interpreted by the fiction of your senses, you perceive as the body. Thus the blueprint for your body is not held in the chromosomes at all; they are simply a physical reflection of the true blueprint and stand symbolically containing the body's structure within each cell. This symbolizes the constant, impossibly complex web of communication that takes place among all "points of intention" that support your body, unseen.

Therefore, given the blueprint for the species and your greater entity's desire for a given contour, each "point of intention" that you may imagine standing behind the creation and sustenance of a single cell will therefore remain constant throughout your life. Behind your physical liver lies an unseen grid of intent whose purpose is to create and sustain a liver. Thus, when new elements and materials assume the place of those washed away, they are simply falling into place along the structure determined by the invisible grid of intent standing behind that cell, that organ or that function.

An analogy would be pouring liquid gelatin into molds of varying shapes and sizes. The gelatin—the raw material—is the same; but the contours of the molds in which it is poured determine its physical expression. The same principle holds for the maintenance of your body's discrete organs and features, as a few basic, elemental building blocks are poured into the nonphysical "mold" determined by the grid of intent that lies behind.

While there are certain "givens" in the aging process—the child becomes the adult regardless of whether it consciously intends to—there is great leeway in the rate of aging. You are not wind-up toys puttering about the earth with your springs unwinding at a steady buzz. You know there are cultures on the earth whose members live far longer than you, on average, and in better health.

In your own society, a look at the statistical tables will show that those living in cities die earlier than those in the country. And blacks die younger than whites. Why?

We must return to our earlier discussion of probable selves. Remember that an infinite variety of paths lies open before you, and the physically experienced events of your life are those you have pulled into actuality through the magnet of belief. For instance, if you are young and you think ahead to when you will be sixty, what do you think? Do you look forward to it? Do you dread it? Do you expect not to see it at all?

Understand that if you are young, there exists an infinite number of "yous" at age sixty. Some lines will have you leaving physical life before that age. Some will have you suffering under severe disease and pain. Others will have you in good health. And others will have you positively effervescing with love of your life.

Now you see the danger in all the negative programming you receive daily from science and government about the dangers of the world, how you are forever susceptible to disease. Coupling this with your scientific belief that death is the end of all existence, you find yourselves fearing the aging process, certain that it means only decay and disease. And what happens when you fear something?

You energize that probable path. If you are young and you fear age sixty, certain that you will be a physical wreck at that point, then you energize that possibility above all others. And when your life's path brings you to the age of sixty, the decrepit condition will be the most likely to fall into place due to your belief that such was the inevitable course.

You have many, many examples of hale, hearty, exuberant, active, inquisitive and productive old people among your society now. Best that you get to know them! For in their company you will find that each stage of life brings fresh growth, that there is no end to the learning and fresh experience that can accrue to the balanced and happy individual.

Not only is it possible to ensure yourself a happy, productive and healthy old age, but it is also possible to reverse the aging process.

Before you use this book for kindling, hear us out.

You understand now that your body is maintained by an invisible gridwork of points of intention, each standing behind a single cell of your body, carrying the code for that cell's unique specialty, apprising all fresh material of its role and structure.

As you grow and age, your beliefs will affect the points of intention standing behind your body. In a life of inner awareness of the trinity of mind, body and spirit, an appreciation for the fresh growth each stage of life brings, each point of intention lying behind the body will retain the polish, energy and vitality that lay behind the newborn it once created.

If, on the other hand, your beliefs about aging are that it must necessarily be an unhappy slide down the slippery slope to decay, your beliefs then encrust those points of intention, literally prevent full energy and vitality from easing across the membrane into physical existence, thus literally creating the decrepit body you so ardently believe in and prepare for. Your beliefs, then, determine the condition of your body as you age.

Now, at any point, if you change your beliefs, you may not only change the present condition of your body, but you may literally rewrite your body's history such that you find swelling within you an exuberant flow of healing energy that can literally reverse the aging process.

All time is simultaneous. All physically experienced events carry a "polish" or charge not carried by those events never brought into physical expression. Therefore, whatever age you believe you are now, understand that all other ages of your life, from birth to death, exist now also. If you change your beliefs in your "now" from thinking of aging as a process of decay to one instead of growth and opportunity, you literally reach back in time, discard the "polish" that carried the belief-charge in your past, replace it with the new belief-charge and therefore rewrite your body's history.

In other words, as fresh material takes its place in a cell, it lends its strength to that cell along the lines dictated by the blueprint, or point of intention, lying behind the cell. If you believe aging to be a process of decay, then the material entering the cell is "instructed" that it is part of a gradually weakening structure. The material then fulfills its duty along the instructions given it. If, through conscious belief work, you remove the "instruction" that aging is decay and replace it with an affirmation that all of life is growth, then that prior directive, carried as part of the point of intention, is released. Thus, when fresh material enters the cell, it is now instructed that it is helping to maintain a vibrant, healthy cell, one which expects to remain so throughout life; the new material, like our gelatin, compliantly assumes the contour of that instruction.

You understand now that with the principles of cellular communication, simultaneous time and probable selves, you can indeed change the past!—and enjoy a far healthier future as well!

When we said earlier that all illness reflects an unfaced or unconscious conflict, we may have led you to believe that you must tremble at the appearance of a cold or flu, that such necessarily represent some karmic backlash from the twelfth century coming back to haunt you. With your love of good and bad, seeing illness as always "bad," you lose sight of the fact that all paths are creative, that they all lead to greater understanding.

Again, events will always first appear in your life in highly attenuated fashion, bouncing on their cycles at an oblique angle, later finding fuller expression if unrecognized and unexamined. Therefore, a slight flu or cold often represents a symbolic disease state of far more serious nature, literally acted out in the body as a way of releasing the conflict that lies behind it.

For instance, you may be overworked, concentrating so hard on professional pursuits that you are ignoring the satisfactions of family and friends. You are not meant to live such a life. You may thus find yourself coming down with a cold or flu. And how do you react? If you recognize that such a condition always represents an unfaced issue, you might think to yourself, I must be overworked, and take to bed for a few days. In this case, you are releasing the charge behind the appearance of the flu, acknowledging the signals your body sends you; that respect for the body's integrity literally strengthens you. The conflict passes, then, in that you have granted yourself a period of relaxation in the company of family, that you otherwise would not have.

If, on the other hand, you consider a flu an inconvenience, an attack on your body from without by some Oriental virus, and continue to charge ahead with your daily professional life, you have only strengthened the conflict bringing on the flu. Now, the flu itself may well pass, the "event" of illness bouncing back away from your existence, but it shall return, duly strengthened. Remember that events always present themselves in steadily increasing expression until you face them and resolve the charge that lies behind them. If you have no time for a flu, could you take time out for pneumonia? How about a heart attack?

Just as you may not violate another with impunity, just as you may not plunder the world without consequence, so you cannot ignore your body's signals, faithful reflections of your life's deeper truths that they are, and expect that your body will sustain you forever in good and trouble-free health.

Any physical "cause" of a physical condition is simply a reflection of the deeper meaning that event holds. Viruses, for example, which you perceive as being transmitted person to person, reflect that the belief behind the disease state is easily transmissible, one to the other; thus you find communities falling prey to the same "virus" at the same time. If you believe the body is susceptible, tell your children the body is susceptible, gorge on vitamins to fend off the attack, then indeed you are most susceptible; and as these beliefs are epidemic in your society, so too will be the virus.

If, on the other hand, you break your leg falling out of a tree, thus impairing your mobility, the reasons will almost always be highly personal, private. Nobody's legs crack beneath him upon viewing you in a cast. It is your private conflicts that would manifest in such a bodily condition.

And that, ladies and gentlemen, leads us quite nicely to the crowning achievement of your civilization: the AIDS "virus."

CHAPTER THIRTY-THREE

AIDS

We call the AIDS virus the highest creation of your civilization precisely because, as we shall see, it so perfectly captures, in its crude and primitive form, the grand political, religious and scientific currents of your time, the final battle between fear and understanding which is the fundamental issue of your day, and throws in the follies of science, medicine and prejudice as well. For not only are there no closed systems—as we have maintained throughout—but our examination of the AIDS phenomenon will demonstrate that your culture is indeed a melting pot, with the once discrete ingredients —politics, religion, science—now commingling their essences, flowing through one another, creating an indivisible gestalt that finds symbolic expression in this most despised and feared viral creation.

To begin, let us examine the phenomenon from a purely physical standpoint, laying out its contours as you presently perceive them.

First, you understand the AIDS virus to be a crude, primitive and frail strain, dead on contact with oxygen. As such, it can only be transmitted through direct exchange of bodily fluids, blood or semen.

It therefore afflicts three groups, primarily. The vast majority of victims are gay men. The second group is intravenous drug users, sharing dirty syringe needles. Finally, the statistically slight genetic disease of hemophilia includes its sufferers on the list, transmitted through blood products, received through transfusions.

Despite its primitive shape, the AIDS virus mutates at a maddening rate, outdistancing any effort to pin down the genetic code and render it harmless.

The virus is now beginning to make inroads in the heterosexual population. Women contract it from men with bisexual experience and pass it along to their infants either in utero or during birth. Thus, the virus appears to have broken out of afflicting only the three major groups listed above and threatens to endanger the populace as a whole. The virus has a strong foothold in Africa, but indeed the entire world is finding itself afflicted.

These are the physically perceivable, commonly agreed-upon parameters and characteristics of the virus itself, the populations it attacks and the danger it holds for the entire society in the future.

Remember that all physically perceivable phenomena are reflections of deeper realities hidden from your conscious awareness. Applying what you have learned up to this point, let us now place this AIDS virus under the microscope of Divine Grace and see if we cannot unravel its true origin, purpose and meaning.

First let us examine the populations the disease has afflicted.

Intravenous drug users are unlikely candidates for good citizenship awards in your society. For by falling prey to addictions, to illegal substances, they violate both your laws and your moral sense. Addictions of this extreme repulse you precisely because you recognize intuitively that anyone who organizes his/her life around a substance, to the extreme of that substance being the motivating force for all of one's actions, represents a capitulation to second-hand reality—a physical substance replacing more life-affirming motives like love, pride and satisfaction. Drug addicts refuse to create their own reality, refuse to take responsibility for their lives, slaves as they are to the irrefutable, imperious demands of a body demanding more, even though satisfying that urge can lead only to the body's further destruction.

Drug addicts are symbols, then, the distilled essence of your society's general disease. You worship and crave second-hand reality—money, status, fame—while refusing to face the destruction you wreak both upon the natural world and on the body politic. You do not want the responsibility for creating your own reality, lest you be forced to face up to the consequences of your actions and realize that only you can save yourselves. Money, status, fame—they are all drugs, metaphysical drugs, and the society has existed far too long as an insatiable junkie, feeding its hunger for second-hand reality while ensuring its own self-destruction.

A tangential reason for the involvement of drug addicts in the AIDS crisis is precisely because you so despise them. Do you then stand back and watch them die agonizing deaths as their immune systems fail? Are you able to feel compassion for these, the very lowest on the totem pole of your society's morality?

Hemophilia is a genetically transmitted disease, manifesting in a sex-linked recessive pattern, passed from hemophilic father to carrier but unaffected daughter, then on to hemophilic son. Thus, the disease is intrinsically bound to the media of conception: sperm and blood.

Remember that the reputed agent of a disease state will always reveal the greater reality behind it. On a global, historical scale, this is also true of genetic disease. Every genetic disease of which you are aware is thus a symbol of certain lines of development that remain in the gene pool, sometimes in as few individuals as a dozen or so per hundreds of millions, and remain as latent **symbols** and **potentials** for the society as a whole. Under certain conditions, if the path of a society warrants, certain of these strains will suddenly become more prominent—congenitally defective children born to families with no history of the disease—as a means of alerting the society that the symbol behind the disease state, the deeper meaning it represents, has come to the fore.

For example, all cultures have a certain percentage of congenitally retarded individuals, those incapable of developing full reasoning and intellectual abilities. The symbol behind such a state is thus the emotional qualities of the species, which in a healthy individual are balanced with the intellectual faculties to ensure an equilibrium. In a society emphasizing intellectual, reasoning and verbal qualities above all others, you will necessarily find a rise in the number of mentally retarded individuals, precisely as a way of ensuring on a mass level that the balance between reason and emotion is maintained. For a retarded individual cannot meet you at your intellectual level; if there be any contact at all, it is you who must limit your expression to an emotional content. Thus is balance maintained, both in the individual family—reincarnational issues often being involved—and in the society as a whole.

Knowing that genetic diseases are symbols of latent developments and attributes in the society, what can we determine about the symbol the hemophiliac represents?

First, we must clear up popular misconceptions about the disease.

As you understand it, whenever injury occurs and blood vessels are broken, the body stanches the flow of blood by forming a clot. It does this by triggering a series of proteins, each protein necessary to the process; like falling dominoes they activate the next in line, helping to form the glutinous mass that becomes a clot. In the hemophiliac, that protein you call Factor VIII (or, in some cases, Factor IX) is missing, either altogether or to some degree. Thus, with one "trigger" in the chain of activation missing, the body cannot form a complete clot. It takes longer for a clot to form, in other words, than in a normal person.

No hemophiliac ever died from a scratch, as your folklore would have you believe. Simply applying pressure to the broken skin stanches the flow of blood. The great danger in hemophilia lies in internal bleeding. Every time you move, walk, run, jump or fall, you break blood vessels within your joints, organs and tissues. In a normal person such ruptures are never noticed; clots form, heal the damage and you are restored.

In a hemophiliac, however, without the full and immediate clotting, blood can continue to seep into damaged areas. The joints are particularly susceptible, since they are the focus of so much wear and tear; and if blood flows unchecked in the joints, it acts as a corrosive, literally eating away the muscle, tendons and cartilage that hold the joint together. The result, over an active boyhood, can be permanent loss of full use of the joints, even permanent crippling.

You know that blood is your life's very essence; if the heart is the organ most closely resembling Divine Grace as it creates your world, then blood is Divine Grace's truest agent, ensuring that the constant exchange of materials, the elimination of dead cells or toxins, the delivery of oxygen, the battling of foreign invaders, all take place constantly, automatically, without a conscious thought. Blood, then, is life itself. In the hemophiliac, blood can be his worst enemy, for it acts against the very body it is designed to sustain.

Here is our clue; here is our symbol. The hemophiliac symbolically represents a house divided, turning upon itself. Hemophilia has been with you through all ages, through all cultures, standing as the latent and statistically tiny symbol of a house divided, turning upon itself.

As an historical footnote, you can see now that it was no coincidence that the last male heir of the Romanov line, the Tsarevitch Alexis, was a hemophiliac. For his body's condition—a house divided, turning upon itself—mirrored and presaged the fratricidal Bolshevik Revolution that ended his family's rule and his own young life.

In your society, in your time, whether you are aware of it or not, the incidence of spontaneous mutation resulting in hemophilia has been on the rise. That is, mothers with no history of the disease in the family find themselves carriers, producing hemophilic sons. When a symbol, manifested in a genetic disease, rises in incidence, occurs spontaneously, you know the deeper meaning behind the symbol has become germane to a society.

A house divided, turning upon itself.

Some may have protested, when we placed drug addicts at the bottom of your society's morality ladder, that such a station belonged to homosexuals instead. Indeed, as we have seen, few groups have been so reviled and persecuted throughout history. What has the result of this sexual genocide been in your society?

Until very recently, and even now only in large cities, homosexuals could never openly declare their desires, live openly with a lover and integrate their sexual preference into the community at large. As a result, emotional attachments being too difficult to maintain, the homosexual community has been forced into reducing that great arena of love and commitment—sex—into a purely physical act, stripping away the emotional undergirding that enhances the physical act. Rampant promiscuity with multiple partners was the result, and few could maintain long-term bonds resembling heterosexual marriage.

Homosexuals thus divorced love from sex—a house divided—and sought affection solely in the ultimately self-defeating emptiness of compulsive promiscuity—turning upon itself.

To expand our discussion of why homosexuals are the primary victims of AIDS, we must make what will appear at first to be an irrelevant digression to a brief look at your closest cousins on the planet, the cetaceans.

Scientists, of course, with evolutionary blinders firmly in place, claim your strongest link is with the apes, as they most closely resemble the human species in form. But it is the cetaceans who most closely resemble your species in consciousness. Later we will explore why; but for now, know that all the characteristics of your species—social organization, the manipulation of symbols and so on—are also the fundamental qualities of the cetaceans, literally, in a different medium.

From time to time you are shocked, if not horrified, to find a pod of whales throwing themselves up on a beach, committing mass suicide before your eyes. Such whales will resist any effort to keep them alive, to return them to the sea. The decision has been made; they will die. Why?

Just as your nose brings you information about your environment, without your needing to see the source of an odor, so the cetaceans are aware of the condition of the medium in which they live, the sea. For you, the sea is one gigantic landfill, is it not, into which you dump toxic wastes—out of sight, out of mind— assuming the ocean floor will hold the products of your folly forever.

Secondly, if your government and that of the Soviets would release such data, you would find a strong correlation between mass whale beachings and the presence of nuclear-equipped submarines in the area. For whales know—they **know**—the **intent** that lies behind the missiles carried on the subs, the desire to **murder one's own brothers.**

Combined, using the seas as a dumping ground for the poisons your science has created and using the ocean as a giant cloak behind which to hide your instruments of death, you create a situation—like the nonbreeding animals in the zoo—in which the creatures involved **will not live by your terms.** If you so cavalierly toss your poison into their life's medium; if you have strayed so far from the natural order as to create implements of death—the malicious intent of nuclear fission turned against one's own species—then the cetaceans **will not share the planet with you.** In deeper terms, there can be no extinction, no death at all, but on the earth you have created, certain species have disappeared, not because you made their lives impossible, but because you **did not deserve their company.**

The cetaceans, being your closest cousins on the planet, finding evidence that you have not kept your end of the bargain and have forgotten the natural order from which they never deviated, **will not participate with your species by remaining on the planet.**

And when you rush to the beach—literally, the bridge between your realities— and frantically seek to succor your behemoth cousins, you look into the great knowing eye; and as your gravity crushes the life out, that eye meets yours not in spite or anger but in the bewilderment of love betrayed: brother, how could you?

Homosexuals have chosen their preference as a means of exploring, in concentrated distillation, what it means to be male or female in your species. They are specialists whose learning and experience benefit the entire society, just as every private life enriches the whole, on levels hidden from you. Homosexuals, then, are students and teachers in the meaning of sexuality, whose findings are disseminated throughout the culture on levels unconscious.

For century after century you have refused to see this; your church, driving a wedge between flesh and spirit, stuffed the wound with festering idiocies of guilt, condemnation and sin.

Pain and suffering are something all in your society have known; all can relate to the agonies of another, remembering one's own moments of suffering.

Homosexuals, then, your brethren explorers in the field of gender, have suffered so long at your ignorant hands that they literally beach themselves on the bridge between realities—pain and suffering being universal—immolate themselves on the pyres of your prejudice—for you have not kept your end of the bargain, have scorned them for performing what you asked them to do—

and they will literally pass into extinction before your eyes, their agonized death throes their last hope to evoke the compassion around which you have constructed centuries of ignorance and condemnation.

Brothers, how could you?

Let us now expand our discussion from exploring the discrete groups affected by the AIDS virus to a broader view encompassing the interrelationships involved. We must observe two parallel strands, one in the homosexual community, the other in the treatment of hemophilia.

In a way we must jump a bit ahead of ourselves, for it is later, in our discussion of the decade of the Sixties, that we will see that period as one in which the theme of "group" was explored in every corner of your society. There are no closed systems, and this emphasis on group infused both the ascendance of the homosexual community to greater visibility and the medical approach to hemophilia.

The Sixties were a time in which the various downtrodden groups in your society—everybody except white, heterosexual males—banded together and stormed out of their respective closets, no longer willing to chafe under the onerous strictures and oppression they had suffered until that time. Civil rights—the black movement—and feminism—the women's movement—were the predominant groups raising voice against the status quo, but other groups, including homosexuals, began to test the waters, to see if they could not make themselves visible and accepted.

That homosexuals should need to do so at all demonstrates how many, many houses your society was divided into! In the field of sexuality, then, the heterosexual majority had long turned upon its homosexual counterpart. Seeking to mend the breach, the rising homosexual population sought to make themselves as acceptable to the majority as possible. They did this by engaging in a variety of philanthropic and charitable causes. One such cause was the constant need for fresh blood; through concerted campaigns among the homosexual community to contribute, the society benefitted from their generosity while the community gained the respect of the majority. The group consciousness of the homosexual community, then, found one avenue in participating as blood donors.

Let us now observe the progress in the treatment of hemophilia. You create your own reality; even those who choose to be born with a genetic disease have great leeway as to the **effects** of that disease. In your western culture, divorced from the natural order, viewing the body as a machine—in this case, a profoundly defective one—you have never understood the body to be simply a **reflection of spirit** and as such, eminently under the control and direction of the conscious mind. Every hemophiliac will tell you—if you ask—that moods and emotions have a profound effect on his body's condition, its susceptibility to bleeding. Dental work is a nightmare for hemophiliacs, as you can imagine, yet there are dentists who, through the use of hypnosis, can literally bring a hemophiliac's clotting time to the same as an unaffected person. What all this means—and what science does not want to hear—is that the mind controls the body; the body is spirit in flesh; and an understanding of the source of genetic disease, its purpose, would truly empower the afflicted to reduce that disease's effect to virtually nil.

Insisting on a purely physical treatment of hemophilia, medical science discovered hemophilia's "cause" to be the missing protein, Factor VIII, and began to transfuse hemophiliacs with the blood of normal persons, the normal person's Factor VIII supplying the hemophiliac's body. As this procedure was first introduced, only whole blood could be transfused; thus only a small fraction of the body's total need for Factor VIII could be supplied and the bleeding thus only slightly lessened.

By the threshold of the Sixties, however, science had advanced to the point where it could split the blood into its various components—a house divided—and thus provide a concentrated dose of missing factor to the hemophiliac. What this meant is that each dose given the hemophiliac was provided by a large number of people—group transfusion. While initially this was a cumbersome process—the solution needing to be kept frozen until use, then thawed—recent advances have refined the process to where the factor is now available as a powder that needs only to be mixed in an aqueous solution before transfusion.

Thus, science—with the best of intent and in total ignorance of the body's true source and workings—created a process by which the hemophiliac was exposed, in a single transfusion, to the blood of literally thousands of people—group transfusion indeed!

At the same time, the homosexual community was opening its veins in blood drives—as a group charitable effort.

You see now the incredibly complex—and yet eminently obvious—strands that intertwine and connect all phenomena in a culture.

The hemophiliac stands as a symbol, a house divided upon itself, his disease passed through the generations in the sperm, manifesting in a crippling of the body by its life's very essence, blood.

For centuries the field of sexuality has been a house divided, heterosexual against homosexual. The homosexual became a house divided, emotion and commitment divorced from sex, fidelity replaced with promiscuity.

Seeking a return to a house restored, the homosexual community demonstrated its compassion for the society that scorned it by participating in charitable blood drives.

Seeking a return to a house restored, soulless science devised a treatment for hemophilia that resulted in each afflicted individual being subjected to the life essence of thousands.

The AIDS virus, as you understand it, works by crippling the immune system, leaving the body as a house divided, playing host to infections that should be attacked and routed.

As you understand it, the AIDS virus is passed through the semen during sexual activity, where it lodges and festers in the blood.

The hemophiliac, infusing himself with infected blood factor, becomes a house divided, the body turning upon itself; once again, he passes his misery on to the next generation through the semen.

Let us now turn our attention to the supposed cause of all this trauma, the AIDS virus.

Again, you perceive it as a weak virus, unable to survive when exposed to oxygen. It thus must work its evil by passing directly from body to body, through the penis, a needle or the birth canal.

Remember that the apparent cause of a disease will always serve as a clue to the deeper meaning the disease represents. Knowing this, what can we determine about the AIDS virus and its presence in your culture?

First, a "virus" is by definition an organism that can pass from one person to another. If the virus is hardy, a sneeze in the vicinity of an affected person may lodge the microbe within you. AIDS needs more personal contact, as we have seen. But in every case, a virus multiplies its avenues of activity through interpersonal contact.

Beliefs work exactly the same way. Those growing up in a given culture will invariably have inculcated from the first the traditions, mores, attitudes, prejudices and beliefs of that culture. As such, these can remain invisible unless critically examined. It was simply natural, beyond question, to the slave owner, that the black race was inferior to his own. There was no question, no need to sit and ponder the issue. It was self-evident. Such beliefs, then, were passed from generation to generation as surely as was the genetic code.

In the workings of a virus, you are meant to consider that all phenomena are "transmissible" from one individual to another. Further, that some such phenomena — like beliefs — may have negative effects, may be unhealthy in their expression. With an understanding that you create your own reality, you can consciously fend off any such attack. You are at the mercy of no virus, then, just as you are at the mercy of no belief you do not care to absorb.

Viruses are symbols of the invisible workings of belief, their unconscious transmission from one to the other, and your freedom to reject that which you find incompatible with your life's highest fulfillment.

Examining the routes of transmission of the AIDS virus, understanding that this will lead us to those beliefs that made the disease necessary, will lead us to the very source of the scourge.

What is the primary route of transmission of the AIDS virus? The penis. Observe the church, how in its history it came to restore Mary's virginity posthumously, to thereafter equate chastity with divinity, to elevate a virgin to the highest exalted throne. Men of the collar became celibate, their sexual organs mere decorations or, worse, sites of guilt and shame. And where does all this belief-baggage lead us? The penis is a tool of defilement. If the Son of God was born of a virgin, if the religious leaders abstain from all sexual activity, then sex must be blasphemy, and its instrument the tool of the devil.

Building on this, even in a self-proclaimed society without a state religion, nevertheless the proscriptions and shame of religion have permeated your society; you have laws seeking to regulate sexual conduct—that most private act—even delineating which acts are acceptable and which not.

Science pitched in, of course, and while claiming neutrality and impartiality in examining and cataloging the world and the body, its perception of the body as a mere machine, an accidental one at that, being the result of eons of natural selection, could only cast a further pall on the issue of sex. For if life is a battle of natural selection, determined by genetics, then the very focus of that great, furious battle was the sexual organ. The most lethal stick a man could carry in battling his neighbors was right between his legs.

The result was centuries and centuries of belief, feeding and building upon each other as religion, government and science all conspired to reduce sex to an arena of shame, guilt, repression and death.

Yes, death. Your beliefs create your reality, and you will always find manifested in the physical world the true expression of your beliefs. If sexual pleasure condemns you to Hell, if sexual pleasure is to be proscribed by the state, if sex is the basis of a great worldwide battle for survival, then you now find miraculously reflected in the AIDS virus precisely what you have been building up to all these centuries: **sex is death.** That is the belief, among but above all others, that has brought this scourge into your existence.

Now you begin to understand why we claim that AIDS is your highest creation, your most ingenious construction. For in the equation "sex is death," we find miraculously joined the two great fears of your era: anarchy and annihilation. The fear of anarchy is the fear of impulses, and the sex act is the most impulsive, irrational act of which you are capable. This is why conservatives rail against sex, sex education, homosexuality, premarital sex, post-marital sex and so on. They intuitively sense that in its great, exuberant pleasure, sex laughs in the face of the conservative's frightened need for order and structure.

The liberal's great fear is of annihilation. Knowing no divine source of the world, condemned to view death as an insult, an outrage, instead of the doorway to greater learning that it is, the liberal's highest value is his body. And AIDS—meaning certain death to those afflicted—must thus evoke unmitigated terror.

As your society moves toward the final showdown between fear and understanding, your two greatest fears have been joined in one simple equation, translated into one primitive virus, the better for you to face all your fears, all your erroneous beliefs, all at once.

Narrowing our microscope's view to the virus itself, what do we find?

If yours is the time when fear must either be dismissed from your reality or destroy it, then in the AIDS virus we find the physical manifestation of unfettered, unbridled, unadulterated fear.

First, you know that the virus is a very primitive structure, beneath its coat. Fears are primitive structures, in that they are by definition a result of divorce from the natural order. The universe is safe; therefore, any fear must be based on ignorance of this fundamental law. Fears, then, are always primitive, always crude constructs built on divorce from the natural order.

The AIDS virus shields itself in a coat that is maddeningly mutable, mutating before your scientists can pin down its genetic structure. Remember that fears always disguise themselves by latching onto whatever legitimate belief will give them credence and authority; to disguise their true nature, fears will don a mutable variety of disguises, often resulting in the seeming contradiction of opposing viewpoints held by those whose policies are driven by fear, not reason.

The AIDS virus is a weakling, contact with oxygen killing it instantly. Remember that any fear, however intractable and deeply rooted, will wither under the piercing glance of a single rational mind. One cold, hard look at a fear will demolish it. You exist to experience physical life through the filter of a rational mind; as fears are by definition irrational, you can render them impotent with a single uncompromising review. Oxygen, which you depend on for your very life, kills the AIDS virus instantly. Reason, which you depend on to guide you through life, does the same to fear.

The AIDS virus does not in itself cause death; it attacks the body's immune system, leaving other opportunistic infections to finish off the host body. Remember the Attorney General's pornography report*– how fear wrenched an illegitimate cause–and–effect relationship between pornography and violence, thus doing its damage while dropping entirely out of the picture. The AIDS virus does the same. It sets the body up for destruction but leaves the dirty work to others. A precise replica of the insidious workings of fear.

Now, the connections laid out here may seem so obvious as to be ludicrous. Again, with your love of thinking life a mystery, a battle, an insolvable riddle, you reject anything so plain, so simple, so obvious. You want life to be difficult, incomprehensible; you want to leave it to the experts of government, science and religion to tell you what to think and what to do. Yet, as we have pointed out, the universe always operates by demonstrating in as clear and unfiltered a manner as possible the physical results of your thoughts and beliefs. Yours is the era of fear; the AIDS virus is the literal physical manifestation of fear; thus the virus works precisely as fear works. Just as your body is the physical reflection of your spirit, **so is the AIDS virus the physical reflection of fear.**

There can be no cure until this is understood.

Let us now look briefly at the broadest picture, the ways in which AIDS weaves itself through the entire fabric of your society.

Yours is the age of fear versus understanding; this present decade is the one setting the stage for the final showdown yet to come. In the three areas of society–government, science and religion–you must face the fear driving the policies of those in charge, or allow them to lead you into the abyss.

---

*In 1986 Attorney General Edwin Mees's Commission on Pornography claimed to find a causal link between pornography and violence toward women. Two members of the Commission dissented, arguing that this conclusion "simply cannot be accepted."

The AIDS virus was first identified in your year 1981, the first year of the present decade. In that same year you inaugurated the present president and his administration. Now, there is no cause and effect, certainly not between presidents and viruses! But as AIDS is the medical expression of fear in your society, so at the same time did you also usher in the most fearful political administration of this century. Further, this administration was elected in large part by the rising fundamentalist Right, the religious bearers of fear.

So you see—and we will explore this later in greater detail—your present decade is one in which the three great institutions of your society—of any society—reveal themselves driven not by reason but by fear. And, in all cases, you see the first glimmers of the results of not facing those fears—death. The religious Right are perfectly happy to bomb abortion clinics in order to save the lives of fetuses. They are perfectly happy to pray for the death of those who disagree with them. Your fearful administration wishes to string a lethal butterfly net across the skies, increasing the likelihood of a nuclear exchange. And the AIDS virus, as you understand it, is a death sentence to those who contract it.

Let us now affirm our version of a fundamental law you have ignored for so long that it can now only manifest in deadly form: **fear is death.** Face your fears and they will wither away. Refuse to face them and they will decimate your society.

If you think yourselves the victims of a plague from the hand of an angry God, or the victims of another of the cold universe's cruel attacks on your accidental existence, you will never understand or be able to cure the menace of AIDS.

There is no punishment, no retribution, no cold, accidental universe. There is only the **physical manifestation of your thoughts and beliefs.** Remember that any event will manifest itself in your awareness in incrementally increasing strength. We earlier saw the progression from polio—leaving you crippled—to AIDS— leaving you dead. And as horrendous as are AIDS's effects, as devastating as it can be to your society, understand that it is not the most destructive version of "disease" that can be made known in your society. It is only because you have insisted on limiting yourselves to the physically perceivable, on treating disease on a purely physical level, that you find yourselves with the genuine misery and horror of this disease. But there are other diseases that, while also sharing AIDS's certain fatality, are easily transmissible through casual contact. How would you protect yourselves from such a disease? Wrap yourselves head to toe in condoms?

We wish not to frighten you but simply to point out that the universe works always for you, works toward your greatest fulfillment; when you stray from the path of Divine Grace, you will be nudged back toward it, those nudges increasing in intensity the longer you refuse to acknowledge the divine reason that is your birthright. AIDS need never have come into your existence, then. And if you do not face the issues behind its expression, you may indeed find even more virulent forms of disease upon you.

You choose.

We have not yet mentioned one key characteristic of the AIDS virus, and we will do so now. One curious aspect of its expression is that the majority of those carrying the virus have not yet succumbed to any ill effects as a result. Thus, there is no automatic equation between acquiring the virus and death. Your scientists can't pin down the precise percentage of those carrying the virus who have not yet found themselves ill. The result is that many infected persons unconsciously spread the virus wider and wider into the population. Men with a few homosexual experiences pass it on to women who now aid its advance into the heterosexual population. Thus the virus is insidious, working its quiet way into all corners of your society.

Now is the time to begin an examination of the **positive** effects of the AIDS crisis. As we will see, every single one of these positive effects, had they come about naturally as part of your society's evolution, would have obviated the need for the virus. But having blunted your easy progress toward the New Dawn with fortifications of fear, you find the AIDS virus forcing into the open those issues you have refused to face.

First, obviously, the entire field of sexuality is suddenly front-page news. No more Victorian prudishness now; ignorance is death, and you best be informed. There is much debate about how to present material on the AIDS crisis to schoolchildren, but none except the insane deny that some education must take place.

Voilà. You must teach children about homosexuality. You must teach them about using condoms—birth control. You must instruct them in the dangers of promiscuity.

Now, had your society evolved in a healthy fashion, all of these topics would quite naturally have been transmitted to children. Homosexuality would be seen as another appetizer at the buffet of life. Birth control would be preached as an absolute necessity for use by adolescents. Healthy sexuality would be seen as linking the physical act with emotional commitment.

Because you have not allowed the easy evolution of these issues into your society and instead have permitted the histrionics of religion to hinder the maturation of views on these issues, you now have been forced by the AIDS crisis to take one giant leap forward where you refused to take incremental steps.

Among the voices debating the proper approach to informing young people of the crisis's dimensions, it has been mentioned that teen-age boys be advised to refrain from homosexual intercourse. What is this! A generation ago, in far more "liberal" times, the very mention of such a possibility would never have been heard from any public figure. Yet there is no time for delicacy now—ignorance is death—and so the society must face what it has wished out of existence for so long.

Finally, we come to the crowning achievement of the AIDS virus as it finds expression in your society. We have seen that one of its attributes is to hide itself in a carrier, unexpressed, without damage to the host, who may never know of its existence within.

Science, and its handmaiden medicine, are stumped completely as to what could trigger the virus from such a latent state to one of active destruction. Until they can spend sufficient billions to find such a trigger, here it is for free: **belief**— they can only counsel carriers to maintain a positive outlook on life, eat well and pursue those activities that bring them happiness.

What is this!! Is this science—cold, clinical science—advancing the proposition that perhaps—just perhaps—**thought creates reality**? That your body's condition is determined by **belief and attitude**?

AIDS is more than a crisis. It is a revelation.

Every phenomenon of which you are aware is a reflection of a deeper meaning. In the deepest terms, there is no such thing as an AIDS virus; you are simply experiencing the results of your beliefs, made manifest and interpreted by you.

While on the purely physical level it is true that the virus is passed body to body in certain modes of transmission, it is the beliefs you hold about those methods of transmission, the symbols they represent, that determine their involvement in the crisis.

You believe homosexuality to be a sin. This is fallout from the church's driving a wedge between spirit and flesh, insisting that any sexual act lead to the possibility of conception. In fact, as we have seen, the sex act is intended to ensure your constant return to the natural order from which you spring, with children being the incidental side effect of sexual activity, not its purpose.

The drug addict, centering his/her life around acquiring and injecting an addictive substance, stands as the symbol for your political state of affairs. You have not two major parties but two major fears: anarchy and annihilation. They work symbiotically, as do your parties, with the liberals agreeing to subsidize the conservative's fear of anarchy while conservatives underwrite the fear of annihilation. In both cases the motivating fears—results of divorce from the natural order—are assuaged by money—second-hand reality. So intense are your fears, so monstrous is the government you have created, that indeed your chasing after an ever greater share of the nation's wealth—like the junkie—will lead, if unchecked, to the collapse of the society—overdose.

Medicine, insisting on limiting itself to the physically perceivable, allowing no thought to a divine source of the world, treats hemophilia—the symbol of a house divided, turning upon itself—by attempting to restore the body's missing clotting protein. A genuine understanding of genetic disease, of the reincarnational issues involved in the choice, and of the great power of the individual to mitigate its effects, would render such treatments obsolete.

In deepest terms, then, the reputed modes of transmission of the virus stand as symbols of the beliefs that brought the crisis into your reality. It is the belief that homosexual behavior is a sin, the belief that you can buy relief from fear of anarchy and annihilation, the belief that you must restrict medical treatment to the physically perceivable, that leads to these modes of transmission serving as the focal points of the virus.

And what is the cure, then? You know, but do not want to hear.
Change your beliefs.

How you roll your eyes, scoff and sneer at such a suggestion! What? Cure a deadly disease by changing our beliefs?

You do not want to believe the universe is an ordered, safe and eminently comprehensible place; you do not want to believe that everything you perceive is a reflection of deeper meaning, instantly understandable to the divinely reasoning mind; you do not want to believe you have such **power**; and you do not want the **responsibility** for the reality you have created.

Very well. Have your virus. Have your crisis. Spend millions, billions, trillions. And what does this gearing up to further bankrupt your society instantly warn you of? Second-hand reality approaching off the starboard side!

True health costs you nothing. Battling reflections of beliefs with reflections of meaning will bankrupt you.
You choose.

We might address those who find themselves afflicted with the disease. We have maintained throughout, reflecting your understanding of the disease, that it represents an automatic death sentence.

Now, is this so? Is there no chance of recovery, of conquering the disease?

Remember way back in our discussion of grids of intent, particularly in regard to the difficulty in overriding the intent of your greater entity that you experience a given condition. If you are born in poverty, you do so because your greater entity desires a life of destitution to balance one of opulence; although you can override that initial intent, it takes that much more energy to do so.

The AIDS crisis is one in which you are having to face your two greatest fears—anarchy and annihilation—molded together into one equation: sex is death. Given that the intent behind the virus's appearance in your reality is to force an examination of the root beliefs that cause it, and given the intent of those who choose to beach themselves on the shores of society as a way of forcing a sense of compassion for those formerly scorned, you can see that it is most difficult to override that intent and restore good health.

No one is condemned to death. All paths lie always open, and great healing can occur. The difficulty is that the gridwork of intent behind the AIDS virus is of such a configuration that it would require an individual of virtually omniscient insight to truly grasp the reason for the disease, its manifestation in a given individual, and to override that initial intent. For instance, as long as you consider your body a frail instrument, prey to virus and germ and disease, you are strengthening the grid of intent behind the AIDS virus. As long as you carry any residual beliefs that sex is in any way wrong, sinful, unhealthy or dirty, you are strengthening that grid of intent. As long as you believe that you must turn to the government to provide you with a cure, you are strengthening that grid of intent, along with your belief in your own weakness and incompetence to create your own reality.

Thus it is exceedingly difficult for an individual in your society to have thoroughly worked through, moved past, all those limiting beliefs, to the extent that one could then override the intent of the AIDS virus and restore full health.

There is no sacrifice involved here; death is **always** chosen, but in this particular case—similar to the Holocaust—an oppressed group will choose to make a joint statement by their deaths. Private reasons are always first and foremost in the selection of time, place and method; but as there is strength in numbers, so too can a communal death force to the greater society's attention those issues it has long refused to face. This is precisely what the AIDS crisis is doing, and its disproportionate assault on your society's outcasts—gays, drug addicts, blacks, Hispanics and prostitutes—is intended to force compassion where there was none before, to restore you to a house indivisible.

Now, as we have stated, if you wish to eliminate the scourge of AIDS from your society—not develop a vaccine, but eliminate it entirely—**you must change your beliefs.** Otherwise it will be with you forever, to be superceded by even more deadly strains if you do not face the root issues involved.

Remember when discussing nuclear power and its toxic waste products, we stated that the solution to the enduring toxicity of those waste products will fall into place as easily as did Three Mile Island and Chernobyl—once the beliefs allowing the violation of atomic fission are abandoned in favor of those cherishing and respecting the earth. Any "negative" manifestation of an issue is simply the flip side of its solution.

You have come far enough in our work to begin to assume responsibility for your reality, to understand how you create it, how all you perceive reflects deeper meaning. With this understanding, what clues might we be able to discern about locating the cure for AIDS?

Remember that AIDS is a reflection of your most central battle, that against fear. We have seen how the virus replicates precisely the workings of fear.

What can we conclude about its potential cure?

Simply **flip the picture over.** What is the AIDS virus? The physical reflection of fear. How does fear operate? By donning a disguise. Knowing this, knowing that it is futile to attack fear's disguises, that you must instead strip it bare and apply withering reason to fear, you can see that those researchers who are hoping to unlock the virus's secrets by concentrating on the virus's outer coat are off the track. You cannot fight fear by fighting its disguises. You cannot fight the AIDS virus by fighting its outer coat. You must attack the very **source.**

Remember that any fear is by definition irrational, a result of divorce from the natural order. The AIDS virus has within its primitive structure an element or configuration never before discovered in your experience with the natural order. It defies the natural order, as does any fear, in a way as yet overlooked, because you have no experience in looking for it. The clue relates to the arrangement of proteins; if you can examine the genetic structure of the virus, there will be an anomaly, a novel configuration that because you have no experience with such, you are likely to overlook. Fear is irrational, and the construction of the genetic blueprint of the AIDS virus is thus irrational, in the sense that it defies your traditional understanding of genetic structure and the resultant proteins.

Remember that any fear will be immediately dissolved by the incisive glance of a rational mind. You see the reflection of this in that the AIDS virus is dead on contact with oxygen, but there is more. The best physical replica you have of a piercing rational thought is the laser. You might find it a useful tool both in conducting the research we mentioned above, searching the genetic code for anomalies, and also in rendering the virus harmless. Again, you have not yet employed this technology—lasers—for this purpose precisely and may find the suggestion without merit. That is your choice. But there are ways in which a laser beam can "read" a genetic code, reduce it to a series of mathematical equations, which can then be studied for the source of the anomaly in that code. There will lie the source.

We will not and cannot create your reality for you by handing the formula for a solution to you on a silver platter. The AIDS virus is your creation, your civilization's crowning achievement, and we will not rob you of the joy at finding that you can indeed change your reality by altering your beliefs. That is the lesson of the time ahead, the lesson of the AIDS crisis. Most importantly, we do not sit on our lofty perch with the secret formula in hand, chortling over your ignorance! For just as any physical phenomenon precisely reflects the intent behind it, so will your cure, when found, precisely reflect the state of your society and its beliefs at that time. For that reason, it is impossible for us to offer more than the suggestions above; we know no more than this, for the cure will change over time, keeping up with and precisely mirroring the condition of your society. And since the future is far too fluid a medium to allow much in the way of predictions, we cannot know when your society will allow itself to end the scourge; we thus cannot know the configuration that the cure will take at that point.

Again, the most important element of finding a cure is to change your beliefs. The mechanics of the cure, as we have hinted at above, will simply reflect the change in belief.

And until you change the beliefs that brought the virus into your existence, you can have no cure. Spend yourselves into oblivion if you wish; the virus will eat its insidious way through the heartland until you finally come to face the universe's fundamental law: you create your own reality.

To conquer AIDS, you must conquer fear. It is that simple.

CHAPTER THIRTY-FOUR

Cetaceans

As we promised earlier, let us now take a closer look at your soul mates on the planet, the cetaceans.

Why do we claim that they are your closest cousins with respect to **consciousness**, when other land-based mammals are so similar in **form**?

In deepest terms there is no time, but in terms of time as you understand it, the world was seeded and thrust into physical existence all at once. It was created with the intent that it be a self-sustaining, self-balancing mechanism. Although constantly refreshed by the eternal energy of All That Is, this energy simply flows into the extant structures, which are themselves designed to maintain the earth in constant balance.

Humankind's distinguishing feature is a rational, reasoning mind. Until now we have engaged in the subterfuge—your vanity being what it is—of stating that you were the only creatures on earth possessed of this quality. In fact, you share the characteristic of reason with one other species, the cetaceans.

When it was determined that there should be lines of development that would lead to the exploration of physical life through the filter of a reasoning mind, the task was divided into two counterparts: the land-based humans and the water-based cetaceans.

For while the human form most closely resembles the ape, and the whale's form more closely resembles the fish, you are both mammals, are you not?

Thus, the task of exploring the physical world through the conscious, reasoning mind has been divided precisely as a way of ensuring that all the earth would be so explored. From the mountaintops to the depths of the sea. The challenges and issues are the same: social organization, manipulation of symbols and relationships, harmony with the natural order and symbolic expression of intent. On land, these qualities manifest as your four great races. Under the seas, the same division holds, as you find great variety in form among the cetaceans, from the dolphin to the blue whale.

Remember that those of your species depend most heavily on the sense of sight for an accurate assessment of their position, to read the accumulated knowledge of the race and to communicate symbolically with others. The sense of hearing serves as background material, filling in the highly focused picture with a generalized cocoon of sensation. The primary sense of sight is buttressed and enhanced with the background of sound.

In the cetaceans, this hierarchy is reversed. For the cetaceans, sight is a means of maintaining a generalized picture of one's environs, while serving as background for the principal sense of sound.

You know this already. If you stand atop a mountain and wave your arms at the fellow on the next peak, he can see you and wave back. If you yell at him, can he hear your words and respond? He cannot. Thus, in your atmosphere, light waves travel with far greater fidelity than sound waves.

If you dive underwater, you find that your sight is diminished by the uneven play of sunlight on the surface, sedimentary murk, plants and other obstructions. Yet if you call to your friend underwater, the sound travels cleanly through to his ear. Thus, under water, sound travels with far greater fidelity than sight.

As part of the intent that the world be both self-sustaining and balancing, then, the two primary senses of sight and sound were divvied up between those based on land—you folks—and those underwater—the cetaceans.

Cetaceans communicate to each other with sound, often traveling hundreds of miles, to be picked up by all within earshot. There is no need for a telephone system underwater, you see; simply speak your mind and everyone horns in on the party line.

To you, the sounds produced by cetaceans—the dolphin clicks, the whale songs—while being of mild interest, nonetheless seem crude, limited, flat.

What would happen if you held a Rembrandt before a dolphin's eyes? It would be able to ascertain that you held an object a certain height by a certain width, that it had certain splotches of color and that it was, well, flat. Beyond that, the dolphin could not interpret the meaning of the painting, as you can, with your superior sense of sight.

Grant the cetaceans the same! If the dolphin's click seems flat to you, it is only because you have no idea how to interpret it! A single "click" can carry as much meaning as the Sistine chapel. For cetaceans communicate on different frequencies, just as you do with your radios and televisions, and a single "click" can be the acoustical result of many channels of information being layered together, to be unraveled in the mind of the listener. For instance, a cetacean can apprise its companions with a single brief sound that it has encountered a source of food, exactly what the source is, how large, how many others can reasonably be expected to share in it, and then provide precise directions. This you hear as a single "click." How primitive!

Have you ever seen photographs or movies of human researchers attempting to teach dolphins human language? And do the dolphins not always seem to be positively hysterical with laughter? Know that there are no coincidences.

For your language is but the crudest approximation of what the cetaceans can achieve with the medium of sound; it is their symbolic carrier of meaning, just as written language and all your visual arts are to you. Thus do you have the world "covered," so to speak, between the two great cousins in consciousness.

Perhaps you want proof that humankind and the cetaceans are truly cousins in consciousness.

Embryologists will confirm that there is a stage in the development of the human fetus, very early, when it resembles nothing so much as a fish or cetacean. It has gill slits. It has a tail. In shape it is the spitting image of a creature of the sea.

Puzzling over this, your scientists have postulated that perhaps the human fetus passes through all the stages of evolution, from primordial ooze to human, in its development in the womb. Yet you no longer believe in evolution. What could the explanation be?

Further, you know that whales carry within their flippers a replica of the human hand's bone structure. This is completely useless to the whale, of course, it being impossible to bowl underwater. Again your scientists propose an evolutionary theory, but this time only at the peril of betraying their own beloved theory. If man evolved from the creatures of the sea, what use have those who stayed in the ocean for man's prehensile hand structure? Did man hop back in and become whales?

We leave the conundrum to your scientists. Now let us examine the reality.

The whale carries a replica of the human hand, and the human fetus passes through a moment of cetacean form, **precisely as a reminder of the bond between you.** Humans and cetaceans are the two species exploring the world with the gift of reason, and they share vestigial reminders of that relationship.

You know how children will pledge to be "blood brothers" bound by friendship and loyalty forever and ever. They seal this pact by pricking their fingers, commingling their blood, each absorbing the life essence of the other as a symbolic expression of their unity.

The human fetus assumes cetacean form.

The whale carries the human hand structure.

Blood brothers.

PART FOUR
ART

CHAPTER THIRTY-FIVE

Introduction

Why is there art?

When we apply our two-pronged Truth Test to this subject —Does it matter in the woods? Does it matter to a three-year-old?—we find a novel divergence. Animals know nothing of art. Young children are bursting with it. Why?

Again, as part of the "package" of your species, humankind was granted two avenues of activity that would ensure a constant restoration to the divine source of your world. One such avenue was sex. To keep our discussion simple, during our discussion of sexuality we claimed that sex is the act that most closely resembles the creation of your physical world, and is meant to ensure your constant refreshment from the divine fountains of your existence.

Now we expand our discussion to see that while sex is the **private** act that restores you to the divine natural order, art is the **public** act that both mirrors the creation of the physical world and restores you to its divine source.

For while you are each unique and individual, you are inextricably bound to the fate and concerns of your fellows. You were thus granted two avenues of activity mirroring the creation of your world and ensuring your bathing in the unseen seas that sustain your world; one is highly private, the other public. Sex and art.

Art has the further quality of being unique to the human species precisely because it involves **manipulation** of physical reality into **symbolic** expressions of meaning. Your species alone deals with symbols. (The cetaceans do so, but only mentally.) Any act of art, therefore, is a marriage between your reasoning mind and the nonphysical realms from which you spring, an attempt to wrestle into symbolic form those sensed but unseen truths and realities that lie behind your world.

Given this brief introduction, we might ask what the ultimate **source** of all art is. Are there nonphysical blueprints for all humankind's works of art, which artists simply tune into and replicate on the physical plane? Or is something more involved?

In deepest terms, the source of art can be considered to be an undifferentiated bank of energy specifically created to be drawn upon and manipulated by all peoples, in all historical periods, as a means of creating symbolic representations of truth. In other words, there is a greater source of Truth standing behind this Art source; this vast undifferentiated Art stands between the deepest truths creating your world and all others, and the physically experienced earth that you know. Thus, deepest Truth is **filtered** through the source of Art, which is then perceived in highly individualistic fashion by every artist, who employs the medium of his/her greatest talent to create a symbolic expression of Truth that others can share.

A fundamental principle in our discussions of art, therefore, will be how clear and undistorted the channel between artist and Art is. The artist with the truest channel can ride that connection to artistic expressions as pure and truthful as your species can create: Michelangelo and Mozart. To the extent that the channel is distorted by restrictive beliefs of the time or motives like ego, prestige or money, the resultant art will be a shallow product indeed; you name them.

Each artist, then, draws upon the vast source of all art, which we term Art, for the inspiration and power to grant symbolic expression through the unique and private experience of the artist.

Genuine art, the product of a clear and undistorted channel with Art, is not coy, shy, respectful, humble, graceful or subservient. Genuine art bursts into your world like the newborn babe, dripping with blood and shouting with promise. It seeks acceptance from no one, cares nothing for the approval of critic or peasant, and bristles at the thought of being bought and sold. Genuine art, the result of an artist's dedication, integrity and commitment to his craft and inner vision, stands aloof from the ebb and flow of the society into which it is born, for as we shall see, genuine art always **presages** the next wave rather than reflecting the current state of a culture.

Let us examine this further.

You know that events travel on cycles. You know that they first manifest in highly attenuated fashion, inserted at a highly oblique angle in your reality, leaving but a trace of their full strength in your awareness. As we have seen, this allows you to choose to alter a course when you find the first hesitant outcome of that path to be deleterious.

While this occurs on an individual level, each person being constantly made aware of the potential future paths before him/her, the same holds true for society at large. Life is energy and energy is motion; therefore, change is inevitable, the march of society impossible to halt. And while most in a society are not consciously aware of the evolution of theme and purpose until the full strength of an event is upon them, the artist can ride the connective strand with Art to the cycles only dimly perceived by the bulk of society, can tune into the potential evolution of society, can literally **behold the future** and fashion that intuitive knowledge into symbolic expression: art.

For while artists always symbolically express the society as it stands, they are also able to infuse their art with prescience, to announce in symbolic form to the society what it may expect to literally experience in the future. Again you see you are not cast adrift in some cold, dark universe; you were granted Art and artists as a means of supplying you with a constant source of the probable paths ahead of you, the better to examine them and choose the course of most benefit.

In addition to this, a society's artistic expressions will always reflect—no closed systems!—the technological, political and societal conditions of the era. Art rides the intent of the artist by using the extant structures of a society as raw material from which to fashion the truest symbolic expression of that given time and place.

This explains, why you look with awe and wonder at the paintings of the Impressionists, the Romantics, the great European Masters, and ask yourselves: Why have we no such masters among us today? Why do we paint soup cans?

You may similarly wonder why your century has not produced a single symphonic composer of the stature of those thundering to your ears from the 1600s and 1700s. Why did one era get Bach and Beethoven and Mozart and Vivaldi while we have...no one.

The reason, as we stated, is that a given art form will always reflect and build upon the extant technological, political and societal contours of its era.

Look at your own century. Consider your premier art forms. What is their single unifying characteristic? What is the single most important technological achievement of this century? The widespread use of electricity. **Every premier art form of the twentieth century requires electricity.**

The visual artists have set down their palettes and are loading their battery-powered cameras. Your greatest musical invention through the first half of the century was the electric guitar. Since then, the synthesizer and digital revolution have taken over. And the premier art form of your century is entirely dependent on electricity for its creation and display: film.

How do you know genuine art from its false stepbrothers? Again, your language carries great intuitive clues.

Whatever the artistic medium, one universal phrase that indicates that one has been touched by truth is to say, "It moved me." Remember, life is energy and energy is motion. A work of art that "moves" you does so because it taps directly into the source of your world, all worlds, and therefore all life.

You thus find yourself physically reacting to what may be an entirely stationary work of art. You may gasp. You may shake your head. You may point and squeal. You may stomp your feet and sing along. You may stand up and cheer. You may boo and stomp out. All physical responses, all firsthand reality as opposed to reading a dry critique of an art form.

And if you are so "moved" that none of the above actions can possibly contain and express your emotion? You cry. This process, which rises to the fore in any time of great emotion or truth, is profoundly symbolic. First, your emotional reaction causes a physical creation—a tear. You thus unconsciously replicate the very creation of your world by squeezing thought into physical reality. Your thoughts, your emotions, literally create a physical substance. Further, what is that substance? It resembles nothing so much as salt water, one more unconscious connection with your cetacean cousins; for in times of deep emotion or revelation, you literally strip away the barrier between the media in which the two species live, as your body creates the medium sustaining the cetaceans.

Admittedly, the eyes' ability to tear serves a utilitarian purpose should a foreign object lodge in the eye. But building on that automatic and unconscious process is your body's deep recognition of how the physical world is formed, and a subliminal nod to your cousins in consciousness.

Returning to our discussion, we can see that genuine art will be that which evokes a **physical response** in the viewer. By this may you know genuine art from its imitators!

Remember that the fundamental quality of white European culture is divorce from the natural order. Now. Compare the singing of hymns in a white Presbyterian church with the same activity in a black Baptist church. Which is closer to the source of truth?

Any work of art that leaves its audience bored, numbed, confused or stunned has revealed itself as a pale imitation of genuine art. This holds true only when speaking of newborn art, freshly created, presented to the public. For as time marches on, what was once a profoundly moving spectacle will necessarily lose its force as society evolves and finds new avenues of expression.

For instance, it is difficult now to believe, observing those who attend symphonic performances, that this art form ever excited the populace. When was the last time such an audience rushed the stage in sheer exaltation? Why, they might lose their jewelry. Understand that symphonic music was accorded a far different reaction in its time and place, the audience behaving far closer to those at rock concerts today. For instance, upon hearing the second movement of Beethoven's Seventh Symphony, as close as mortal ears are likely to come to the song of Divine Grace, the audience virtually rioted, threatening the orchestra with death if they did not play it again! Prudent musicians that they were, they complied. However stirring Beethoven's music is today, and you can see what a true arrow he rode to the heart of Art by his music's effect now, know that his music's impact was literally overwhelming on its contemporary audiences; it was almost more than one could stand to hear the divine song of the universe roaring through every pore of the body.

The truest judge of art, then, is not one's friends, contemporaries, critics or little statues, but history. For if a work of art speaks to generations unborn when it was created, you may know that it has been carved with vigor and abandon out of Art itself, its truth so profound that even as the technology and society that formed its expression disappear, that work of art still rides so powerful a thrust from the source of all Art that it laughingly leapfrogs the evolution of technology and society, diving unhindered into the heart and soul of all who behold it, in any time, in any place.

Thus may you know genuine art.

Perhaps you now see why art is so threatening to tyrannies of the Right and Left. For genuine art speaks the Truth, capital T, while it presages the society's evolution and mirrors its condition. Tyrannies of the Right and Left—based on fears of anarchy and annihilation, fears by definition being irrational and divorced from the natural order—must frantically squash any expression of truth, of symbolically revealing to the society both where it stands and where it is headed.

Art suffers more under the Right than the Left, for the conservative's great fear is of the anarchy of impulses, and what is more impulsive than the creation of genuine art? Sex, which of course is equally repressed. But art is far more dangerous, for however cleverly disguised in symbolic wrappings, Truth always lurks within, secretly apprising any viewer of the present and future and thus representing a profound threat to those tinpot trashers of truth.

In your time, in your society, art is not so much controlled by the state as it is by commerce. Money. Second-hand reality. You see now the great battle lines drawn here.

Art always **rides the next wave.** Commerce, seeking the security of past performance, wants nothing to do with future cycles but restricts itself to past cycles. Since life is energy and energy is motion, to seek to slam on the brakes and remain in a past cycle is by definition stasis, stasis being death, death being the antithesis of genuine art.

Any art field that is the site of shenanigans over money is therefore one whose channel to Art has been sullied, muddied, the firsthand reality of Art being wrenched to perform for the sake of a second-hand reality, money. While every art field does manage to produce artists of quality despite money's presence, and frequently to enrich them, the pressure to imitate what was nascent on a past cycle will necessarily result in stale, meaningless drivel.

This is especially true in your fields of popular music and film. Great artists excel in these media, but you find bandwagons full of shallow imitators, accountants and lawyers in tow, their feet firmly planted in the past, jumping on a wave that has long since crested and producing "art" that cannot last ten minutes.

Nowhere is this more evident than in the medium of television. For the major networks exist solely to make money; thus they must be safe and unoffensive to everyone in the audience. Genuine art, in contrast, swaggers up, smacks you in the face and demands that you accept it on its own terms or be damned. You can see now why all the cries for improvement in television programming are futile; it can only emit an unrelenting stream of dross.

If, as we have maintained throughout, everything that is physically perceivable is simply a reflection of deeper meaning, then how is art able to "move" us? Why should a painting evoke resonances that the skyscraper cannot, if they both are mere reflections of deeper reality?

We must examine precisely how art is wrestled from the nonphysical banks of Art into the various forms that you physically perceive. Much of this is virtually inexpressible in your terms, but let us make the attempt.

Any work of art is the result of interplay between the vast undifferentiated Art source and the artist's highly individual interpretation. It is the process of physically creating a work of art that holds the clue to our discussion.

Remember that all physically experienced events carry a "charge" or "polish" as a result of being brought into physical life. A work of art has its genesis in deep realms of truth far too vast to be comprehended by a single mind. It is as if each artist pulls off a little chunk of this vast Art source, pulling a handful of clay from an infinite sea of the material. In deepest terms, the artist's initial intent is not to create a work of art but to feel truth resonating within, to ride that next wave, to tap into the undercurrents flowing hidden beneath the society. The **intent** of the artist propels him or her to a realm of nonphysical experience, the confluence where technology and other societal currents meet; the urge to **share** this experience with others of the species results in creation of a **reflection** of that initial experience: a work of art.

This is a good illustration of how, in deepest terms, there is no time, yet you experience a progressive series of moments. The **key** experience is the artist's tapping into the deep wellsprings nourishing your world; it is later, in your time terms, that this event finds a physical reflection in a work of art.

The artist bolts out of bed, gripped by inspiration, rushing to the easel, the piano, the pen and paper. The resultant work of art will reflect the profound non-material experience that gave it birth.

When an artist wrestles this nonphysical experience into physical form, he or she necessarily "charges" it with the coating of physical reality. In the process of doing so, the artist imbues that "charge" with his/her own personality and frame of mind when creating the art, the state of the society in which he/she lives. In a manner most difficult to describe, all these highly personal factors are "locked in" the work of art, to be "decoded" by the viewer, such that the viewer will, in a diminished fashion, literally be transported to the time, place and mindset of the artist who created the artwork.

You have a perfect example of this in that your technology—electricity—allows you to record music and play it back whenever and wherever you like. Wherever you are when you hear an old song by a particular artist, you are transported back to that recording session. You hear the outer expression of that experience, but on levels unconscious you are also riding along with the artist's initial intent to the heart of Art.

You may find yourself attracted to certain types of art, certain styles of painting, certain music forms, sometimes centuries old. In many such cases there are reincarnational factors involved; you recognize, on deep unconscious terms, the flavor of the society in which the artist—and you—lived at the time of the art's creation. With your physical body firmly planted in "today," you can literally rip through the psychological barrier of time and re-enter a society long since dead, in your time terms.

This occurs whenever you find yourself so engrossed in a work of art—watching a movie, reading a book, listening to music—that when the experience ends you are amazed at how much time has passed. "I just wasn't aware of the time!" you say. Indeed. For while you rested quite securely in your comfortable physical world, you were psychologically in another era, another time, another place, riding the intent of the artist and infusing your consciousness with the intertwining strands of the society in which he lived.

Just as a recorded piece of music can be reduced to a series of electrical impulses, to be interpreted and amplified by your stereo equipment, so does every work of art carry the "charge" of its creator's private and public lives. You **literally travel through time** when a work of art thoroughly engrosses you. You know this; you feel an inexplicable rush of emotion, an unusual flood of sensation, when viewing old works of art. You are riding the artist's intent to the milieu of the art's birthplace, finding yourself in strange territory indeed!

Genuine art, being firsthand reality, carries you straight to the heart of Truth; while Truth is immortal and immutable, its expression changes with every sweep of the clock, and your experience of that Truth will be carried and cushioned by the flavor of the artist's time, place and private inner drama.

With this material as introduction, let us now examine the various art forms in more specific detail.

CHAPTER THIRTY-SIX

Paint

Let us first turn our attention to the strictly visual arts, especially painting.

Your species has, from the very first, worked to create symbolic expressions of the physical world. The crude drawings you find on cave walls, the ancient Indian carvings in your Southwest and so on, all testify to the innate urge to replicate the natural world in symbolic fashion. What utilitarian purpose could be served by carving pictures on a cave wall? There was no thought given to function or necessity then, as now, but it was simply the undeniable urge to record the world symbolically.

It seems patently obvious, but you see how the march of technology has accompanied the advancement of visual depictions of the world. The cave dwellers used stone, plants and flowers heavy with dye, as these were the only tools available—literally, elements fresh from the natural world, no second-h..nd reality or technological processes standing between intent and execution. Pick up the stone, smear the flower into the wall for color, and voilà: cave art.

The march of technology and the species' evolution, in your terms, brought about the use of tools, representing both a retreat from firsthand reality but also a leap forward in technological and intellectual terms. These tools allowed far greater freedom to the artist than the cave dweller restricted to stone and elemental dye. For with creation of the paint brush and the experimenting with various bases in which to mix the dye, a far greater range of expression was granted.

Your European legacy as captured in paint is almost exclusively devoted, among the early works, to depictions of the Christ story. This is a point worth exploring in some detail here. For as we shall see later in our discussion of the stages of life, each cycle from birth to death carries with it a certain "filter" through which events will be experienced and interpreted. A day at an amusement park is a vastly different experience for the parent and child, though they walk hand in hand, sharing every physical moment together; it is the filters of their life cycles that result in their profoundly different experiences of the day.

As this holds on an individual level, so is it also true of the evolution of society through its cycles. Because you are couched in twentieth-century technological society, it is difficult for you to step back from yourselves and appreciate the vast difference in the human mind's functioning in times past. You see your evolution as being simply a one-line advance from the ignorance and terror of the cave to your present condition of technological achievement and concomitant peace and harmony for all humankind(?). Yet as each cycle from birth to death carries within its boundaries challenges and growth not possible in any other cycle, so does every era of your history represent a given set of challenges, opportunities for growth, not present in any other era. You are not simply stumbling blindly forward, then, but experiencing physical life through a variety of filters, one aspect of which is a certain advancement in technology; but that is only one attribute of the march of society. For as we have seen, there are no closed systems and the technological advance, while imbuing all other qualities of an era with a certain cast or contour, is also dependent upon the changing filters of the species as a whole at different eras in "time."

Thus, the "mindset" of an individual in the fourteenth century was vastly different from that in your day. Such individuals were not merely ignorant and superstitious, as you would like to believe, but simply experiencing life through a different filter. The technology of that era both reflected and was dependent upon all other qualities of the society.

We have gone on at length about this because it comes to bear so significantly on the issue of painting and its evolution. For in the seemingly endless renditions of the Madonna and Child through the centuries, you find era after era driven by a search for meaning, the church being the source of meaning, and driven to wrestle that search into symbolic expression. In your pluralistic era, it is difficult to conceive of the mindset of those living in times before the church was split asunder. While the church held sway, as both the religious and political source of knowledge and morality, certain issues were constantly uppermost in mind while others were never even considered.

In your day, for instance, your society is driven to a large extent by the liberal's fear of annihilation. That fear, based upon the ascendance of science, Marx and the downfall of religion, was simply unknown to humankind before your era.

When you look back and observe the condition of the culture, vast multitudes living in wretched poverty while royalty and, to some extent, the church wallowed in riches, you are incensed. Why? Because your filter leads you to believe that all such economic divisions in a society must be eliminated or at least ameliorated to the point where no one is starving. We are not passing judgment on your era or theirs but simply pointing out that their filter held no possibility of such thought but interpreted the same physical reality—destitute poverty among the many—as God's will. And if you then scorn their God, understand that the presence of an omniscient and ultimately benevolent God imbued every nook and cranny of that era's consciousness, such that even the most destitute felt safe and valued by their Creator. In your time, the liberal has no such sense of security, living in his accidental universe. So while you disdain past societies for their treatment of the poor, understand that if you could meet those poor now, they would not trade their position for yours. Live in a world without God? Where is life's meaning, then?

Another long digression, but again this simply points out how inextricably are bound together the strands of art, technology, religion, politics and all other aspects of a society.

Because religion provided a secure framework of meaning that imbued all of creation, it was natural that artists would seek to represent the source of that meaning, the church's birth in Jesus and Mary. The drama of the Christ story was far more vibrant, had a far more profound impact on that society than it does in yours. You reduce that drama to one hour a week at best, most of you. In that era, it infused every moment with meaning. Thus, instead of pastoral scenes or portraits of common folk, the artist, striving always to wrench truth into physical expression, naturally turned to the nexus of truth, morality and meaning: the church.

When you visit a museum and observe the works of the European Masters, certain qualities may strike you. For one thing, such paintings are enormous. This is particularly true of any religious theme but also of those works depicting monarchy. Such works were hardly designed to be lugged home and placed above the fireplace!

Now, why the enormous size? Why not simply reduce it on a scale of ten and render the product more manageable?

Because when dealing with the grand, all-encompassing issues of religion and monarchy, the artist was literally depicting larger-than-life issues on a grand canvas. All the world was infused with the sense of the divine, a sense that life was greater than the physically perceivable, and the artist unconsciously chose such an enormous canvas on which to express his interpretation of such insight. A merely human, manageable, compact picture could not contain the majesty and grandeur of a world suffused with divinity. For when you stand before such a painting, it literally fills your field of view. It therefore commands your entire consciousness, sight being your primary arbiter of reality. In its time, the sense of the divine infused the entire consciousness with meaning. By literally filling your eyes with the painting, then, the artist symbolically replicates his world in which all creation was filled with a sense of the divine.

The colors in such paintings are also highly revealing. No pale pastels and watercolors here! The colors in such old paintings are rich, bold, defiant, compelling, stirring, insistent and powerful. Again, these qualities all result from the filter of the era, where the church provided a secure framework of rich and compelling drama, stirring pageantry, bold heroics and unearthly power.

Do you remember the quality of genuine art, how it walks up and smacks you in the face? Can you argue with one of these huge, majestic paintings? Can you talk back? Can you reason with it? Can you reduce its impact to verbal expression? You cannot. The power of such paintings thus derives directly from the mindset of the era in which they were born, where life was ruled over by an omniscient and not entirely benevolent God. Would you argue with Him? Talk back to Him? Talk things over with Him? No! You simply absorbed His presence in every corner of creation, just as you now stand before the painting, passively absorbing its stirring image, not even considering the possibility of refuting it. In your day, in your democracy, art is much more open to criticism and evaluation, is it not? And artists are more open and receptive to what critics and the public feel about their art. In the days when these magnificent paintings were created, such a "filter" was entirely foreign to the artist. The artist's relationship with you, the viewer, is precisely the same as that between God and the world that infused the artist's creation: Take heed and don't even think about talking back!

Again, as we mentioned, any time you behold a work of art you are literally "decoding" the intent and milieu of the artist who created it. When you stand before such paintings, you may feel an unexplainable rush of stirrings and emotions within, a sense of falling humbled before the work, do you not? You feel a strange sensation—strange to you because it is foreign to the filter of your era—of grand, sweeping drama and meaning, do you not? All these were precisely the thoughts of the artist, unconsciously, when creating the work. You are simply "decoding" the painting, stepping into the psychological milieu of its creation, stepping into the time, the place, the very room where the art was created. You do this in a highly attenuated fashion, of course, and the fact that the initial intent of the artist is so vastly reduced, yet results in such a storm of emotion within you, should give you a hint as to the power of such issues when given full expression in the artist's era.

With the sundering of the church, this "filter" was lost. No longer was all of creation imbued with the intent of its Maker, speaking through the Pope and the kings by divine right. Now there was a **choice**. And the long-held framework of irrefutable meaning and divinity was sullied. For while most still chose one church or another, the essential unity of the world to that point was lost. Thus the power behind the world's creation was splintered, scattered among the various sects and branches.

This gave rise to schools, then, whose creations in paint became more "human." Gone were the enormous canvases filling the eyes with bold and dazzling color. Your words carry great clues, always, and a school calling itself "impressionism" is by definition taking a step back from firsthand reality, now offering its "impressions" of the physical world. You see the step here from one in which the artist considered himself as a part of a world suffused always with divinity, to one where the instinctive oneness with all of creation was loosening, to be replaced with "impressions" of reality rather than stirring brushstrokes of divinity.

Taking this line even further were the pointillists, who literally reduced physical reality to a series of dots. We are not passing judgment!—simply pointing out the evolution of your world as reflected in the society. Actually, in profound terms, pointillists were tapping into a great wellspring of truth. You remember how the world that you know is the physical reflection of grids or patterns of points of intention. And it is your senses, fiction that they are, that interpret those points of intention as physical reality. The pointillist does precisely the same. If you step right up to the painting, stick your nose in it, you see but a series of dots—points of intention, each given a specific color. But when you step back, and the gaps between the points blur, you are left with a cohesive, coherent picture—precisely the way you convince yourself of the solidity and permanence of physical matter.

Now, none of this was conscious to the artist! It was a strand evolving from the divorce from the natural order, picking up on developments that would later manifest, in your time, in the television, the newspaper photograph and recorded music. All were reducing physical reality to a series of impulses or dots, which at a sufficient distance you interpret as a coherent whole.

Notice some other characteristics of the various schools of paint after the church's split. Paintings became reduced to a human scale. You can cart your Van Gogh or Monet around the block as often as you wish, with one arm free to pet the dogs you meet. Thus the grand, sweeping canvas that was the world in times divine became reduced to one eminently human.

Further, observe the subject matter of the paintings. Gone were the cherubs, the passion of Christ and the battle between good and evil. In their place, we find Cezanne's apples and pears, Van Gogh's portraits, Monet's landscapes. Once again, all eminently human images: the natural world, the people in it, food. There is no divine wind rushing through these creations. And while you may marvel at the technique, it is difficult to feel the full swelling of power you feel before a Rembrandt when you stand before a Monet. For the intent and mindset of the artist, couched in the filter of his era, has radically changed from a world infused with irrefutable divinity to a world turning toward the strictly physically perceivable, one reduced to the human scale.

Thus, in size of the canvas, in colors employed and in subject matter, we find quite unconsciously represented the very evolution of the species' technological, religious, political and social realms.

Now, as we mentioned, in your era the technology has advanced to the point where those of keen visual ability are most likely turning to photography. This represents two twin strands: first, the use of electricity in the creation of art; second, that your world is moving toward a more "realistic" understanding of the world, a total divorce from the ethereal brushstrokes of the Masters, to one of literal images, captured on film. We shall explore this later.

The absolute cutting edge of visual art has evolved beyond photography now. The field attracting the very best and brightest in the visual arts is that of computer graphics. This is the most "exciting" visual field to be in, precisely because it represents a brave new world, just opening up. This is always the case with the evolution of art, Art riding the technology as it forever seeks new avenues and modes of expression.

The computer is also highly evocative, for a reason we will cover more thoroughly in our music chapter. But by mentioning that application, you see, you find that the computer is infusing every art form with new modes of expression, generally making it far easier on the artist to simply concentrate on creating. In the field of literature, a computer can be used as a word processor, as we use it now. In music, the MIDI revolution allows multitracking and instantaneous playback without the bother of recording on tape. In computer graphics, images can literally be created and manipulated that previously would require animation or elaborate techniques for capture on film. We will keep our secret about the very basis for the computer's involvement in all these fields until our last chapter in this section, on music.

As technology advances, certain art forms will find their channel to Art growing dimmer. This is the case now with the field of painting. Of course brilliant work is still being done in the medium of painting; for woe be to the society that tosses out its legacy the instant a new technology arrives. Any artist picking up a palette in your time draws upon the centuries of work preceding him, and there is still much power to be expressed through painting. But you do not celebrate those scratching crude figures on cave walls, do you? That technology is so far behind you as to be lost entirely as a medium of expression. Ultimately, such will also occur with the field of painting. For those strongly visually inclined, as we mentioned, are for the most part turning to photography.

This explains why much of the "modern art" in the field of painting resembles the bulletin board in a first-grade classroom. The channel simply isn't there in full strength any longer; Art always rides technology and society to the next wave, and the field of paint rides on a prior wave.

Still, you have within this century a fine representation both of the evolution of the field and how it intuitively taps into the undercurrents and future of society.

Picasso is perhaps best known for his works that literally scrambled the human figure—portraits where the face's features were scrambled out of proportion and position, both eyes on one side of the face and so on.

Knowing that art always presages the next wave, the future of society, what can you deduce? Perhaps you would rather not.

For you see in such paintings Picasso's unconscious riding upon Art's intent

233

to the future and coming back with pictorial depictions of the path on which science is leading you. Cold, soulless science. Fiddling with the genetic code of the species—to result in mutations of which you cannot presently conceive. Splitting the atom, the basis for all life, again promising, as we earlier mentioned, that your children may mutate into hideous caricatures of human form. Would you like to pull out your wallet to show friends pictures of your grandchildren, and flash them a walletful of Picassos? Know that such is not beyond the realm of possibility!

Further, Picasso's works represented the state of your society as a whole, as it literally unravels at the seams, the great institutions of politics, science and religion turning belly up in the great Lemming Sea where all institutions divorced from Divine Grace must ultimately fling themselves.

Art presages the future precisely as a means of warning you about the probable earth the artist has seen, a means of awakening a slumbering populace to what may lie ahead. What **may** lie ahead. Nothing is predetermined! You need not carry Picassos in your wallet, your grandchildren's eyes planted on one side of the face. You need only turn away from the technologies that create such a possibility—nuclear fission and genetic manipulation.

Picasso also drew a simple, clean little drawing of a dove carrying an olive branch.

You choose.

CHAPTER THIRTY-SEVEN

Photography

The leap from painting to photography is such a quantum jump in so many ways that we must pick apart the differences one by one, the better to understand the significance of the medium.

First, observe the time that photography appeared. It was about a century ago, or earlier. The same time Darwin was poking about the Galapagos. The same time Marx was outlining his thoughts for later presentation to the world. And these trends were the heirs of the Reformation, the splitting of the church, beginning the long, slow march away from the intuitive sense of the divine in the world.

So the rise of photography as a medium of recording the world both resulted from and furthered the divorce from the natural order.

Once again, of course, the technology of the era had to be far enough along to permit such a contraption. The physics of light had to be understood for there to be photographic plates and paper. All these trends, then, converged with the developments in the religious and social spheres.

In its infancy, photography was a cumbersome process indeed; the film and camera required long shutter times for proper exposure. Thus the early uses of the camera were primarily for portraits—the subjects holding their breath for hours on end—or nature scenes. The camera was too bulky, the film speed too slow, to allow any peripatetic photojournalism!

Consider now the fundamental difference in intent between the Renaissance painter and today's photographer. The painter felt stirring rushes of emotion, divinity, the eternal themes of good and evil and salvation, rushing through his every pore, which he struggled to render on canvas. The painting was thus a replica of the artist's inner storms and fires.

Photography, on the other hand, is an essentially passive medium on the part of the artist: point the camera and shoot. While great artistry and beauty can result, the intent is to portray the world as it is rather than to depict the unseen forces behind the world manifesting on earth.

Photography is a mechanical medium, then, of exposure, shutter speeds, film speeds and lens focal length. Painting was a far more direct experience for the artist, the hand placed in service of a soul swelling with divine inspiration.

So as your divorce from the natural order intensified—via Darwin and Marx, among others—the art form expressing the visual sense of the world became more of a mechanical process, a passive rendering of the world, rather than an active interpretation of that world and the forces behind it.

At the same time, your world is indeed marching toward a time of increased "realism" in every aspect of its existence. The New Dawn of which we foretell will be a time in which the entire facade between physical reality and the unseen energy that sustains it will be ripped away, leaving your world with a far more realistic understanding of how the world works, how you create your reality.

Photography, then, can be considered a more "realistic" art form precisely because it presumes to offer concrete images of what is rather than the product of someone's imagination.

This advance also brings you closer to understanding what we have maintained all along: that the artist's intent, mindset and milieu are always "locked in" to a work of art, to be decoded by the viewer. In this case, the photographer accomplishes this quite literally. You "lock in" to the physical parameters of the artist's viewpoint, and all who observe the subsequent photograph are quite consciously apprised of where the artist was at the time of the photograph's creation, as opposed to the Renaissance paintings that unconsciously transmitted the same material.

For the photographic film literally replicates the human retina, beholding the image and recording it. The difference is that your eye observes a constant flow of moments, while the photograph freezes one single moment in time.

For what is a photograph, then? In deepest terms, it is like the fossils your archaeologists dig up. It is a reflection of a probable existence that was physically materialized and apprehended by the photographer. It represents one line of development of your species, your time, that photographer's life, frozen that others may later behold a replica of that probable path.

In deepest terms, all time is simultaneous; no event is ever "finished"; there is no past or future. In those terms, then, a photograph is a reflection of our stating that any event pulled into physical experience will carry a certain "polish" or "charge" that nonphysical experience does not. A photograph is just such a polish or charge, lending weight and credibility to one probable path of development, one which was physically experienced by the photographer, the resultant photograph representing "proof" of the event's occurrence and therefore granting it greater weight among the viewers than if the photographer simply related the event verbally. A photograph is thus the "polish" that physically experienced events carry as the badge for having been pulled into physical actuality.

Note also that photography is a far more "democratic" art form than painting. Before technology allowed the wholesale printing of painted works, there was only one way to view a painting: You had to track it down and stand before it. Again, this replicates the religious flavor of the day, when you struggled to work your way into the benevolent sight of God.

The technology of photography, however, permits an unlimited series of prints to be made from a single negative, thus making it far more egalitarian and democratic a medium. You will note that the camera was not invented in a medieval fiefdom.

Despite carrying far more weight as a "realistic" depiction of the physical world, photography is a legitimate art form because so much depends upon the photographer's eye for detail, the deliberate composing of subject matter, the juxtaposition of subject with background, light and shadow, color and texture. Remember in our discussion of perception how a given grid of intent, standing behind any object you can perceive, will be interpreted differently by all who perceive it. If you gave cameras to ten people and told them to take a picture of your house, you would most likely end up with ten very different interpretations of the house. Some would choose a simple broad shot encompassing the entire structure; others might zero in on little details often overlooked. So while representing a move toward a more "realistic" medium of expression, photography nonetheless depends just as much on its creator's interpretation.

In the progress of photography, the medium traveled from the limits of black and white to the far more "realistic" color film stocks available today. And yet many photographers insist on working with black and white; indeed, you can attest that the most beautiful portraits are almost always in black and white. Why this retrograde refusal to depict the world in as "accurate" a form as possible?

Black and white photographs strip away the surface elements of a scene or object—color—and reduce it to light and shadow, to varying shades of gray, to texture, to form, to line and to contrast. As such, a black and white photograph manages to capture a deeper truth than color can. For black and white renders the themes while color offers the particulars. This is an unconscious recognition of our maintaining that everything you physically experience is a reflection of a deeper reality, a deeper meaning. The physical world that you experience is the particulars; behind it lie the themes. Recognizing this, and especially in the field of portraiture, the human face being the most evocative image you can view, many prefer black and white for its stripping away the superficial details and leaving you with the heart, soul and character imprinted on film.

Thus you can see that while photography renders a more "realistic" product than painting, it nonetheless is a highly subjective art form, dependent upon the photographer's perception of an event, and it often renders the most beautiful image when stripped of the patina of color.

If taking a photograph is simply a matter of pointing the camera and pressing a trigger, why are some producing works of genius while the vast majority can only crank out snapshots?

Again, remember that how close one comes to the Art source depends upon two items: the artist's native talent and his/her channel to Art. It is the interplay between these two factors that determines the quality of the resultant artwork. While the technology of photography is democratic—anybody can own a camera and learn to operate it—do not think that pure channels to Art are passed out quite so indiscriminately! It is always a select few in a given era who can ride that arrow to the heart of Art. There is literally a difference in two persons shooting the same scene at the same time with the same equipment, then, as the one gifted with a clearer channel to Art will produce a more evocative photograph, one more likely to hold your attention in appreciation, even awe. Remember, in deepest terms, nothing physical exists; it is your perception of the grid of intent behind the photograph that determines its effect on you; as you "decode" a photographic image, the intent and purity of the artist's vision will infuse the work with a unique and highly individualistic flavor or tone. Once again, you are literally transported to the time and place where the artwork was created— literally, on all counts, in this case—for you both behold a precise replica of the scene in the viewfinder and that image is also imbued with the photographer's connection to the Art source. If that channel is clean and pure, you have the work of a genius. If it is absent, you have a snapshot.

By our discussion we hope to have helped you to see that while photography is a more "realistic" art form than painting, it nonetheless still remains a highly personal interpretation of reality, one influenced by the photographer's intent, perception, thoughts and, most of all, channel to the Art source. To the viewer, a photograph is a frozen moment from a physically experienced probable past— thus it represents one possible version of an event, not the definitive version! There is no definitive version of an event, ever, for all paths lie open, both toward the future and stretching back into the infinite past. A photograph commands your respect as having a certain validity, representing an irrefutable truth, but know that the event the photographer experienced and recorded was only one version of that event, the one pulled into physical actuality through the intent and beliefs of the photographer, and thus it is an entirely subjective record of an event. You need not bow humbled before this art form and grant it omniscience! For the event recorded to be registered on film at all, it must first be pulled into physical actuality by those involved; another person or group, in the same place at the same time, might experience an entirely different version of that event, pulling into expression a different probable path. A photograph has no more validity as a record, in deepest terms, than does a painting.

As politics and technology evolve, they weave their way through the art world. The decline of religion and a sense of a divine world, coupled with the growth of democracy, the march of technology and knowledge of physics, and your progression toward a more "realistic" understanding of the world, all led to the creation of photography. Because it is infused with these elements of your present civilization, it is therefore more attractive to those seeking to express Art through a visual medium; as true artists always ride the next wave, most have set down their paint brushes and picked up their cameras.

There are no closed systems; there are only open shutters.

CHAPTER THIRTY-EIGHT

Dance

Like music, dance is a universal art form, known to all cultures, in all periods of time. For nothing is necessary to dance but the human body; if one is alive at all, one has all the technology one needs to engage in this art form.

Dance ranges from the intrinsic happy step and sway of the young child to the ritualistic celebrations of native cultures, to the formality of ballroom dancing in your culture. Because the technology remains the same—the human body—it is the social, religious and political currents that shape the expression of dance in a given culture.

Dance is such a direct connection with the divine source of the world precisely because life is energy, energy is motion. And while the natural world knows its own order, that order is determined by impulse, not rigid logical structure. In native cultures living in harmony with the natural order, dance is often used as a ritual of storytelling, of ceremony, of celebration, of preparation for war and the bringing of rain. Such dances can best be viewed as ordered impulse, the body gyrating wildly but in an ordered fashion, not simply spinning randomly. Thus is the natural, spontaneous order of the natural world filtered through the human conscious mind to create dance.

You must confess that the sight of scantily clad natives chanting and swaying around a fire makes your European sensibilities a bit nervous. For in your divorce from the natural order, you see only the impulse and not the order, the order of the natural world. Besides, they're half naked! To view such a native ceremony is often vaguely or overtly threatening to the European eye, then. It is too free, too unrestrained, too impulsive, too irrational for your taste.

European dance, then, filters the impulsive desire for motion into a highly rigid, structured tradition. First, everyone is properly dressed from head to toe, the men in dark formal wear, the women glittering like the colors of the rainbow, but a demure rainbow at that!

The man leads, as God leads his followers, as the king leads his serfs, as logic rules over intuition.

Every dance is a sequence of highly technical movements, laboriously learned, every participant moving with precision in movements carefully delineated and from which one must not stray. Just as one must not stray from God's straight and narrow path. Just as one may not contradict the king's divine right.

European ballroom dancing, then, funnels the intrinsic need for the body to move to music into a highly structured, tightly controlled and ordered sequence of movements, rendering it safe to the culture divorced from the natural order. No impulse here! No spontaneity here! No embarrassing individuality rearing its impulsive head! Order. Tradition. Hierarchy.

In your country, never having known monarchy, what is your "native" dance? The square dance. A far more informal affair than the palatial ballrooms of Europe. Dress, while still carefully shielding the body's impulsive beauty from head to toe, is not so rigidly prescribed. The movements, while following a given pattern, allow much more freedom in execution. The male leading the female is retained.

Most important of all is the flavor of a square dance. It is democracy galloping at full tilt, is it not? Everyone working together for the common good, and while under the command of a caller, he does not set himself up as God incarnate, does he? He does not order you to do-si-do or be condemned to Hell, does he? He does not command you to promenade or face the guillotine, does he? The whole flavor of European culture, of a rigid hierarchy leading from God through monarchy to serfs, is replaced with a sense of partnership, of mutual effort, of enjoyment. For those not dancing can stand on the sidelines, clapping along, singing along, cheering and laughing—all societally approved actions, of course, but still much more impulsive than could ever be permitted on a European dance floor.

Thus we see that the form dance takes is, like all other art forms, an expression of the societal, religious and political currents of the society.

European culture, and yours also, have dance formalized into troupes or companies that filter the world of dance through a variety of styles and techniques. Most formal is ballet, highly technical and ritualized, the choreographer assuming the role of monarch. This is a direct import from Europe, so the influence remains strong.

As an aside, what do you think of boys in your culture who study ballet? Sissies, are they not? The fact that boys and men dancing ballet are monsters of muscle appears to escape your notice; for even when channeled through the highly ritualized field of ballet, dance still always expresses an impulsive need for the body to replicate the unseen energy behind the world, and as men are mere robots in your culture, lockstepping through life, the slightest deviation from the automaton mold is deeply threatening and, therefore, often seen as homosexual. How else to explain it?

Again, notice that ballet is presented in a theater to which you come and watch the performance, passively absorbing it—just as you had to search out the works of the European masters and stand before them, absorbing their grandeur. Again, shades of monarchy and an imperious God.

Modern dance troupes in your culture have discarded much of the stifling formality of ballet while retaining emphasis on technique and ritual. You must know what your partner is going to do, especially if you are to leap into his arms! But as dance becomes more "free form," it unconsciously expresses the progress of your culture, moving away from the formality of European culture into a realm of far more impulsive movement, random order, unpredictable, full of surprise. Thus, while still presented on stage for an audience, your world of dance unconsciously nudges the society back to the natural order from which it sprang, back to the native's chanting and whirling around the fire, back to Divine Grace.

And while the world of dance progresses upon the stage, it does so also in the heir of your country square dance: the boogieing rock and roll dance club. Rock is the premier music form of your era, as we shall later explore, and nowhere is this more evident than in its effect on those beholding it. What do they do? They get up and dance! And their dance is highly individualistic, is it not, a jumble of impulsive spontaneity, much to the consternation of their tradition-bound elders! Remember that the fundamental quality of genuine art is that it will move you, evoke a physical reaction. When young people in your culture hear a Strauss waltz, do they leap to their feet and pair up, hand in hand? They do not; both the music and dance of that era ride on a long ago-crested wave. And if someone cranks up the rock music at a party? Can you keep them in their seats? You cannot. Thus do you find that rock is the premier music form of your era; in its effect upon its listeners you see the literal presaging of your society's progress toward a more impulsive, spontaneous and natural order.

Remember that your body is simply the physical reflection of the impossibly complex gridwork of points of intention that sustains it. That gridwork is essentially electromagnetic energy, formed into patterns that find physical expression in your body's various features. The body itself, then, is created and sustained by energy. Energy is motion. Thus, any time you dance, you are restoring your body to the natural order, cherishing the wellsprings of energy from which you spring, acknowledging the divine source of the world. Dance literally springs from the unseen energy that sustains your world as it flows through the grid of intent behind your body. As with your other art forms, it is meant as a link between the physical world and that which sustains it, unseen.

Do animals dance? Does a bear wear a tutu in the woods? It does not need to. Every motion it takes springs from the natural order. Dance is unique to the human species—and your cetacean cousins!—as a means, again, of ensuring that the logical, conscious mind would not lose sight of its divine origin. Thus is it present in all human cultures, at all times, the particular expression dependent upon the religious, political and social themes of the era.

CHAPTER THIRTY-NINE

Humor

The inclusion of humor in our section on art may be a source of some, well, amusement. We confess it does not carry the outer trappings of the other art forms, but it does share one important characteristic, which we shall later see. Further, you go to see comics just as you do musicians and movies, so there is that further quality of art.

How does humor work? What makes you laugh?

In many cases, humor is evoked by a deliberate scrambling of your strictures and mores. This holds true in any time. The more oppressive the area of life, the more likely avenue for humor. Thus? Your "dirty" jokes, filthy limericks, etc. Since sex is an area of confusion, guilt and sin in your society, it naturally follows that humor—which always ferrets out such repressed themes—should be present in abundance in your experience of sex.

Why? What is a laugh?

Remember that any "event," events being grids of intent that must be unraveled and inserted into your linear time perspective moment point by moment point, will take a certain amount of "time" to play itself out, depending upon how tightly woven, how compact is the initial grid of intent which is its source. For the most part, in most situations, it holds true that a given grid of intent will require a certain length of "time" in which to play itself out.

You do have a shortcut, however, to release an event more quickly. That release is laughter. For when you burst out laughing, you are releasing a sudden jolt of energy, are you not? What lies behind that jolt of energy is the grid of intent holding an "event"; by thrusting it suddenly into your awareness, releasing it and dissipating it, you may ease its way out of your awareness that much more quickly.

Now you see why any taboo area will be ripe for humor. There are no taboos in the natural order! It is your unconscious recognition that you must release such suffocating strictures of belief that compels you to literally attack the repressed topic with humor, laughter biting away huge chunks of the grid of intent behind the belief, releasing them at once, the better to ease your society toward a life more in harmony with the natural order.

There are also situations where events are of such horror that humor is used as a balm on your offended sensibilities, and to release the shock. Any time a major tragedy occurs, in which many people die, for instance, soon thereafter you will begin hearing the first hesitant jokes about the event. You recoil at first— "Oh, that's terrible!"—and five minutes later you are running up your long-distance phone bill, telling everyone you know. For by sharing the humor with others, you help to release that communal grid of intent, the shock and sorrow, you necessarily feel when learning of the sudden deaths of others of your species. It is thus a healthy attribute, one restoring you to balance much more quickly than if you simply let the event drip moment by moment out of your reality, imbuing your days with inconsolable sadness and bereavement. Because humor allows a sudden, explosive **release of energy**, it is employed as a balm to the wounded psyche, releasing the horror, allowing you to restore yourself to balance and move on.

Again, notice how your body unconsciously confirms that humor is indeed an art form, by our definition. When you find something hysterically funny, how do you react? By raising an eyebrow? No, you shake all over, you gasp for breath; you may fall on the floor, rolling if you cannot release the intent behind the humor any other way. For your body literally struggles to replicate the unseen event in which it takes part, and just as humor serves to release a grid of intent, so does your body literally shake, writhe and roll to do the same. Once again, if something is sufficiently hilarious, you may start to cry; and we have explored what that means. All these **physiological reactions** clue you in that genuine truth is involved, a restoration to the natural order, a genuine art form finding expression.

Humor can take many forms. It can be strictly visual, scrambling the standard visual themes of your society—a man wearing a dress, a chicken bearing a cow's head, a person with purple hair. Again, these are all surreptitious pokes in the ribs of your beloved physical senses, urging you to not take physical reality so seriously; you unconsciously recognize the undue importance accorded the images of the senses by laughing at such sights—laughter indicating your unconscious recognition of the truth behind the scrambled image.

With your love of verbal language, much humor derives from a "play" on words, a wrenching together of rhyming words, puns, alliteration and limericks. Again, your laughter reveals your unconscious recognition that verbal, written language is simply the outer coating on the deeper meaning that wells up in preverbal thought, later to find expression in words. When you begin speaking to someone, with an "idea" of what you intend to say, do you know every word you will speak, every pause, every inflection? It simply spills off your tongue, does it not, without your conscious effort to translate it into words. And by using written or spoken language as the source for humor, you demonstrate your recognition of the essential meaninglessness of language, its use as a medium of information exchange, not the information itself.

For consider: How often do you hear jokes about the truly significant aspects of your lives? Can you recite the last limerick about maternal love you heard? How about the last one-liner exploring the origin of the universe? The last pun ridiculing God? For you see, the themes of genuine importance are not to be dismissed from your awareness; it is only reflections of meaning, which you can mistakenly assume are the meaning itself, that need to be taken down a notch or two from time to time. Your language is second-hand reality, then; your sexual mores are anachronistic hand-me-downs from the fourteenth century; your strictures on diet, behavior, dress, appearance and so on are all fair game for they are all second-hand reality.

Humor, then, is a gift granted your species to ensure it would never grow too serious about the reflections of meaning that are necessarily the product of a species endowed with a conscious mind. You are meant to laugh at the mores and strictures of your time, the better to release them from your reality. Humor is a beneficent corrosive, eating away at the encrusted barnacles of belief that prevent your living in harmony with the natural order.

What is your image of those who know no humor, who find nothing amusing, who never utter a silly word? Are they the dynamic movers and shakers of your time, to whom all flock for guidance? You are repelled by such persons, precisely because you recognize that humor is the great equalizer, the puncturer of hot air balloons, the milker of sacred cows, and those who allow themselves no humor allow themselves no growth, no balance, no harmony.

Which is the more divine act? Dragging your child to church, where he/she may sit in benumbed catatonia? or instead spending that Sunday morning telling jokes, singing silly songs or tickling each other?

Stasis is death. Life is energy, energy is motion. The child rolling on the floor under the incisive tickling finger of a parent is far closer to Heaven than his comatose friend cemented in a pew.

Thus does All That Is, the source of your world and of humor, have the last laugh.

CHAPTER FORTY

Literature and Poetry

Before we begin an examination of literature, we must first pause to explore the medium through which this art form is expressed: written language.

As we have stated before, written language is a symbolic retreat from firsthand reality, a means of reducing the contours of existence into little squiggles hinting at the greater meaning that they reflect. This demonstrates in perfect fidelity what we have maintained about art all along: The initial intent is "locked in" or codified by the artist, to be decoded by the viewer. This relationship is obvious in the field of literature; the writer wrestles his/her ideas into written form, to be decoded—read—by the viewer.

Your use of the alphabet is also instructive and symbolic. At its very base, the energy that creates and sustains your world is a vast, undifferentiated sea of energy, which "specializes" into various patterns and grids to create every physical object that you can perceive. Your thoughts, dreams, hopes, ideals and emotions all have electromagnetic reality also, patterns or grids of energy. These you cannot physically perceive—you feel them—but they are as valid in terms of an electromagnetic source as any perceivable object.

So the vast energy source of your world rearranges itself in patterns of differing contours, ultimately to find expression in the features of your world. The alphabet works the same way. Every object of the physical world, every action, every person, every thought, can be reduced to a series of squiggly lines, symbolically representing the source material, to be interpreted and understood by the viewer. Literature and reading, then, replicate the process by which you perceive a physical world.

For how is it that words, mere scrawlings on a piece of paper, should be able to amuse, anger, threaten, console or create? How is it that little scribblings should literally evoke physiological reactions in your body?

If we offer the word "kucf" to you, what is your body's response?

If we rearrange the letters to "ufck," would you become nervous?

If we further unscrambled them to read "fukc," would the blood quicken?

Now, we will not rearrange the letters to full glory and risk cries of plagiarism from your era's literary giants. We merely wish to point out that words, mere curvy lines on a piece of paper, evoke physiological reactions within you; for as you read, you "decode" the intent behind the words, move past the symbolic barrier into the writer's initial intent.

Literature differs from the other art forms in that the beholder has the ultimate power over how, where and when the art will be perceived. You can cart a book to the beach, the mountains or to bed; can you do the same with a Rembrandt, a square dance, a symphony orchestra? It is thus an eminently egalitarian art form, which accounts for your society's preference for literature over those art forms flavored by monarchy and divine right. In times past, in European culture, only the learned had access to books; but with the invention of movable type, progressing to your technology today that churns out vast quantities of paperbacks, literature has become eminently accessible to everyone.

What accounts for the fact that some literature stands through time while most falls by the wayside? Why do you thrill to *The Odyssey* while last month's pills-and-thrills novel is lining bird cages?

Remember that the duration of an art work through time is determined by how clear a channel the artist rode to the heart of Art. Those springing from the very Art source will endure for millennia, while those created to reflect a society rather than explain it, particularly when cranked out in hopes of making money—second-hand reality—spring directly from the binder to the wastebasket.

Almost always, your enduring stories are tales of heroics, of men and women struggling against seemingly impossible odds, only to triumph in the last chapter. Note several aspects of this. First, your heroes, those enduring through time, are always models of morality. Frequently the temptations they endure are those that would veer them off the straight and narrow path of rectitude; and you know—*you* know—such can only lead to disaster. While your literary heroes can be full-blooded characters, with an occasional lapse into temptation, can you name any enduring literary hero who was an uncompromising crook? True literature draws you into every page by the force of your identifying with the hero; who wishes to identify with a scoundrel? Because you instinctively know right from wrong, because you are born with an innate sense of justice, you are drawn to those characters who exemplify the very best your race can become.

Secondly, your grand tales compel you because the odds seem so impossible, the battle so long and arduous. Who wants to read a novel about a housewife making it through another day? You want challenge in your literature. This reflects your deep, intuitive knowledge that **you create your own reality**, that no obstacle is too great to overcome when tackled by a determined spirit. The more arduous the journey, the better, for the greater the obstacles, the more deeply you resonate to the thrill of a challenge overcome. You know you create your own reality; you thrill to every literary depiction of this immutable law, just as when you read in the newspaper about a handicapped person overcoming seemingly impossible odds to triumph. Examine your literature, your heroes; do they not **endure, conquer and triumph?**

So it is heroics you thirst for in literature. Particularly in your society, where so many live as cogs in someone else's wheel, you turn to literature for that rush of adrenalin and purpose missing in your lives. You vicariously live the challenges and triumphs of others as a way of bringing balance to a life whose contours are not quite so sharp.

Literature is the most "realistic" of your arts because it precisely replicates, word for word, your speech. While a painting or a symphony or dance may evoke certain feelings within you, may impart certain themes, literature carries the initial intent of the writer on symbolic breath, which is then "decoded" by the viewer, stripped of its verbal patina, to return to the initial feelings and themes of the writer. There is a symbolic middleman, then, the written word, between the artist's intent and your interpretation. This is what speech represents, of course. Because your society is so heavily dependent upon speech as a means of communication, it follows that the written word is your most "realistic" depiction of reality. For the written word can be funneled into an infinite variety of uses: from the hard news of the front page to the gossip of the society column to the human drama of the advice columns to the humor of the cartoon page to the opinions in the editorials. The instrument is the same—the written word—but you see how even in one daily newspaper the intent can vary so dramatically, as can the themes and fields to be explored, or reduced to symbolic form.

As your society moves toward a more realistic understanding of the workings of the world, it naturally follows that you would find yourselves crushed under the sheer volume of words churned out in your society: newspapers, magazines, books, journals, pamphlets; no one can read it all. Your technology also permits instantaneous transmission of the written word from anywhere in the world to virtually anywhere else. You are coming closer to an understanding, then, of the unseen reality behind your world, of the instantaneous communication between every point of intention sustaining your physical earth, each apprising all others of the conditions in its locale while "holding its place" in the overall scene. Knowing that a written word is a **symbol** of a greater reality, you edge toward a new comprehension of your physical world, coming to see that it is a symbol of deeper realities, "read" by your senses to a depiction of a physical world, when in fact it is a reflection of far deeper events and realities.

On our plane, there is no need for the written word as thoughts are transmitted instantaneously one to the other. Those capable of such a process on your plane you know as telepathic. Stories are legion in your culture of those suddenly seized with concern for a loved one, only to later find that, at the moment of concern, the other had died or suffered great trauma. Science cannot explain this, so instead of disposing of science, you deny yourselves the validity and power of your minds. But the time is coming when the barrier between the physical world and its nonphysical source will be ripped down, and then will science be seen as the haughty emperor marching pompously around in his "new clothes"! Only to have a child—your closest link to the natural order—cry out that the fine physical coating on the imperial autocrat—science—which the adult world all "sees" without dissent—is but an illusion, behind it lying a naked body—**the natural order.** And you thought this was a cute little fable! You may have chuckled at the wisdom intrinsic to this tale, but its profundity will soon come roaring from the heart of Art and leave your autocratic monarch, science, parading around with its sagging flesh displayed for all to see!

Like all other art forms, literature, true literature, rides the intent of Art to the next cycle, carrying hidden prescience while couched in the society of its origin.

You have a particularly evocative tale that rides on its own cycle, coming to the fore every Christmas season. Dickens' *A Christmas Carol* features a penurious old miser named Scrooge, whose tightfistedness deprives his clerk Bob Cratchit of time with his family at the holiest of seasons and threatens the life of Cratchit's crippled son, Tiny Tim.

On Christmas Eve Scrooge is visited by three ghosts, those of Christmas Past, Christmas Present and Christmas Future. Each presents him with a vision of his life as it was, as it is, as it may be. If he does not change his course, Scrooge beholds a future in which Tiny Tim's crutch stands unused by the fireplace, its owner having passed out of physical life due to Scrooge's greed. Duly chastened and reformed, it is a new Scrooge who arises on Christmas morning, bringing a feast to the Cratchit household. "God bless us every one," offers Tiny Tim as thanks.

This story is so profound, so evocative, so thick and rich with meaning that we shall carefully pick our way through the strands to see why it bears such importance—and warning—for your own time.

Dickens was British, European. Your culture is based on his. The fundamental quality of European culture is divorce from the natural order. Above all others, the most significant symbol of this divorce is money. Money is a reflection of meaning; in a culture divorced from the natural order it becomes meaning. Those who chase after it, lust after it and hoard it, consider it a source of security, are leading second-hand lives, shallow, superficial, devoid of meaning and true connection with others.

An accurate description of Scrooge, perhaps? An accurate description of your society, perhaps?

At night, in the dream state, Scrooge has laid out for him his past, how it leads to his present, and how, if unchanged, his course will lead to a certain future.

You do the same every night in the dream state.

Scrooge is apprised of past, present and future not by his own thoughts but by ghosts, nonphysical entities come to warn him of impending tragedy.

That is precisely what we are doing now. We and all other entities speaking to those on earth are bursting through the barrier between physical and nonphysical worlds lest your society leave only forlorn crutches as evidence of its existence.

Having been apprised of a possible future—a probable path—Scrooge turns away from the second-hand reality of lust for money and embraces the firsthand reality of love, love expressed through the giving of money to aid others. For where is true security to be found—alone in a bank vault surrounded by cash or gathered round Christmas dinner with loved ones?

Scrooge chose.

You choose.

What finally awakened Scrooge's deadened heart was the probable death of a child. You know that children are your closest link to the natural order, but there is more. They will be the first to go. The first to starve. The first to mutate. The first to be eaten alive by genetic disaster. They will suffer first and most.

Scrooge was transformed on Christmas Eve, just the other side of the day celebrating the birth of Christ.

We speak to you now on the cusp of the return of the Christ entity to your world. Christmas would have arrived with or without Scrooge's reformation. He chose to embrace the spirit of Christmas. Know that the New Dawn will arrive with or without your reformation. Will you choose to embrace it?

"God bless us every one."

You must acknowledge the divine source of your world.

Dickens' tale is so powerful, speaks to you year after year, precisely because it carries such profound prescience, resonates so deeply with the great intuitive knowledge you were born with and have forgotten.

As with all great literature, it is a tale of triumph, is it not? The triumph of firsthand reality over second-hand reality, of familial love over money lust. Of a probable path avoided when its horrific outcome was beheld. Of the life of a child over a vault of "security." Of the divine spirit of Christ over secular sterility.

These are the choices before you now. Which will it be—a celebration of family, love and warmth, or a discarded crutch?

You choose.

Poetry is built upon the same foundation as literature—the written word—but fashions it in far different constructs to express the artist's intent.

For while a literary description of a place, a thought or a feeling may go on for pages of explicit detail in an attempt to evoke in the reader the writer's precise intent, a poet is far more parsimonious in his use of words, offering them as triggers to light the reader's imagination and evoke the feeling or mood of the author's intent without literally spelling it out as does the prose author. Words are thus used less to describe as to **evoke** a reaction within the beholder, true to the artist's intent.

Poetry is the bridge between literature and music in that it uses words constructed in a rhythmic pattern to transmit its meaning. There is a cadence, then, a bounce to many poems that resonates deep within the beholder, as indeed the poem connects with the deep, unseen rhythms that sustain your world, while riding that rhythm to evoke physical images or feelings within the viewer.

Poetry often employs rhyming words at the end of each phrase, in a variety of constructions. There is something deeply satisfying about this, is there not? A sense of completeness when the inner ear rides the rhythm and rhyme to a gentle flow of meaning and beauty, the deep unseen rhythms flowing like an undercurrent on which ride rhyming waves of uniform shape and sound, resonating deeply within while pleasing the ear.

The poet also straddles a bridge between literature and paint. For the poet paints with words, using them as a painter does his colors, to create a picture that, when beheld by the viewer, evokes certain responses, certain meanings, within. Even a series of seemingly jumbled, unconnected words, as in more modern poetry, will inspire a **feeling** within the viewer, if the rational mind can be held at bay and the **rhythm** and **image** allowed to come to the fore. Poetry is partially a visual art, evoking a series of images in the viewer's mind's eye while also pleasing the inner ear and resonating with its rhythm.

The progress of poetry through time can be seen to fulfill our understanding of the history of art as it has progressed in your culture. Shakespeare, for example, wrote much of his dialogue in rhyme, meticulously and precisely employing rhythm and rhyme in the service of dramatic speech. There is not much room for interpretation by the beholder in this instance, because the poetry is used to inform, to keep the story moving. It follows that the use of poetry in such a fashion would spring from an era when monarchy and divine right still held sway—little room for personal interpretation of the words expressed, more a passive acceptance of their meaning, in the context of a larger drama. The same as with the words of God or a king.

Influenced by European culture to a large degree, your early poets remained true to the rigid structure of Shakespeare's poetic form, while moving toward a greater dependence on the viewer to interpret the images created by the poetry. A more democratic use of poetry, you see. One that respects the individual rights of the interpreter.

Moving forward in time, particularly in this century, you find many poets dropping the use of rhymes entirely. This allows the poet greater freedom, not being bound to the limited number of rhyming words in the language. It also frees the viewer, to some extent, from the dependence on structure, order and tradition, through which a rhyming poem is funneled. It is a move, then, toward a freer expression, moving away from the monarchical poetic form to one allowing greater freedom to both artist and viewer.

This also allows each phrase of a poem to stand on its own—"April is the cruelest month"—rather than standing in the service of a greater whole. Again, this is an evolution in which the very phrases of poetry advance from dependence upon a greater being—the entire poem—for their value and worth, to one where each phrase can stand alone—another move toward democracy and individual supremacy.

Taking this even further are those poets who deliberately offer only a scramble of words, placed irregularly on the page, without capital letters, deliberately turning the language on its head. All this is an attempt to break the viewer out of a specific traditional use of language, wrenching words loose from their previously unchallenged structure to one of far greater spontaneity, freedom and individual expression. Again, a move from monarchy, through democracy, on to a celebration of individuality, in which words themselves break free from the shackles of the past, as expressed in traditional poetry, each word now freed from dependence upon the whole to determine its meaning. While such poetry often seems frustratingly nonsensical, if you can suppress your confusion long enough to get through the poem, you may find a certain theme or feeling resonating within you, evoked quite unconsciously by the meaning of each word jumbling together with the other words' meanings to create a synthesis, a melting pot, in which the strength of the overall work depends on the fierce independence on each of its members, joining their energies while refusing any subservient bondage to rhythm or rhyme.

You see, then, that the evolution of poetry mirrors that of every other art form. The technology remains essentially the same—the written word on a page—but in structure, form, construction, rhythm, rhyme and layout, we find a progression from a rigid traditional structure where each word holds meaning only in the context of the larger picture to your modern poetry, celebrating the unique meaning of each word while combining them to create gestalts of meaning and power no word alone can command. The progression from monarchy to a democracy's celebration of the individual.

CHAPTER FORTY-ONE

Drama and Film

Drama is related to literature in that the story is played out for the physical eyes instead of the mind's eye. Drama has been a part of European culture as far back as you can trace it, for it rides both on your culture's love of language and the need to express the species' highest motives and purpose, to share the experience of a restoration to the wellsprings of intent and purpose from which your species springs. Like literature, then, drama concerns itself with the grand sweeping themes of your species: bold heroics, great tragedy, love, betrayal, honor, challenge, victory over evil.

Drama is a communal event, from the amphitheaters of ancient times to the theaters of your culture. Aside from the obvious monetary benefit of having a larger audience rather than one spectator, this communal quality to drama affirms the underlying commonality of the themes portrayed, their universal resonance within all of your species, and the need to drink from the wellsprings of your existence with others of your species as a means of ensuring your continued conscious awareness of the profound bonds lying beneath the unique and private part each of you plays in the great drama of life.

Ah ha! All the world's a stage. Indeed, quite literally. For just as you sit before the proscenium arch and deliberately forget that you are in a theater watching a performance, being sucked into the drama and truth of the production such that you lose sight of its essential subterfuge, so is physical reality itself a falsehood, which your conscious mind pretends to interpret as "real" for the duration of your own private drama, your span from birth to death. The great themes of your species are literally "played out" on scales both massive and solitary, as a means of exploring those themes from as many angles as possible. Drama is so compelling because it precisely replicates the very existence of your planet and your species' place upon it. In deepest terms, the physical world is a fiction, but you pretend not to know this and allow yourself to be fully drawn into the sweep and drama of your era, your life.

Thus, attending a dramatic performance is a communal experience, for it precisely replicates the communal experience that is your physical world and your place upon it. You are all actors, each of you shoved on stage with a few brief instructions from the director—your greater entity—there to improvise your way through and hope the audience finds your performance satisfactory! And if not—there is always another day, another play!

The traditional three-act play follows a set structure. In the first act, the characters are introduced and the dramatic conflict is established. Who is the hero, what does he want and what stands in his way of achieving it? The second act is one of development, of focusing on the hero's struggle to achieve his goal while further complications heap upon his shoulders. The third act holds the resolution, in which the hero either succeeds or fails; but in either case, the story is resolved, brought to a satisfactory conclusion.

Why should this be the traditional structure for a drama? Why not simply watch someone go through the motions of a routine and ordinary day? Why would this not be nearly as compelling?

Again, in your art you seek confirmation of your intuitive knowledge of the workings of the world. You know you create your own reality. As with literature, you thrill to watching someone create his reality, against seemingly impossible odds, struggling courageously against whatever opposition the world can offer, battling the forces of evil, until final triumph is achieved. You do this every day, on scales small and grand, as "problems" manifest in your life to be acknowledged, confronted and overcome. The greater the problem, the greater the challenge; it is your inner understanding of the satisfaction derived from triumphing over adversity and evil that compels you to the bold heroics of your dramatic figures.

Again, your heroes are always battling evil for the sake of good. Evil is often presented as caricature in drama, persons of bottomless malignant depravity, the better to demonstrate in distilled form what everyone faces in daily battle against the temptations to trample morality for the sake of expedience and personal gain. You root for the righteous hero holding fast to his values against such temptations because it resonates with your own deep, inner understanding that true happiness, a life well lived, can only come from living in fidelity with the universe's fundamental law: Create your own reality and allow others the same.

Drama, then, is a communal event depicting the grand themes of your species and remaining vibrant through the passage of time, as indeed the deep intent and purpose from which you spring remain immortal and immutable, granting fresh breath and expression to every era, every culture, while buoying them in an eternal sea of truth.

You know that children thrill to dramatic spectacle, whether as audience or participant. They thrill to the puppet show, the play, the mime; because they live with one foot in the natural order from which they spring, they find it far easier to strip away the distractions—the stage, the noise in the audience and so on—and plunge headfirst into the dramatic themes presented. A play is real to a child in a way unknown to adults, for the surface elements are discarded—whatever the setting, whoever the actors—the better to behold the deeper truths intrinsic to the work.

Children are also all actors, are they not? They love to play dress-up, to imagine themselves adults, living in other times and places; or gathering in the back yard for a game of good guys versus bad guys, cowboys and Indians; and to explore the great moral issues intrinsic to your species. Like adults, they wrestle always with the dynamic tension between doing what is right and what may bring personal gain, however transient. To play good guys versus bad guys is to explore the very nature of your species and its conflicts as it seeks a balance between the reasoning mind and the natural order. Drama is thus intrinsic to children, as is all art, as a means of allowing constant exploration into the nature and meaning of your existence.

Again you see how the evolution of technology has aided the progression of dramatic form from a monarchical event—you will show up at the theater at 8:00 sharp—to the egalitarian television. While we still maintain that television is not an art form as much as an emetic, still you see what great freedom it allows you to view what you wish, when you wish. The further video cassette recorder revolution has even permitted you to record programs while you are gone, to view them later at your leisure. The television is thus the ultimate egalitarian form of dramatic presentation. Again, it rides upon your society's widespread use of electricity, as do all major art forms of the twentieth century. What is lost in the process is the communal event of observing a dramatic presentation at a theater; it serves thus to isolate you from others of your species. To some extent the family group replaces the theater, as all may participate in watching a favorite show. While something may have been lost in this progression, it nonetheless nudges you in the direction of the future: the celebration of the individual, supreme above the group. Again, technology lubricates the movement from monarchy to democracy to individualism, in this art form as in no other.

In your society, born of monarchy but never experiencing it directly, your vestigial need to worship royalty surfaces in your approach to dramatic artists. In your day, film stars play the part of royalty; in the past, stage actors did the same. They literally play the role of monarchy and royalty for you in their flashy lifestyles inconceivable to most of you—the respect and adulation accorded them by the public, your following their every move and utterance and marriage du jour. You pin your admiration on the artists in this field, as opposed to others, precisely because through their work they are, literally and figuratively, larger than life— magnified on the big screen while exploring grand themes of your society. You root for them in the roles they play, and with your atavistic need for royalty, you similarly worship them outside the theater.

This provides a fine segue into our discussion of film.

Film is the premier art form of the twentieth century. Why?

Yours is an era, as we have stated throughout, when all the previously discrete elements of your society—your political, religious and scientific institutions; your ethnic groups; the fields of economics, education, art and so on—will increasingly be seen to be a part of a gestalt from which no single element may be extricated without affecting all others. Your society has been a house divided turning upon a house divided turning upon a house divided since its very inception. You are moving now toward an appreciation of the **interrelationships** among all elements of your society, their **interdependence** upon all others, moving from viewing yourself as a certain sex, a certain age, a certain race, a certain profession, to appreciating your essential **unity** with all others of your species.

Film reflects this evolution as no other art form can because **it is the unity of all other art forms.** You begin with a story, a dramatic piece. This drama is rendered as a visual medium, photography. The visual depiction is cushioned and enhanced by the use of sound and music, both to communicate dialogue and to musically create mood. The medium is dependent upon actors, individuals possessed of the talent to dramatically portray the themes and problems of your society and species. A host of invisible technicians work behind the scenes to render the image on film, to process the film, edit the picture and sound, render it suitable for presentation.

This art form is thus dependent upon a company of professional artists, each a master in his/her own craft, each in the service of a project greater than any individual. The actor brings his training and talent to bear on a dramatic rendering of the words; the words were written by one steeped in the tradition of dramatic structure, seeking to give it fresh expression (though not always!); the cinematographer paints with light and color in rendering the story on film; the director stands at the helm, priming the actors, positioning the camera and its movements, serving as the vital source of energy radiating intent to all employed in the project.

Film, then, is the most egalitarian of your art forms; despite your love of the director and your habit of deifying him, the fact remains that any film is the product of collaboration. Film is the premier art form of your century precisely because it so perfectly mirrors the evolution of your society, moving from discrete and independent groups to one of cooperation and an appreciation of the talents of the individual in the service of the whole.

Film is also the most "realistic" art form in that it presents the world as you experience it with your eyes and ears. You see moving images, people talking, living, loving and warring; your eyes cooperate in the essential falsehood by pretending to see three dimensions where there are only two. Filmmakers call it the "suspension of disbelief," your conscious mind's retreating from its ever-critical examination of what comes to your senses, permitting you to sink into the drama on the screen as if it were actually occurring before you. As your society moves toward a truer understanding of the nature of reality, then, film naturally rides that next wave as it replicates the process by which you experience physical life: You conveniently "forget" the hidden source of your world, from which every physical object springs, "pretending" to yourself, for the duration of a lifetime, that what you behold with your senses is truth.

There is a further feature of film, in its presentation, that nudges you closer to this understanding. It will also infuriate the scientists, so we cannot resist.

When you view a film, you are not watching a string of film being dragged smoothly and continuously before the projector bulb, to be projected to the screen. Instead, each frame of film is held stationary before the bulb, its image projected; then the shutter blacks out the screen while the pull-down claw pulls the next frame into position. The shutter opens, the next frame is projected and so on. With film running at twenty-four frames a second, then, each frame is projected, as a stationary photograph, for 1/48th of a second, followed by 1/48th of a second of darkness while the next frame is pulled into place. This is why the soundtrack is "read" **after** the image has passed through the projection stage, where indeed there is a continuous, smooth flow of film.

In other words, while you sit and pretend to yourself that you are watching a film lasting two hours, what is actually occurring is that you are watching one hour of film and one hour of black screen.

And you thought Hollywood wasn't giving you your money's worth!

Now, you are not aware of the black screen because your mind eliminates it from conscious awareness, leaps from the moments of blackness to the next image, sewing them together in a cohesive whole, convincing you that you are watching motion when in fact you are watching a series of stationary photographs.

This relates to your evolving understanding of the nature of the world in this way: **Every physical object blinks "on" and "off" all the time.** We told you we would infuriate the scientists. What you perceive as bedrock physical reality is in fact the "picture" presented to your senses, which leap over the moments when the physical world before you has "blinked off," back into the unseen source of your world. You have proof of this, as we just demonstrated in the presentation of film. Your senses lie to you every time you see a film, convincing you that you have gotten your money's worth for two hours of film! By the same token, in the same fashion, your entire world is constantly pulsating between physical expression and nonphysical retreat; it is your senses that deceive you into perceiving a constant, steady physical reality.

Again, film is the one art form entirely dependent upon electricity. Photographs can be made with pinhole cameras, although the evolution into battery-powered cameras was a great advance. Music needs no electricity, though in your era it rides that current to amplified rock and roll and recording. Dance needs no electricity. Paint needs no electricity. Literature needs no electricity. Film is unique, then, in being entirely dependent upon electricity for its recording and presentation. As the widespread use of electricity is the single greatest technological achievement of your century, the art form entirely dependent upon its use is necessarily your premier art form.

Film thus rides your technology—electricity—while mirroring your society's evolution to a comprehension of the interdependence of each upon the other—the various crafts working in unison to create a film—and in its presentation, replicates the fundamental creation of your world: every object "blinking" on and off, read by your deceptive senses as consistency.

Genuine art always employs the time and place of its origin as a springboard from which to explore the deeper truths undergirding your world, and to presage the next wave in your society's evolution.

Those films you know as "classics," those enduring through time, thus couch grand themes in a given genre, time and place. For your classic films almost always feature a hero struggling against seemingly impossible odds, with only his/her integrity, courage and tenacity as tools to battle the forces of evil. As with literature, as with drama, you flock to any depiction of a hero **creating his own reality** against the overwhelming forces opposing his happiness and dedication to truth.

When an old film moves you, you may know it is genuine art, struck on the anvil of Truth. When you find an old film hokey, campy, unintentionally hilarious, you know it is reflecting the time and place of its creation rather than explaining it.

Children, **and** adults, continue to thrill to *The Wizard of Oz*, do they not? Does it matter that the special effects cost 69¢ in constant dollars? As with Dickens' *A Christmas Carol*, this film is worth a closer look.

First, notice the use of photography. The film's drama is sandwiched between opening and closing segments taking place at Dorothy's home. These segments are filmed in black and white. Now, those who have visited Kansas may simply feel this the most accurate means of presenting this locale, but there is more. Remember that black and white photography is so evocative precisely because it strips away the surface patina of color, reducing image to form, contrast and theme. Given that Dorothy is literally wrenched from her home—by a tornado—it follows that her time spent in the bosom of her family—the comfortable womb from which she springs—should be reduced photographically to theme and content, rather than flashy color. Just as the physical world you perceive is the outer reflection of deeper realities, so is one's home, one's hearth, one's family, the source of meaning from which one may spring to do battle with the world.

Once propelled to the land of Oz, what do we find? A **child**—Dorothy—and an **animal**—Toto—cast adrift in a strange land. Just as young children and animals are your closest link to the natural order from which your culture has long been divorced.

Dorothy is aided along her journey by the munchkins, miniature people—literally, adults in the bodies of children—representing the triumphant synthesis of reason and the natural order. It naturally follows that these should be considered good characters, as they represent the synthesis that the truly enlightened in your society attain.

Dorothy is further aided by the good witch—again, an incarnate source of good, replacing Christ in your secular society.

And whom do we find opposing Dorothy's quest every step of the way? The evil witch! Now! Notice how she is constructed. First, she is robed head to toe in black. In your culture, black is the color of evil, darkness, satanic malevolence. Further, this witch is literally the embodiment of fear, as manifested in your society. For, as any fear is irrational, the witch's skin is green, a color no human ever bears, and is therefore an irrational depiction of your species. And what does the witch want? She wants Dorothy's ruby slippers—for what purpose? To increase her power. Power over others can only hold in a society divorced from the natural order; it is thus a second-hand reality she chases after. What cares the witch for Dorothy's loving family? Such is anathema to the witch, calcified chaser of second-hand reality that she is.

And who are Dorothy's companions on her trek down the yellow brick road? They are all grown men in various guises—the tin man, the scarecrow, the lion. And what do they represent? Dare we say it? No heart! No brains! No courage! Need we say more about the deep wellsprings of truth this film taps into?

Your society, in its divorce from the natural order, has **abandoned reason**—no brains—**betrayed divinity**—no heart—and is left cowering before a host of **fears**—no courage. It is no accident that such qualities are embodied in adult men, those who represent the furthest divorce from the natural order in your society, who have abandoned reason, betrayed divinity and cower before fears of their own making.

And all such grown men are led by a **child**, a **girl**—the female still maintaining some semblance of intuitive connection with the natural order. She has enough **brains, heart** and **courage** for the four of them! As does any child.

For what does Dorothy put herself through the ordeal of tracking down the wizard? For money? fame? power? No; it is **firsthand reality** she's after!

"There's no place like home."

Is there a heart so cold, so dead, that it does not flutter at the profound truth in that plaintive line? Home, one's womb, the source of one's life, the site of un-qualified love and acceptance—the wellspring of life from which you sally forth to face the world.

And when Dorothy and her companions finally come face to face with the exalted wizard, this lofty and scornful bearer of all truth and knowledge, what do they find? Such is all an **illusion**. In your own time, you run from politician to preacher to guru to physician, investing them with omniscience and insight because you have forgotten that you are the master of your life, the keeper of the gates of your reality; you contain all knowledge necessary for your own fulfillment.

The wizard, while a humbug, nevertheless launches into a series of brilliant speeches on the nonsense endemic to your society, regarding love, brains and courage; the tin man, scarecrow and lion all miraculously find that they held those resources within all along—they simply needed someone to show them.

Dorothy, too, as she is bade good-bye, is told by the good witch that she knew all along what she needed in order to return home. When the scarecrow angrily demands to know why the witch didn't simply tell Dorothy, the witch replies, "Because she wouldn't have believed me. She had to learn it for herself."

In our own modest way, we are offering the same to you now. In your divorce from the natural order, you have forgotten what every child is born knowing. You may not believe what we have to say. But you will learn it for yourselves.

How is the witch disposed of? The evil witch, the personification of fear. By a muscle-bound cretin bearing a submachine gun? By a fancy display of martial arts? By tossing her off the castle? No; as with any fear she is literally **dissolved** by a single brush against the **natural order**—water. So are fears, all fears, dissolved—by a glance from a reasoning mind couched in the security of its divine origin.

And does Dorothy triumph? Does firsthand reality triumph over second-hand reality? Do the child's heart and mind triumph over adults' no brains, no heart, no courage? Is the pompous posturing and sham spectacle of the wizard and those he represents not revealed as so much literal smoke and fire, masking ig-norance, to be exposed by the divine reasoning mind of a child? Do you not con-tain all knowledge necessary for your own fulfillment, but refuse to see it?

Is there no place like home?

Do you understand now why this film will play forever?

Remember that genuine art will always move the audience, evoke a physical response.

In your time, you find a glut of "action-adventure" films, language reduced to monosyllabic grunts as evil is combatted by firepower instead of reason.

Yet the audience for these films is great, and the cheering and footstomping of the audience clues you that fundamental truth is being displayed. What could that truth be?

Remember that any theme or idea, as it plays itself out, will send off a super-charged spark or version of itself as its dying gasp, the better to come to the attention of your conscious mind before being dismissed from your reality. What you find in these action-adventure films is the last, dying gasp of violence as a means of righting wrong. Your society cannot survive, cannot continue, if you persist in mistaking weaponry for strength. As this idea plays itself out, then, you find the century's premier art form acting as the springboard from which this theme emits its dying gasp. The audiences cheer because the battle is still presented as good versus evil—as drama has always been—and there are those in your society, as in any society, who cling to the past, the prior wave, the security of familiarity, even when such can only lead to self-destruction. These you find cheering the action-adventure films, applauding the last foamy spray of a long-crested wave as it expires on the sands of time.

For there are many in your society genuinely repulsed by such mindless depictions of violence; and these ride the next wave. Your experience in Vietnam serves as warning to any reasoning mind that violence can solve nothing—the boys there dying for nothing—and that your only hope of salvation is in a return to reason and divinity.

Between the two forces of your society lies the dynamic tension of your era. Will the old way—the resort to violence, the abandonment of reason, the betrayal of divinity—surrender to the new wave—the restoration of reason and divinity? This is the fundamental challenge of your era, among others, and it naturally follows that the premier art form should play such a powerful role in literally bringing to your eyes the battles being waged, unseen, beneath your society.

For you have just as many examples of reason triumphing over violence. Your *Star Trek* series spoke to just such a healthy evolution, projecting a future in which violence was used as a last resort, not the first response of choice. Even when attacked and violated, a violent response was withheld, representing your evolution to an understanding that you only strengthen the concept of violence by resorting to it, even when attacked. No more eyes for eyes, teeth for teeth. You must grow up. And in this television series, you find projected a future in which reason and restoration to divinity have triumphed, although there are still many in the universe lusting after the second-hand realities of money, power and territory! The crew of the Enterprise was of broad international flavor, was it not, again tapping into your evolution toward an understanding of the essential unity and cooperation underlying your world, despite superficial differences of color.

So your mass media, those most powerful in your society, present the dynamics of your era's greatest battles and conflicts. Which is the greater victory? Rambo standing atop a heap of corpses, or Captain Kirk employing reason and divinity to lead his crew to triumph?

You choose.

While "mainstream" films retain the three-act dramatic structure that is drama's ancient legacy, there are those utilizing the medium of film to ride the next wave, to fracture the traditional structure. Just as poetry has broken from its meticulous rhyming verse to fresh expression in form and structure, so are there "experimental" films that break the mold of tradition and fashion new experience from familiar technology.

Specifically, the potent duo of sight and sound can be channeled into creation of mood, without any recognizable structure to a piece. You may watch a series of fleeting images, not logically connected, which nonetheless leave you with a certain feeling or mood. Just as modern poetry can achieve. Such pieces thus by-pass the traditional structure, through which theme was funneled into traditional dramatic expression, to be unconsciously interpreted by the viewer. In the case of these experimental films, the dramatic structure is by-passed, leaving you with a direct experience of mood. It is thus a more realistic use of the medium, in that since all genuine art returns you to the unseen source of your world, an experimental piece that directly—rather than subconsciously—evokes a mood or feeling has achieved art's purpose in truer fashion.

Experimental film, that which springs fresh from the heart of Art, nudges your society closer to a more "realistic" experience of the world.

Let us turn our attention to the industry behind the world of film.

Again, all art flows through the political, social and religious currents of its era; as film is the premier art form of the century, and your country's film is the most universal and global in its appeal, we might be able to detect the condition and future of your society by observing the film industry.

In film's early years, the studios were king. They hired and fired, put actors under contract, determining which pictures they would play in, held all production facilities within their walls, and thus controlled every aspect of production.

Monarchy, is it not?

The combination of antitrust regulations and the increasing independence of actors and others involved in the industry ultimately led to the collapse of the studio as king. Then the individual became king. Stars were free to choose their projects, for the studio of their choice. Technicians became free agents, taking work wherever it could be found. Directors and writers went free-lance, looking for producers to provide them with work.

A more egalitarian system, is it not?

Yet as you look at the state of the film industry today—churning out so much garbage—you wonder how we can claim that this is the premier art form of your century.

The problem, of course, is money. Making movies takes big money, and successful movies make big money. Thus are the parasites drawn like moths to the flame. And, as we have seen, what happens when commerce infects an artistic medium?

Commerce seeks the security of past performance, the prior wave. Genuine art always rides the **next** wave. When art is forced to perform for commerce, it ceases being art. It becomes sequels.

The current state of the film industry mirrors your society. Money lust is the driving force—second-hand reality trampling over the firsthand reality of art. The studio system has gone berserk, paying actors more per picture than most workers earn in a lifetime, while unions featherbed and pose so many restrictions on a film's production that art necessarily suffers. This mirrors the state of your society: Wall Street crooks, wealthy beyond all need or reason, bilking the public for more, while your fears of annihilation and anarchy underwrite a bloated government that places so many restrictions on you that freedom necessarily suffers.

Films cost so much to make that only the safe, the sure, the tried and true—the past wave—can be made by the studios. For studio executives are placed in a literally impossible situation. They are required to accurately predict the next wave—what audiences will want to see two years ahead—while always performing for the bottom line—the security of the past. There is not a person on earth who can perform such a job.

Rising against this bloated studio system, then, are the independents—those freed from the shackles of union rules and regulations, not paying their stars the gross annual product of a Third World nation, working with a small crew, working quickly and efficiently. This mirrors the rise in your society of those who have turned away from money lust to return to firsthand reality. In the field of art, these filmmakers may never have a "smash," but they are far freer and happier working in the service of genuine art.

Further, your technology—again—encourages such independents. For the explosion of avenues and markets for film—video, satellite, foreign, cable and so on—virtually ensures that any well-made low-budget film will at least return its investment, if not provide a handsome return. Thus do you know that this is a healthy development, for the technology of a society will always aid the truest expression of genuine art. In providing such a variety of markets, your technology encourages the independent filmmaker, for his/her moderately-budgeted work must work long and hard to lose money.

You see how the evolution of film necessarily mirrors the evolution of society. From a monarchy to democracy evolving into bloated bureaucracy, to a rise in independence and free thought.

Further, your technology allows far greater freedom to the viewer. For one thing, films can be shown continuously throughout the day, as opposed to live drama, thus allowing greater freedom of choice.

While the thrill of watching a film on a big screen in the company of a crowd will never be lost, film is a far more democratic medium. At home, television and the video cassette revolution allow you to view any film of your choice, whenever you choose. Technology rides the evolution of society as it progresses to a celebration of the individual, supreme above the mass.

Technology, society, politics and the evolution of your culture—they all find expression in your era's truest art form: film.

Pass the popcorn.

CHAPTER FORTY-TWO

Music

We have saved music for last, as in many ways it is the best. For your species it is the truest art form, for it alone by-passes your dependence on visual imagery and is thus able to soar directly to the heart of your soul without cogitative distractions. In addition, in its very creation it reveals profound truths about the nature of the reality standing behind your world and your place upon it. Finally, in modern times, it edges you closer to a comprehension of the unseen mechanics behind the reality you know.

Let us begin, then, by examining the physical properties of music as you understand them.

You know that all sound travels on waves, or cycles. These waves are interpreted by your ears and brain into the infinite variety of sound that you are capable of perceiving. You enjoy puzzling over the question: If a tree falls in the woods and no one is there to hear it fall, does it make any sound? The answer is that it sends off vibrations that may be interpreted as sound by anyone within hearing distance.

You know also that animals have different ranges of the sound they can perceive. Dogs, for instance, respond to whistles inaudible to the human ear. So, however grand your experience of sound, understand that the range available to you is one more parameter of perception granted your species, for a reason, and that other species will interpret sound in far different fashion. Not less, but different.

With an oscilloscope you can examine the physical properties of sound. There are only a few basic sound wave forms. Each such wave pattern will be modified by an "envelope" with four parameters: attack, sustain, decay and release. A host of other modifying factors come into play, as there are very few "pure" tones available to you in the natural world. Almost always what you hear is a combination of wave forms, modifying each other in an infinite variety of patterns and sequences, bringing to your ears the full richness of sound you can perceive.

So sound travels on cycles, or frequencies. The faster the wave or cycle moves, the greater the "frequency" within a given unit of time, and the higher the "pitch" you perceive. The top note on a piano sounds much "higher" than the lowest note because it vibrates at a much faster "frequency" than the lower note.

There are mathematical values and equations involved in all of this. For instance, if you play two notes on a piano, an octave apart—say, middle C and the next C above it—the higher C is vibrating at a frequency precisely twice as fast as middle C. This is the physical or mathematical definition of an octave. You perceive this relationship as a similarity—calling both tones "C"—while acknowledging their difference in sound due to their differing frequencies.

Music, then, is at base an intrinsically mathematical field. As the digital revolution has proven, and as we shall later explore, all of music can be broken down into a series of mathematical values, to be "read" by a laser and presented to your ears as sound.

Now, we do not wish to put you to sleep with a physics lecture. Our point in offering this introductory material is to couch our further discussions in the framework of the deeper reality lying behind all music, the knowledge that all music can be essentially reduced to properties of physics and mathematics.

The reason music is prevalent in all cultures, in all eras, without exception, is precisely because it restores you to the unseen realities lying behind your world. Its appeal springs precisely from its restoring you to the unseen source of your world; it acts as a bridge or conduit leading you to drink from the wellsprings of existence.

We have seen that music travels on waves, on cycles or frequencies.

Your body is created precisely the same way.

Behind your world, your universe, lies a vast, undifferentiated bank of energy that is the source of everything you know. This undifferentiated storehouse of energy creates everything of which you are aware—both physical and nonphysical. It is the source both of the chair you sit upon and your attitude as you read this book. It is the source of your hopes, your dreams, your sorrows and your refrigerator. It fuels your automobiles, nourishes your children, inspires you to bravery and leads you to love. As we have maintained throughout, the physical world is a fiction, presented to your mind as fact through the senses. Because, in deepest terms, there is no barrier between physical and nonphysical, this vast energy source creates both thought and physical reality. It does so by specializing into an infinite swirl of variety, an endless series of configurations and patterns. At base, all is electromagnetic energy. Your body is created and sustained by electromagnetic energy. Every thought you think has an electromagnetic reality. Every belief your society holds has an electromagnetic reality.

Your body works precisely the same way, does it not? From the single fertilized egg cell, it specializes, differentiates into the impossibly complex construction that is the human body. In doing so, it precisely replicates the very creation of your world and universe. From that single, undifferentiated source all variety springs forth, working together in a **cooperative** framework that respects the **individual integrity** of each entity while each discrete part works for the good of the **whole.**

This seeming digression ties into our discussion of music because, as we have said, music by-passes the reasoning mind entirely, its dependence upon the eyes, and restores you to that **field of energy patterns** from which you and your world spring. Music travels on cycles. So do you. Music takes a few elemental relationships and configures them into an infinite variety of form. Such is your body.

Music, then, leaps the membrane between physical and nonphysical, shoving you back into the lap of All That Is, Who gave you life.

Since every thought you hold has its own electromagnetic energy, since your body is created and sustained by electromagnetic energy, it stands to reason that you will be affected by contact with any other source of electromagnetic energy. You are. This is why music is so powerful: It leapfrogs the reasoning mind and burrows deep into the energy patterns of your body. Music moves you as no other art form can, does it not? It literally vibrates with your body.

Why does an out-of-tune instrument grate on you so? Because the strings are not tuned to complementary frequencies, are battling each other with discordant frequencies, rather than working together to create a smooth and unified whole. Because these battling frequencies resonate with the core of your body, they evoke a feeling of dissonance, of discomfort. You are vibrating to each string of the instrument, and when they are not—literally—in harmony, the normally smooth and unified flow of your body is disturbed.

Most disturbing to your system are those sounds created by your species, unknown to the natural order. A car horn honking. A sidewalk drill. A chain saw. Such sounds all result from your divorce from the natural order, and as such they will necessarily grate on your body's inner core, fry it with discordance and battling frequencies, as a means of alerting you to the violation taking place.

Back to music. Your body works on the same principle music does. All its frequencies, when you are happy and healthy, are operating in harmony—a cosmic theme and variations. Out-of-tune instruments or discordant trash grate on you because they upset the natural harmony of your body's energy pattern.

Let us examine an octave on a piano keyboard. The main keys, the white keys, are laid out in octaves, each octave composed of eight tones laid out in a diatonic scale. Crouching above the white keys are five black keys, configured in a pentatonic scale.

While you could get away with none but the white keys, the resulting music would be uniform and bland very quickly, would it not? No thrilling sevenths, diminished chords, sustained chords, to spice things up.

Such is your body, your world, created. Your body has an overall energy pattern behind it, a standard configuration that you retain from birth to death. These are the white keys. But the richness of life, the variety, lies in your pulling into existence infinite variations on that basic form, as you move from infancy to old age—the black keys.

The added element of integrating white and black, diatonic and pentatonic, into a whole of greater richness and variety than either alone can produce, offers an additional insight into your races which by now is obvious, if not a cliché.

So, as you see in these few examples, music literally replicates the creation of your world and your body in a way no other art form can. Music can be broken down into a series of physical and mathematical equations or patterns—as can your body—and for this reason it literally resonates inside you.

Music, in whatever form, is entirely dependent upon what? **Rhythm.** Whatever the style, whatever the instruments, any musical expression always rides atop a beat, a pattern, a speed. Again, this is a fundamental quality of the creation of your world. For there is a rhythm to the natural world, a deep steady beat, from which the variety of expression springs. You see this as the rhythm of your seasons, the rhythm of your tides, the rhythm of the earth's rotation, the rhythm of the moon's path across the sky, the rhythm of the stars, the rhythm of rain beating against your window, the rhythm of birds migrating and the rhythm of the life cycle from birth to death. Every aspect of your existence is couched in a deeper rhythm; but beneath such differentiated rhythms lies one sure, steady beat, the intent of All That Is as It lovingly sustains your world.

Let us examine music as we have the other art forms, as a reflection of the technological, societal and religious themes of your society's progress.

Primitive man was restricted to very elemental instruments, as the technology had not evolved to allow great elaboration. Rhythm, being the most elemental backbone of music, can be provided by the human body alone: two hands clapping. With a stick and a rock, we can take a mighty leap forward. A group chanting and slapping sticks together in unison is a communal form of primitive musical expression. So while one person standing alone can provide himself rhythm and music—with hands and voice—so can such be combined to create a whole of greater strength and power. Just as each element of your body, just as each element of your world, stands alone in its own integrity, also serving to enrich the greater whole.

Perhaps the earliest known music that remains with your culture is the Gregorian chants. Here we find what? A religious theme, often performed by monks. No technology other than the human voice was employed. From that era, we find evidence of an irrefutable sense of the divine in the world, couched in the most private and personal experience of the world—the human body.

Moving up in time we find primitive musical instruments appearing. Again, such instruments always ride the technology of the era. One must learn to chop down trees and work tenderly and gently with their substance if one is to create a guitar, a violin. The technology of the era, the use of tools to create objects both of utility and beauty, allowed the first musical instruments to appear.

You know that by blowing your breath over a bottle, you can create a tone as your breath resonates with the interior of the vessel. This was known to primitive man in blowing upon grasses, or listening to the wind in the trees and upon water. Building upon this ancient knowledge, as technology progressed you were able to produce the first of the wind-powered instruments, the recorder and harmonica representing vestigial reminders in your day of the first crude attempts to marry wind and wood to render music.

Woodworking became a craft in its own right, an art form in its own right, by the time of the Reformation and Renaissance. Far from strictly utilitarian uses, wood was shaped by tool into rich and intricate patterns in the service of utility.

A table, a dresser, a door, while serving utilitarian purpose, could also look beautiful. There is an unconscious recognition that the basic undifferentiated energy source of your world is enhanced by variety and beauty.

This technological advancement also permitted the concomitant evolution of musical instruments. The first crude stringed instruments sprouted into violins, violas, guitars, mandolins, harps and so on. Wind-powered instruments blossomed into the flute, the piccolo, the trumpet, the French horn and the oboe.

And while each such instrument can stand on its own as a source of beauty, it came quite naturally that each discrete instrument could be combined, with the result that the harmony and beauty of the whole was greater than that of each individual part.

While there is great beauty to be found in the small chamber music groupings, what is the most powerful musical form of the era? The symphony, the unity of all extant instruments in the service of a work of power and strength no solo instrument could ever command.

Now, what is a symphony? A symphony is musical monarchy.

The composer (God) records his expression on paper (stone tablets and Scripture), gives it to the conductor (the king ruling by divine right), who in turn leads the orchestra's musicians (dutiful serfs).

The hierarchy, then, flows from contact with the divine source of your world, the composer's expression in musical form, which is interpreted by the conductor and rendered by the musicians, who have little leeway or freedom, following both the composer's notes on the page and the rhythm established by the conductor.

You see now why the symphony was the premier musical form of its era. It rode the technology—advances in woodworking—the religious—imperious God before which you tremble and obey—the political—monarchy—into creation of a society—the orchestra—which functioned as a cooperative whole, each part contributing to the majesty and harmony of the whole.

You see now why the geographical birthplace of the symphonic masters was Europe—Germany offering Beethoven and Bach, Austria producing Mozart. Monarchy was born, centered and flourished in Europe.

You see now why your country has never and can never produce a symphonic composer to rival the European masters. Your soil has never known monarchy. As a symphony is musical monarchy, it follows that a land unknown to monarchy cannot produce the highest and truest expressions of that musical form.

As we earlier stated, it is difficult in your time to appreciate the profound, overwhelming impact symphonic music had on its audience. For all the grand themes of the era—the technological, societal and religious strands—lay crouched beneath the jumble of notes, springing on the audience with a ferocity that was virtually more than the body could stand. Your conscious mind is constructed to absorb only so much information at a time, and to behold an art form that thrusts in unfettered expression the profound themes of an era has a literal physiological impact which the faint of heart would do well to avoid! As we saw, such was the impact of the second movement of Beethoven's Seventh that the audience, stunned by the profound truths spoken as from the very lips of God, had to hear it again. Once was not enough; too much information lies coiled within the deceptively simple theme and overlaid melodies, and it requires repeated hearings for the body to absorb, assimilate and comprehend it all.

You have an example of this process in your own era, as we shall later see.

The era of symphonic music's greatest achievements, then, naturally flowed from the strength of monarchy, the church and technology.

For what have you in your day as the descendent of the symphonic form? Now you see how the channel to Art shifts over time to ride the currents of a society to the next wave of progress. Are there any symphonic masters in your era, in any country? Anyone to rival Beethoven, Mozart, Vivaldi? There are not. The symphonic form, which rode the extant political and religious themes of its era, no longer reflects the state of your society. You are left, then, with those working in the symphonic form producing works stripped of the power and beauty of the great symphonies.

As proof of this, one such strand labels itself "minimalist." At least no one is violating any "truth in advertising" laws here! Is there anything "minimal" about genuine art? Does a Rembrandt sink into the wall, its pastels blending in with the surroundings? Does rock and roll music, played loud, allow you any choice but to be overwhelmed? Does great literature, great photography, great film ever come across as "minimal"? By very definition, by the self-imposed mantle of "minimalism," you know that the channel to the symphonic form has long since atrophied, withered, shriveled.

You have even known of performances of minimalist music where the audience charged the stage, begging the musicians to stop! Or walking out in the middle of a piece. Or bursting into applause halfway through, as a means of bringing an end to the numbing boredom such music evokes. While the snobs among you, who would not know genuine art if it slapped them in the face, as genuine art always does, would scoff at such behavior as the boorish ignorance of philistines, remember that genuine art always **moves** you and **compels** you. Where audiences once rioted to hear Beethoven's music again, now they riot to force the music to stop! You need look no further to see that the channel to the symphonic form is dead.

Where, then, is that channel in your era?

Where is your technology? First, the single most important technological achievement of your century is the widespread use of electricity.

The electric guitar is the single most important musical achievement of the first half of this century. For it adapted itself to all styles of popular music, from playing rhythm with the big band, to more prominence in rhythm and blues and jazz, rising to prominence in the premier musical form of your era, rock and roll.

What is rock and roll?
Where is your political evolution headed?
Rock and roll is musical democracy.

Instead of musicians dutifully following a score written by someone else, interpreted by someone else, rock and roll musicians democratically work together, usually writing their own music, but always interpreting it in their own idiosyncratic style. While certain members of the group, because of the instruments they play or their personalities, may predominate, rock and roll nonetheless is an eminently democratic musical form. Group consensus is vital for the healthy functioning of the band. As with a symphony, every instrument is essential to the overall sound, but you see the evolution from obedience to a higher authority (composer) to a commitment to group consensus.

Rock and roll, then, necessarily achieved its greatest prominence in England—moving from monarchy to a parliamentary form of government—and your country, which has known democracy from the start.

Further, notice the content of the rock and roll song as compared to that of classical music. As the symphonic era was couched in the irrefutable presence of the divine in the world, its masterworks flowed from this source: Handel's Messiah, Vivaldi's Four Seasons and Beethoven's thrilling conclusion to his Ninth Symphony, the ode to joy and brotherhood.

As your secular society has toppled God from His throne and you modestly installed yourselves at the top of the presumed evolutionary ladder, the content of your musical form has necessarily changed. What do rock and roll singers sing about?

Above all else, they sing about love. Not love in any grand, cosmic sense, but simply: gotta get a girl. Gotta have sex. Remember that in your culture, men, haunted by fear of touch and feelings, must seek out solace and warmth in the arms of women, and only then in the sex act. This is their crippled and maimed attempt to restore to their lives the divine sense of purpose, meaning and importance that every person must feel. If God is dead, if the political leaders are crooks, one must find one's source of meaning immediately at hand; and if touch and feelings are to be avoided except in the arms of a woman, then the need for sex becomes desperate.

The clear sense of the divine, which produced the Hallelujah Chorus, has now been funneled into the secular sex act: let's do it oh yeah.

We are not passing judgment. We are simply pointing out how the evolution of your society will always be faithfully mirrored in your art forms. As rock and roll is the premier musical form of your era, the content of the songs reveals profound truths about your society. That so many songs would be concerned with love and sex indicates your profound confusion over this area of life, your using it as a substitute for the irrefutable divinity that infused the world in eras past.

Rock and roll, then, flows from the technological—electricity—the religious—God is dead—the political—democracy—to stand as the premier musical form of your era.

Remember the viewer standing before the enormous Renaissance canvas, the image literally filling the field of view as a means of commanding his attention? You know, or have been curtly informed by your children, that rock and roll is only rock and roll when played loud. Why? Once again, the ascendant art form commands your attention, allows no distractions, no back talk, no questions. You simply listen; and if so moved, you get up and dance, your body literally replicating the patterns of energy of which the music is composed. Again, genuine art, riding the highest wave, overwhelms you, permits no argument, no distraction.

Rock and roll is most often based on a three-chord pattern of 1-4-5. This essential simplicity, compared with the complexity of a symphony, represents an evolution toward a more accurate comprehension of the unseen mechanics lying behind your world. Your world springs from a vast bank of energy that specializes into grids or patterns of energy, manifesting as all the objects you know. In the Renaissance and beyond, when such was entirely hidden from view, the extant musical form weaved an intricate pattern of melody and harmony, as the patina of notes virtually obscured the rhythm underlying the piece. Rock and roll is a progression, then, in that its simple building blocks more closely replicate the foundations of your world. You still have an infinite variety of songs that can be written atop the driving three-chord structure, as lyrics and melody change, but you are much more aware of the underlying rhythm and structure of the piece, the building blocks. Your next wave, the digital revolution, takes this a step further, as we shall see.

Following our custom of zeroing in on a specific work of art as a means of exploring in detail the grand theory we present, we will now examine closely not a song but a rock and roll group. It is a free cosmos and ghosts are entitled to their opinions, so we shall cast our lot with those who consider the Beatles to be the premier rock and roll band of your time.

Let us see why. We will do so while respecting the privacy of the individuals involved and therefore keep our discussion general.

First, what was the geographical origin of the Beatles? England—moving from monarchy to democracy. British society is much more stratified than yours into upper class and working class. Which class did the Beatles spring from? The working class. Why? Because the upper class, the scions of monarchy and privilege, are riding the past wave. The working class, those struggling to gain rather than maintain, are the next wave. It is thus natural that the individuals involved would spring from the lap of monarchy, riding the next wave of political evolution.

The four involved were men. This is true of almost all rock and roll music. Why? Again, European culture, and men particularly, are the furthest divorced from the natural order; and their dominance in the era's premier art form serves to restore your society to that natural order, to return you to a comprehension of the divine source of the world. Rock and roll, in general, and the Beatles in particular, rode the next wave of societal evolution.

We have already seen how the technological evolution resulted in the Beatles' instrument of choice: the electric guitar.

Genuine art always reflects the themes of the era and society in which it is created while pushing it forward. Knowing this, why should the Beatles have made such an enormous impact?

Again with the utmost respect for the privacy of those involved, from what you know of their personalities and interests, you can see how each represented a given **theme** of the era. One was an angry activist. One a poet-balladeer. One an introspective mystic. And behind these three, providing the beat, an amiable everyman.

Sums up the Sixties, doesn't it? Growing political awareness. An explosion of poetry and song. A search for spiritual truth. All played out against the steady **rhythm** of mainstream society.

Thus the Beatles, with their combined interests and abilities, could ride a clear and unhindered rocket to the heart of Art. Thus could they churn out hit after hit, wrestling basic chord patterns into an infinity of melody and beauty, which spoke to you in a way that most other music of the era could not.

For remember that genuine art is always the product of two elements: native talent and a clear channel to Art. When the individuals composing the Beatles joined their energies, they literally replicated the grand themes of the society, resulting in a power and influence unrivaled by any other band.

The Beatles were far more than a musical phenomenon, then; their influence spilled over into dress—wild colors replacing drab business suits—hair—restoring men to the impulsive beauty of longer hair—openness to new experience—use of drugs—and so on. The release of each new Beatle album was an Event, capital E, was it not? For literally encoded within the music, to be decoded by the listener, was the very evolution of the society.

Remember the effect Beethoven's music had on its listeners, its overwhelming impact. What occurred during the Beatles' concerts? One could hardly pass judgment on the Beatles' musical technique for all the screaming drowning them out. Was the music that bad? Was it that good? Why didn't everyone simply sit down, shut up and enjoy it?

Because the four young men standing on the stage were but the physical reflection of the entire **evolution of society in all its themes.** Awakening political consciousness, poetry and song and spiritual search were combined into the gestalt of the Beatles, and in comprehending this the audience was literally overwhelmed. Again, it was more than the body could stand to be assaulted with so much profound truth all at once. It was more than the conscious mind is equipped to handle. To literally see the very essence of a decade standing upon a stage, the different themes working in unison, was too much. It is no accident that pubescent girls were shrieking the loudest; for while sexual awakening was involved to some extent, more germane is the fact that the female has retained the intuitive connection with the divine order that the male has lost, and the young ride the next wave far easier than the old.

A Beatles concert, then, was the modern equivalent of God announcing his next ten-year plan, complete with lightning and earthquakes.

The Beatles' recorded music was enhanced by a further factor. Their recordings were produced not by a contemporary rock and roller but by a classically trained musician and composer, a generation removed. This man literally represented the past wave, upon which the Beatles could ride to the next wave. For no art ever appears out of empty space; it always flows from its antecedent form. Couching the Beatles' thematic replication of the Sixties in the sage hands of one steeped in the musical form of monarchy perfectly mirrored the evolution of British society, and the world.

To this day, the Beatles' records sell as well as many new releases. If rock and roll is the premier musical form of your era, and the Beatles—as we opine—are the premier rock band of your era, it naturally follows that their music will appeal as long as rock and roll lasts. There is something happy about their music, is there not, something that triggers good vibrations when you listen. Again, you are decoding the intent of the artists, returning with them to that grand, tumultuous decade, exploring it anew through the cooperation of individuals exploring the era's themes individually.

You may have felt that the work of the individuals involved, after the Beatles' dissolution, does not always live up to the genius of their work together. Did they all wake up the day after the divorce with their talent gone? Of course not. The native talent remains, but the channel to Art, which they rode through the combining of their personalities, was lost. And while the individuals involved still have much to offer musically, it cannot spring with such fidelity from the very heart of Art, for the channel is not as strong and sure.

The Beatles, then, represented a new development: a **group genius.**

Thus did they mirror the evolution of your society toward a truer understanding of the nature of reality. Yeah yeah yeah.

The Seventies were a decade of rest and consolidation, as we shall later explore in detail. There was not so much innovation as there was **absorption** and **reflection** over the events of the Sixties.

While rock music grew throughout the Seventies, it did not offer any fresh burst of originality as were the Beatles and the other preeminent bands of the Sixties. The musical form was built upon as technology progressed but was not as stunningly original as the Beatles' music, say.

Just as rock and roll represents a progression toward a tearing down of the old structure of music in the symphonic form, so did you have a further step in this direction with the advent of disco music. This was an elemental music form indeed, in which the lyrics became meaningless, providing vocal overlay to the essential rhythm of a song. This was dance music, and it thus represented a positive step forward in that dance serves to restore you to the natural rhythms from which your world springs, and a musical form that makes no intellectual demands—no intricate lyrics—allows the rhythm to predominate. Your discos were full of people trying out a variety of steps and styles, experimenting with sundry structures placed upon the rhythm of the beat. Exactly how your world is created.

The loss of lyrical meaning, while retaining the rhythmic beat, hastened the decline of the traditional musical structure. We are not passing judgment, not proclaiming this a negative development. It mirrors the tearing down of societal structure that must precede the arrival of the New Dawn.

Rising from the ashes of disco was a new musical movement, infused with political fire, that of the punk or new wave movement.

This musical form built upon the legacy of the Sixties and Seventies. It furthered the decline of traditional musical structure by rendering both music and lyrics unintelligible—a driving wall of undifferentiated sound—while restoring the Sixties' emphasis on political meaning to music. Thus the lyrics contained harsh indictments of society yet were spewed out with breathless rapidity, in a monotone, over a driving blast of unmelodic steam. Politics was restored, then, while the progression away from traditional musical structure was enhanced.

Few over thirty find anything positive or progressive in this musical form! For indeed it assaults the ears in an unpleasant way. But there are clues to be found, always, riding on the new wave.

Again, as with disco, punk music furthers the decline of standard musical structure, mirroring the decline of the traditional societal structures. If the music sounds like chaos, observe your society and see if there is not a correlation.

Most instructive of all is the dance form employed by those listening to punk music. Called "slam dancing," its devotees break the boundaries of chivalry and respect that even the most ardent rock and roll dancers observed. A slam dancer closes his eyes, jerking about in seemingly epileptic contortions, falling to the floor, spinning about, smashing into other dancers, utterly oblivious to anything but his own inner fire and need to physically express the music flowing through him. The dance is an utterly individual one, then, a swirl of frenetic energy characterized by randomness.

Does this ring any bells? Do you remember Chapter One? How the first hesitant expression of physical matter is the electron, whose mad spinning dance is characterized by randomness?

Your slam dancers, frenetic fools to the eyes of middle age and polite society, are in fact the very heralds of the New Dawn. The human body assumes the dance of the electron. The circle is complete. O brave new world.

Technology, in the form of the computer, has further aided music's evolution and your edging closer to an understanding of the nature of reality.

The digital revolution has brought unprecedented freedom to the artist, while allowing far truer fidelity to the initial music. You know that your analog systems—tapes and records—always produce a certain degree of background hiss, the result of the needle gliding through the grooves or tape rolling past the heads. In a compact disc player, this is entirely eliminated. A laser reads the digitally-encoded information, offering a far cleaner, truer sound. Separation is enhanced. Everything seems crisper, more vibrant, more alive.

The march of technology has also aided the artist in the profusion of electronic gadgets available to the musician. Anyone with a rudimentary command of the keyboard can now produce complete works without the need for other musicians. Drum machines and the multivoiced synthesizer replace the human band. While this brings a certain loss of human involvement, it enhances the freedom of the individual—just as the march of technology has brought you out of the communal movie house and before the video cassette player in your own house.

A composer returns to the method employed by the symphonic composer—assigning different parts to the different instruments—while allowing far greater freedom in execution—for the musician can literally hear his composition, in all its full glory, as he composes. There is no slack time, no need for rehearsal with assembled musicians. Thus, building upon the symphonic form, riding the technology, moving toward the celebration of the individual above the mass, today's musician can be both jack-of-all-trades and master.

The digital revolution, the use of computers, has aided the musician even further. No longer need he lay down the various tracks on tape and mix them. Now, the computer stores the information digitally to play it back through the synthesizer. One can play a synthesizer and find the notes duly recorded on the staff by the computer, edit the notes and then have the computer play back the edited piece! Remember that technology always aids the ascendant wave of an art form, and the time saved in such a process is time left for composing.

Now we come close, very close, to an understanding of the very creation of your world. Your technology reveals it. How does the digital recording of music work?

As we have seen, every sound of which you are aware travels on waves, the basic wave form being modified by a host of factors to result in a unique shape, interpreted by your ears as a distinct sound.

Digital recording operates by the "sampling" technique, in which the sound waves generated by the musical source are "sampled" at specific intervals in time. Your present technology allows a sound wave to be sampled about 40,000 times per second. This means that the contours of a sound wave are measured and recorded 40,000 times a second. The entire sound wave, then, is not reproduced in total fidelity. But your ear cannot hear 40,000 distinct units of sound in a second's time, can it? As with the presentation of film, your ear leaps the gaps in sound, tells itself it is hearing a cohesive flow, when in fact it is listening to a series of discrete musical values.

For each of those 40,000 values, recorded per second, is reduced to a mathematical value. Now, let us be sure we understand this. Every sound that your ear is capable of hearing can be reduced to a series of mathematical values. These values are then further broken down into bits and bytes, the essence of the computer, built upon the binary system which, at its very base, knows only two values: "on" and "off."

As the laser reads a compact disc, it is reading a series of mathematical values, each of those values itself composed of a complex chain of "on" and "off" commands, spewing these into electronic impulse to be interpreted by your ear at such a speed that you are convinced you are hearing a smooth, steady flow of music. Instead, at the very base, you are hearing an impossibly rapid series of "on" and "off" commands. Again, your conscious mind is designed to handle information only at certain parameters, and while you can intellectually conceive of 40,000 discrete sounds per second, you cannot possibly hear such a series. They blur, blend, in your mind's interpretation of them.

This returns us to the very source of your world. The source of your universe and everything in it is an infinite field of energy, specializing and differentiating as it approaches your plane, reconfiguring into grids and patterns of a variety impossible for you to grasp. At base, everything of which you are aware—every thought, every object—is your **interpretation** of an energy pattern that at its base is simply energy blinking on and off, in and out of your existence. Just as every physical object blinks on and off all the time, so does every thought that you can hold, in ways virtually impossible to describe. There is a constant flux and flow, then, between your world, your body, your life and the unseen source of it all.

And it is your senses that convince you of a physical world rich with color and sound and variety, when in fact you are merely perceiving the blur of energy rushing through and around you with such inconceivable velocity and frequency that your mind simply cannot intellectually comprehend it. You perceive the blur, the blending of these discrete energy units, and convince yourselves of a bedrock physical reality.

You know this. Your digital revolution shows it to you. The symphonies of Beethoven, the bouncing rockers of the Beatles, the whine and growl of the synthesizer—all these are reduced to a series of "on" and "off" commands, rushing past you so quickly you blend them together into the fiction of a cohesive whole.

So is your world created. So is your body created. Energy, the music of the universe, whirling past you, past all hope of conscious awareness, painting the picture of your physical world with an impossibly complex, an infinite, series of commands:

On and off.

PART FIVE
THE AGES OF LIFE

CHAPTER FORTY-THREE

Introduction

Scientists stutter incoherently enough when asked how you grow and age **physiologically**, but they are rendered virtually mute when asked how you grow **psychologically**. While various schools of psychology have sprung up, attempting to explain the nature of psychological growth through the span of life, still they are limited to describing cognitive or developmental growth, not explaining what lies behind it. Why should the infant not be able to read? Why is youth so idealistic? Why do people grow more conservative as they age? Why are the elderly possessed of wisdom? You know that these phenomena occur; but you do not know why.

Limiting itself to the physically perceivable, psychology, a branch of science, views the life span like a statistical bell curve, in which the child grows out of its foolishness into the years of productivity, gradually to decay and decline into senility and death. Youth is thus the pinnacle of life, aging a cruel punishment and death the final insult.

Now let us examine the reality.

Your fixation on growth generally ends with adulthood, when presumably all growth has ceased and the individual assumes his/her role in society, until decay and death remove one from the scene. In fact, **each stage of life** carries a **unique** and **essential** challenge and opportunity for growth. This does not cease with the physical body's maturation to adult size. A full life is composed of an endless series of unique, specific tasks, flowing from the psychological and physiological state of the individual.

While the bell curve may be an evocative symbol of the stages of life, a more accurate interpretation is to see that the process of growing to adulthood is one of increasing commitment to physical reality, the prime of life—middle age—representing that period of most highly concentrated physical activity, followed by a gradual **release** of physical life. Not decay. Release.

A long, full, rich life, then, is one of endless challenge, growth and learning. At each stage, the physical body will mirror the psychological progress in highly symbolic form.

There are a few basic concepts we must impart before turning our attention to each specific stage of life.

Remember that the span of seven years is highly significant to human life. You consider the number seven to be "lucky," though no one knows why. You have heard of the "seven-year itch." Most significantly, you know that every cell of your body is completely replaced every seven years. There is not an element, an atom or a molecule inside you now that was there seven years ago. What holds you together, then? How do you remain you?

Looking at the span of life, you see significant mileposts approximately every seven years. From birth to around age seven the child is preliterate. At age 7, about the time of first grade in your culture, the child has matured to where it can begin to grasp symbolic relationships, written language, mathematical functions.

The next significant change occurs at puberty, about age 14.

The next milestone is about age 21, when career and family choices are made.

The milestone at about age 28 is not so apparent, but nonetheless important, as we shall later see.

Age 35 often brings the "mid-life crisis," a time of intense searching and introspection, a sense of years rushing by, and an honest appraisal of how much can be accomplished in one lifetime's span.

While the seven-year stages are not so obvious beyond age 35, they exist, and we shall explore them.

So you see, in your culture, that your species goes through dramatic change, physical, mental and social, approximately every seven years.

We have two essential principles to guide us through our discussion of the stages of life.

First is that all-important juncture between seven-year stages. This we shall term the **cusp**. The cusp is that point where one stage gives way to the next, and what occurs at the time of the cusp deserves close examination.

Remember that all time is simultaneous. Given that, at the moment of birth there is a "you" already in existence at every moment of life, from birth to death. An infinite series of "yous," which we have termed parallel selves, you pull into existence by the force of your thoughts and beliefs. Each day you live out one probable life, one **version of yourself**, as a result of the choices made before and the nature of your thoughts.

Remember also that events travel on cycles, dipping close to your physical plane, then bouncing away. There are "times," then, when events can manifest with greater ease, when poised just on the other side of the membrane separating physical from nonphysical worlds.

This principle applies to each human life, and it is here that the seven-year cycle is significant. For at every cusp, every seven years, all of your future and past selves swarm into your awareness as at no other time. This is why the cusps are imbued with such **searching**, such **introspection**, hopes and dreams evaluated against past progress. For every past moment, every future possibility, is with you in intense and urgent proximity, as at no other time.

Further, most significant at the cusp is that the parallel selves that will be "you" at the next cusp will manifest more clearly and strongly than any others, will literally plant psychological and physiological seeds to prepare you for the next cusp. The immediate future cusp, the one awaiting you after seven years, has the strongest impact, reconfiguring your psyche and body as **preparation** for the tasks to be faced at the next cusp.

As an example of this, at puberty the body begins sexual maturation. The first hesitant romantic contacts are made. Does this mean the 14-year-old is ready for marriage and parenthood? Of course not. All this has been triggered by the next cusp, that of age 21, so that when the age of 21 is reached, the groundwork will have been laid, the body strong, vigorous and ready to reproduce, and psychologically prepared for the responsibilities of parenthood. Thus, the parallel selves awaiting the attainment of age 21 reach back in time, plant the psychological and physiological seeds that blossom into puberty, as a means of laying the groundwork for the tasks to be confronted at age 21.

While the immediate future cusp is the most significant, all prior and future cusps swarm close to the individual with every cusp. This is why such intensive searching of the past occurs, as one's past selves present themselves for inspection, the better for you to evaluate them and change course, if need be. And those cusps far in the future make their presence known as a means of ensuring that the decisions intrinsic to each cusp are balanced with an appreciation of the lifelong goals and dreams each individual holds.

The end of each seven-year period, then, we call a cusp. It is the time of introspection and planning, when the unseen selves from your past and future cusps swarm into consciousness, most significant being the immediate future cusp, planting psychological and physical seeds as groundwork for the healthy evolution into the next cusp's tasks.

A second principle we will employ in our discussion of the stages of life is what we shall call the **filter** of each stage of life.

There is a certain psychological framework or filter through which each stage of life is experienced. These mirror the evolution from childhood, to full-scale concentration in physical life at middle age, to a gradual release of physical bonds in old age. Each stage of life, then, carries a specific **task** or **focus**, and this essential challenge imbues the entire stage with a psychological flavor unique to that stage. You know that children literally see things differently than adults. While they may stand beside you, watching the same physical event, their experience of that event is far different, because the filter through which it is interpreted is so different.

We have seen, for instance, in our discussion of sexuality, how the middle-aged parent is aghast at the compulsive, impulsive, noncommittal sexuality of the adolescent. Each is therefore viewing the same phenomenon—sexuality—from a different filter. The adolescent is not guilty of licentiousness but is funneling sexual experience through the unique filter of youth. Those in middle age, where sexuality is best used to cement commitment, can only view the adolescent's sexual explorations with alarm. The event is the same—sexuality—but the filters are so different that there can rarely be a true meeting of minds, except among those middle-aged who remember the filter they carried in adolescence, when they pursued sexual experience with heedless abandon.

Each stage of life, each span of about seven years, carries a specific set of tasks, a unique package of challenges and learning, all experienced through a unique filter.

With these principles in mind, let us now turn our attention to each of the stages of life. With a tip of our hat and a ruffle of our Freudian slip to those cognitive, developmental and psychosexual researchers preceding us, let us see if we can integrate our understanding of Divine Grace, the nature of reality, and the cusp and filter, into a more comprehensive understanding of how you grow.

CHAPTER FORTY-FOUR

Before Birth and Birth

In this book, our initial work, we have concentrated on explaining how the unseen mechanics behind your world create the physical reality you know. We have thus avoided lengthy discourse on issues having no immediate physical result. Dreams, reincarnation and so on have been mentioned only in passing, therefore. When we have mentioned reincarnation at all, it has simply been to buttress your understanding of a larger physical phenomenon. In doing so we have simply posited reincarnation as fact, without offering proof. Of course it is a fact from our perspective, though we realize there are many who find it distasteful, incomprehensible or unbelievable. Perhaps in another work we can delve into the topic more fully, but for now, as throughout, we will simply treat reincarnation as fact.

Reincarnation enters our discussion of the stages of life because it is so intrinsic to the prebirth process. There are no accidents or coincidences, ever, and certainly no accidents of birth. Every parameter of one's birth—time, place, society, parents—is chosen beforehand as a means of exploring certain aspects of the whole gamut life can offer.

We have spoken throughout of your "greater entity," the source of all your reincarnational lives. Again, we cannot provide lengthy explication of its nature. As an analogy, your greater entity views your entire life span as you view a single day. While each is unique and carries intrinsic challenge and opportunity for growth, it also slides seamlessly into the larger fabric of your life. So does your entire life fit into the overall learning and growth of your greater entity.

Your greater entity, then, casts about, looking for times, places and circumstances that will best lead to challenge and growth in the areas of interest to it. Just as you have a personality, interests and aptitudes, so does each greater entity. You do not spring from an undifferentiated intent but from a greater entity with its **own** personality and aptitudes, its own interests. And each such entity belongs to a larger family of consciousness, groupings based upon similar interests—but don't get us started!

So the time, place and circumstances of each life are chosen by the greater entity as a means of focusing on a specific angle or slant to the overall set of interests. Reincarnation enters the picture in that the greater entity will always seek to **balance** its various lives, one against the other. Once a given theme is chosen for experience, that theme will be experienced in all its facets. A life of great wealth will be balanced with one of great poverty. A life of unbroken happiness, where good things seem to "happen" without interruption, will be balanced with a life of struggle, where the most rudimentary satisfactions come hard. This principle, of balance over a series of lifetimes, holds sway when the greater entity searches out the birth site of each incarnation.

Some have a series of highly unique, contrasting lives. Others choose a series of relatively calm, uneventful lifetimes. Again, the nature of the greater entity determines on which end of the spectrum the choice is made.

Highly significant will be the immediate past life, in your time terms. Of course, in deepest terms, there is no time, but the greater entity works within the parameter of time as you experience it on the physical earth and seeks a progression of growth. If challenges are left unmet from the immediate past life, these will be recast into the next. The need for balance will be addressed. All these factors are considered in the time of choice.

Of all we have said throughout, perhaps no thought will be so attacked as our stating that **you choose your parents.** Choose them? you cry. What on earth for!

The very reaction to this thought carries a host of clues as to the nature of your life's challenges. Perhaps you are delighted to know that you chose your parents as you maintain fine, warm and loving relationships with them. Perhaps you are repulsed at the thought, finding them an endless source of anger, scorn, derision and interference. Whatever the nature of the relationship, it carries within it deep importance as to the challenges of the life.

Further, remember that free will always operates. The greater entity is not a puppeteer, pulling your strings. It treats you the way the sage parent treats children: Do your duty and then set them free. So, over time, the original intent of parental choice may be perverted; life may bring unexpected hardship to the parents, rendering previously empathic parents cold and bitter. Nothing is predetermined. So do not think you set yourself up for every encounter with your parents! Their free will, and yours, always reign supreme over any prebirth choice.

There is much debate in your society, particularly when discussing abortion, about when a fetus is considered human. Is it when the fetus can survive on its own outside the womb? when it has a heartbeat? at the moment of conception? Science, religion, ethics and law are hopelessly deadlocked, as each views the process from its unique filter, and there can be no meeting of minds when coming from such disparate perspectives.

The answer is that free will operates at the very moment of selection. Only very rarely will a soul latch onto a zygote at the moment of conception. For the mother's loving intent sustains the fetus, is strong enough to carry it, imbue it with sufficient consciousness, that the fetus can thrive. There is no need for a distinct new consciousness to enter immediately at conception, then.

It is even possible that no consciousness will have "claimed" the infant at the time of birth. Again, the mother's loving intent can sustain the physiological functions of the body, but there will come a point where the separation from the mother has gone too far for the mother's intent alone to sustain the baby's physiological function. If no consciousness has entered by this point, the infant dies. This occurs in almost all cases of "crib death." However wrenching a bereavement for the parents, there is no tragedy in the sense of a life lost, for no life had entered the little body to be lost. In all such cases, then, there is a **purpose** to the parents' choice to have such an experience, as difficult as it seems for the bereaved parents to understand.

Assuming that a new consciousness enters the fetus, usually somewhere between the third and ninth months of pregnancy, there is a period of "anchoring" into the body of the fetus, a need to relearn the lessons of physical manipulation. Fetuses toss and turn, kick their legs, wave their arms and put up a constant fuss. They are simply learning the ropes of physical activity from scratch; though recalled from prior lifetimes, the gross motor movements have to be tried out within the new body.

Couched inside the mother's body, and in her loving intent, the new consciousness finds the womb is the splashdown site into physical reality. The greater entity chooses each such site with the greatest of care; its **intent** to experience physical life gradually anchors in the fetus's body, strand by strand, dipping back into the immediate past lifetime, then leaping forward into stronger commitment to the present one. There is a flux or flow, then, between the physical and non-physical, the soul dipping its toes into the sea of physical experience, then drawing back, seeking the security of the greater entity's loving intent and the familiarity of the past lifetime. Finally, if all seems propitious, the strands will be nailed down, the commitment to physical life made irreversible and the joy of existence embraced without restraint.

The physical act of birth is the best replication of the creation of the physical world that you can experience. Just as mother earth and Mother Nature grant you life, just as you pull into physical experience across the membrane all the events of your lifetime, so now does the thrusting, loving intent of the mother propel the child from the womb into physical life. Notice—as another connection with your cetacean cousins—that every person begins life in a sea of liquid, from which it springs into the atmospheric standard of human life.

Birth is the most dynamic, powerful and aggressive act of which your species is capable. It frequently involves excruciating pain. While we do not wish to belittle the agony many women suffer—we have been through it ourselves, thank you—in deepest terms it **enhances** the experience, does it not? For it mirrors the very essence of life: from struggle, from pain, comes triumph. If it were easy, a process like washing the dishes, would it carry such meaning? Would it be as satisfying, as imbued with power and meaning?

You see also in the fetus's movement through the birth canal another analogy of life itself: how infinitely **malleable, adaptable** and **resilient** the human body can be. The little baby's body is twisted and contorted, subjected to pressures inconceivable to the adult mind, and emerges **intact, triumphant**. A fine metaphor for the later **metaphysical** struggles that, however daunting and seemingly insurmountable, can lead to exultant triumph, if the spirit be willing.

Because the consciousness is so tentatively anchored in the body at the point of birth, the entire birth process does not carry the pain or suffering you would endure if subjected to similar pressures. The neonate is not nearly as sensate, as sensitive to the physical reality about it, as the adult is. The anchors of physical life, the strands binding consciousness to body, are tenuous. There is no pain, then, in the birth process, from the fetus's perspective.

Yet every child, popping triumphantly from the womb, certainly makes its presence immediately known, does it not? From your filter, you perceive the cries as pain. From the baby's viewpoint, there is no such experience.

The baby is simply announcing to all within earshot: Whoooooopeeeeee! Another crack at the joy of physical life! I'm here! Let's get the show on the road!

Your species knows many expressions of triumph, shouts of joy and victory, but none compares to the **power**, the **intensity**, the unbounded **joy** of the babe fresh from the womb.

Mom! Dad! I'm here!

CHAPTER FORTY-FIVE

Early Childhood

In discussing early childhood, it is impossible to entirely divorce the natural growth of the child from the childrearing practices of a society. For given that a young child is your closest link to the natural order, the question becomes: Do the childrearing practices of a culture enhance or obliterate that natural, easy bond with the divine order?

We have seen that the fundamental quality of your culture is divorce from the natural order. Given that every infant dwells entirely in the natural order, what can we deduce about the socialization of children in your culture? The process of growing up in your society is one of relentless **divorce** from the natural order, the squashing of all intuitive knowledge, betrayal of all intrinsic divinity in a child.

How else to explain the natural curiosity of the child perverted into the scientist's creation of atomic fission, artificial conception, genetic manipulation and nuclear weapons?

How else to explain the child's intrinsic love and empathy for all living creatures blunted into the senseless depravity of sport hunting?

How else to explain the child's constant delight in firsthand reality—love, art, creative play—mangled into the mindless pursuit of second-hand reality—money, fame, power?

Your society, then, is one whose socialization process holds one intrinsic and overriding goal: to divorce the child from the natural order.

In examining the growth of the child, therefore, we shall both explore the child's **natural** progress and the concurrent approach to childrearing of your society. Sadly, these paths rarely converge.

First, what can we say about the fundamental task or filter of the first seven-year span of life? What is the intrinsic and supreme challenge of this stage?

The young child's essential task is **security.**

The child is born with unlimited capacity for adaptation into whatever culture it lands in. At birth, the child of the Stone Age tribe is the same as the child of the space age culture. The process of growing up, then, is one in which the root parameters of a society are imparted to the child, as a means of providing a **secure** framework from which all future growth can spring.

As an example, you know that children are born with the capacity for learning any language. The lips and tongue of the infant are infinitely adaptable and malleable, can assume any idiom: the lilting song of Chinese, the guttural bite of German or the fluid poetry of French. Yet as the child grows, certain sounds will be emphasized while others are lost. If you learn a language in adulthood, you will always speak it with a strong accent, the filter of your native tongue. The young child has no such handicap but has the entire gamut of verbal expression in equal potential for fluency.

This is one example of how the infinite variety of human culture is carried within the infant; in growing up, one emphasizes certain strands, qualities and characteristics while neglecting and forgetting others.

In this sense, the young child seeks the security of learning the parameters of the culture in which he/she lives.

Further, of course, the child needs to feel that the **world is a safe place.** For what good is growing up if the world seems harsh and cruel? As we have seen, the act of breast-feeding itself subliminally transmits to the child that it is loved, appreciated, as the suckling babe gazes naturally on the face of the mother and comes to associate the human face with love and sustenance.

You can see in the faces and bodies of infants improperly cared for the results of neglect. While the physical, nutritional needs may have been met, such infants look terrible, do they not? They are unresponsive, immune to touch and loving words. For the essential task of early childhood, security, has not been met by the world; the young child withdraws, rather than set itself up for further hurt.

There can be no overstating of the importance of constant love and affection for the infant. It is impossible to smother them with too much love. They soak it up, each such moment cementing the sense of security that the world is a safe and happy place, that the decision to rejoin physical life was well made.

There is some debate about whether one should always respond to a crying infant. Some say they need to learn that their needs cannot always be instantly met, that they must learn to delay gratification, that they must operate on schedule.

Babies are not airplanes. They do not operate on schedule. They know nothing of your second-hand reality of alarm clocks and lunch breaks. They have only one fundamental task—security—and if you are unable or unwilling to instantly respond to the cries of an infant, you had best go childless.

Notice the physical shape of an infant. Remembering that the physical condition of each stage of life mirrors the psychological progress, what can we deduce about infancy?

First, the infant is a cuddly, round ball more than anything else—pudgy, soft, lacking line and form. This physically reflects what we mentioned earlier: The child is born infinitely malleable, and the process of growing up is one of assuming the contours of its society. Line, form and stiff spine can come later; in infancy the whole gamut of human experience lies as a latent possibility, and the indistinct shape of the infant reflects this.

Further, what can we say about the infant's head? Is it not—from your adult perspective—grossly out of proportion? Huge compared to the rest of the body? Why? Because it is the brain that is the site of symbolic manipulation which is intrinsic to your species. Your species is distinguished by its conscious, rational thought, and it naturally follows that the site of that quality would be oversized at birth, as a means of emphasizing the essential tasks of the life ahead. Observe kittens and puppies; are they born with their heads so grossly disproportionate? They are not. Their neonatal bodies more closely reflect the adult shape of their species, for dogs and cats always remain in the natural order. The human species' use of rational thought sets it apart from the animals, and thus the head—the site of rational thought—is emphasized in the form of the infant.

In infancy, the flux and flow between physical and nonphysical worlds occurs constantly. You do the same every night in the dream state. This explains why infants sleep so much, and why less sleep is required as one ages and anchors more solidly in physical reality. The infant is drifting back into the intent of the greater entity, comparing the intent of the life's creation with the physical experiences so far, drifting back into the prior lifetime as a means of ensuring that those challenges carried over are understood and brought forward. The infant, then, literally straddles the reality between physical and nonphysical, both anchoring in the security of physical life and reviewing the material that drove the choice of time, place and circumstances.

The infant can make sounds but not language. When you speak, it is your intent that is understood by the infant. As with all other creatures anchored in the natural order—your pets—it is the **sound of your voice**, rather than the words you speak, that imparts your meaning. You can tell a baby it is the ugliest thing you ever laid eyes on, but if you do so in a loving voice, it will thank you for the compliment! For the infant knows only firsthand reality—direct emotional contact—and knows nothing of second-hand reality—the subterfuge of words.

The infant and young child are masters of their own reality, understand they create it, and consciously do so themselves. They employ visualization constantly. They learn to grasp by seeing the hand clutch the object before their motor skills permit it. They learn to walk by seeing their clunking progress across the room, before their legs can carry out the plan. They see the future—deliberately and consciously construct it—and then physical experience naturally follows.

For the young child knows nothing of fear, that bugaboo of adult society, cowering behind nuclear warheads and Bibles. If the child were to rationally consider what would happen if it fell while taking its first few steps, it might never make the attempt! The child understands consciously that thought creates reality, that the **intent** to walk will result in the **ability** to walk, and thus there is nothing—ever—to fear. Have you ever known a young child to say "I cannot"? Young children will make seemingly outrageous claims about their physical abilities, will promise to uncomplainingly carry a fifty-pound backpack up Mt. Everest if only allowed to join the expedition. While this seems amusing or exasperating to the adult ear, the child **literally believes** it to be true, for **nothing is impossible to one who consciously creates his reality**, and the child knows this. There is no obstacle too great to be overcome. Only adults know despair, defeat and resignation. Children know only conquest, growth, challenge and triumph.

The natural order.

In your culture, as we have seen, as women move into the workplace in greater numbers, the issue of day care for small children rises in importance. Two-career couples assuage their guilt over abandoning their children by promising to compensate with "quality time."

Of all the bones we have to pick with your society, this is truly a mastodon femur.

First, only an adult could come up with a phrase like "quality time." Every **moment** of a young child's life is suffused with a quality unknown to adulthood, distracted as you are by countless worries, reliving of the past and fretting over the future.

The child sitting on the beach with a bucket and shovel—or even bare hands—is having time of a quality you cannot conceive of, for he lives entirely in the **now**, focuses every strand of consciousness and intent on the task immediately at hand, and experiences a far richer, fuller time than the parent sitting beside him, reading the paper full of the usual travesties while worrying about tomorrow.

While there is no intrinsic harm in dragging a child to the museum, the zoo, the theater, the library or Grandma's in a desperate effort to compensate for abandonment, such is entirely unnecessary. If you lie on the floor beside your child with a pile of blocks or paper and paints, and see what you can come up with, the child's essential task is entirely met—the **security** of your presence.

You need not even be actively engaged with your child at all times. He or she can be perfectly content playing on its own, but only when in the security of knowing **you are there**. If he or she cries out for you, for no apparent purpose, and you respond, expecting some demand or inquiry, you may hear only silence. And what was that all about? The child simply needs to know **you are there**. **Security**. It is the fundamental task of early childhood, and you provide it simply by being there.

Now, if the burden of this discussion seems to fall on the shoulders of women, this demonstrates how far you have yet to go. For to the extent that feminism has succeeded in women assuming traditional male jobs and work patterns, it would be more accurately termed masculinism. Women becoming men. This is the opposite of what must occur for the evolution of society. Instead of accepting that the traditional female qualities of nurturance and warmth are detriments to the proper functioning of society, there must be a **return** to those qualities lest both men and women become robots. Your pejorative phrase "working mother" is not matched with "working father," is it? It is acceptable for the father to abandon the children. Yet your language implies that the woman is somehow at fault if the children are not properly cared for.

Now, in native societies, it naturally happens that men, the physically stronger, should go out hunting, if that be necessary, while the women remain with the children. As we have seen in our discussion of art, however, technology always aids a salubrious development in society. It does not require bold, masculine heroics to bag a pound of ground round from the supermarket. Anyone can do it. You thus move toward a society in which the intrinsic differences between male and female will be **appreciated** and equally **valued**, while also realizing that to a large extent they no longer hold.

The issue is not one of working mothers. This is the smoke screen sent up by those who wish to avoid a hard look at the very basis of your society. What is this process, jumping from the delivery room to the boardroom, the child dropped into a sea of equally needy and wailing colleagues at the day-care center? The single most important element of human life, you will grant, is the depth of connection with others, the ability to love, to cherish, to nurture another's spirit. No man is an island, you say, recognizing this. You are an intrinsically gregarious species, and nothing rides above the importance of learning deep emotional contact and commitment.

And if the young child is shuffled from home to day-care center, to be cared for by well-meaning strangers, but strangers nonetheless, the lesson is that life is shallow. That one must not expect profound relationships. That one should not bother making the effort at profound contact, for the revolving door of caretakers makes it impossible.

How many truly profound relationships do you have? How many genuinely deep, abiding, eternal bonds? How many relationships where you can tell **anything** and **everything** to the other, to have it accepted in love and trust?

There is no higher purpose to human life. By shuffling your children from crib to day care—"well, it's good for her to play with other kids"—you betray the fundamental task of the child's early years: **security**. And with that foundation shaky, all of life will be diminished.

You can see the progress in the child, from infancy to first grade, as it comes to learn symbolic expression. The infant can neither speak nor understand language; it exists in a cocoon of pure firsthand reality: emotion, drive, hunger, love. With the acquisition of spoken language, at about age two or three, the child makes the first leap into the human species, whose unique feature is rational thought, symbolic manipulation. This is not intrinsically a step backward, for indeed the child who never learns to talk will find itself bereft of the challenge and achievement of human life. There is no derogatory intent, then, in our stating that the child moves from firsthand reality to the second-hand reality of verbal expression, for such is an intrinsic part of your species and occurs in every tribe, however "primitive" to your eyes. It is a fundamental quality of human life.

And the child delights in verbal expression, for it no longer absorbs the conversations of others but can actively participate. How actively, we need not tell young mothers! The child knows only triumph and joy, and the assumption of verbal expression is one more conquest, one more challenge resulting in increased competence. While understanding that language is always the outer patina on a deeper, preverbal truth—like the physical world itself—the child nonetheless gladly assumes its place in human society, participating as a full-fledged, full-throated contributor to the tower of babble that is your world.

Somewhere along the line we will have to address the issue of whether hitting children is ever justified, so we shall do so now, even though the principles involved carry over to later childhood and, indeed, all of life.

Remember that violence is always the result of **reason abandoned** and **divinity betrayed**. Since these are the two fundamental qualities of your culture, it naturally follows that your society should be so violent. People who cannot **reason** with each other, in an atmosphere of **respect** for the unique divinity in the other, pick up their Magnums and decide right with might.

You know no question of morality can ever be decided at the point of a gun.

You know that strength lies not in weaponry but in reason and divinity. It is only in a culture divorced from the natural order that we find such knee-jerk retreat to the cowardice and passive surrender of violence.

With that understanding, you see what a heinous violation it is to strike a child, especially if the blow is any more than a light slap to underscore the verbal message accompanying it.

The child's fundamental task is to learn **security**. It needs to know that the world is a **safe, rationally ordered place**, in which reason and divinity work in tandem through the filter of the conscious mind. It asks "why" constantly, because it needs to understand the mechanics of the physical universe. It knows there is a **reason** for everything, and it needs to know **why**.

The child looks to the parents for the security of love and to help it understand the nature of physical existence—the "why." If young children ask you a million questions, it is because they respect you, look to you as the source of all knowledge and truth. They automatically imbue you with reason and divinity.

When you hit a child, you not only violate its bodily integrity but far worse is that you topple yourself from the pedestal of reason and divinity. Every child knows that violence is passive surrender, and to have the all-important parent, the arbiter of truth, approach the child with violence is to communicate that **the parent knows nothing. The world is an unsafe place. Reason and divinity have been abandoned.**

The implications of this are too profound for words. The child's body will recover from all but the most vicious attacks. But the psychological scars—the wrenching from the secure cocoon of parental reason and divinity—are permanent and etched deeply into the psyche.

Even the most tolerant of parents may find themselves at wit's end from time to time, or so frightened by the danger in a child's act—like walking in front of a car—that the message is underscored with a smack on the bottom. This is more a release of the parent's emotion than anything calculated to benefit the child, is it not? And while the qualitative difference between such a swat of concern and the vicious beating of a child is enormous, still the essential violation remains.

There are cultures, there are families, where children are only touched in love.

There is no more effective tool to ensure the divorce of a child from the natural order than to beat him or her regularly. It sums up every aspect of your crippled society—abandoned reason, betrayed divinity, unbridled fear—all in one fell swoop, or swat.

Some old folks among you are fond of proclaiming that they were routinely beaten when they erred as children and it didn't seem to do them any harm. Oh yes? And what kind of world has that generation left behind?

Parents of young children frequently cry in exasperation that their young ones won't listen, won't pay attention, won't follow orders. This is interpreted as evidence of willful disobedience, to be ruthlessly weeded out. It just goes in one ear and out the other.

Indeed, quite literally. The young child listens not to words but to the breath on which they are delivered. It knows only firsthand reality, not the symbolic retreat of language. It literally lacks the neurological structure to retain a blast of oratory bombast and change accordingly. Men particularly, the furthest divorced from the natural order and therefore utterly without a clue as to the nature of the young child's mind, are fond of imparting paternal "lectures" as a means of harnessing the young feet into the lockstep of adulthood.

The child learns not by words but by example. Again, it depends on its parents for its understanding of the nature of physical reality and the culture in which it was born. Nothing is hidden from the young child; they are the most telepathic creatures on earth. They **know** exactly what you are thinking, though you build a fortress of verbal mendacity around your intent. And the child imitates your **intent**, not the endless stream of verbiage you feed it.

If the parent treats others with instinctive kindness and warmth, the child learns that others are to be trusted and cherished, unless they prove otherwise. If the parent deals with everyone honestly, the child learns honesty. If the parent demonstrates respect for the child and other small creatures, the child learns to value all expressions of divinity, whatever their size.

We need not go on at length about this; you know quite well that the child learns by example, not lecture. We simply wish to emphasize again the importance of the parent in providing the framework through which the remainder of life will be experienced.

Because you view life as a progression toward physical mastery and manipulation, your society holds little respect for those who don't produce like proper capitalists. Young children and the elderly are thus so much baggage, your treatment of them one of impatience, waiting for them to grow up or to die. Thinking middle age the prime of life, the age when physical mastery is greatest, you fail to appreciate the intrinsic **challenge** and **growth** of each stage of life.

The child is not a miniature adult. The child is a being with its own set of challenges and tasks, which have nothing to do with those of middle age. The **filter** is different. The **purpose** is different. When you match your physical looking down on children with intellectual looking down on them, you cheapen their lives and yours. They are not impulsive little animals, bent on bringing chaos to your secure little world, but sparks of divinity, masterpieces of flesh and bone, set upon their own unique challenges and intents. What they need from the adult world is **security**, a basis from which all the rest of life flows.

For instance, how many of you, when meeting a child, kneel down to meet him or her face to face, eye to eye? And would you ask permission to touch the child, kiss it, hold it?

Ask permission of a child! What nonsense! you cry.

And when your friendly neighborhood molester drags the child behind the bushes and has his way, who are you to complain? The child is merely performing as you have taught it: its body is not its own. It is the possession of adults.

As one small step toward the evolution your society must make or perish, try this exercise: When you meet a child, bend down, proffer a finger that it may grasp if it likes, greet it with respect and a smile, and ask if you may hold it.

Once this exercise is mastered, perhaps you can extend it to all the creatures of the earth—the young child's companions in spirit—and the world may yet be restored to reason, divinity, the natural order.

To sum up, the young child's fundamental filter is to learn **security**. It needs to know that the world is a safe place for exploration and growth; that the love of the parent is unconditional, unqualified; that bodily integrity is respected; that the world—suffused with Divine Grace—is respected in every manifestation, the child included.

Thus do you set a child upon its happy path to adulthood.

CHAPTER FORTY-SIX

Later Childhood

efore beginning our exploration of the second seven-year stage of life, we must examine the all-important cusp between the first stages.

Remember that while all past and future selves swarm to the fore at each cusp, most prominent will be the immediate future cusp, imbued with the fundamental task or filter of the next stage of life.

The cusp occurring around age seven is therefore suffused with the nature of adolescence or youth. The task or flavor of youth is that of exploration and experimentation. This message having been sent back through time, at the cusp of seven years the child finds planted in its body and mind an urge to grow toward the tasks intrinsic to the next stage of life.

How is this manifested?

The fundamental task of youth is exploration. In order to explore the world, one must be physically and intellectually in command, secure in one's competence to meet the challenges of life in the greater world, burning with desire to know, feel and search. Thus the intent of youth is sent back to the seven-year-old, sparking both physical growth and the assumption of symbolic manipulation that is essential to effective mastery of the world. Thus the seven-year-old is able to learn the alphabet and basic mathematical functions, the laws of science, the legacies of religion, the process of government. All this is preparation or groundwork for the achievements of youth.

Thus we deduce the fundamental task or filter of the second stage of life. It is **mastery**.

Building upon the security of early childhood and stretching toward the exploration of youth is mastery. Mastery of the physical world—through increasingly fine motor coordination, added muscle and progress toward the adult shape—and mastery of rational thought—language, mathematics and the legacy of culture.

Schooling begins in earnest for the seven-year-old in your culture, though you may push it back to six or five. You sense that the child is ready to begin to assume its place in human society, steep itself in the cauldron of your culture, stepping toward adulthood.

Nowhere is the divorce from the natural order that is socialization in your culture more evident than in your manner of schooling.

Remember that life is energy and energy is motion. Are little children not bundles of perpetual motion? And how do you approach this, in the context of education?

Sit still! Sit up straight! Pay attention! Stop squirming! No talking! And on and on, ad infinitum, ad nauseam.

It is perfectly possible to impart all a child needs to learn in your culture while respecting and working with the child's innate energy and motion. But you train children from the very start for their later jobs of numbing repetition and stasis.

Further, you upset the natural rhythms of the child's body with a rigid schedule, period after period followed by lunch, then back to the rigid slavery of the clock. There is an intrinsic, natural rhythm to all of creation, and the child's body floats on this rhythmic, natural sea, if you let it. But by imposing the adult's harness of enslavement to the clock, you snatch the child from its bobbing contentment on that natural sea and straitjacket it on the hard and rocky shore of adulthood.

You see, the battles over various educational methods in your society obscure the fundamental process which is of far deeper import. You can bicker all you like about which subject matter should be taught, which methods should be employed and so on. But the fundamental method of schooling—strapping children to desks, slaves to the clock—is rarely questioned. This is why we will not join in any discussions about the **content** of your educational system; it is the system itself that requires revolution.

Ugh! Revolution! Don't say that word! Turn to page 116 now, class, and follow along as we study the events of 1776.

The years of older childhood are those of increasing investment in one's peer group, those of one's age, rather than the parents. The parents have done their most important job—either provided security or failed to do so—and the task of mastery requires an evolution into dealing with one's fellows. It is natural that those of similar physical and mental progress should be attracted, as they can use the common base of their cognitive and emotional growth as background to explore the varieties of personality. Some will be bullies, some wallflowers, some leaders, some delinquents. Observing this, intuitively understanding each to be equals in growth, the older child sees laid before him the gamut of human personality, the variety of approaches to life's problems and dealing with others. Is the child who instinctively strikes out when upset the most popular in the class? How about the one who cheats and steals? the blabbermouth? the braggart? While there can be a certain delicious attraction to those who flaunt the rules of adulthood, the most natural and revered leaders among children will be those who treat others with **reason** and **respect**—those who employ their rational minds and accord all others their natural divinity. These are looked up to as no others, for they are the first to make a successful link between the natural order of early childhood and the rational thought of adulthood. By being fair, impartial, respectful toward all, the young leader stands as a symbol of the very best the species has to offer and is naturally gravitated to by those peers eager to soak up the essence of this successful synthesis.

As with the younger child, the older child lives life in far more direct fashion than the adult. Every little crisis appears to be the end of the world, the weary parent will agree. If a toy is swiped by another, a howl of protest to wake the dead will ensue. What's one measly toy, asks the adult mind. But to the child, a **violation** has occurred, and violations are always to be **protested without cease** until redressed. There is no thought of perspective, of balance, of addressing the issue at a later date. When violated now, the child must have satisfaction now.

And to whom does the child run for justice? To the parent. And what does the wise parent do? He or she brings together the two offending parties, hears two wildly conflicting stories, as if each child was in a different state at the time of the event under discussion, and seeks through **reason** and **respect** to find a satisfactory conclusion. The child guilty of a violation knows perfectly well what he or she has done and is relieved to be exposed and forced to make amends. This increases the **security** learned earlier, reinforces the **mastery** leading to successful **exploration** in youth.

It is enough that the violation has been discovered, the child made aware of the adult's displeasure, and recompense made to the one offended. Punishment is not only superfluous and irrelevant, it is damaging; it prolongs the child's experience of the event. The child lives in the **now**. When a violation occurs, it should be remedied, the child being told in **rational** and **respectful** tones why the behavior cannot be condoned, and the event is **finished** in the child's mind. To prolong it by sending the child to his room, forcing a meaningless task as compensation, deprivation of food—never!—or any other favored adult punishment is to deprive the child of **now** and force a miserable extension of a past. The punishment means nothing to the child, does not drive home the message with any greater force, but simply robs the child of the next experience it could have.

Your approach to punishment of children simply mirrors the way you punish adult offenders. Those who prove themselves unfit to enjoy the freedoms of your society are incarcerated, deprived of mobility. This is suitable as it is freedom and mobility that are most dear to the adult; in addition, those posing a physical threat to others have no business inflicting their depravity on others.

The child's mind works far differently, and if you approach it as simply a miniature and unformed version of the adult mind, not only are you demonstrating disrespect, but your punishment will not work. A period of enforced solitary confinement is not interpreted as compensation for any violation committed because it bears no resemblance to the crime. It is simply seen as an arbitrary punishment meted out by an adult divorced from reason and respect.

Children will sometimes do the most outrageously immoral things—stealing, lying, hitting—and if you ask why, they say, "I don't know." They are not being evasive. **They don't know.** Knowing that immorality exists, they try it out to see how it feels, how the act of committing a violation resonates inside. It is essential to the achievement of mastery that life be explored in all its facets, both good and bad. When caught in a violation, therefore, it is enough to sit the child on your knee and explain why the act is wrong, why it cannot be tolerated in a society based on reason and respect. The child will already feel bad inside because of the violation, and to have that feeling confirmed by the adult's reason will drive the point home as nothing else can. To prolong the experience with punishment is to smother the child's native grace and comprehension with the arbitrary and irrelevant abandonment of reason.

The child wants nothing more than to please the parent, to live up to expectations, to grow to **master** the world as does the adult. Transgressions are the child's determination to explore every facet of existence; the child will feel the violation as a discordant resonance within; coupling that with reason, in the form of explanation, is how the child learns to master the world and those impulses that are best left unexpressed.

To subject the child to the arbitrary and capricious anger of the parent is to re-create the Biblical flooding of the world when the human species brought displeasure to God's eyes. You have graduated from that image to a God of love, have you not? Allow your parenting techniques to follow.

You will notice that older children tend to rigidly separate themselves by sex. Boys and girls live in different worlds, regarding the other with revulsion or, at best, indifference.

Why? For one thing, the special synthesis of male and female is expressed and strengthened through the sexual act. Prepubescent children are obviously incapable of such behavior.

That synthesis, again, derives from the unique qualities of each sex. While your technological society may diminish the rigidity of sex role differentiation, not even two decades of the most strident feminism can obliterate the foundation of your species!

The male is more concerned with **physical** reality while the female concentrates on **inner** reality.

Boys naturally love to play war, cops and robbers, cowboys and Indians, to build spaceships, forts and tree houses, form secret clubs, roll in dirt from head to toe, hunt worms and snakes and frogs. All these are a physical manipulation of the environment, either playing out certain grand themes of your society—war—or reveling in the natural world—earth and its creatures.

Girls, concentrating on inner reality, share experience just as intense but without the outer manifestation. They are more actively dreaming, planning, thinking, wishing and hoping. Girls seem to chatter an awful lot because through verbal expression they share their inner storms and fires with each other. Boys are more likely to communicate in monosyllables. Girls concentrate more on **nurturance**—of pets, dolls and babies—as opposed to boys' mere **collecting** of the creatures of the earth.

The raging battle over what is innate and what is cultural has so obscured your understanding that there are some claiming that there are no differences between boys and girls, save their anatomy. And what of their anatomy? Which displays an **outer** device for all the world to see, and which an **inner**, hidden from view?

Your bodies always reflect inner truth.

It is only your culture, divorced from the natural order and trampling inner life for outer, second-hand reality, that would consider the bearer of inner truth, the female, to be inferior. Differences—yes!—but inequality—no!

Remember that children are your closest link to the natural order. If you doubt the innate differences between boys and girls, plunk a bunch of ten-year-olds together and observe what happens. Observe the groupings and the nature of their conversations. This is not socialization at work here. This is nature.

Observing parents with their children, you may feel sorry for those young ones whose parents so shelter them from any and every possible mishap that they live virtually in a cage. This bothers you for deep reasons, resonates discordantly inside you, yet you may not have known why.

It is because you intuitively understand that the central task of later childhood is to learn **mastery**. To learn mastery means that one must learn one's limits, throw oneself up against the parameters of physical life and see where one lands—to bump and scrape and fall as a means of learning one's limits. Parents who deny their children such explorations are in fact stunting their children's growth as no hormone deficiency ever has. The parent's job in early childhood is to provide security; in later childhood, the parent is to supervise the child's mastery of physical life. Obviously, there are many dangers inherent in the world; the wise parent learns to distinguish them and to explain to the child with reason why certain avenues are not to be permitted. Anything threatening permanent harm to the body or psyche is to be avoided. Those paths leading to the possibility of physical harm of a temporary nature are to be granted. Such is the child's **job**.

Is there any sight sadder than a child stuffed into a military uniform?

Again, as your culture is divorced from the natural order, you seek to impose the filter of middle age on all other ages, leaving childhood and old age lacking, in your eyes.

The military is not only an adult expression—building upon the strength and competence of adulthood—but in your society it is institutionalized fear. As we have seen, the young child knows nothing of fear; such is the exclusive domain of adults. To smother the child's natural rhythms with the lockstep of shiny black boots; to pollute the natural, trusting sympathy with the cowering fear of adulthood; to trample the intuitive sense of divinity with instruction in evil, represents perhaps your society's supreme depravity.

To sum up, the older child's central guiding task or filter is that of **mastery**. While the body moves toward a stronger and more adult shape, the mind comes to grasp symbolic manipulation and the history and contours of its culture.

All this is groundwork for the next phase, youth.

The wise parent of the older child, having furnished the requisite security in early life, withdraws to the extent consonant with the child's need for safety, permits the child to explore the world in as unhindered a manner as possible, understands the rising importance of the peer group, and that each child is born with its **own** intent and search for fulfillment, which may contrast sharply with the adult's beliefs about what gives life meaning. While ever present to deal with questions, battles and injustice, the parent takes a step back, allowing the beloved child to float on its sea of security to the land of mastery.

CHAPTER FORTY-SEVEN

Youth

The cusp between late childhood and youth is the most significant, the most traumatic, the most fraught with challenge, of any in the span of life. If you doubt this, visit any junior high school.

The parent watches in horror as the previously sweet-natured and compliant child seems to devolve into an atavistic replica of its simian ancestors, in behavior and appearance.

What is occurring here?

Remember that each cusp brings a rush of intent and energy from the parallel selves waiting at the **next** cusp, planting psychological and physical seeds to ensure proper growth for the successful entry into the following stage of life.

Youth, as you will grant, is the stretch of years between childhood and adulthood.

There is thus no juncture, or cusp, that is so wrenching to the psyche. The child exists in a mental and physical world all its own, which the adult may glimpse only rarely and crudely. To push toward successful entry into adulthood requires that the psyche literally be unraveled and rebuilt from scratch. All of the learning, the security and mastery of childhood are incorporated into an entirely new structure, allowing the assumption of full status as an adult in your society. The cusp of youth, then, at about age fourteen, is so fraught with trauma because there is no life point where the psyche is so rent asunder, restructured from the ground up.

You may thus find wild mood swings, sudden growth spurts, snarling disobedience, foul language to embarrass a sailor, experimentation with drugs, and rejection of the toys of childhood and the strictures of adulthood.

The early adolescent is a gangly, uncoordinated creature. The body always reflects the inner condition. The psyche is literally unraveling, sorting itself out into new configurations, and this activity finds reflection in the physical awkwardness of early youth.

We are not speaking figuratively. Everything physical on your earth is but a reflection of electromagnetic reality. Each person's psyche is composed of patterns or grids of electromagnetic energy; the shape and contours determine personality and all other individual attributes. In early adolescence, particularly at the cusp, these structures dissolve, except to the extent required for the continued sustaining of physical life—the autonomic bodily processes—while the personality elements of the psyche are entirely reshaped. Reflecting this, the early youth is impulsive, moody, often depressed, alienated, confused, angry and feels unanchored.

For those who can get past the language and mood swings, this age group can offer unparalleled joy to work with. For at no other time is the adult world so embraced, in the form of hero worship. At the cusp, the soul of age twenty-one calls back in unprecedented intensity, and the urge to grow successfully to that age propels the early youth into the arms of role models seeming to meet the lofty standards to which the youth holds himself.

This is why young adults can hold such sway and magic over early youth. Observe the unlimited love and devotion early youth grants a wise and irreverent counselor at summer camp. No other age group clings to adults with such tenacity as, looking in the eyes of the young adult, early youth finds reflected the hoped-for successful evolution to adulthood.

The fundamental task of early adulthood is **choice**. Age twenty-one, in your culture, brings issues of career, college or graduate school, whether to start a family or maintain independence.

Building on the mastery of late childhood, growing toward the time of choice lying at the next cusp, the onset of the stage of youth evokes the fundamental task or filter of that age: **exploration**.

Having mastered the rudiments of symbolic manipulation, having grown to an extent permitting active participation in the physical world, the youth's task is to explore every nook and cranny of existence, the better to make informed decisions at the later time of choice. A corollary task, then, would be experimentation — sampling all the goodies at the buffet of life.

Early youth is the most likely time for homosexual experience. In part this is due to leftover revulsion toward the opposite sex that characterizes later childhood. Yet these rushing, raging hormones have to go somewhere! And as the body suddenly brings new and delicious pleasures, it is natural to want to share the experience with one's friends. It is an exploration, then, both of the body as it sprouts new sensations and of joining with friends in the new world of sex.

In your society, with its rampant drug culture, it is natural that those in early youth will both be exposed to and likely to participate in the use of drugs. This area is so laden with fear and genuine concern that it is difficult for even the sagest parent to know how to react. On the one hand, a certain degree of exploration, of experimentation, can be considered healthy, in that early youth is the best time for it, the central focus of that age. On the other hand, drugs can carry great physical danger, as well as the possibility of addiction. Every experience in early youth is so crucial because the psyche is in the process of unraveling and reshaping itself, and an unhealthy investment in one area of life — like drugs — can warp the psyche out of healthy development and retard successful attainment of adulthood.

By early youth, the opportunities for parental intervention and control are diminished. The groundwork must have been laid earlier. Does the parent head straight for the liquor cabinet upon arriving home after work, or in moments of stress? Or are life's challenges faced directly, without retreat to the escapism of drugs and alcohol? Does the child observe the parents and his friends occasionally enjoying alcohol or other drugs as a means of enhancing a convivial evening? All these impressions are duly stored away, to be unlocked at early youth. Proper education about the role of drugs, then, begins when the child is too young to speak.

In early youth the first hesitant romantic attachments may be made. Again, this is the result of the next cusp, age twenty-one, calling back and planting the seeds to sprout throughout youth so that when twenty-one, the time of choice, is attained, there will be sufficient romantic experience from which one can make clear and intelligent choices about partners.

Physiologically, puberty brings about a sudden growth spurt. You see, the body does not follow an even, deliberate path from infancy to adulthood. Infants grow like weeds. Later childhood brings a gradual increase in stature and muscle. But at the cusp of youth, with the urgent entreaties from young adulthood, the body leaps into action, pouring hormones into the bloodstream, working overtime to struggle toward the physical shape of adulthood, much as the psyche unravels to assume the contours of adulthood.

The unbalanced psyche is reflected in the bodies of early youth. Most excruciating is the appearance of acne, just at the time when the opposite sex becomes of interest, just when appearance assumes unprecedented importance. Is this some cruel cosmic joke? No, the body reflects the psyche and there is such imbalance in the psyche's form that the body reflects this in secretions gone haywire.

The peer group assumes importance as at no other time. For in late childhood, while the child would prefer playing with those of his age, he is perfectly content to return to the lap of the parent, to be cuddled and stroked.

And what would happen if you tried the same with your fourteen-year-old? The child is repelled from the parents because the call from the next cusp, the time of choice, requires a rejection of childish dependence. Choice can only be made if one is secure in one's mind, body and competence; the urgency with which it is called back to the early youth compels a sudden break with the formerly important parents. No more hand holding now! No more kisses good-bye in front of one's friends! Nothing that indicates the slightest dependence on one's parents.

Parents can often find this stage almost as traumatic as the early youth, for it is so bewildering that the formerly close and trusting relationship has seemingly been tossed out the window. Again, the wise parent anticipates this, appreciates the unique path of the child and withdraws.

Do not think you are not still cherished and loved, O wounded parents! Your children just can't tell you the way they used to, but the **feeling** is still there, riding on the **security** you provided in early childhood and the **mastery** you permitted in later childhood. But open professions of love and respect will have to wait until the next cusp, when the urgent need for distance has healed to acceptance and friendship as equals.

Youth seems such a wondrous and magical time from the perspective of adulthood because it is the time when all paths lie open, life is without limit, the whole world lies ripe for discovery and exploration. Those in middle age, however content with the choices made, cannot help but cast a somewhat envious eye upon the freedom and limitless potential of youth. This is how the adult world perceives youth, and it is valid as far as it goes.

But from the filter of youth, such limitless choice and opportunity can also evoke panic, anguish, indecision and fright. For while intuitively sensing that the time of choice is approaching, there can be too many choices and no clear guidance as to how to select from among them. Youth is the time of deepest insecurity, for coupled with the psyche's unraveling and re-forming—evoking the eternal lament of "Who am I?"—the infinite field of choice can result in quiet terror. For the psyche is unable to choose during youth, is working toward the time of choice, so the crush of possibilities and options can be overwhelming.

Youth is the time of deepest insecurity, then, the phase of life when all paths lie open but without the maturity to effectively choose among them. Time, only time, will bring the maturity and insight to step into full adulthood.

Youth is a time of idealism, as in no other stage of life. Why?

The world of the child is egocentric. One learns that oneself is secure, and one then masters one's own physical and mental processes. The child lives in a cocoon quite divorced from the world of adults. The child cannot tell a capitalist from a Marxist, despite the horns and hooves on the latter.

In youth, as the psyche is wrenched apart to allow the influx of adult cognitive and emotional development, the child is suddenly thrust into the greater world. The grand themes of the culture will rush into the psyche, seeping into the gaps left by its reconfiguration, evoking urgent and compelling interest in the events of society and the larger world.

The child simply accepts whatever culture it is born into. Speak French? Fine, mais oui. Spanish? Sí, claro. English? You got it.

But in youth, as the critical faculties of adulthood are thrust upon the psyche, the child is wrenched from mere passive **acceptance** to **active** participation, as indeed any fully functioning adult must become aware of and participate in the larger society. Suddenly yanked from the security of childhood, without the full cognitive structure of adulthood, the youth is left enthralled by the workings of larger society, while stunned by the enormous gap between real and ideal.

The functioning adult understands that change comes slowly, that there is much misery and suffering in the world, that one must narrow one's focus to those few avenues of activity likely to bring greatest benefit. The world holds an infinity of problems while each life holds a finite number of days. Growing up is learning to channel one's energy into those avenues bringing personal and societal growth, leaving the remaining battles to others.

Youth, lacking this comprehension, is simply scandalized by the state of society. Sensing the ideal rushing through every vein and fiber, the evidence of one's eyes revealing how far the real falls below the ideal, youth turns its unlimited energy to protest and indignation: What is this mess you grown-ups have made of the world?

Youth is a time, as no other, when the **genuine** source of the world's creation flows into consciousness. The unhinged psyche permits this infusion of intuitive understanding, a means of restoring to the psyche those fundamentals every child is born knowing but that, particularly in your culture, are trampled during the socialization process. The fundamental principles of your world are thus restored once again—you create your own reality; the world is a rationally ordered, divinely inspired corner of creation—and thus compel the youth to compare this intuitive knowledge with the state of society. In your culture, with the gap between intuitive understanding and physical reality so enormous, youths are understandably outraged.

There is a great danger, then, that this gap will be perceived as so huge and unbridgeable that the youth surrenders, gives up, withdraws from active participation in life. In extreme cases this leads to teen-age suicide (one of other factors, of course). If the real world falls so far short of the ideal, the sensed divine, natural order, the youth can throw in the towel, find no reason to crawl out of bed every morning.

Again, growing up is a process of learning that while no one can confront every problem confronting a society, there are battles that, if zeroed in on and pursued tenaciously, can result in victory. This is true both on a personal level—creating one's own life—and on the societal level—narrowing down the focus to one or two societal issues and attacking them relentlessly.

Youth is scandalized by the adult world's seeming indifference to the problems of the world, the monotonous regularity of each work day, appearing devoid of purpose and satisfaction. The purpose or filter of middle age is not exploration but consolidation, and it naturally follows that one's battles, having long ago been chosen, do not carry such urgency as they do for the youth, feeling overwhelmed by the state of the world.

There is little the wise parent can do for the young person, struggling to make sense of a world seemingly gone mad, falling so very far short of the sensed natural order. The groundwork will have to have been laid in childhood, when the child views the parent approaching each new day with **purpose**, meeting problems head on and tackling them with courage and tenacity. This teaches the young child that the world **makes sense**, that **action leads to consequence**, that **one creates one's own reality**. These lessons, while not consciously available to the youth, are nonetheless tucked inside the nooks and crannies of the unraveling psyche, and will sustain the youth through that anguished era of real versus ideal, landing him or her safely on the opposite shore, young adulthood, with security and mastery intact, exploration pursued, ready for choice.

We have seen, in our discussion of sexuality, how this issue raises more conflicts than any other when middle age meets youth.

Since the filter of middle age is of consolidation, it is a time when emotional commitments are to be cemented. This is accomplished, among other ways, by a long-term romantic relationship enhanced by sex.

The youth is incapable of such long-term commitments. The time of choice and consolidation lies ahead. The youth's task or filter is exploration.

Your society is burdened with so much encrusted belief, gunking up what should be an arena of guiltless pleasure, that it is the rare parent who can deal honestly and effectively with the adolescent child's sexuality.

Many parents simply refuse to deal with it. They refuse to acknowledge the sexual awakening of their children, refuse to believe that any experimentation is taking place. They could never muster the courage to speak to the child about it. The child, sensing the parent's profound discomfort, will do his or her best to tiptoe around the subject, not leave any blatant clues lying around, and suffer a burden of guilt and secrecy, not knowing why such pleasure should be the source of such repression.

On the other extreme are the parents who shrilly rail against any sexual exploration, stuffing their children's heads with the detritus of the millennia, hauling out ancient Biblical proscriptions devoid of any application to today, suffusing the arena of sex with guilt, shame and condemnation to Hell.

Such parents are generally still working through their own youthful sexual conflicts.

The youth is growing toward a time of choice and commitment, but is not there yet. Youth is the time of **exploration**. In addition, there is an urgency in the uneven rush of hormones that compels the youth to sexual experience. This is precisely the intent of the twenty-one-year-old self in triggering puberty: that the youth literally conduct countless rehearsals of the sex act, in preparation for the time of choice, when such experience can be used as a basis for intelligent decision.

While there is a romantic component to much of adolescent sexuality, such is generally superficial. The puppy love of early youth gives way to longer-lasting relationships, but none can carry the true depth of adulthood. That lies ahead. Again, youth conducts rehearsals of the challenges waiting in the future.

Compounding the distance between middle age and youth over sexuality is that middle age often brings a decline both in desire and performance. There is a certain amount of envy, then, when observing the supple, young bodies cavorting without commitment. Envy results in prohibition against the joy of others, and this is a further nail in the coffin of rational discourse between parent and youth.

The fact remains: Whether you ignore it, wish it away or condemn it, they are going to do it anyway. This is their job, their task. The time when the parent exercised total control over the child's actions has been gone for ten years.

Now, we do not wish to imply that all youths must engage in sexual conduct or be considered misfits. While most will choose sexual exploration, there are those who will not, either for reasons of shyness, immaturity, fear or simply having other avenues for expending one's energy. There is no shame in remaining a virgin, just as there is no shame in surrendering it. Variety is the signature of Divine Grace, and as each youth is set upon a highly private and unique path, an infinite variety of experience will result. We do not mean to imply, then, that those bowing out of sexual exploration are somehow deprived for the choice.

Given that most adolescents do choose to explore sexuality, what course can the wise and concerned parent steer?

Again, the groundwork must have been laid earlier. There must be an appreciation of the body, a recognition of its divinity and an embrace of the sensations it brings. Seeing the parent enjoying the body—not in sexual activity but elsewhere—teaches the child that the body is a source of pleasure and happiness, to be cherished and appreciated.

Building on that will be the parent's romantic status and the nature of that attachment. If the parents are married, affectionate with each other, have been through ups and downs which left the bond bruised but intact, the child learns that one of life's greatest rewards is to share the path of life with a partner at one's side. This will carry over to the adolescent's sexual explorations and hesitant romantic approaches, urging the youth forward to a healthy evolution to adulthood.

Finally, the enlightened parent talks to the child about sex. There will be plenty of questions from young children, and if they are answered honestly, openly, with neither shame nor a retreat to technical terminology, the child learns that sex is a natural part of life, one more facet of a happy existence.

It is the rare adolescent who maintains such intimate bonds with the parents that much verbal information can be exchanged about sexual practices. If the parent has been open and calm about the subject in childhood, however, the youth may well seek an adult understanding from the parent. This is a privileged moment for the parent, a badge of honor atop all the purple hearts* childrearing wrought.

There is one fundamental issue that simply must be insisted on by parents. That is the use of birth control. Nothing is more devastating to the task of youth than to have the filters of later stages of life—choice and consolidation—suddenly thrust upon one's time of exploration. The psyche of the youth is literally unequipped to handle the responsibilities of parenthood, resulting either in defective parenting when the child is young—and we have seen where that leads—and/or the blunting of the youth's exploratory ventures, the psyche left warped and unfinished.

Again, parents who want to wish away their children's sexuality will never broach the subject of birth control; those who condemn it will refuse to discuss it, viewing it as acceptance of behavior they cannot condone. Of course the church jumps in with its Dead Sea Scroll barnacles of sin and guilt and never blocking God's way, should He care to hop into the process and ruin the young lives of those He claims to love.

In a world choking with overpopulation, with your understanding of the youth's central task of exploration, the inability to accept the mantle of responsibility concomitant with parenthood, no sane or loving parent can choose otherwise: Discuss it, approve of it and buy it if your children ask.

Youth can be an excruciating time for those who fail to "fit in" to the values the society, and particularly youth culture, holds as the standard.

Youth is the stage when one literally rehearses for the later induction into society. Part of functioning as an adult member of society is learning to express one's individuality within certain limits designed for the good of both one's self and the society. While conformity can be stifling if carried too far, nonetheless there are certain ground rules in every culture as to what behavior is tolerable and what is not.

In youth, playing with the themes of adulthood but without the cognitive and emotional development to absorb them maturely, the importance of accepting society's standards can result in an obsession with fitting in.

The peer group reigns supreme; within it, groups form based on intellect, talent, delinquency, politics and athletics. The issue of acceptance into a larger

---

*A purple heart is a military medal awarded to those wounded in combat.

group is explored as a means of stretching toward the adult's functioning in society.

Again, the distraught parent may well worry about the low-lifes one's child hangs out with. To make an issue out of it is simply to ensure enhanced fidelity to the group. The child is struggling with the future responsibility of adulthood, in an incomplete and attenuated fashion due to the unraveled condition of the psyche. It is simply a matter of time, then, healing the psyche's wounds and loosening the dependence on the peer group.

The adolescent body is stronger, more resilient, powerful and flexible than the body at any other stage of life. While the body can retain fine physique and musculature for the entirety of life, it requires some work to keep it in condition once past youth. The youth can lie in front of the television all day, smoking cartons of cigarettes, and still climb Mt. McKinley on an afternoon field trip.

The body's condition always reflects the state of the psyche and the purpose of one's stage of life. The youth's psyche hums with the rush of intent being sent back from the future, urging it toward adulthood, and the adolescent body's growth into strength and flexibility represents the anchoring into physical reality required for later consolidation in middle age. Further, it naturally follows that the stage of life infused with exploration should require a supremely powerful body, the better to carry it to all its adventures and provide it with endurance, whatever it faces. To **explore** requires **strength** and **flexibility**; the body of youth mirrors the intent of the psyche in providing an engine of unequalled power to carry out such explorations.

Youth, then, is the age of exploration. Bursting from the insular cocoon of childhood, stretching toward the commitments of adulthood, the youth's psyche literally unravels, incorporating the lessons learned in childhood, absorbing the rush of future growth and commitment, consolidating them in an incoherent jumble resulting in impulse, idealism, romance, sex and passion—all the contours of adult life, played out in exaggerated fashion. It is a wondrous time, indeed, but one also suffused with trauma and inner hurt, even panic. Like the child, everything hurts deeply and it hurts now. The balance and perspective of adulthood lie ahead.

Successful adolescence means exploration into every corner of creation one finds of interest. Marching securely forward on the mastery of childhood, rushing to embrace the freedom and achievement of adulthood, the youth hangs suspended in an atmosphere of unlimited potential, grasping at every flavor and twist life can offer, living **deeply** and **now** as it builds a bed of experience on which adulthood, the rest of life, can lie.

CHAPTER FORTY-EIGHT

Early Adulthood

The cusp ushering in early adulthood is where the security, mastery and exploration of childhood and youth meet the challenge of stepping into full responsibility as an adult. This can be a time of great indecision, even panic, as one may still not have a clear sense of one's purpose in life, which paths will bring greatest happiness, and the results can be either paralysis—refusing to choose—or premature decision making—jumping into a secure niche before allowing oneself time to allow the answers to well up from within.

For while the task of early adulthood is **choice**, this does not mean that all life choices must be made at the cusp, any more than those at the cusp of youth are as confident and sturdy in their explorations as are those in later youth. The cusp of early adulthood ushers in the time of choice but does not demand that all choices be made at that time.

Again, well-meaning parents can interfere to their children's detriment by shoving them into secure little paths, pressuring them into marriage and grandchild-rearing, forcing them prematurely into the consolidation of middle age. Again, the filters differ, and from the filter of middle age—where one had best have made one's choices—the floundering and indecisive early adult can appear simply lazy, apathetic or unambitious. The well-meaning parent can step in and force the child onto a path the parent would find of benefit—or **has** found to be of benefit—without appreciating the unique path each individual must tread, at his or her own speed, in his or her own direction.

Left alone, things will sort themselves out. The decisions and choices will be made. To hurry them, to impose middle-aged values on them, is to rob the child of living a life of his or her own manufacture.

Most crucial at the cusp of early adulthood, about age twenty-one, will be the call from age twenty-eight, reaching back in time to impress upon the early adult the urgency of choosing. Remember that while no life can conquer all problems presented to it, a life well lived will choose a few select challenges, zero in on them and work without cease to see them through to triumph. While age twenty-eight, the cusp at that time, carries no special and urgent task—as do all the cusps preceding it—it represents a time of reflection or review on the progress made so far. To that end, the cusp at this age calls back to the early adult, urging and guiding him or her to make choices that one will find, upon reaching twenty-eight, to have been the best possible for personal and societal growth and satisfaction.

The cusp of early adulthood, then, initiates the process of decision making, without requiring that every decision be made at that point. It simply gets the ball rolling.

In your culture, those attending college are automatically granted a certain leeway in the form of extended adolescence. They continue in a world strung halfway between adolescence and full adulthood, living freed from parental control but still ensconced in an institution with their peers, subject to the rules and regulations of their elders. This can provide a safe cocoon within which to complete the exploration of youth and anticipate the time of choice lying ahead.

Panic can set in, however, if by the senior year a graduate school path has not been chosen, and one's life is not mapped out to the day for the next fifty years. Until this time, one has always known the expectations parents and society held, whether or not one chose to live up to them. With youth's end, one must set one's own expectations, standards and drive.

In your culture, divorced from the natural order, you define people on the basis of their careers. The mantle of profession determines the worth of an individual above anything else. There are no awards, no citations, no medals handed out for sage and loving parenting, for respecting the divinity of every creature on earth, for cherishing the unique path of every individual. None of these attributes can be translated into second-hand reality and are therefore disregarded in determining the worth of an individual. Money, status, fame—all second-hand reality—are the standards by which you measure a person's worth.

There can be a certain dread, therefore, coming from the exuberant restoration of intuitive knowledge surfacing in youth, to surrendering the sensed natural order for the harness and bit of corporate life. Many early adults seem to drift without inner compass because they sense the violation of the natural order that is the world of work in your culture, and there is a period of dynamic tension between the two worlds.

Ultimately, unless one is to live off the land or in a monastery, the early adult in your culture casts his lot with second-hand reality. The divorce from the natural order, begun in earliest infancy, is complete.

At age twenty-one, those parallel selves that have followed one throughout life, and whose future projections soar back in new intensity, jostle for attention at the time of choice. Any child will feel leanings toward a variety of paths and professions, except in rare cases, and the time of choice is when those paths must be consciously and realistically evaluated. Given time, that path most conducive to one's later fulfillment will resonate with greater intensity, will feel better than the other paths. The choice can then be made and the path pursued with vigor.

We emphasize again that this need not occur at age twenty-one but that the process is initiated then. It can be of great benefit to hold a variety of short-term jobs in the fields of interest, to see which sparks the greatest interest and enthusiasm, holds the greatest potential for personal and societal growth. Then the choice can more realistically be made.

Those electing not to attend college are left floundering for a while, for the age of choice, ushered in at the cusp around age twenty-one, is yet to come. Yet one must make some choice, unless the parents are willing to relieve one of the burden of creating one's reality and allow continued living at home without responsibility. The great mistake of those at this age, prior to the cusp, is to select a path or profession and never deviate from it. This should be considered the final stage of youth's exploration, and no better time to travel, hold a variety of different jobs and sample widely the variety of life. Then, at the time of choice, the early adult will be that much further along in choosing intelligently.

You are all set upon a highly unique and private path. While an inherently gregarious species, who at base share far deeper commonality than difference, still the superficial elements of personality and aptitude will vary markedly. It is often the case that artists will spring from families devoid of artistry, as a means of both bringing art to the deadened family group and to provide the artist with the security of routine in early life, from which later explorations can spring. There is nothing wrong with the early adult choosing to see the world, any more than with the one who knows from birth that he wishes to be a doctor or engineer or painter. Variety is the hallmark of Divine Grace, the ink with which you each write your life's history on the ledger of the universe, and the wise parent and society will be those who permit each child to grow toward the sun of his own choice.

In addition to questions of professional choice, the cusp of early adulthood brings to the fore issues of attachment, marriage and parenthood.

Building on the romantic and sexual explorations of youth, stretching toward the consolidation of middle age, the early adult faces, for the first time, the opportunity to establish a long-term relationship with a partner. Again, around the time of the cusp, such a possibility will just be beginning to blossom, and it is unreasonable to expect all such young adults to immediately settle down for life. There is much jockeying and playing of romantic musical chairs in early adulthood, then, as the sensed urge toward long-term commitment sorts itself out from the peripatetic explorations of youth.

Those who have grown to early adulthood without security, mastery and thorough exploration will feel cast adrift, unable to find their bearing from an inner compass. They don't know who they are. They are unable to enjoy solitude. Such early adults may thus spring into romantic attachments with fervor, as a way of relieving the fright and boredom of being alone. Yet what have such to offer a partner, if they do not know themselves?

Your statistics demonstrate that the earlier the marriage, the greater probability it will not last. Certainly almost all teen-age marriages are doomed from the start. There is still far too much work ahead on a personal level to allow oneself to be submerged into the greater identity of a twosome; further, as each partner grows in his or her unique path, the likelihood is great that those paths will diverge down the road.

The later in life the marriage—the more strands have been nailed down, the more choices have been made, the more secure one is in oneself—the longer the marriage will last.

There are some, however, who do a thorough and conscientious job of sorting out the choices before them and realize that marriage and parenthood are what interest them most. Since relationships with others almost always provide greater challenge and sources of satisfaction than one's career choice, it naturally follows that one's true "work" in life is more likely to be centered in the home than in the office. A strong urge toward parenthood, then, is not only the recognition of this but also includes, quite unconsciously, the sensed but unheard cries from one's unborn children, who have chosen their parents and await the time of conception.

Again, only in a culture divorced from the natural order would you hold the successful mother in lower esteem than a garbage collector. The greatest challenges and rewards come from relationships with others, and there is no triumph on earth like that of the parent raising sane, happy, self-directed children. Sensing this, hearing the call from the future selves echoing back through time, the early adult may choose marriage and parenthood when still at the cusp.

You will notice a difference between the sexes in this regard. Women are more likely to demand a depth of emotional commitment to a relationship, while men would prefer to continue the youthful scampering a bit longer. While the child is best raised by two involved and loving parents, the fact remains that the burden of childrearing—the literal possibility of childrearing—lies with the mother. Building on the young child's need for security, then, the woman moving toward motherhood will naturally look for the same. How else to explain the phenomenon of young women marrying older, and invariably richer, men? Is there an equal occurrence of young men marrying older women, whatever their wealth? Sensing the approach of motherhood, sensing her child's need for security, the young woman will appraise her prospects more coolly, more realistically, not so eager to engage in carnal gymnastics with every suitor at her doorstep.

The young man, on the other hand, more concerned with continued exploration of the physical world, is not so compelled to nest building. He would prefer to hold onto his freedom as long as possible. There is no urgency, therefore, in the young man's thoughts of marriage and fatherhood—no sense of needing to weave a cocoon of security.

The result can be like two species from different galaxies communicating with crude sign language. The drive, the impetus, differs; the two sexes literally do not see eye to eye on the subject of marriage and commitment. The needs are different.

The rigid straitjacket of manhood thus works to the woman's advantage in your society. For if the man could find his needs for affection and touch fulfilled by his buddies, there would be no urgency to seek it in the arms of a woman. There is a trade-off, then, the man surrendering some freedom for the continued presence of a woman, he having met standards of stability and security.

Now, almost all of this is relative to your culture. It is innate that women consider more carefully the welfare of their children than men. The maternal bond is more all-encompassing than the paternal bond, however much delight the father takes in his children, and they in him. The male is more able to relegate fatherhood to one compartment of his multifaceted attention, while motherhood colors every aspect of a woman's life. This is innate.

You see this among animals in the wild, among native peoples. The degree of male participation in childraising differs from species to species, tribe to tribe. But it is never the case that children become the responsibility of the male to a greater degree than of the female.

All of this ties in with our discussion of early adulthood and the cusp at that point, in that issues of security and searching for a life partner will present themselves with greater urgency to the female. There is the additional factor of the biological clock ticking away. Motherhood cannot be postponed forever, to be enjoyed in retirement after one's career is over. It must be addressed fairly early in adulthood.

For the male the issue is not quite so pressing. Women observe in exasperation that men just "won't make commitments." Of course they can. They simply do not feel the urgency to do so.

The time of choice can be one of intuitive acceptance of one's healthiest path or one fraught with indecision or panic, depending on one's connection with the inner self. If one has come to trust impulse and intuition as the divine urgings that they are, the time of choice will be relatively painless; the best path will simply present itself and be accepted. If one has been taught to distrust one's impulses, to ignore the whispers of parallel selves, the time of choice will be as if one is cast adrift in a hostile sea without compass or rudder. In such a case, a choice is often made to clutch to the security of second-hand reality rather than follow the inner wisdom of one's intuition.

This explains why those with careers in commerce and banking are almost invariably conservative. The conservative's motivating fuel is the fear of impulses. Since impulses are the whispers of life itself, urging one to a life in firsthand reality, those taught to fear and repress impulses naturally flock toward fields entirely divorced from firsthand reality and the natural order: banking and business. It is not that those who join these fields later become conservative. The initial decision is propelled by the conservative's central fear of impulses.

Those who retain an intuitive bond with the natural order and their inner selves, despite your culture's every effort to squash that understanding, will feel no inner panic when the time of choice arrives. Such choice is not so much a process of conscious, rational thought but one of **inner listening**. All time is simultaneous; all parallel selves will present themselves for inspection at the cusp of early adulthood; and simply considering each, one by one, and feeling how each **resonates** inside will lead one to the choice bringing greatest fulfillment over a lifetime. This pack of parallel selves, which has followed the individual through childhood and youth now lines up, their future counterparts calling back the likely outcome of a life lived on each of their paths, and one such path will resonate, will **feel** better, than any other. The choice is then simple.

There are those born knowing without question or debate what they want to do when they grow up. In this case, most likely the intent of the greater entity in setting up the life can only find truest expression in one specific career choice, and while other parallel selves will mill around, offering constant free will, most likely one will never deviate from the initial intent.

Early adulthood, then, builds upon the security, mastery and exploration of childhood and youth and makes the first few hesitant steps into adulthood. The process cannot be rushed without detriment to the healthy attainment of an adulthood based on one's private and unique path toward fulfillment. Inner listening, recognition of one's impulses and intuition, will invariably lead to that path most conducive to a happy, satisfying and challenging life.

The cusp occurring at age twenty-eight is not so significant as to warrant in-depth discussion. This cusp is a bridge between the time of initial choice at age twenty-one and the more comprehensive life review that occurs at age thirty-five. The "mid-life crisis," as you term it, is when one intensively examines one's goals and ambitions for the life, compares them with the progress so far and makes readjustments in accordance with what can reasonably be accomplished within one lifetime's span.

The cusp at age twenty-eight is thus a halfway mark, a way station, between the time of choice and the time of evaluation. While no choices need be made at the cusp of early adulthood, the inner processes by which those choices are made should be triggered, and by age twenty-eight some clear sense of one's future goals and challenges made apparent. Not to choose is a choice, and there are those whose lives are richest from never carving a niche in any particular field, but using the earth as a workshop from which to fashion an endless variety of experience. Those who can live such a life successfully, meaning that it becomes the best possible route, are relatively rare. Most find greatest satisfaction from hunkering down with a narrower set of challenges, including career and attachment, and working them through.

Age twenty-eight is the time when the choices made, or not made, beginning at age twenty-one, are examined. Again, most significant is the parallel self calling back from the next age, thirty-five, imbuing the process with a sense of urgency, lest age thirty-five be reached with nothing to evaluate! The mid-life point thus calls back to the late twenties, urging along the process of choice, if it has not already been satisfactorily completed. The cusp around age twenty-eight acts more as a bridge between life periods, then, rather than as a discrete challenge in itself.

CHAPTER FORTY-NINE

Middle Age

It is fair to say that the cusp occurring around age thirty-five ushers in the stretch of years you call middle age. From this point on, the cusps and filters of life are not so rigidly demarcated as they are earlier in life, with the acquisition of symbolic manipulation at age seven, puberty at fourteen, career and romantic choice at age twenty-one. Middle age is essentially a process of consolidation, turning one's full energy into those avenues selected during one's twenties, hunkering down with one's self-selected set of challenges, working to bring them to satisfactory fruition.

The filter of middle age, then, is **consolidation**. Where the energies of youth and early adulthood can be scattered in a million directions, as the world offers both unlimited opportunities and an infinity of problems, by middle age one has selected one's focus, one's set of challenges, and has allowed the rest of the world to tackle those battles not chosen.

The cusp occurring around age thirty-five can often contain a "mid-life crisis" because, as at all other cusps, past and future selves swarm in for evaluation and review as at no other time. The unbounded energy and dreams of youth have given way to a realistic appraisal of what one can reasonably expect to accomplish in one lifetime, and as those past selves rise in force once again, there can be a certain feeling of nostalgia for the glory days of youth, those halcyon years of limitless potential, unbounded energy and infinite opportunity.

At the same time, one's future selves drop into consciousness, presenting themselves in heightened vitality as a means of ensuring that one remains clear regarding the paths most likely to lead to a challenging and satisfying life, to change course if need be. Again, there will always be a path rising in prominence above all others, if the individual involved can quiet the conscious mind and open the inner ear. Often this results in a sudden career change, a return to graduate school or some other sharp break. If a marriage is not working out, the cusp of thirty-five is frequently when it will be discarded. In these cases, often the time of choice, in early adulthood, was rushed, the choices made without inner listening and in too great a haste. At age thirty-five, when the panic of early adulthood has subsided, the process of early adulthood, the time of choice, can literally be replayed, this time with the calm of middle age, and may result in the choice of an entirely new career and attachment direction.

Again, as always, the immediate future cusp calls back in greatest intensity. While all of middle age can be considered the stage of consolidation, and the future self at age forty-two does not represent a radical new direction, this future cusp calls back to ensure that one has honestly and thoroughly evaluated the choices made earlier and compared them with the time left and the reasonableness of one's expectations. For if one has not made substantial progress in one's career of choice by age forty-two, chances are one will not do so. Similarly, if one has not started a family by that age, one has most likely opted out of marriage and parenthood; for women, motherhood is a virtual impossibility much beyond this age. By the early forties, then, one should be fairly well set in one's course; and this cusp calls back to age thirty-five, sparking your "crisis" as the choices of youth are compared with the need for consolidation lying ahead, the better to make conscious adjustment if necessary.

None of this is meant to imply that life should be a constant narrowing of one's circle of interest, a shunting aside of any distracting, irrelevant diversions, a grim and single-minded beeline toward career success or the burdens of parenthood.

The best-lived life is one in which a concerted effort in one area of concentration is enhanced and enriched by an endless stream of new experience, a constant influx of fresh insight and knowledge. Remember that all time is simultaneous; while the filter of middle age is one of consolidation, it can only be enriched by the continued bursts of exploration intrinsic to youth. Further, in parenthood one finds the joy of early childhood all over again and can delight through the child's eyes in first marveling at the colors of a butterfly, waves lapping at the shore or the embrace of the natural world through a house full of pets.

All too often, middle age does become a time of increased complacence, a turning away from the issues of the larger world, settling into a comfortable routine and never budging. Life is far too rich to be fully experienced through evening after evening of falling asleep before the television with a drink in hand. The beauty of your planet is precisely that it is too large to ever permit anyone to tread every square foot of its surface; the avenues of intellectual pursuit far too vast to allow anyone but a fraction of all knowledge; and the flesh-and-blood miracles of children provide a constant stream of delight and rapture to the involved parent.

While middle age naturally brings a narrowing of one's focus, as a means of ensuring the satisfaction in creating one's own reality after hard and determined effort, such a focus is enhanced by the constant influx of fresh experience, keeping one dancing far too fast to ever settle into a rut.

In the arena of relationships, the middle age filter of consolidation should bring a new maturity, a new sense of commitment, of long-term fidelity to one partner.

Before we proceed, let us again affirm that variety is the signature of Divine Grace, and not every person needs a life partner in order to live a satisfying life. There are those whose purposes are best served by solitude, without the distractions and energy drain intrinsic to a long-term relationship. There is no suggestion that such individuals are misfits, then.

For the majority who do find themselves capable and desirous of long-term commitments, however, middle age is the time when such commitments are to be nailed down in earnest. Those who continue the youthful exploratory conquests into middle age indicate a lack of appreciation for the flow of life through the span of years. Often, as your society views death as a descent into the great black void, any evidence of advancing age can only be viewed with panic; by continuing to act young—playing libidinal musical chairs into middle age—one can pretend that one remains young. On deep levels you cannot fool your psyche—it knows exactly how old you are—and this knowledge can gnaw at those unaccepting of life's progress, propelling them into even more inappropriate, youthful behavior.

This is more true of men than women. Again, those women who wish to experience motherhood know they best find themselves a mate and get down to business. Building upon the young child's need for security is the woman's determination to find a stable and responsible mate, one likely to fulfill obligations to family. Men, lacking this inner drive, are more likely to want to continue the sexual hide-and-seek of youth.

The purpose of sexual experience in middle age, in keeping with its filter of consolidation, is to cement a commitment. Since it is the most pleasurable act of which you are capable, and practice in any field makes perfect, there are few aspects of life more fulfilling than a long-term romantic relationship cemented with sex. In youth, sex is simply a physical urge, perhaps accompanied by an attenuated romantic attachment. In early adulthood, the first romantic attachments cannot carry the **depth** of middle-age bonds. It is only in the time of consolidation, when the psyche devotes its full attention to pouring energy into those long-term choices, that the deepest and most satisfying relationships can occur.

Sex is the glue that holds such relationships together. As with any other aspect of middle age, sex can become stale and routine if neglected. You are blessed with minds brimming with unlimited creativity; do save some for the bedroom! For the relationship riding both on the satisfactions of long-term commitment and a concerted effort to infuse the relationship with fresh experience is the most deeply rewarding experience you can know.

There is no need to envy youth and early adulthood in their frantic backseat explorations. As we have said, all such is simply rehearsal for the magical union of sex and commitment that finds fullest expression in middle age.

Again, the body always reflects the state of the psyche and the filter of a given age.

Those in middle age may observe with concern and dismay their bodies of youth losing their fine, sharp edges, as the bathroom scale seems determined to torment you at every opportunity, the flexibility of youth giving way to awaking with new and unwelcome aches and pains.

Remember the filters of life. Youth is the age of exploration, the span of inquisitive and searching experience in every facet of life. Flowing from this, early adulthood is a time of choice, when much exploration may still be required to choose effectively.

By middle age, most choices are made. What need has the middle-aged adult for the strength and agility of youth? There is no reason, given the filter of consolidation, why that body need be maintained.

The psyche supplies a constant flow of energy into your life. In youth, that energy is almost all directed into the body, its construction, growth and explorations. In middle age, with exploration behind, that energy is better spent **intellectually**, in meeting the demands of one's career, marriage and parenthood. It is not that the body is in decline but that the focus of one's energy shifts from pure physical activity to physical activity **driven by intellect**. The psyche is thus reconfigured to devote more energy to the mind, to focused concentration on the choices made, rather than frenetic activity.

Now, as you are seeing in your day, there is a rise in the number of men and women who can continue to perform athletically almost as well as they did in youth. Once again, your beliefs built upon the medical model of a body decaying from birth are being laughed off the planet. There is no reason whatsoever why the body cannot remain fit, vigorous, vital and active for the entire duration of life; indeed, this is the plan. It is only when you saddle the body's innate resilience with beliefs about aging, about death, that you find the literal results in the breakdown of so many elderly bodies. As one more slap in the face of science and medicine, then, as the New Dawn approaches you find middle-aged and elderly persons demonstrating athletic prowess to put to shame many in the stage of youth.

We say this to emphasize that, while the psyche does refocus its energy into the intellect, rather than youth's exclusive concentration on activity, there is no suggestion that the body must decline in resilience or strength. It may require more **work** to maintain that tone, however.

The body reflects the filter of middle age, though the site of consolidation—the waist and hips, primarily—can inspire a longing for the filter of youth, acne or no!

The psyche literally reshapes itself throughout life. Each seven-year stage carries a different fundamental task or set of challenges, and the psyche is literally reconfigured to focus concentration on each successive task. This explains why everyone, from young children to the elderly, finds most of their closest friends among their own age group. There is an intuitive, common understanding among those viewing life through the same filter.

Because the psyche reshapes itself with each successive stage of growth, it is entirely possible to completely forget what it felt like to experience life through an earlier filter. Restricting yourself to the physically perceivable, you may envy the carefree freedom of children while forgetting the enormous challenges inherent in struggling to gain mastery of the world—the view of the world as an infinite mountain on whose flank one seems to make only incremental baby steps. Youth will also be regarded with nostalgia or jealousy, for its freedom, muscle tone and sexual license; entirely forgotten is the inner panic youth can bring—

the suffocating crush of paths and choices without clear direction as to how to choose effectively among them.

While it is natural that one should view life through the filter of whatever ꞈtage one is in, the very best-lived life will be one that retains enough memory of the inner challenge each earlier stage carried, not just the superficial physical coating. All too often, adults have entirely forgotten how their minds worked as children, how they struggled to make sense of the world in youth; and they will apply the filter of consolidation backwards into the past, comparing the relative calm they feel now with the indecision and activity of the children and youths one meets in daily life, and conclude that children have just gone to Hell, but boy, things were different when I was a kid!

They most certainly were not. You were just as impulsive, just as cranky, just as moody, just as indecisive, just as testing of authority. Because you no longer carry the filter of those ages, all this may be lost to you.

While the psyche does literally reconfigure itself throughout life, and it is thus impossible to ever fully live life through the eyes of those in another filter, a conscientious effort at recall, coupled with close attention to the words and deeds of those in other stages of life, can result in returning to a close approximation of the earlier stages of life.

This is so important to those in middle age who have chosen parenthood. The sad fact is that parenting in your culture is essentially a process of divorcing one's children from the natural order into which they are born. This is accomplished because the adult has entirely forgotten how differently one's mind worked as a child; the culture has cut the strands, one by one, connecting one with the natural order, and one thus quite unconsciously sets about replicating the damage by turning one's own children away from the divine natural order.

It is virtually impossible for the adult to truly comprehend the mind of the young child or infant. The urgency of now, the complete absorption in a world of sensation devoid of rational thought is virtually incomprehensible to the adult. This is true of all cultures; the very process of assuming human adulthood is the mature use of the reasoning mind, casting off the filters of childhood. But one must respect one's children where they are, rather than interpreting their actions in the light of adult mastery.

Again, children are not miniature adults. Their minds are not simply crude and amorphous versions of adult cogitative ability. They function in an entirely different fashion. For the infant and young child, there is only one question: Is the world safe? The answer is derived from these questions: Am I loved? Are my needs promptly taken care of? Am I responded to quickly when I cry? Am I fed whenever I ask? Am I hugged and cuddled and stroked whether or not I can return the affection?

The answers to all these questions boil down to the young child's fundamental task of security. If all of the above are answered in the affirmative, day in and day out, the child learns that the world is a safe place, that it is loved and wanted and appreciated.

Thus, there can be no sense in imposing the middle-age filter of consolidation, of order and structure and routine. Feedings on the hour. Nap times on the hour. Toilet on the hour. To subject the child to the routine of adulthood is to deny the very essence of early childhood, which is to enjoy the security of knowing that one's needs and desires will always be met. Now, woe be to the adult who carries such a filter! But to the young child, the very randomness of demands made on the world is a way of determining if one's security is always responded to. In addition, there is so much work going on in the sleep state, drifting back to the greater entity and to the prior lifetime, that one's daily routine will be split in even intervals of sleep and wakefulness, not two monolithic blocks as with the adult. The young child needs more frequent sleep, returning to the nonphysical sources of its life, and upon awaking to the chosen physical life it must know—it **must** know—that the choice has been well made, that the hue and cry set off upon awaking will be responded to by the parents.

There is only damage, disrespect and harm in approaching the young child like a miniature adult, expecting it to perform on schedule.

Similarly, the older child can be a source of exasperation both because of its incessant questioning and because it can so often fail to heed the strictures of the adult world.

Building upon the security learned in early childhood, knowing that the world is a safe place, the older child needs to be certain that **the world makes sense.** For what is the purpose of struggling to achieve mastery of rational thought, if reason is without value? Intuitively sensing that the world is a rationally ordered place, the child needs confirmation from the adult world that this is the case. Everything has a place, a time, a season; the child knows this. It knows it in general but it needs to learn the specifics of the culture into which it was born. There is no crime in saying "I don't know" to a child. The felony occurs when that phrase is not followed by, "Let's find out."

Parents may be puzzled, if not shocked, by the seeming immorality of their older children. Again, it is simply their attempt to master the world, to experience its every facet, to feel the resonance of a violation. For children operate not out of reason but feeling; every experience they have is not stored away intellectually but is filed according to the emotions and feelings it evokes.

You can catch a glimmer of this process as an adult if you daydream, allowing your mind to wander. You may suddenly "come to," realize you are thinking about something entirely unrelated to your initial thoughts. But if you follow the chain back, you will find a string of associations connecting the images and thoughts. The connection will not be a rational one but one guided by the feelings of the events involved. While you consider the outer surface of an event, your daydreaming mind will strip away that patina and ride the emotion intrinsic to the event, building its chain of association upon that feeling.

This is how the child's mind works. It operates not so much out of a desire for knowledge per se but to determine how new experience **feels** inside. Though you grant little validity to feelings, emotions, intuitions and whims, these are the **principal building blocks** of the older child's mastery of the world. What feels good is good, and will be filed away as such. Committing a violation, the child will feel bad, and this alone will serve to steer the child away from such a course, particularly if that feeling is buttressed with reason from the adult. For it is reason for which the child yearns but has not yet fully mastered.

We go on at length about childhood here, perhaps repeating ourselves, because those finding themselves parents in middle age can fall into the trap of imposing their own filter—consolidation—on the stages of childhood, thus robbing children of their unique challenge and viewpoint. The child is entirely unable to consider your filter, O middle-aged parent! It is you who must work to bridge the gap, to couch the child's search for security and mastery in a rationally ordered environment, both respectful of the child's unique path and still urging him or her toward the reason of adulthood. Yes, you must explain things at length, over and over, until the inner resonance your explanation evokes in the child vibrates with sufficient intensity that the lesson is stored and available for recall. To answer the child's question "Why?" with "Because I said so" is to abandon adult reason for which the child looks to you so intently, to affirm that the world does not make sense.

The inner drama of childhood can only rarely, vaguely, be glimpsed by the adult, even by the most attentive and loving parent. The filters are so radically different, the interpretation of each physical event so varied, that one must realistically resign oneself to not truly knowing one's children until they attain adulthood. The sensitive parent is the one who buttons the lips and opens the ears, for every child will offer a host of clues as to its inner storms and fires, if it finds an adult willing to accept these offerings without judgment or disdain. **The world in which the adult lives is not the world in which the child lives.** As we have seen, all perception is relative; the ant does not perceive reality as you do, and neither does the child. While you can only partially and crudely glimpse the child's-eye view of the world, you can nonetheless be of enormous value to the child by establishing that the world is safe and that it makes sense.

If we have robbed the adult world of many of its favored approaches to childrearing—corporal punishment, food deprivation punishment, go-to-your-room punishment, "Because I said so" punishment, paternal lecture punishment, and every other tool in the bag of tricks divorcing the child from the natural order—we have at least handed you one potent weapon in the battles which may lie ahead in youth.

When the angry adolescent cries, "I didn't ask to be born! I didn't ask you to be my parents!" you may now, in full truth and understanding, reply, "Oh yes, you did!"

As we mentioned earlier, the path of life is constructed like a bell curve, with the focus of one's energy and attention gradually concentrating more and more on physical reality and manipulation. This reaches its apex in middle age, during one's "productive" years, as one contributes to the society along the lines of one's talents and interests, actively involved in the dynamic physical mechanics of sustaining the culture.

The psyche of those in middle age, then, is one configured to allow most intense concentration in physical reality. Gone are the dreams and terrors of childhood and youth, for the most part. The focus now is on carving one's niche in a profession, sustaining a long-term commitment (if that choice has been made) and raising one's children. There is little energy left over after these aspects of life are taken care of to be actively daydreaming without regard to their application to the physical world.

Every life is set up with a specific challenge or set of challenges. No one is here for the ride. The mark of a life, then, is how one deals with the problems that arise: head on or duck tail and retreat. It is rarely the case that one's professional choice will carry the full, intrinsic challenge of a lifetime. Your greater entity is not interested in your resumé. It wants to know how you handle those challenges you have chosen ahead of time.

Since relationships with others provide such a fertile bed of opportunity for growth and exploration, as well as for degradation and defeat, most often one can sense the focus of one's life by evaluating the state of one's relationships with friends, family and the world. Is there a particular trouble spot, a source of anxiety that has never been confronted and dismissed effectively? This could be a clue that this touchy area is that chosen by the greater entity as the focus of your life.

So while the time of choice—in your culture—entails selecting among the variety of professional options, and while professional achievement certainly brings feelings of satisfaction, it is rarely the case that one's profession is the site of one's central life task.

The cusps and stages of life occurring after the mid-life point, while occurring with the same frequency, are less clearly defined or demarcated than those previous. In any culture, the tasks of security, mastery, exploration and choice must be met, followed by the consolidation—the intense focus—of middle age. Whether or not one has successfully worked through all these tasks en route to adulthood, chances are one's approach to life will not differ much once adulthood is reached. The baby deprived of love will most likely be unable to become a tender and caring spouse or parent. The challenge has not been met. All of life will inevitably be diminished.

Having said that, understand that you create your own reality every moment, and you are at the mercy of nothing, including your "past." It can just be that much more difficult to override the experiences of the past, to find within oneself the sources of security and mastery that the world failed to provide.

Moving on into middle age, then, the cusp ushers in not so much a new direction as a further consolidation, a narrowing of the focus, a more intense concentration on the tasks and challenges chosen earlier. It is enough to be parent to adolescent children without searching out new avenues of challenge!

Each cusp will serve, as do all others, to bring into awareness the past and future selves, the better to appraise your progress along the course you have chosen to chart. Adjustments can be more easily made at these cusps, as one is aware to a greater degree of what the future can hold and which path will lead to one's greatest fulfillment.

As one ages, one may find that one has less energy in middle and late-middle age than in youth. While this may appear to be a sign of decay to those limiting themselves to the physically perceivable and considering death a terminus, in light of our discussion you should see that there is no purpose to maintaining high energy levels throughout all of life. The exploration of youth and the agonized time of choice of early adulthood are past. One has made one's choices, for better or worse, and middle age is when those paths selected are followed. There is no need for youth's exuberant energy when one is simply focusing on a few discrete tasks. The loss of energy in middle age is not a sign of decay but actually a sign of **progress** in the sense that the energy once frittered away on endless avenues of exploration in youth is now **focused** in middle age, and the psyche has shifted the bulk of its energy output from the physical to the mental. It takes thought to climb a career ladder, to maintain a long-term commitment, to raise children effectively. One's energy is not lessened or lost but **rechanneled.**

To sum up, the cusp of thirty-five ushers in the era of middle age, the long span of "productive" years when one's attention is most highly focused in the physical world. It is a time of narrowing one's focus, concentrating on a few select avenues of activity, the better to achieve mastery and the satisfaction of effort well expended. It brings professional achievement, long-term relations with a life partner and the raising of children.

It is rightfully called the "prime of life," for at no other time are all the faculties working so well and in such harmony. The body is strong, the mind is keen, the paths are chosen and the goals are set. With one foot in the adult world of professional choice and the other in the nursery, middle age is the time of greatest concentration in physical reality, while the plaintive wails from the crib, confounding the adult's sense of order, cannot help but serve as constant reminder of the natural order from which you, parent and child, spring.

Children are granted during middle age lest you take yourselves too seriously, think yourselves omniscient, all-powerful or possessed of decorum at all times. The little monsters will show you just how much you know, how polite you can be, the limits of your insight and endurance!

It is life's most magical time, in our view, for the dreams of youth become the realities of adulthood; the mastery of childhood becomes the achievements of productive work. One treads one's highly unique and private path with a sure foot, the time of choice behind, the satisfaction of accomplishment at hand.

CHAPTER FIFTY

Old Age

By late middle age, if one has lived a life along the cycles of most, the focus will have shifted. The children will be gone, making those first, fledgling attachments and career choices of early adulthood, beginning the process anew. Grandchildren may be squawking on the horizon. In professional life, one nears retirement, signaling an end to one's active participation in the mechanics of sustaining your society and economy.

Because your capitalist society judges a person's worth solely on the basis of his or her contribution to the economy, because your medicine and science view life as an accident, careening from birth to decay and death, there is perhaps no age of life more misunderstood and underappreciated than old age.

While childhood is virtually incomprehensible to the adult world, there is no similar excuse for your attitudes toward the elderly. They have already been through every stage of adulthood and can communicate with a **wisdom** that only they hold. By shuffling them off to nursing homes, you deprive yourself of truth and insight unknown to any other age of life.

You see the elderly bodies declining, losing their resilience, reducing in size, becoming more brittle, running on less energy, and you believe this evidence of decay. It is not. Again, life is like a bell curve, with childhood and youth leading up to the full and total concentration in physical reality of middle age. Following this, when one's active participation in the society has lessened, the body **reflects** the inner reconfiguration of the psyche.

Old age is no more a period of decay, in the natural order, than is childhood. They are simply reflections of **growing toward** and **drawing away from** the intense physical focus of middle age. Old age, then, is not decay, decline, loss. It is **release.**

Since childhood is a process of growing from one's first hesitant appearance in physical life at birth, nailing down the strands of physical existence, one by one, learning language, symbolic manipulation, social relations and so on, the period of old age is when those strands are released, one by one, in preparation for the **next stage of growth** that lies beyond the portal of death. You do not simply jump out of physical life but gradually **release** yourself from it.

Now, your beliefs about old age so gunk up the natural progress of this stage that you are indeed left with the sad spectacle of many losing their health, their minds and their resilience, representing the psyche's way of forcing the release that your society's beliefs will not allow. In the natural order, such is not necessary.

Observe, for instance, animals in the wild. They do slow down in old age; there is no need for them to maintain the physical strength of the stages of mating and raising young. And when an animal senses that the time of release is at hand, it goes off by itself, lies down and passes on. You do not find dead animals littering the landscape, do you? They know perfectly well when the time has come, and they accept it with their great, knowing intuition, and remove themselves.

Your pets will often do the same. When the time comes they may wander off, hide themselves from your grieving eyes, lie down and die. Death never sneaks up suddenly on those in tune with the natural order; when the time of release arrives, it is accepted gracefully, calmly, with the intuitive understanding that it is as essential to life as birth.

Your science has so divorced you from the natural order, knowing nothing of the challenges lying beyond physical death, that you are left quaking in terror at the prospect. With your culture's fear of annihilation, the liberal's sole expression of value the life of his physical body, indeed you must wail in horror at the prospect of death.

The animals know better.

Remember that the body's condition always reflects inner truth, specifically in this case, the configuration of the psyche.

With one's contributions to the world essentially behind—in that the bulk of one's work is finished, one's family raised—there is no need for the high, focused concentration of energy that sustains middle age.

Remember the progression from childhood through youth to adulthood. In the early years one's psyche is configured to pour its energy into physical manipulation as the child learns mastery, as the youth explores. In middle age, this energy flow is refocused, flowing into sustaining a strong body but also nourishing the intellect. For the mind is necessary for consolidation to a degree not necessary for exploration.

In the time of old age, the time of release, you can see that there will again be an alteration in the flow of energy from one's psyche.

Let us take this very carefully now, one step at a time. You know that your body is the physical reflection of a grid of points of intention, each point of intention standing behind a molecule of your body, "holding its place" in the overall scheme of things. Each such point of intention is constantly blinking on and off, into your physical world, then back into the nonphysical source of energy from which it springs. The psyche stands as a middleman between your physical body and the intent of your greater entity. The psyche mediates the constant flux and flow of energy between the greater entity's desire to explore physical life and the purely physical mechanics of your body.

While the blueprint, this grid of points of intention, remains consistent throughout life, what occurs is that in early childhood, many of those points of intention never blink on into physical life. While the constant flux and flow remains, it transpires solely between the greater entity and the psyche. The psyche's configuration at that stage does not permit all energy to flow through it to the physical body. There is no need for it to do so; one is not yet fully anchored in physical life.

When we say that childhood and youth grow toward full, intense focus in physical life, we are not speaking figuratively. Growing into adulthood is a reflection of the mechanics of the psyche, as it literally turns on additional points of intention throughout growth, allowing the energy of the greater entity to flow unhindered into the physical body. The psyche can thus be seen as a switchboard, with the great pulsating energy of the greater entity meeting either resistance or conduction, flowing either into physical life or back to the greater source.

The time of greatest physical focus, middle age, is thus when all points of intention receive full energy from the greater entity. The psyche stands with its floodgates wide open, permitting the intent of the greater entity to experience physical life in full and unfettered expression. This allows the concentration of energy necessary to sustain both the strong body and the lucid mind of middle age. At no other time of life is there such an unfiltered and undammed flow from one's greater entity.

In the time of old age, those points of intention all flowing at full speed in middle age will one by one be turned off. Note that there is no loss of energy involved, in deepest terms. It is simply being refocused. There will be less energy flowing to the physical body, but the slack is being **returned to the nonphysical realms** precisely as a way of preparing the way for death. For what you are will never be lost, never be annihilated, and it is in preparation for your returning to the nonphysical source of your life that the psyche concentrates the flow increasingly in the nonphysical realms, so that when death comes it will carry no shock; you will already be on the other side!

The bulk of your energy, of your soul, of your life's work, will be waiting for you when those last few points of intention are shut off and you step into the realms from which you sprang. Do you begin to see that there can be no thought of decay in such a process? It is simply a **refocusing** of one's energy, performed out of **loving intent** that death be no big leap, no shock, but that you will literally meet yourself on the other side!

So the decline in resilience, in strength and in stature that can occur in old age is not decline, not decay, but simply **preparation for release.** One by one, those points of intention are turned off like little spigots, **refocusing** your energy elsewhere.

In your culture, divorced from this understanding, believing death the universe's last cruel laugh on your meaningless existence, you confound this process so thoroughly that you are left with the genuine decay and collapse of many of your elderly.

It is the elder's job to release physical life. If that cannot be done naturally, as with animals and native peoples, then it must be forced upon you, not out of spite but out of love, for indeed you must prepare your bed to await you on the other side. If you cannot face the physical release with grace, then it will be thrust upon you. Thus you find a host of ailments endemic to and epidemic among the elderly, both physical and mental. We are not a medical school so we will not catalog them for you. But you know the loss of eyesight, the loss of hearing, that so many elderly experience.

Even more upsetting is the loss of mental function. This is **entirely unnecessary**, as you are meant to be lucid and alert to your last breath. But, again, if your mind cannot observe the changes in the body with calm and appreciation for the blessed release of death, then the mind itself will be shut down in order to allow the process to occur unhindered. You see the rise of Alzheimer's disease in your society, for instance. You will never find a single case of this occurring in any native population, those in tune with the natural order. It is a **creation of your culture**, reflecting your quaking fear at the prospect of death, your ignorance of the eternal divine flow of energy between physical and nonphysical, and your part in that cycle. If the mind will not naturally and gracefully accept the decline of the body, it will be crippled to allow that work of old age to occur.

You see what a vicious cycle you have running in your society. First you cast off the elderly because they no longer contribute to the economy. Then you view their physical decline with horror, turning away from the terror of death such represents to you, and thus literally cripple your old people in body and mind.

The elderly of native populations know nothing of the panoply of diseases from which your elderly may select. They know nothing of aphasia. They understand that the physical body **reflects** the grand spiritual design fueling the world and calmly accept their place within it.

You know that the elderly are accorded positions of respect high above all others in native cultures. This you find quaint and amusing. As a result, you have Alzheimer's. Do you consider this also quaint and amusing?

The elderly, those who have lived full and rich lives, are possessed of wisdom precisely because they have tested their beliefs and assumptions against the physical world, day after day, year after year, and have drawn conclusions as to what matters and what does not. If you ask the elderly for their advice to young people, almost always you will hear admonitions to take chances, take risks, spend more time in youth exploring, living a variety of experience, not settling down too young.

This is the precise opposite of the advice the parents of young people will offer! For from the middle-aged filter of consolidation, where one's focus is highly concentrated in a few fields of activity, the concerned parent urges the youth and early adult toward the same stage. The danger is that in doing so, the youth will be robbed of its primary task, that of exploration.

The elderly realize that a life devoid of challenge and variety is a life not worth living. They may well regret having taken the easy course, having abandoned their dreams when young, seeking instead the security and familiarity of routine and a paycheck. There may be some regret over those choices, for from the long view of old age one realizes that life is best lived not as a search for security but as a search for **experience**.

In the natural order, your security is guaranteed, given, granted, free. Building upon this, you search out a life rich with new experience.

The elderly know this.

They know that for all the frantic corporate ladder-climbing of middle age, such amounts to virtually nothing when taking stock of a life. As the elderly feel that fresh influx of energy from the nonphysical realm, cushioning their approach to physical death, they are naturally infused with the very wisdom of the ages, of their greater entities. Your professional achievements count for very little in the ledger of the universe. You do not hand your resumé to your greater entity upon death and consider that the mark and meaning of your life.

What matters is **how you lived**. First, did you love yourself? Did you pursue those avenues of interest to you, regardless of the opinions of family and friends? Did you stand your ground when tempted to compromise your principles and integrity? Did you hold true to your beliefs? Did you treat others with respect? Did you find time to love? Did you listen to your children? Did you encourage, nourish and support them on their own unique and private paths, not hampering them with meaningless strictures? Did you contribute to the life of your community? Did you make yourself available to your neighbors, to the extent they desired? Did you respect the natural world? Did you live a life attuned to the natural order? Did you make an effort to maintain contacts with those in every stage of life, from young children to the elderly? Did you listen to them? Did you seek out avenues of fresh experience and learning? Was boredom unknown to you, busy as you were exploring a world that can never fully be known? Did you laugh, long, hard and often at yourself? **Did you live?**

These are the questions the greater entity seeks answers to when you pass into spirit. Your fancy car, your fancy house, your fancy title, your fancy clothes — dust.

Sensing this intuitive rush of spiritual understanding, the elderly are in a better position than any to evaluate life. For they have not only their own store of experience from which to draw, but this is buttressed with the swell of cosmic comprehension buoying their last days.

The elderly are rarely inspired to fight. They will remain on the front porch, rocking in their chairs, observing with sadness as their grandsons lace up shiny, black boots, shoulder a rifle and go off to die on some foreign rice paddy because their leaders have lost all touch with reality. The elderly do not join not only because their bodies will not permit such excursions, but because they know better. How many lasting peaces has your world known? How many questions of morality have been decided at the point of a gun? How much lasting improvement in the world can you point to as a result of all of the blood spilled? How much genuine progress in the evolution of your culture is traceable to bombs and bullets? How many times have arch enemies become allies, then back again, in the endless paranoid swirl of national alliances? What has ever been solved by war?

So the elderly will rock on the front porch, knowing that today's enemy is tomorrow's friend, that genuine progress in society is never inspired at the point of a gun but by reason and divinity, that the chants, the slogans, the songs, the marches and the medals are all so much garbage, tossed on the trash heap of history in preparation for the next war. Nothing lasts; nothing stays the same; and to lay down one's life for an ephemeral paranoid fantasy is the ultimate display of contempt for life—one's own.

The elderly know better.

Middle-aged parents may often observe in bewilderment as their adolescent children—who consider them oppressors from the black lagoon—and their parents—the adolescents' grandparents—get along famously. The generation gap leapfrogs the parents, the young and the elderly embraced in a unity of understanding, leaving the poor parent out in the cold. Why?

Because both adolescent and elderly are in the **process of unraveling**. The adolescent psyche is unraveling to reshape itself into that of an adult. The elderly psyche is unraveling to prepare for the growth beyond physical death. There is thus an **intuitive understanding** between the two ages. Remember that one will always find closest comfort in the company of those sharing a similar filter of life. As proof that you are never cut free in the cold universe, the youth is comforted by the presence of the grandparent, intuitively sensing that both elder and youth are in a similar condition, though headed in different directions: one **toward** physical life, one **releasing** physical life. In the interim, while both psyches reconfigure, strand by strand, there can be much growth, much benefit to both ages as they meet on that common ground.

And what compares with the delight of grandchildren? All the delight of having children with the work handled by others!

Again, since the elderly possess a far deeper understanding of the relative importance of life's issues than those in middle age, the child naturally turns to the grandparent for a sense of what matters. The child's job is mastery, and what better teacher than one who has lived the entire span of life, the better to evaluate what is worth bothering with and what is worth ignoring.

Thus you find the grandfather sneaking his grandson out the back door to go fishing when there are studies to be attended to, Biblical passages to be memorized. Dust. Knowing this, knowing that an afternoon in the sun, in the natural world, is of far greater benefit to a child, the grandfather joins hands with his grandson to engage in an activity of genuine importance.

For if we have maintained throughout that young children are your closest link to the natural order, let us now expand the list. To the extent that the elderly have lived full, rich lives, have seen through the nonsense and hewed to the truly valuable, they are also prime links to the natural order. Just as the child has sprung from nonphysical realms, so does the elder prepare to spring toward nonphysical realms; in both cases, the sense of **connection** with the natural order is more vibrant than at any other time.

This is the link between grandparents and grandchildren. Again, there is a common understanding, a common base for exploration. Both have one foot in the physical world and one in the nonphysical realm. One is stepping in, the other stepping out. While they share that dual existence, such relationships are of incalculable benefit to both.

The stage of old age, then, is the time when one's life is reviewed, the hopes and dreams of youth either met or defeated in middle age, the children grown, the life's work mostly finished. One by one, the strands holding one to physical life are released, returning to the spiritual realm to prepare the way for return to the unseen source from which the infant sprang so many years earlier.

It is the stage of **release**, a gradual letting go of the pressing cares and woes of day-to-day living, infusing each day with a fresh inflow of divine energy and wisdom, easing the transition from physical life to that which waits beyond.

No decay, no decline, no loss. **Release.**

All in preparation for that magical moment when one steps through the portal into the glorious realm lying beyond the physical world.

CHAPTER FIFTY-ONE

Death

Death. How you tremble before the word! If you subscribe to the ignorance of science, restricting itself to the physically perceivable and hopelessly entangling itself in reflections of meaning while true comprehension eludes it, you view death as an end, the universe's last cruel laugh on your short and accidental existence.

The religious, those adhering to traditional dogma, may find themselves quaking before the thought of throwing oneself prostrate before God, knowing full well that one has failed to live a life of rectitude and slavish obedience to the infinite strictures on behavior the religious leaders so willingly provide. Death will thus be seen not as an end but as the beginning of a process one might prefer to avoid!

Now let us examine the reality.

As we have seen, in old age the points of intention sustaining the physical body are gradually shut off, one by one, sending their energy back into the nonphysical realm as a means of preparing for the day of physical death.

Just as the infant constantly flows between physical and nonphysical reality, so do the elderly. There is no "moment of death," either. There is no clean, precise breaking point. The release proceeds at an even pace for a time then at the point of optimal benefit to the individual, the bulk of the points of intention sustaining the body will be redirected toward the nonphysical realm. The physical body can thus no longer operate in the physical world; its fuel has been shut off. Yet there will still remain a few points of intention easing energy into the body, after the "moment of death," as a way of easing the transition, providing the flux and flow between the physical and nonphysical that always couches the young infant.

Nothing is lost. Nothing is ended. Those points of intention, each a funnel of energy from the greater entity, are simply **refocused** back into the nonphysical realm from which all physical reality is created.

There will come a point in time when the majority of those points are redirected, and this you experience as the moment of death. But the flux and flow of energy continues for a time after death as well, as a means of dipping back into the familiar physical reality before fully anchoring in the next field of exploration.

As a footnote, it is therefore a good idea to wait a few days after death before cremation, if that has been the choice. It will ease the transition of the departed into the spiritual realm.

Again, everything you physically experience is a reflection of deeper meaning. Your scientists are beginning to discover that the body does indeed emit an electromagnetic burst at the moment of death.

As we have stated throughout, the entire cosmos is composed of electromagnetic energy, and your body reflects that. Remember that each experience you physically pull into your life from the infinite swirl of probabilities carries a certain "polish." That polish is in fact an electromagnetic charge, imparted by the act of pulling the events of your life across the membrane between physical and nonphysical. Like everything else, that membrane is itself composed of electromagnetic energy, of a highly specific configuration, and any event—a pattern of energy—easing through that membrane will therefore carry the mark or flavor of the membrane's configuration. We have not been speaking idly or metaphysically, you see. We are speaking literally. The infinite swirls of probabilities about you are electromagnetic patterns and grids. When your thoughts and beliefs—themselves electromagnetic patterns and grids—rise to the membrane and latch onto those probable events of similar contour, the combined energy can propel that event across the membrane into your physical life. Such an event will always carry the charge of that membrane as a means of apprising the greater entity that such an event, such a version of an event, has been physically experienced.

All such events are therefore stored up in the grid or pattern sustaining your physical body throughout the course of your life. This is how you hold memories of your life, despite the cells of your brain being entirely replaced every seven years. The brain cells simply reflect the functions of the psyche in holding the charge of those events you brought into physical life.

You see now why it is so difficult to remember events from very early childhood. At that time, the membrane between physical and nonphysical is far looser in a way, far more permeable, as the infant naturally straddles both realms. With its looser configuration, the membrane can thus not impart as great a charge to the events chosen for physical experience; and it will therefore be much more difficult to recall the events later in life, as they do not carry such a compelling charge, forcing them into awareness.

We may appear to have been sidetracked off our discussion of death, but here is the connection. Each event of your life that you have pulled into physical experience is stored within the psyche as a grid or pattern of energy, imbued with the highly specific charge or coating of the membrane between physical and nonphysical.

At the moment of death, this entire highly charged energy pattern, which is the sum total of your life experiences, is suddenly released, thrust back through the membrane into the nonphysical realm, as a way of imprinting the universe with the story of your life. As an analogy, each day of your life is like a page in a book. As you leave physical life, you insert those pages into a lustrous binder of your own creation and place the book of your life on the shelves of the universal library, from which all may read and benefit.

You see that nothing is lost at the time of death; what you were in physical life will remain forever imprinted on the universal memory of the race and world. Every moment of the life, then, is available, throughout all eternity, as the permanent record of the series of moments that strung together into the flow of your life.

For do you imagine that you will remain "you" once you cross over? There is no need for eyes, ears, nose, taste buds or touch in the nonphysical realm. Those are the parameters by which you experience physical life. Once released from the physical, they have no reality. And as you grow and develop further in the nonphysical realm, you will **expand beyond** what you were in life, building upon the physical experiences just as you build each day upon all those that preceded it.

While your essence thus continues its growth forever, at the close of each physical life you tie up your life's experiences into a bundle and contribute it to the universe's store of knowledge. Thus you leave behind an imprint of your life, which is not you but a **reflection of you, a record of you**, and beyond which you continue to grow and expand.

Let us now examine what occurs to the individual at the time of death.

Assuming for the moment that our subject is one easing out of physical life in a natural, gradual manner, there will come a point where the bulk of one's energy has returned to the nonphysical realm, and one senses the end of physical life at hand.

One by one, the points of intention sustaining the physical body are refocused back into the spiritual realm. Those of least importance are redirected first. Thus you find, in those dying, that the extremities lose sensation first. The legs, the tips of the fingers, the arms, gradually relinquish the possibility of physical action.

Those points retaining physical activity to the end are those most central to your physical life, most reflective of Divine Grace as it creates your body. The heart, the lungs and the brain remain until the end. This can evoke medical debate about which is the official point of death: the cessation of brain activity? the heart's retirement? the final breath?

Each case will be different; there is no "moment" of death. It is a gradual process of release, of ebb and flow from physical to nonphysical and back again.

The individual experiencing death will thus find a gradual release of the burdens of the body, beginning with the extremities and narrowing the circle to the core of the body. As the eyes close, cutting off the primary sense through which you experience life, the ears remain, the better to hear one final, sweet song of love from those gathered at the bedside. One last coda of divine loving harmony from the physical plane.

As the psyche shifts its energy back toward the nonphysical, the individual most often experiences a sense of travel, of being transported, of movement.

In this initial return to the nonphysical, you see, your experiences are couched in the framework of physical life. You see things still; you hear voices. In deepest terms, you are carrying forward your dependence upon physical reflections of events rather than experiencing the core events themselves.

This is all part of the plan, that your return to the nonphysical realm be as **comforting** as possible. It would not do to suddenly rob you of the beloved senses that carried you through so many years. You carry them with you and maintain their fiction into the first moments of life beyond physical death.

Frequently, one will experience this sense of motion toward the other dimension by seeing a tunnel, at the end of which is a bright and welcoming light. This is another comfort, offered by your psyche, as a means of confirming that you have made the proper choice, that death has come, and that what lies ahead is better, holds opportunities for greater growth and learning.

Moving into this light, one frequently finds oneself met by historical religious figures. One's religion in life naturally determines the figure one will meet: Jesus, Buddha or Mohammed. In deepest terms, here is what operates. All great religions were brought into creation by the same source, that spiritual self-balancing device established by All That Is to provide constant spiritual insight into your plane. This has manifested as many different persons and dramas over the course of your history. All great religious figures are your interpretation of its entry into your history. Each such drama always speaks in specific ways to the time and place of the entity's entrance. Yet, at base, all are reflections of the same intent, the same truth, the same source.

This carries over into the moment following death. The person leaving physical life and rejoining the spiritual realm will immediately be met by a sudden rush of divine spiritual consciousness, a restoration to the natural order. This sudden encounter with the great spiritual source of your world will then be interpreted by the individual along the lines of one's spiritual understanding during life. If it is Jesus you worship, it is Jesus you shall meet. The same holds for Buddha or Mohammed or Moses. Just as in physical life, you interpret deeper experience in line with your beliefs.

This is provided as a moment of comfort, of easing the transition from physical to nonphysical. To meet the spiritual source of your world in **unfiltered truth** would be **overwhelming** to the consciousness fresh from physical reality—as when you meet genuine art, it is too much to fully comprehend at once. So the process is eased by your interpreting this body of spiritual knowledge in the form of a person—a familiar shape indeed!—and as this person's form resembles that of the religious figure worshipped throughout life, one is automatically imbued with a sense of one's importance. Jesus Christ, meeting little old me! I must not be such a humbug after all!

Thus are you restored to your proper place in the universe: **divine, unique, eternal.**

Following on the heels of the welcoming spiritual entity may be those one knew in life, those who have preceded one into the spiritual realm.

This can in truth be one of two different experiences.

As we have said, there is no end to the growth, the exploration, the learning. As such, one never crosses over into the nonphysical and then remains there, with one's earthly personality intact, for all eternity. One leaves one's imprint behind, sizzles the life story in the ledger of the universe and then moves on toward new growth.

An experience with one long dead, therefore, will most likely not be a direct contact with that person's spiritual entity. What occurs instead is that your desire to meet again with that person will link up with the imprint left by the other at the moment of his or her death, and as that imprint naturally carries a feeling of love for you, this love will be "unlocked" from the imprint, to surround you at the moment of crossing over, as a means of easing the transition. Again, you may interpret this as an actual encounter with the lost beloved, assuming the physical shape he or she held in life, but in deepest terms that physical shape has long since been discarded, and you will hallucinate it into existence by the force of your thoughts. Since you are fresh from physical life, accustomed to interpreting the entities of others solely as physical form, this is how you will experience your encounters with loved ones.

On the other hand, if the beloved has recently crossed into spirit, a more direct encounter can occur. There are planes and levels of growth, then, spiritual hierarchies above the physical plane, and those just departed from physical life will be at a certain level. Therefore, the bulk of one's essence may still be readily available to those crossing over and a more genuine contact made. It will still be interpreted in physical terms—your seeing the human form—but the contact will be less a gift from the imprint of the other and more a direct connection.

In either case, as one leaves physical life one is most often met by a spiritual figure recognizable as the one worshipped while on earth, and upon its heels is a surrounding by one's loved ones, returned earlier to the spiritual dimension.

As there is still enough connection with the physical world, the now-spiritual form may well look back to the physical world and gape in astonishment: What is everybody crying for? Why is everybody dressed in black? Why the long faces? Over my dead body!

The physical voice is silenced, but if only the lips and tongue could dance together for one final song, how they would shout: Shed no tears, you who loved me! Nothing is lost! The very universe lies open to me now!

And the long-ago cry of the infant, bursting into physical life shouting, "I'm here!" in unrestrained joy, now finds its partner on the other side of life, the cry echoing through the very cosmos in exultant jubilation:

I'm free!

CHAPTER FIFTY-TWO

Summary

Through our discussion of the stages of life, we hope we have cleared up some popular misconceptions about the path each of you treads. You see now that each stage carries an intrinsic challenge or task. Each stage, therefore, will be experienced through a **filter** particular to the stage.

Further, the juncture between stages, the **cusp**, calls into awareness the past and future selves, aiding one in appraising the progress made and charting a clear course along the lines of the choices selected.

You are not wound up at birth, springing forth in frantic activity and then winding down, rusting, breaking down into decay. There is a **purpose** behind the body's progression through life, as we hope we have shown.

To step back and take an even broader view, the life you now live is but one of many that your greater entity has established throughout all historical periods as its intent finds focus in a multitude of guises, sexes, races, creeds and professions. Your life stands as one unique and inexpressibly valuable contribution to the growth of the entity that gave you birth.

You might view the stages of life as you do any event for which you prepare and on which you later reflect.

For instance, you may decide to hold a party. You might view all the preparations involved as the stages of childhood. Building on the **security** that you can in fact throw a party, and your **mastery** of how to do so, you can proceed to fashion your own highly unique celebration. As you give thought to the tone you wish to set, the people you will invite, you are engaging in **exploration**, rummaging through the limitless options available under the rubric of "party." Then you make your **choice.** You invite those on your list, arrange for the food, the drinks and the decorations along the lines of the choices you have made.

The party itself is **consolidation**, where all the preparations come to fruition, resulting in the event of the party. The "event" thus is the center of your focus and attention as at no other time; it is your sole concern during its duration. You are therefore entirely focused in the physical reality you have created.

After the last guest has departed, the immediacy of the event subsides as it takes its place in your store of memories, of "past" events. You think it through, replay it in your mind, evaluating its progress, what you might do differently next time, which drunks you won't invite. There is the further physical work of cleaning up the mess. In the days ahead, guests may call or send cards, thanking you for the good time they had. Thus do you gradually **release** the event of the party from your awareness, bit by bit, until it fades entirely from conscious attention.

We choose our analogies carefully.

Life is a party.

PART SIX
YESTERDAY, TODAY AND TOMORROW

INTRODUCTION

In the final section of our work, we hope to tie together the many issues we have covered throughout in the context of examining the recent history, the present and near future of your society.

As we do so, we must return to our earlier discussion of the Christ entity and its return to your earth, in your time.

Remember that the Christ entity is the name we assign to that spiritual self-balancing mechanism established by All That Is to ensure that the earth never strays too far from the principles of Divine Grace, the medium through which All That Is grants life to your planet and the universe you know. You are not cut loose, then, but are nudged back to the divinity and reason that are your birthright by this body of spiritual energy which returns to your planet every two thousand years.

We call this spiritual body the Christ entity because the last time it appeared on earth, it did so in the form of the man you call Jesus. Understand, though, that this spiritual body has entered your time continuum every 2,000 years from the very beginning of the planet's existence, in your time terms.

Like all events, the return to the earth plane of the Christ entity does not simply fall from the sky into your unprepared laps. It manifests first at an oblique angle, so to speak, then bounces away, allowing a period of rest and consolidation while the extant culture absorbs the impact of its first contact. Then it returns again, this time increasing the strength and impact of its appearance. This is the time of struggle, of conflict, as it polarizes the era's society into two distinct camps: those clinging to the old order and those stepping into the new. In the Jesus drama, for instance, you found the simple teachings of a carpenter to represent such a threat to those in power that the man was crucified. And did the crucifixion turn back the clock, back to the old order? It did not. The words of Jesus speak to you today, infused still with humble brilliance and divinity.

There is no stopping the evolution of society. There is no possibility of preventing the return of the Christ entity, nor its radical and all-encompassing push toward a new understanding. The question, the area of choice, is in how difficult you will make the transition—how many will cling desperately to the familiar security of the old order, though it bring them only ruin, and fight those urging the society's stepping into the new order.

This challenge, as you know, resulted in the crucifixion of Jesus and the persecution of his followers.

And what will your reaction be?

CHAPTER FIFTY-THREE

The Sixties

The Sixties was the decade of the Christ entity's first, hesitant return to your plane. For all the upheavals of that turbulent and wild decade, understand that such represents merely the **first approach** of the Christ entity in your time.

Until the decade of the Sixties, your country had steamed along in self-satisfied contentment, sure of its especial favor in the eyes of God and of its divine role in bringing the benefits of civilization to the globe. Yours was the freest country on earth, the strongest, the most vital and vigorous, the most creative; with the wonders of technology, political and artistic achievement, little thought was granted to the need for self-examination.

In the decade of the Sixties, this unshakable security of purpose and rectitude was shattered by uprisings and upheavals such as your country had not known since the Revolution. Children dropped out of the culture, grew their hair long, took acid, burned their draft cards and defied every institution, every authority figure, every previously sacrosanct value. One by one, groups traditionally oppressed by the culture in power—white males—raised their voices in protest and anger, demanding equal rights, equal opportunity, for blacks, women, homosexuals, children, the disabled and every other downtrodden group.

The country was further rent asunder by your participation in the Vietnam War. This polarized society into two camps—doves and hawks—and the debate flavored every contour of society: politics, religion, music and personal relations.

The decade was marred by assassination as, one by one, prominent leaders in politics and civil rights were murdered.

The society, previously rolling along in smug contentment, seemed to suddenly have gone mad.

Now let us examine, piece by piece, what occurred.

The ideal hero of your society has always been the rugged individualist—the man standing alone, apart from the pack, following his own vision, marching to the beat of his own drum, without regard for the opinions of others. In your folklore, such individuals find ultimate triumph for having pursued their idiosyncratic, even iconoclastic, course.

While such a folk hero rises from the admirable emphasis on individual liberties embedded in your Constitution, it also led to a sense of separation from the others with whom one shared the common ground of your country. Naturally flowing from the emphasis on the individual was your economic system of capitalism, rewarding the entrepreneur, the inventor, with great monetary riches as acknowledgment of their contribution to society and their right to benefit personally from such contributions. Such a system led to stark contrasts in wealth between the industrialist and those who labored to make his fortunes possible.

And preceding the industrialists, of course, was the institution of slavery, in which one race owned another. From the very start, such a system ensured that your culture was based on **separation** from others of one's species rather than on a comprehension of the essential unity binding all persons, all races.

Such a system allowed the extraordinary economic growth of your country, buttressed of course with the bounty of natural resources to be found as the westward push expanded the nation's boundaries. For a time, the rugged individualist reigned supreme, his rights secured by the Constitution, duly rewarded in return for his effort and intellect, free to speak his mind and cast his vote.

In the Sixties, above all else, the society was wrenched in a new direction, that of **group consciousness.** The emphasis altered from holding the individual supreme to a rising chorus of **groups** clamoring for the rights and privileges so long denied them. There is strength in numbers, and those in similar situations of prejudice and disenfranchisement—whether based on race, sex, age or any other factor—pooled their anger into the ascendant movements of the Sixties: civil rights, feminism and so on. This represented the first nudge of the Christ entity, moving the society toward a new comprehension of reality. The rugged individualist, while serving his purpose, stood also as a symbol of separation. In your era, the essential goal or intent of the Christ entity is to restore your sense of **community** with the others of your species. The rugged individualist can thus no longer hold. As the culture was infused with fresh spiritual insight, it naturally swung from an emphasis on the individual to a rise in **group consciousness.**

The premier musical form of the era was rock and roll: group music.

The single greatest technological achievement was landing a man on the moon: group scientific effort.

The most heinous and infamous crimes were the Manson slayings: group murder.

The ascendant sexual arrangement was the orgy: group sex.

The emergent familial structure was the commune: group living.

The most powerful political statement was the mass rally: group protest.

The premier creative form was film: group art.

Television made its way into every household: group entertainment.

In every nook and cranny of society, from art to politics to sex, the culture was wrenched from the supremacy of the individual toward **group consciousness.**

Before proceeding with our examination of the Sixties, let us observe several more qualities of the Christ entity and the manner in which it manifests in your world.

First, while its initial approach will serve to wrench society from its secure moorings into a new direction, that new direction is not the **ultimate aim** of the Christ entity. It is the **first step** toward infusing the world with a new consciousness.

In the case of the Sixties, then, it is not to be inferred that group consciousness remains the ultimate goal of your society's evolution. It is not. But it is the background on which the remainder of the drama will play itself out, as we shall see.

A further characteristic of the Christ entity's appearance is that it will necessarily lead to excess. If you conceive of a pendulum swung far to one side, as an analogy of a culture gone astray, the Christ entity does not restore the pendulum to dead center and consider its work finished. The pendulum must swing equally far in the opposite direction before it can come to rest at its center point.

You are not to infer, then, that the Christ entity's ultimate intent was that everyone drop out of society, take LSD, and refuse to bathe or wear shoes. All such were reactions against the stifling of individual expression which had encrusted the society before the decade; the pendulum must swing an equal distance away from the mores and structures of the society undergoing change.

With those points in mind, let us now return to the decade under examination.

The Sixties were ushered in with the administration of the youngest president* ever elected in your country. Your young president was the very embodiment of man in his prime: brilliant, handsome, steeped in art and literature, possessed of vigor and energy.

While this man was no visionary, politically—reflecting your twin fears of anarchy and annihilation in his policies—far more important was the **symbol** he represented.

For not only did your society move toward a group consciousness, but more significant was the crossing over of those in one group to aid those in another group. While most groups had a common attribute, then, each such group was buttressed by support from outside its unifying feature: whites supporting civil rights; heterosexuals rallying for gays; men advocating feminism.

This significant feature of the society's evolution was reflected in your president. He was a millionaire evincing concern for the poor. He was a white man dedicated to equal rights for blacks. By crossing over the boundaries of his race and social standing, this president stood as a symbol of the next step beyond group consciousness: a flow from group to group, a move toward unifying society into one cohesive whole.

Again, this president's policies reflected the times. Visionaries are never elected president in your society. Your culture was fueled then, as now, by fears of anarchy and annihilation, resulting in a push toward the liberal's goal of increased government involvement in the society, and the conservative's Cold War need for security in the form of weaponry.

This president learned early enough—during the Bay of Pigs—about the limits of the generals' wisdom. Still, it was he who first involved your country, however slightly, in Vietnam.

*John F. Kennedy

This president thus performed a balancing act, standing as the symbol of the evolution of society into the new order while retaining some policies and traditions of the old order.

Assuming office upon your fallen leader's death was a man* more deeply rooted in the old-style political world. This man picked up the twin strands of his predecessor—old and new orders—by launching a panoply of social programs ushering in the Great Society, while at the same time involving the country far more heavily in Vietnam.

The schisms in the society grew wider, more strident, more unbridgeable. As time passed, the culture increasingly polarized—liberals versus conservatives, hawks versus doves—over the nation's direction in domestic and global affairs.

This is another attribute of the Christ entity's appearance, remember: increasing polarization in the society between those clinging to the old order and those ushering in the new.

Remember that youth is the age when one is infused with a sudden rush of divine spiritual energy, a restoration to the knowledge carried at birth but trampled by your society. It thus naturally follows that youth, on the whole, fell into the camp working toward the new order: dropping out of mainstream society, protesting the war, urging on the civil rights and feminist movements, and working for the poor.

It also stands to reason that those in the period of middle-aged consolidation would most vociferously cling to the old order, as it is in the security of the old that one grew to adulthood, has made one's plans and is finding one's success. Such is not to be abandoned lightly or without protest.

The polarization, then, ran along age lines, although many in each age, again, crossed over to the other camp.

Significant also was the rising ecological movement. The infusion of the Christ entity into a culture cannot help but restore many to a sense of balance with the natural order, and your society had strayed so far from this native understanding—viewed the earth as one giant natural resource—that a rising chorus urged the culture back toward an appreciation of the divinity of the earth, all its creatures, to restore your species to its proper place: one of countless species upon the earth, no more worthy than any other.

Perhaps you can see now where this polarization is leading. Until the decade of the Sixties, you see, all your great battles were fought over second-hand reality.

You might say the major battle of your century is that between communism and capitalism. Certainly this has been the preoccupation of your leaders, the justification for an enormous military build-up, the rallying cry terrorizing the populace and returning the most strident voices to office again and again.

Yet, what is this struggle about, in deepest terms?

Economics. While the ideological battle—between freedom and tyranny—is employed by leaders on both sides to buttress their oratory, the battle is essen-

*Lyndon B. Johnson

tially between two competing economic theories. Does the individual stand supreme, or does the state?

As we have seen, money is a mere reflection of meaning, not meaning in itself. A battle over economics, therefore, is a battle over second-hand reality. Where do questions of love, of faith, of art, of integrity, enter the debate? They do not. They, firsthand reality, are irrelevant to a debate over reflections of meaning.

So the great battle of your century is in fact a squabble over second-hand reality, both sides proclaiming that they provide greater liberty and fairness to their subjects, both sides using the alleged threat from the other to justify increased state interference in the private lives of its citizens and to enrich the merchants of death.

In the Sixties, then, the entire focus of society's battles changed. For the struggle between the old order and the new order was an entirely fresh battle: that between **second-hand reality** and **firsthand reality.**

In the civil rights movement, what was it black people wanted? Money? Status? Fame? They wanted **respect.** Remember that respect is the way you acknowledge the Divine Grace, the divinity, in another. While the battle over poverty was the outer shell on this battle, the fundamental struggle was to restore blacks to the human race, from which the white majority had long ago dismissed them. Those clinging to the old order, therefore, hiding their cowardice behind white hoods, grasped at skin color as a measure of worth—second-hand reality in the raw— while those pushing for civil rights were asserting that **all persons are created equal**—firsthand reality, divinity.

A similar battle was fought in the feminist trenches. Because in the ancient order your species required a division of labor between hunters and child bearers, men and women naturally assumed different roles. In your technological society, such roles no longer need hold. Again, women fought for **respect**—for their intelligence, talents and insight—while those opposing them clung to the prehistoric order—quite literally—as a way of boosting their self-esteem. While there are innate differences between the sexes, these are rendered negligible in a society such as yours, and clinging to sex as a badge of superiority is a retreat to second-hand reality: outer attributes determining inner worth. The truly secure sense their worth in every moment. It is the insecure who must cling to race or sex to provide the self-esteem they lack.

Perhaps nowhere is the schism between old and new orders, between first- and second-hand reality, so clear as in the environmental movement. For here there is no personal gain to those urging the society forward, as blacks and women stood to personally gain from their movements. A clean and healthy earth benefits everyone in general but no one in particular. All can breathe the air, smell the flowers, hike the trails, listen to the birds.

This is why the environmental movement is so infuriating to those opposing it. The battle is no longer being waged strictly on the battlefield of second-hand reality. Those clinging to the old order, therefore, viewing the earth as existing solely for plunder and profit, can only sputter incoherently at their opponents, as the rules of the game have been changed. The battle is not over money. It is over **consciousness**, an **approach** to the earth. Is it one giant sandbox, to be ripped apart by avaricious children, or is it divine natural harmony, to be preserved and protected? There can be no common meeting ground, then, as the two sides speak different languages. The old order views a redwood forest and salivates at the profit potential. The new order views the same forest with reverence.

This is why those protesting against environmentalists can only resort to contradictions in terms, terming their opponents "nuts"—saving the earth is insane?—and "elitists"—do not all benefit from a clean earth?—because there is no common meeting ground. The battle is between old order and new order, secondhand and firsthand reality. It is no accident that conservatives—whose root motive is fear of impulses—should fall decidedly in the camp decimating the natural order, for the natural world stands as a demonstration of the miraculous harmony of spontaneous impulse, laughing the conservative's root fear off the planet.

In every area of society, then, as the Christ entity infused the world with its approach, the battlegrounds shifted from second-hand reality—how much should we tax the rich to feed the poor—to battles between second-hand reality and firsthand reality: respect versus prejudice, respect versus chauvinism, respect versus plunder.

We might touch briefly on the assassinations, though in a general way.

Again, the time and circumstances of one's death are always chosen, are always meant first and foremost to fulfill private purpose. Yet such choice can also serve to make a statement about the condition of the society, to leave a greater imprint by the manner in which death comes.

Two factors were involved in the assassinations.

First, since your culture is based on divorce from the natural order, you are therefore divorced from each other. If you cannot feel the divinity infusing your world, how can you see it in others? If you cannot sense your place within the divine natural order, how can you recognize that all others have their equally important role to play? With your divorce from the natural order comes the inability to communicate, to recognize any commonality between you and your neighbor, leaving you focusing on the superficial differences while ignoring the fundamental unity.

Only in such a society can we find such a resort to violence. If you cannot sense the divinity in another, if others are mere walking caricatures of race and sex and status, then it is no loss to the world to simply eliminate those with whom you disagree. Your culture's fascination with firepower reflects your profound insecurity, your fears of anarchy and annihilation; coupling this with your divorce from each other leads to the instinctive reach for the pistol when others fail to live and believe as you see fit.

You will notice a common attribute of those falling prey to assassins in the Sixties: They were all **progressive**, all urging the society toward the new order.

No major reactionary figure was so felled. Why? Because you needed to learn the lesson, again, of the Christ entity's last appearance: Kill the bearer of the message, if you wish, but you cannot halt the evolution of society.

Again, private reasons for leaving physical life were always foremost; the Christ entity does not randomly pick off those who seek to do its work! But there will always be carry-over from one appearance to the next, and as the words of Jesus have hardly penetrated into your culture after two thousand years, in a sense the drama was replayed, reenacted, as a way of hammering home the message: Silence the lips who speak truth, but you will never silence truth.

It is fair to say that certain members of your society cheered each assassination. While each gunman may have acted alone—**may have** acted alone—no event of such significance ever occurs in a vacuum; the trigger fingers took direction from more than one brain, either literally or figuratively.

And those who cheered the assassinations, then? Planting their feet firmly and proudly in the prehistoric muck of the old order, such represent the core disease of your society, which the Christ entity has returned to cure.

The Sixties brought revolution to the world of art and entertainment the likes of which no previous era had seen.

First, observe simply the use of color. Psychedelic posters and paintings, often rendered hallucinatory under black light, fed the eyes a stunning palette of color. The premier musical form, rock and roll, assaulted the ears with the overwhelming drive of power and rhythm, urging the body to replicate its force with spontaneous and uninhibited dance.

More, the senses were by-passed entirely in the flood of drugs into the culture, offering their users hallucinatory experience no eye, no ear, could ever manufacture.

Dress became freewheeling, outrageous or nonexistent.

As art is the truest public expression of Truth, pulling society forward into the future, it naturally follows that the world of art should undergo such revolution upon the return of the Christ entity to your plane. Music, paint, photography, film, poetry, dance—all underwent total immersion in the sea of Truth supporting your world, baptizing the society's evolution into the new order.

Perhaps no other issue so consumed your society than the Vietnam War. It infused every aspect of the culture, every debate, every household, every conversation, with the central conflict of your day: peace versus war.

As we have seen, as war plays itself out in increasingly ludicrous and grotesque expression, the better to be dismissed by all rationally thinking persons, you found in Vietnam a situation where you were fighting a war over a purely metaphysical concept—communism. Your territory was never endangered. No swarm of kamikazes pulled you into the conflict, as with Pearl Harbor. It was your choice to go, to spill the blood of your youth upon foreign rice paddies over a concept, a thought, an idea.

Before we proceed, let us pause to simply examine the concept of war itself, divorced from any specific application.

War is so ingrained in your culture, like the church presuming authority to address your sexual behavior, that it seems invisible, an inevitable condition of human society. Instead, understand that it is your culture, your beliefs, that make it necessary and sustain it.

It is true that all races can recount their history through a recitation of the wars fought. It is not unique to your European culture, but common to all races.

You will note, however, that there are groupings within each culture that refuse to participate in war. You know of "peace-loving" tribes among your Indians, for instance. You have discovered Stone Age tribes with no weapons, no word for "war" and, considering them quaint, call them primitive. There are nations in your world that steadfastly maintain neutrality in times of war, refusing to accept the premise of most that questions of morality are ever decided at the point of a gun.

So war does indeed seem intrinsic to the human condition, although there are always a few exceptions that you find quaint or infuriating, depending on your mood.

What is the basis for war? How is the game played? It is simply this: Whichever side kills the most people on the other side wins.

War can thus only hold in a species divorced from the natural order. The great danger in setting up a species with rational thought is precisely that it would move in such a direction, would forget its divine origin and hold reason supreme above the natural order. The initial intent of All That Is was that the human species should explore the physical earth through the reasoning mind, but also couched in the security of the divine natural order. It is this you have forgotten—that you and all others are divine creatures—and thus your fall into the use of war to settle disputes, where reason and divinity have failed.

Nothing is predetermined. No Great Being is pulling your strings. In the history you acknowledge—one possible strand of many—you have thus strayed from your intrinsic sense of divinity, held the rational mind the supreme arbiter of reality, but then abandoned reason and resorted to force, mere brute strength, to decide conflicts.

So the human race has abandoned both elements of its setup as a species: reason and divinity.

It is no accident, you can see, that men should be the warriors. They are granted the focus on physical life, on outer experience. Women, granted inner life, have remained closer to the divine source of the world—as carrying a child cannot help but ensure—and thus have largely remained out of men's endless murderous squabbles over territory, prestige, ego and psychosis.

All paths are creative. In deepest terms, there are no "good" or "bad" experiences, only growth and learning. This holds true of every war ever fought. With your reason, look back in history and ask yourselves, what has war ever solved? What has ever been accomplished with firepower?

Now, you may well point to skirmishes where you perceive a beneficial outcome—your Revolutionary War bringing independence; the Civil War freeing the slaves; World War II halting a madman's charge through Europe—and declare that war has proven itself of benefit.

This is to engage in ex post facto confusion of cause and effect. In all these cases **war would have been unnecessary had society's evolution been unhindered by those clinging to the old order.** You see, you cannot stop the evolution of society. You can only make it unpleasant for yourselves, as those clutching to the old order retreat to firepower when they realize they hold no moral basis for their views. Had England recognized that the move from monarchy to democracy was a healthy one, and granted your independence without a fuss, the Revolution would have been unnecessary. Had the South acknowledged that blacks were in fact members of the human race, entitled to the same rights and privileges as all other citizens, the Civil War would have been unnecessary. Had Europe—the site of divorce from the natural order—not closed its eyes to the plots and schemes of a madman, capitulated to his demands, and refused to protest the carting away of the Jews, buttressed by your country's hibernation from reality until the cries of "Tora! Tora!" awoke you, World War II would have been unnecessary.

In each such case, then, when you point to war as necessary for the preservation of the moral, the "right," you see that it is only your betrayal of the moral, the good, that leads some to pick up their arms when their cause has shown itself a betrayal of divinity and reason.

In a sane and divine world, no madman like Hitler could ever exist. It would not occur to anyone to blame anyone else for the shortcomings of an individual or nation; it would not occur to anyone to help himself to the territory of others.

War, then, boils down simply to this: mass psychosis.

Because it is so utterly divorced from your twin pillars of reason and divinity, war must necessarily be dispensed with if the society is to return to its proper course. As we have seen, any philosophy or idea divorced from Divine Grace will display itself in increasingly grotesque and ludicrous form, waving larger and larger red flags until your slumbering eye finally opens.

Thus your Vietnam War. Nothing was at stake. Your country was not endangered. No one uttered a word against your security. Yet because your leaders have convinced you that communism poses such a dire threat to your society, and that one nation "falling" to it will necessarily result in every other nation on earth following suit, you were convinced, some of you were convinced, that you were required to battle the installation of a communist government in Vietnam.

So you lost your tens of thousands of boys, of sons, of lovers, of husbands, of fathers. And for what? What can you point to now as the beneficial outcome of your involvement there?

There is none. The men died for nothing.

Worse, the Vietnam War carried with it, as proof of the need for you to examine war or have it destroy you, the concomitant strands further damaging your society: an enormous drain on the economy, flushed down the Pentagon, and an unrelenting stream of deceit from your leaders and generals.

Again, you create your own reality, individually and en masse, and when you find yourselves being lied to daily by your leaders, do not point your fingers at them in blame. The blame lies with you. You want to be lied to. You want to hear that your country has the right to impose its will on the rest of the globe. You want to hear that God blesses your missiles as they wreak havoc on native peoples. You want to hear that your own boys, sacrificed on the altar of American business interests, died noble deaths. You want to believe that your leaders have your best interests at heart. **You want others to create your reality.**

Vietnam served, as did every other issue in society, to polarize the culture into two distinct camps. On one side were the hawks, convinced of your country's especial blessing by God, granting you the divine right to shoot everyone with whom you disagreed and to sacrifice your own sons in the name of "peace with honor." On the other side were the doves, wondering what you were doing over there in the first place, refusing to lay down their lives for those pulling the strings in the secure comfort of Pentagon and boardroom, refusing to accept that any moral question can be decided by firepower.

A retreat to weaponry is always a **surrender of reason**, a **betrayal of divinity.** You can only shoot another when you cannot see the God inside him. You can only pick up a gun when your reason has failed. As one band of society stepped toward the new order, refusing to go along with the participation in Vietnam, the old order climbed back down into the primordial ooze, dusted off its weapons and fought bitterly to retain the comfort and security of psychotic evil, which is war at its base.

It should be no surprise that the division into hawk and dove camps fractured along age lines. Youth, suffused as always with a rush of spiritual understanding, protested against the middle-aged exercise in futility on foreign soil.

Nowhere was this fracture more evident than in the event that slammed the book closed on the Sixties in the ledger of the universe.

Four college students died in a hail of gunfire on an Ohio campus*. The students were unarmed. Reacting as cowards always do, the authorities called in the National Guard—a retreat to firepower, the abandonment of reason, the betrayal of divinity. In a hail of bullets, middle-aged authority demonstrated the moral vacuum in which it operated, the abandonment of reason brought to brilliant irony for its employ on the soil of a university—the alleged shrine of reason.

The Sixties, ushered in on a vigorous presidential voice and the poetry of Frost, ended with the death shrieks of your murdered children and the inscriptions on their tombstones.

The New Frontier and the Great Society were dead.

---

*On May 4, 1970, the National Guard opened fire on students protesting the Vietnam War on the Kent State University campus, killing four and wounding 10.

CHAPTER FIFTY-FOUR

The Seventies

As we have said, the Christ entity operates by hesitantly approaching your plane, apprising itself of the spiritual condition of the world, infusing the planet with a fresh burst of spiritual energy, and then retreating while your human society sorts out the good from the bad, the useful from the harmful, in what will always be the excesses of the Christ entity's first appearance.

The Seventies, then, was the decade of rest and consolidation as the Christ entity withdrew, leaving you to integrate the legacy of the Sixties into your culture. It was common, during that decade, to bemoan the seeming loss of energy, of insight, of originality, that imbued the Sixties. Yet this is the plan. While there was not so much outer drama, you will find that each strand leading to the new order was consolidated, solidified and strengthened during the Seventies.

In your culture, projecting your personal power onto government and expecting it to run your lives, much of the work involved legal codification of the advances of the Sixties. Building on the Civil Rights Act of 1964, barrier after barrier to blacks' full participation in society was outlawed; discrimination—which was always immoral—now became illegal. Women also struggled to write into law their demands for equal treatment; again, many such barriers were eliminated. The environmental movement sprouted a host of new laws and regulatory agencies to ensure that the wanton destruction of the natural order was at least slowed to the pace of a jet fighter.

In every fiber of society leading toward the new order, then, the initial burst of enthusiasm and outrage of the Sixties was consolidated into law, reflecting the absorption into the mainstream society of those beneficent paths leading the culture forward.

No president in this decade managed to inspire either the fire and enthusiasm of he who inaugurated the Sixties, nor of the one who involved you in Vietnam, relinquishing the opportunity for a final term under a hail of opposition. It naturally follows that a decade of rest and consolidation would not produce leaders provoking such reactions among the populace.

Ushering in the Seventies was a president* elected on a "law and order" platform, and we have seen what that means. It means that one perceives the world as festering with sin and impulse, which must be repressed and controlled by the state lest the conservative's nightmare, anarchy, be loosed upon the world.

*Richard M. Nixon

Again, since such a platform—law and order—is driven by fear, and fear is by definition irrational, it stands to reason that this president's downfall was brought about by his resort to illegal acts in defense of a patently irrational goal: ensuring his re-election.

With the opposition party bent on nominating a candidate who failed to speak to but a small minority of the populace, what could a rational incumbent president have to fear? Again, reason was not invited to the inaugural ball, nor any White House function thereafter. The men surrounding the president were deeply fearful, therefore deeply irrational, therefore profoundly illegal in their activities. Fear knows no law and order. It can only seek to assuage its fright by employing any means to reach its end. Thus the spectacle of the committee to reelect the president engaging in illegal wiretaps against an opposition party bent on self-destruction.

This president also sustained the war in Vietnam, pledging not to withdraw until "peace with honor" had been achieved—honor presumably accruing in direct proportion to the pile of dead American boys rotting under the Asian sun. War is the conservative's first and truest love, as something always dies—something natural, something impulsive—thus granting at least a moment's reprieve from the threatening swarm of impulse that is the natural world.

During this period of consolidation, then, your first president of the decade served to highlight those clinging to the old order, cowering with fear on both domestic and global fronts, resorting to illegalities and firepower as reason and divinity had long since been abandoned and betrayed.

It is always the latter part of a decade that will carry the deepest charge or depth of a theme as the Christ entity returns to your plane. Your president in the latter part of the Seventies*, then, most closely resembled the purpose and intent of the decade as a whole: rest and consolidation.

Notice, though, the symbols such a man brought to the White House, carrying greater significance than his policies, for the most part. For one thing, he was the first president elected from the South since the Civil War. Remember that a fundamental feature of the evolution of society was a move toward group consciousness, then a step beyond, where individuals in one group crossed over into another. In a sense, the Civil War had left your nation divided into two camps for over a century. As evidence of the flow of fresh energy and unity of the species, you elected a president from the "losing" side, the South.

Note also the professional experience and qualifications of this president. First, he was a farmer. In your culture, farmers are those closest to the natural order, taking their place in the rhythm of the seasons, the cycle of sowing and reaping, working within nature's world, rather than against it. Your president thus represented the return of the society as a whole to its place in the natural order.

Further, this president had experience as a nuclear engineer. This gave him a scientific background, science being—to your eyes—the most "rational" field of endeavor. Though we may quibble about that from our perspective, from yours

*Jimmy Carter

the president was thus steeped in the field of greatest reason in your society.

On top of that, he was a born-again Christian—not of the fire-breathing fundamentalist variety, but one whose religion suffused his life with a sense of the divine, of the place of humankind in a grander scheme, of a higher purpose and meaning to life than the mere physically perceivable. Your president thus represented a return to divinity, a comprehension of the innate goodness of the universe and your species, of life rich with meaning and purpose.

Now, we do not wish to deify this president. Again, no visionaries are ever elected in your culture. But you can see how these three attributes combined in one man to represent the evolution of your society: the **natural order**—farming—**reason**—science—and **divinity**—religion.

It was thus no accident that while this president may have failed to incite the population to riots of adulation, he nonetheless set about **consolidating** the strands first sprouting in the Sixties. With the Panama Canal treaties, he ended an embarrassing vestige of imperialism. With the Alaska lands bill, he locked up your last chance to demonstrate harmony with the natural order, the lower forty-eight being devastated. He brought the Middle East closer toward peace than any prior administration could achieve. In racial relations, women's issues and so on, he worked to strengthen the progress made in those areas leading toward establishment of the new order. Reason and divinity—your twin faculties in concert with the natural order. Such is where you are headed. Such represented the quiet work of this president.

In the world of art, you found the fresh energy and boldness of the Sixties losing its steam. Nothing came to replace rock and roll as the premier musical form; for indeed, such is the power behind this musical expression that it remains with you still, evolving but essentially intact. While disco music arrived to enliven the dance clubs, in no way could disco be compared to the revolution rock and roll represented, nor its infusing the entire culture with fresh energy. Nothing arrived to match the impact of the Beatles, for instance.

You may note with interest that several musical versions of the life of Christ were significant cultural events, as albums, as plays, as films. Again, any appearance of the Christ entity will carry with it the traces of its last appearance. This manifested both in the assassinations of the Sixties—kill the bearer of the message, but you cannot stop the message—and in the retelling of the Jesus drama through the premier medium of the era, rock and roll. All in preparation.

Following on the heels of the Sixties' sexual revolution, movies in the Seventies began to display an unprecedented acreage of flesh, provoking institution of a ratings system, lest the little ones learn what all the fuss is about. Always, there will be excess as a culture struggles to right itself; the virtually obligatory nude scene in movies of the Seventies was meant to desensitize this issue, this baring of flesh, and move the culture toward a saner view of the matter.

The art world reflected the purpose of the decade: to consolidate those first steps taken in the Sixties toward the society's return to the natural order, the new order, the New Dawn.

CHAPTER FIFTY-FIVE

The Eighties

The Christ entity operates by infusing the world with fresh spiritual energy, then withdrawing. This took twenty years, the Sixties and the Seventies.

The Christ entity then returns to earth with a fresh burst of insight and energy. What? you cry. The mess of the Eighties resulting from an infusion of spiritual energy?

You create your own reality. You must fight your own demons. The Christ entity's purpose now is to set, in clear and unmistakable terms, the battle between the old order and the new order.

You have only one enemy: fear. We have said this over and over again. In the natural order there is nothing to fear; therefore fears are, by definition, irrational. And as a glance at the morning's paper will apprise you, those leading your political, scientific and religious organizations wallow in the deepest depths of the asylum.

Your religious myths tell you that man's fall from grace was precipitated by eating of the fruit of knowledge, of reason, turning your back on God and divinity.

In fact, it is reason and divinity together that are meant to pilot your course through life.

The real enemy in the Garden of Eden, then, the true serpent, was not reason but fear. Fear is the embodiment of your divorce from the natural order, for in the divine harmony of the natural world there is nothing to fear.

Does this mean you can hurl yourself off a cliff and expect to land safely? To stand naked in a blizzard for an hour and suffer no ill effects? To sit at home, refusing to work for your support because "God will provide"?

In all such cases, you have violated the boundaries and parameters of human existence as granted your species. The universe and your earth are governed by certain physical laws. You are intended to use your reason to navigate with these laws respected. But once your reason is employed to steer your course safely through the physical world, and with the security of understanding your divine origin and your place in the drama of physical life, there is indeed nothing to fear.

If your world seems otherwise, it is your beliefs that have made it so, not the world itself.

Thus, fear is the single stumbling block in the way of returning you to the natural order. It clouds your reason, forgets your divine source and urges you toward paths that can only lead to self-destruction.

Upon the return of the Christ entity to your plane in the Sixties, it absorbed the state of the society and came away with the understanding that there was only one roadblock standing in the way of the society's evolution: fear.

It is not the nature of the Christ entity to magically wave a wand and dissolve your problems. What you will learn in the time ahead, above all else, is that you create your own reality. Every problem facing you now is the product of your own beliefs. It is the Christ entity's intention that you be made aware of those hindrances standing in the way of your successful evolution into the new order. To that end, the Eighties are the decade setting the stage for the showdown yet to come, as the society increasingly polarizes along the lines of those clinging to the old order and those stepping into the new.

You might want to understand how this operates in technical terms. Again, everything of which you are aware is composed of electromagnetic energy—everything both physical and nonphysical, from the ant to the Christ entity.

You know that energy travels on waves or cycles; light waves, sound waves and so on are interpreted by your senses based upon their frequency, their rate of vibration. All energy is motion, vibrating at a certain frequency.

The Christ entity, being the body of spiritual energy granted by All That Is to restore your planet every two millennia, is necessarily vibrating at a far faster frequency than anything presently on the earth plane. As it approaches, those whose beliefs are of a contour most in line with the energy patterns of the Christ entity will feel the greatest burst of fresh insight and spiritual energy. Those whose beliefs are contrary to the Christ entity will feel no such infusion.

As time passes, the earth consciousness as a whole, having its own electromagnetic reality, begins to vibrate at a faster rate. The entire earth is being infused with this fresh spiritual energy.

This explains why things seem to change so fast in your day. Remember that events take a certain amount of "time" to be expressed in your reality, moment point by moment point. The rate of dissipation is determined by the vibrational frequency of those involved in an event. In other words, a given unit of time will allow the passage of more "events" in an individual of greater vibrational frequency than in one of lower vibration.

In your own life, think of people you know who constantly harbor grudges, who constantly replay the past, never letting anyone forget the egregious wrongs they have suffered. Are these fun people? Do you want to be around them? You do not, because they seem a drain on your energy, do they not? What is occurring is that such individuals are vibrating at a slower rate, that rate determined by one's beliefs, which in turn means that a greater number of units of time are required for an event to pass from that individual's awareness—in some cases, forever! A healthier individual harbors no such grudges and eternal resentments but gets on with life, seeking fresh experience.

On a national level, you find racists in the South still fighting the Civil War, which is dead and buried to those who prefer to live in this century. And are such racists the movers and shakers, the geniuses, the artists, the prophets? They are not. Because by clinging to an event occurring before their birth, such people evidence a low vibrational frequency and, therefore, are not open to rushes of divine inspiration that fuel the artist, the thinker and the leader.

Such also occurs on a global level, as the Christ entity infuses the world with a fresh burst of energy, which is at base a flood of energy vibrating at a faster rate than any person on earth experiences.

Now, this rate of vibration will increase as time passes. This is how you experience the increasing polarization of society upon the Christ entity's return. In the Eighties, you see, the fresh infusion of energy is vibrating at a sufficient rate that many, whose beliefs are in line with the intent of the Christ entity, move toward the new order, while those clinging to the old become increasingly hysterical, precisely because there is less energy sustaining them. This is most difficult to express. But as the human race is pulled toward the new order, all upon the earth will feel the infusion of fresh insight; those too fearful to release the old order will cling to it, while the energy sustaining them is literally cut out from under them. This induces the panic you notice among the Right wing in your society, the hysteria, the uncompromising stance they take on every issue.

And you will find, as the energy increasingly is drained from the old order, that such persons fall ill far more frequently than those in the new order. Your body, the physical reflection of a grid of energy, requires constant, fresh inflow of energy from the divine source. Those clinging to the old order are therefore sealing themselves off from the source of divine energy, and you will find an increase in health problems, marital problems and psychological balance among those clinging to the old.

That explains in technical terms what is occurring now. Let us observe the practical effect of these changes.

Any culture has its version of the three elements of human society: government, science and religion.

You began this decade by ushering in the most conservative—and therefore most fearful—administration of the century: the **political** embodiment of fear.

The election of this president was aided in large part by the fundamentalist Christian Right: the **religious** embodiment of fear.

And, as we have seen, modern medicine was stumped by the appearance, the same year as you installed your president, of the AIDS virus: the **scientific** embodiment of fear.

This sets the stage for the battle lines to be drawn.

You see, if your society simply tooled along as it was prior to the Eighties, sensing that things were amiss but not knowing what or why, you might not have faced the issues that must be faced in the time to come. The intent of the Christ entity, then, is to **force** these issues into your awareness, and it does so by polarizing the society as a means of presenting—in clear and unmistakable terms—where the central conflicts lie. And those clinging to the old order, finding the energy sustaining them drained, become increasingly hysterical, precisely as a means of forcing to the greater society's attention the dying gasps of those clutching to the security of the past.

The Eighties are thus the decade in which the issues first raised during the rush of divine inspiration that was the Sixties are brought to brilliant relief. Again, the battle is no longer being waged over second-hand reality but is now drawn between second-hand and firsthand reality.

The old battle between liberal and conservative in your society is, at base, a struggle over money. How much should we tax, and to whom should we give the proceeds? As such, this battle is fought over second-hand reality—money—and entirely ignores the fundamental structure of your economy, which must be faced in the time to come.

To the extent that the women's movement is bogged down in issues like day care for their children and how much money women make compared to men, it remains on the level of second-hand reality; for all such issues ultimately boil down to money. Instead, in the time to come the society must incorporate the inner, intuitive, feminine qualities into the very fiber of society, if it is to survive. The battle will no longer be over how well women can perform like men. The battle will be to restore men—and your patriarchal society—to the divine balance between outer and inner reality that holds in a truly healthy—and liberated—society.

Battles over taxes and welfare, over day care and salaries, are all part and parcel of the old order. As such, they can all be reduced to a root issue—money—which is in itself second-hand reality and carries no power to cause the fundamental changes that must take place in your society.

As fear becomes increasingly apparent in those clinging to the old order, and they grow increasingly hysterical as the energy is withdrawn from the old order, you are forced to face issues that you have long swept under the rug.

As we have seen in the discussion on AIDS, this crisis has forced the issue of homosexuality into the society's awareness as nothing preceding it has done. While the compassion for the downtrodden evinced in the Sixties may have infiltrated the society to one degree or another since, the issue of homosexuality had never squarely been dealt with. No society can expect to join the new order that clings to ancient Biblical proscriptions, wrenched out of context and slapped on your present-day reality. The issue therefore needed to be brought to your attention in clear and unmistakable terms, once and for all, and dealt with by society as a whole.

The AIDS crisis accomplished this. Whatever your opinion of homosexuality, one had to match it with the agonies of those under siege by the virus. Many persons who may have formerly felt revulsion toward homosexuals find themselves feeling compassion toward those suffering, and when the crisis passes from your existence—at the time of your choice—that compassion will automatically restore the homosexual to full standing in the society. The crisis, entirely unnecessary had your society evolved in healthy fashion, thus **forces** the changes you would not permit otherwise.

By the same token, others found the AIDS crisis to be irrefutable evidence of the anger of God toward these sodomites, and His smiting them down with an agonizing, invariably fatal disease their just reward for betraying God's word.

Thus you find society polarized. Either you feel compassion for the victims or you scorn them and watch in satisfaction as God tortures those defying His word. In either case, the issue is brought to conscious awareness, no longer left stewing on the back burner.

Now, had the society as a whole all evinced compassion, the disease need not have progressed any further into the culture.

Because some fell to their knees and scraped their morality from the pits of primordial ooze from which you sprang, holding the suffering of those afflicted to be God's just vengeance, the virus had to therefore attack a seemingly innocent segment of the populace as a way of forcing compassion where none could be felt for the homosexual. It was God's plan, then, some felt, that homosexuals should be stricken with the disease. Now you find a growing number of infants born carrying the disease, their little bodies ravaged from the first moments of life by the carnivorous slaughter of the virus.

AND IS THIS STILL YOUR GOD'S PLAN?

If it be your God's plan that infants have tubes rammed down their nostrils to prevent them from suffocating, then your God is not worth spitting on, much less worshiping.

God's plan? God's plan? God's plan? What sort of God? What sort of plan? What unmitigated evil is this, God's plan?

And are there those among you who still cling to the notion of divine retribution? What is the infant's sin? Why should it suffer so?

Once again society polarizes. Those who condemned the homosexuals to a just death may find themselves heartbroken at the sight of infants so afflicted; once again, this compassion will work backwards, to all victims of the disease, and restore homosexuals to a position of caring and concern in the hearts of those previously unable to feel it.

Yet there are those who still see God's plan in a ravaged neonatal body. There are those who would worship such a God. How much longer, how many more must die before you once and forever dismiss from your beliefs the notion of such a God, of such a plan, of such a hateful existence?

There is only you, your beliefs, creating the world that you know. While you are each divine, sparks of unique divinity, no One pulls your strings. You create your own reality. This you must learn before you can step into the new order.

How many more must be sacrificed on the altar of your ignorance?

Again we confirm that everyone in your society, however histrionic, acts out of the **best of intent.** Even those ardently planning and hoping for nuclear war do so not out of love for the prospect of mass incineration, but because their misreading of Scripture leads them to believe that such is—again—God's plan, necessary to establishing Jesus' kingdom on earth.

No one acts from pure evil. There is only misguided, blunted or perverted good intent.

You must not interpret the Christ entity's intention as being to deliberately provoke battles among your species. It does not infuse both sides, old and new orders, with equal energy and then sit back to see what develops. In your terms, this entity is capable only of "good" and therefore would never empower the old order. It operates simply by infusing the new order with a rush of divine energy, increasing the vibrational frequencies of the entire planet; as a result, the old order will necessarily be cut off from the energy that formerly sustained it.

You see, as of now it is quite possible for you to live in both old and new orders, and most do. You can send off a check to your favorite environmental group and write the next check for the payment on your fine, imported sports car. You can straddle both worlds, leaning toward the new while couched in the familiar framework of the old.

As the Christ entity nears the earth plane, though, and increases the vibrational patterns of the planet, the middle ground will eventually dry up. You will no longer be able to straddle old and new orders. You must make your choice.

This is what we mean when we say that the battle lines are drawn. It is not the Christ entity who draws them. It is you, each of you, choosing which side you wish to live on. And the number choosing to participate on either side determines how much turmoil you must have before all are ensconced in the new order.

You see, free will always operates. No God is pulling your strings. No Christ entity is going to zap everyone with pixie dust and have you all awake on some glorious morning, suffused with divinity, joining hands simultaneously to cast off the old order. **You choose** the circumstances of your entering the new order. Your free will always reigns supreme.

So the Christ entity does not set up battle lines, does not empower both old and new orders and sit back to watch them duke it out. As it increases the vibration of the planet, most will feel stirrings within, which will eventually lead them to step into the new order. There are those so blunted by fear who will cling to the old order, and it is they who will be the source of whatever degree of trauma and pain you must have before the new order is firmly established.

Let us take a look at a few examples in your society now and see how those battle lines are shaping up.

In California, a governmental commission recently voted to restore mountain lion hunting for sport. The commission's reasoning was that it was appointed by the governor—a conservative—to manage the natural resources of the state, and that the cougars are a "resource" to be "harvested" and "managed." Further, the presence of the cougars necessarily diminished the stock of deer available for hunters, leaving less of a "surplus" to be "harvested."

The debate over whether or not to permit resumption of cougar hunting, while to some extent waged over "statistics," for the most part boiled down to simply this: animals' rights versus hunters' rights.

With their guileless plain speaking, the commissioners who voted for resumption of cougar hunting on the basis that cougars are a "resource" to be "harvested" have stated the fundamental challenge of your era, the chasm between old and new orders.

While religion and science stand, for the most part, in opposite corners of the ring, they are engaged in a loving tryst on one point: Mankind is the top of the heap. Judeo-Christian heritage tells you that you were appointed by God to hold "dominion" over all the animals, all the earth. Science, restricting itself to a linear time perspective, proposes the theory of evolution, once again placing man at the top of the endless battles of natural selection.

Both religion and science lead you to believe you are the very pinnacle of all creation, either blessed by God or the victor of mutational battle.

Yes, you are unique. Yes, you are divine.

No, you do not hold dominion over the earth. No, you are not the pinnacle of creation.

You are **one element** of creation. It is only your European culture, divorced from the natural order, which could lead you to see yourselves as separate from, rather than a part of, the natural world. You participate in the earth's divine balance with your unique filter of a reasoning mind, but such a filter is no more valid, no more important, than that of any other creature that walks, swims or crawls upon the earth.

The cougar is not a resource. It does not require your judgment as to when harvest time is due. It is a divine creature—as are you—with the right to seek its own fulfillment—as have you—and to do so without the interference of other species—same as you.

You have a fine analogy in your AIDS virus. Once again, the body politic is reflected in the human body. Remember that the AIDS virus is never even detected in the bodies of most who carry it. It assumes its place in the harmony of the body. It is only when the virus loses its smooth unity with the natural order of the body that the trouble sets in; the virus views the T-cells, your body's front line of defense, as a resource to be harvested without regard for the effects of its carnivorous attack on the body as a whole. It is only when the virus presumes that its right to reproduce and feed upon its host supercedes that of every other element of the host's body that the trouble arises.

Hunters are the AIDS virus of human society.

Nowhere is the line more clearly drawn between old and new orders. Kill a spark of divinity, for fun! Mount its head on the wall as a trophy! Again, as those advocating animals' rights line up against those advocating hunters' rights, you are left with the spectacle of a United Nations with the headsets turned off. There is no communication. One side operates in the new order, the other in the old. There is no common ground any longer. Either you respect the divinity of all the earth or you presume yourselves masters of the universe.

And what happens to the AIDS virus, in its frantic reproductive activity and disregard for the host, when the host finally expires?

In the issue of health care, you have several recent trends. First is the call for a federally funded catastrophic health plan, ensuring that those faced with sudden and debilitating illness need not go bankrupt. There is also the call for increased coverage for the elderly, eliminating old limits on the number of hospital days that will be covered and so on.

There are several strands we need to pick apart here.

First, you find again the projection of one's power onto others—the federal government. You want others to create your reality for you; you want others to pick up the tab when your unfaced conflicts find physical expression; you do not want the **responsibility** for your bodily integrity.

It is no surprise that these developments are boosted by the liberals. Limiting themselves to a solitary lifespan in an accidental universe, clutching to the physical body as the sole standard of value, viewing death as a cruel end, they again seek to cushion the physical body with a cocoon of social programs designed to sustain that physical life to the last possible moment in the hands of the finest your medical science can offer. They view the body as inherently untrustworthy, prone to failure, like a car or refrigerator, helpless to determine its own health.

As far as the elderly are concerned, we see again a confirmation that they are viewed as decrepit, rusting old heaps, clattering toward death, unable to care for themselves, unable to forestall the decline, the decay and the rot that is old age.

All of these strands can only hold in a culture divorced from the natural order.

Your body is simply the reflection of your soul. There is no division between them other than the membrane separating physical and nonphysical life. If you remain happy, directed, confident and vigorous, your body will never fail you. It delights in sustaining your journeys through life. And if you do find the body manifesting anything other than health, you are meant to **examine your life**, for the nature of the malady itself will carry the entire meaning of its entry into your existence. There is no cold, dark universe bent on destroying you, plaguing you with locusts and viruses and bacteria. If you ignore the quiet signals of your body over too long a time, pretend not to hear their whisperings as they urge you toward a healthier lifestyle, then you may well find yourself faced with catastrophe as a means of slamming on the brakes of your life, the only way the body can awaken you to what you have refused to face.

You create your own reality. You create your own body. It is entirely under your control; its condition, healthy or otherwise, simply reflects the condition of your spirit.

You may not lay claim to the wages of others to hand to doctors because you have not faced up to hidden issues in your life!

Old age is not decline or decay, but **release.** It is only in your culture, tossing aside any who do not actively contribute to the economic machine, that you would dispose of your elderly so cavalierly.

We mentioned earlier how your Social Security system is a violation, robbing the young to support the elderly. You need not take our word for it that such a system cannot persist into the new order; simply look at the actuarial tables, at the rising number of elderly, their increased longevity, the reduced numbers of young people.

But ask any elder you know: Which would provide the greater security, a monthly check from the government arriving at a lonely apartment, or living as a cherished and appreciated member of one's family, guiding grandchildren in their path toward mastery?

True social security is granted to the elderly in every native population! Because you have abandoned your elderly, you assuage your guilt by setting up a system in which you pay them to stay out of your hair! Just as you abandon your children, pay others to care for them because you mistake liberation for corporate status.

In such cases, while the liberal proclaims compassion for those allegedly benefitting from such programs, the truth is the opposite: The liberal abandons responsibility, personal responsibility, for the members of one's family and foists responsibility for their care on others. Some compassion!

Your body will sustain you in fine and vigorous health to your last breath, if you would trust it and listen to it. You are not to entrust your body's care to those whose ignorance results in their approaching your spirit in flesh with poison and scalpel. The span of life is granted for a specific purpose: that grandchild and grandparent should know each other, the little one soaking up the elder's wisdom, bound by their common quality of living with one foot in the physical world, the other beyond it.

True health costs you nothing. True security for the elderly costs you nothing more than another place at the dinner table, more than compensated for by the sure and gentle rudder through life they offer to the generations following them.

Such is the new order.

Your government's patent office recently announced that it will grant patents to those genetic engineers whose work results in new "forms of life." The "inventors" of new life forms will thus "own" the rights to life and be able to benefit, as any inventor does, from their creations.

Remember that the further divorced a field is from Divine Grace, the sooner it will collapse in an immoral heap.

The fact that genetic engineering is such a relatively young field and that it has already plummeted to the depths of grotesque depravity embraced by the patent office should demonstrate, to those with a glimmer of reason remaining, that this field is so utterly and profoundly divorced from the natural order that it can only lead to harm, and soon.

Own life! Fiddle with the genetic structure of life, and then **claim the rights to the results of your malevolence!**

If hunters are the AIDS virus of human society, we confess we can find no life form primitive enough to employ as analogy for those who tinker with the structure of life and then claim to own the results. No paramecium, no molecule, no atom, no electron would ever engage in such behavior.

Again, if you do not voluntarily choose to turn away from such a field of endeavor, which has as its basis utter contempt for life, then **destruction of life** is what you shall experience until you are **forced** to turn away from a field that would **never even be contemplated** in a society embracing the natural order.

We do not believe in employing scare tactics, so we offer the gentlest euphemism we could find—you shall watch your children eaten alive from the inside out—when hoping to dissuade you from this path. Do we need to describe it in gory detail, how the "new form of life" that is "owned" by your species begins at the spine, eating its way up the central nervous system, to lodge and fester and wreak havoc in the brain? Must we describe the appearance of a child's face as the brain and skull rot from within?

We need not. Continue on this path and you will behold it for yourselves.

Again, there will be those instinctively appalled at the malicious meddling of those engaged in this field of research, incensed by the actions of the patent office. There can be no common ground between the two camps; you cannot argue it out on the basis of reason or anything else. It is such a **profound violation**, represents such a triumph of the old order, that there is no longer a bridge between the two sides. Remember, as time passes, the possibility of living with one foot in the new order, one in the old, evaporates. You must choose.

Those clinging to the old order, fiddling with the basis of life, will make an array of lofty claims about the "good" for society that will result from their efforts— curing of genetic diseases, manufacture of synthetic hormones, etc., etc.

And do you remember the siren call of those advocating nuclear power? Too cheap to meter! Yes sir! As your utility customers are saddled with the doubling, tripling, of their bills to pay for reactors, some of which will never be turned on, you might pause and consider the veracity of those early claims.

Yes, nuclear power plants can indeed provide electricity. Tell that to those living near Three Mile Island, near Chernobyl. Was it worth it?

Yes, genetic engineering may result in all sorts of marvels. Tell that to your mutated children. Is it worth it?

You need not take our word for this; and indeed, you should not. You should find such a field of endeavor so repulsive that you turn away from it, not out of scare tactics but out of recognition of its profound violation of the natural order.

Ultimately, you will. The question is, how many must die before you do so? You choose.

We have sketched three areas of your society in which the fissure between old and new orders shows itself in clear and unmistakable terms. Ultimately, every facet, every aspect, of your society will split itself as well, between old and new orders. And there will be no straddlers, no middle-of-the-roaders. You can either step into the new order or cling to the old. To do the latter will only ensure that the time of transition will be unnecessarily traumatic.

But you choose.

Now is the time to further expand our earlier discussion of politics, to look more closely at the nature of the fears motivating the two political camps and where they will lead.

The liberal fears annihilation, death. This results from the liberal's disdain for the traditional forms of religion, promising Hell or Heaven, salvation or condemnation. The liberal prefers to live in the physical world, and science is the high religion of this world. Since science proposes that the universe, the world and your body are all accidents, the liberal's greatest fear is of death, annihilation, bringing a close to one's accidental existence.

Because one always fights fear by clinging to its opposite, we thus find that the liberal's motivating fear, of annihilation, of death, propels him to **embrace life.** You find the liberals much more open to embracing alternative lifestyles, to sybaritic pleasure, to tolerance, to concern for the downtrodden, precisely because the liberal's core fear leads him to embrace life, to follow the resignation to ultimate annihilation with the attitude that one might as well enjoy life while one is here. "You only live once." There is thus an embrace of life on the part of the liberal, though because such is motivated by fear, it will result in some deleterious effects—your monstrous government.

The conservative's core fear is of anarchy. Taught by traditional religion that you have fallen from grace, are born in original sin, bound and determined to go to Hell unless toeing the straight and narrow line prescribed by religion, the conservative comes to fear impulses. In religion's view, impulses are the whisperings of the devil, leading one astray from one's righteous path.

In fact, as we have seen, impulses are the whisperings of your parallel selves, urging you to your fulfillment. In addition, the natural world operates entirely on impulse, of a spontaneous order incomprehensible to the conservative's mind.

The conservative thus **fears life itself**—and as one always assuages fear by clinging to its opposite—the conservative **embraces death.**

This is why the conservative agenda reads like the Grim Reaper's Christmas list. If you follow every principle of the conservative philosophy to its logical outcome, you will find one common denominator: death.

More guns, more tanks, more bullets, more bombs. Death.

Snatching food from the mouths of poor children to buy $600 toilet seats for the armed services. Death.

Unbridled destruction of the natural world in pursuit of profit. Death.

Subjugation of native populations into cogs in the capitalist machine. Death.

Smothering the child's natural, impulsive grace with the harness of adult conformity and productivity. Death.

Encouraging the "harvesting" of "resources" by clubs whose unifying feature is their love of weaponry. Death.

Funding genetic research and turning it into a profit center for entrepreneurs. Death.

Capital punishment. Death.

Nuclear power. Death.

In every instance, then, the ultimate outcome of the conservative's agenda is death. Death of the spirit, death of the natural world, death of children, death of native cultures, death of the planet.

Ye shall know the old order by its Orwellian doublespeak! For what banner do conservatives drape themselves in, to buttress their philosophy? "Pro-life"!!

This banner is waved most vigorously when the subject is abortion. If conservatives genuinely care about the fetuses of the world, why would they advocate the slashing of social programs sustaining the resultant human children? The conservative's concern for the fetus ends at birth. Because the conservative's root motive is not concern for life in general but concern for one's own life, fear for one's security in a world ruled by an angry and vengeful God; as so often happens, this inner fear is **projected** onto the world at large, where it finds a **symbol** of the inner helplessness—a fetus—and rushes to its defense rather than face the fear inside.

For these are the same people, as we have seen, who advocate capital punishment! What hypocrisy is this? Is life sacred or is it not?

Again, it is not a philosophy, a coherent, cohesive philosophy, that informs the conservative's agenda. It is simply the fear of life. The result is death.

Remember that as the Christ entity infuses the planet with an increased vibration, those clinging to the old order will feel their energy draining and react with hysteria. This will further manifest in increasingly ill health, difficulties in interpersonal relations and loss of reason.

In your society, do you find the rise of the Right wing matched by an equally vehement Left wing? Do you find Marxists bombing NRA offices corresponding with good Christian souls bombing abortion clinics?

You do not. This is your clue that the conservatives are those clinging to the old order, resorting to hysteria and violence, while there is no similar reaction from the liberal camp.

For the liberal's fear propels him to **embrace life.** The conservative's fear leads him to **embrace death.** And unless you consider the ideal new order to be a cemetery, you can see which way the world is headed.

Further, notice how precisely the two competing philosophies, motivated by fear, interlock and mesh with each other. The liberal **fears death** and **embraces life.** The conservative **fears life** and **embraces death.** Around and around you go, arm in arm, equally contributing to the monstrous budget deficit as you seek to assuage your fears with second-hand reality—money—rather than face the **root issues** in your society.

You ushered in the decade of the Eighties by electing the oldest president* ever in your history.

Now, we do not subscribe to your beliefs about old age, but it is precisely those beliefs that will create your reality. Contrasting with the youngest president ever elected ushering in the Sixties—standing as a symbol of the new order—your oldest president, elected to rule over the decade where the lines are firmly drawn between old and new orders, is necessarily your most conservative president of the century.

If you think us about to embark on a round of president-bashing, you have not yet learned that you create your reality and your elected leaders merely reflect your beliefs.

This man did not storm the palace gates. He presented his platform, his philosophy, openly and honestly.

He promised to cut taxes, increase defense spending and balance the budget.

The abandonment of reason.

He promised to boost the military budget.

The betrayal of divinity.

He warned about the "evil empire" threatening your liberties at every turn, around the globe.

Unbridled fear.

Responding to this, a majority of those voting elected this president.

Has this president and his administration followed through on his promises?

During his administration, the deficit has ballooned in an amount equal to the deficit racked up in the entire history of the country before him.

While the military budget has certainly been boosted, are you more secure? We shall delve into this more thoroughly later.

What you find is that this president and his administration have betrayed virtually **every tenet** of the conservative philosophy and yet continue to be cheered by the conservatives!

Deficit spending is anathema to the conservative. The budget must be balanced. No business could operate the way your government does. Your president has amassed debt at a rate unprecedented in your history, and still the conservatives cheer.

National security is a top priority of the conservative, fearing the world of festering impulse. And while your president has expended billions on researching a cosmic cheesecloth to spread above the globe—which no rational person believes can work—it is no accident that his administration was so lax in supervising security at the Moscow embassy—where it genuinely matters—that the military men—no accident—assigned to guard the structure gladly exchanged your national security for sex! And still the conservatives cheer.

A prime tenet of the conservative philosophy is that each business must stand or fall on its own, without seeking assistance from government. As we have seen, the timber industry enjoys a fine, fat subsidy from the department allegedly as-

*Ronald Reagan

signed to protect the natural world, thus aiding private industry at a loss to the taxpayer. And still the conservatives cheer.

You see, it does not matter what this president does. His supporters will cheer him because **reason has been abandoned**. He could proclaim Marx's birthday a national holiday, and the conservatives would cheer. Remember that as the energy is cut out from under the old order, their reasoning faculties, their health and their relationships will suffer. You can see, then, that among the far Right who most vociferously support this president, the conservatives are losing their minds. They have abandoned all reason and cheer on a president who has betrayed every conservative principle. The debate is no longer on a rational plane. Psychosis is setting in, and you will find the Right wing becoming more and more extreme, irrational, violent and psychotic in their behavior as time passes.

The issue of "national security" merits discussion, as it is so central to this administration and to the conservative's philosophy.

In the recent scandals about selling arms to Iran to fund the Nicaraguan rebels, defying a Congressional ban, and in the Marine Moscow scandal, you find several telling clues, or common denominators.

First, those betraying your security were military men. Yes, your beloved military will be the first to betray your security. Why? Because you turn to the military for security, and that need for security is built on fear, and because what you fear will always bring about the opposite of what you desire. If your fears propel you to turn to the military for security, then the **military will betray your security**.

If we look at the military's history in the past few decades, what do we find? They could not win in Vietnam. They could not rescue the hostages in Iran. They circumvented Congress to illegally fund the Nicaraguan rebellion.

Each step, then, is meant to bring to your awareness that what you desire is the opposite of what you are experiencing. But you have not seen this and have continued to fund the Pentagon as the source of your security.

Thus you now find the truly ludicrous spectacle of Marines—your military's finest—trading national security for orgasms.

How much further need this go on?

You see, the military will continue to fail you, again and again and again, until you come to see that it **cannot** provide you with security. Your security is **guaranteed** in the natural order. When your fears compel you to seek it in armaments, it is the holders of those armaments who will betray your security first.

What was the military's goal in the attack on Libya? To assassinate the Libyan leader with no civilian casualties. And what resulted? The Libyan leader escaped ungrazed while innocent men, women and children died. The bombs, promised by the military men to be so accurate, went far off the mark, scattering death and destruction far from their targets.*

---

*Of the nine Air Force planes sent to attack Kadafi's compound, four turned back after their lasers and target sensors broke down; none of the "smart bombs" released by the five remaining planes scored a direct hit.

And this was hailed as a victory! And still the conservatives cheered.

Can you not see the progression, from the inability to win the Vietnam War to the spectacle of allowing the KGB the run of your embassy in exchange for a roll in the hay? Any philosophy, any area of your existence, divorced from Divine Grace will play itself out in **increasingly ludicrous** extremes until you face the root fear.

How much further will you allow the military to compromise your security? How much longer before you dispense with instruments of death, holding them as keepers of the peace when in fact they only ensure war?

We do not advocate unilateral disarmament. The conservatives running the Kremlin will also find their reason clouded as time goes on and the old order is cut off. The creeping psychosis of the Right wing in your society will be matched by the leaders there, if they do not change.

For it is the world, as one, that must together once and for all dispense with the belief that weaponry is strength, that security lies in the barrel of a gun.

Again, such is a reflection of your belief in your own powerlessness and your projection of your personal power onto others. This is now expressed in the extreme situation of your fate lying in the hands of the Politburo, beyond any hope of discourse within your own society. You must **reclaim** your personal power, refuse to project it on others and to allow them to build tanks and bombs and bullets to ensure the security that is yours, granted, free, in the natural order, but from which you have strayed.

The military cannot provide you with security. They will betray it, in increasingly serious incidents until you order the last general out of the Pentagon to shut off the light.

How much trauma must you endure before that day?

You choose.

The brouhaha over selling arms to Iran in exchange for hostages and then shipping the proceeds to the Nicaraguan rebels deserves a bit of scrutiny.

Once again, you find the conservatives cheering the actions of a president who did the precise opposite of what he said he would: negotiate with terrorists.

The operation was run by military men. If you asked them their motives, they would say they were fighting for freedom and democracy to be installed in Nicaragua, along the lines of your own government.

But because this fear—of communism—is by definition irrational, it will bring about the precise opposite of what is desired. For how was this financial backing for the contras arranged? By circumventing your triumvirate system of judicial, legislative and executive branches. This is the cornerstone of your precious liberty, the guarantor of the endurance of your system, and such was **betrayed** by those who sought to **protect** your constitutional form of government! This occurred because fear, not reason, was driving the actions of those involved, and the result—a private fiefdom of guns and money—was the very **antithesis** of your system.

Now, however scandalous this seems to you, note another aspect of the situation. Did those involved benefit in any personal way? Did they enrich themselves off the public treasury? Did the investigators burst into their offices, to find 12,000 pairs of shoes? They did not. Those involved did so at personal sacrifice, in terms of time away from their families and so on. So the motive was not mere base greed or powermongering, but was based on a genuine love for your system. But fearing that the system was under attack from a tiny impoverished Central American nation—as irrational as one can get—the inevitable result was the establishment of a caricature of a Third World despotic regime, answering to no one, by-passing the law, beyond the reach of reason.

The commission investigating the matter was rather scathing in its view of the president's management style, which could have allowed all this to occur without his knowledge. If, in fact, the president did not authorize these illegal activities, the very best that can be said is that he was asleep.

What better leader for a country that sleepwalks toward oblivion? Your elected leaders, again, merely reflect the state of your society. The man himself is blameless, for he is performing according to the wishes of the populace. You do not want to create your reality; you do not want responsibility for your actions; you do not want to face the root issues of your society, preferring instead to duke it out over the second-hand reality of liberal versus conservative while the very structure of the society—the economy, the Constitution and the natural order—rot from underneath you.

No president has ever performed truer to the expectations and desires of those who elected him, and even those who voted for the opposition. You are all somnambulant, and your actor president has portrayed this with impeccable polish for all the country, and all the world, to see.

Let us pick up the strand mentioned earlier and explore it further.

The fate of your society now rests in the hands of the Kremlin, as a reflection of your projection of personal power onto the world at large.

Remember from our earlier discussion of the Christ entity that the fundamental lesson it will infuse the world with is to move you away from projecting a separate God, an omniscient Being out there somewhere, and come to understand that **God is within**, that you are not cast off from the divine source of the universe but are part of it. Just as there is no separation between your spirit and the body, so there is no separation between All That Is and you.

As an analogy, consider the molecules of your body, taking their place in the liver, the heart, the skin. Now, are those molecules you? They are not. But are they separate from you? They are not. They are part of you but they are not you, nor can they survive when separated from you.

So it is with your relationship to All That Is, the divine source of your world. You are a part of it, not separate.

So when you look for God, you must now move from looking outward to looking inward. There is the divine source of your life.

Remember that the last time the Christ entity engaged the earth, the resultant drama centered on the man Jesus. Because his teachings were so threatening to those in power, clinging to the old order, your myth tells you that Jesus was crucified.

Now. If, this time around, **everyone** is feeling the Christ entity **welling up from inside**, how will the drama manifest itself? It is this: If you insist on clinging to the old order, **you will crucify yourselves**.

You see this already. You do not need us to tell you this. What happens if nuclear war erupts? What happens when genetic disaster is unleashed? What is the AIDS virus doing to your culture? What about poisoned water and air?

You are all being crucified on the cross of your ignorance.

You can no more stop the march of the new order than could Pilate in his day. The only area of volition on your part is how difficult you will make it on yourselves—how many of your brethren you will nail to the cross—before allowing the new order to suffuse human society.

You see, you are **all in this together**. No one person will arrive to save you from yourselves. The Christ entity is working **within you**—now—and the time of transition will be as traumatic or painless as you wish, depending on how many of you allow yourselves to step into the new vibration, the new order, and how many cling to the old.

The Eighties, then, represent the time of the Christ entity's return to your plane, following up its first appearance in the Sixties with an even more increased vibrational frequency, leaving your society polarized into new and old orders, with those clutching to the old ultimately losing their health and sanity.

You are all on the road to Calvary. Will you proceed, or chart a new path?

Such is what you will face in the time to come.

CHAPTER FIFTY-SIX

The New Order

You may wonder, if the battle lines are shaping up between old and new orders in your society, increasingly polarizing into two distinct camps, the air fraught with potential danger, what one who wishes to aid the establishment of the new order can do.

You may well feel that the old order—the alleged primacy of your species over all others, the chasing after money and possessions when true love and contact could not be found, the cutthroat competition endemic to your society—has failed you and that you wish to step into the new. How do you do so?

We are happy to provide the answer from the banks of our infinite wisdom. Ready, ladies and gentlemen? Notebooks open? Pencils sharpened? Breath bated? Ears straining to hear? Bursting with suspense?

Here, then, is what you must do to usher in the new order:

Absolutely nothing!

You see, the new order is already here. It is upon you. You need not leap any great chasm between old and new orders. Just gently step into the new rhythms that are already to be felt everywhere in your society.

Nothing ever falls from the sky upon you. Everything approaches first obliquely, then returns with greater and greater strength. The Christ entity works the same way, approaching, withdrawing and returning. You already feel its stirrings within you.

If you concern yourself with fighting the old order, then what do you do? You simply **empower** it. You give it your **energy**. And while that energy may be born of anger on your part, at base energy is simply energy, and what you hurl as negative energy can then be fashioned into positive energy by your opponent, strengthening the other side. It is best, therefore, if you do not allow the histrionics, the hysteria and aphasia of the old order to consume you, for in doing so you simply empower it.

Now, a fine line must be drawn. In the present state of your society, it would not be wise for those who are environmentally aware to simply turn their backs on the destruction as the old order, the "pro-development" (doublespeak!) forces, rapes and plunders what little is left. To some extent you must maintain a holding pattern, lest there be nothing left to save.

But far more important in establishing the new order is to feel the swelling **inside** you and to follow that to a life of purpose, vigor and happiness. Above all, you must restore yourselves to the **joy** that is life at its base. If you become grim and narrow-minded about battling the forces of the old order, you are betraying the purpose of the new order!

Now, there is a way to synthesize both your rejection of the old order and embrace of the new order, and to do so in the healthiest possible way.

For so long you have reacted to an opponent's nonsense with anger and contempt. Now, as we have seen, such only leads to empowering the other side. In our discussion of art, remember one potent weapon you have in your arsenal that will not only decimate an opponent but make you feel better.

That weapon? **Humor.** If you laugh at your opponents, what happens? You feel better. They cannot continue their bluster, for they know you see through their subterfuge. Thus do you reject the old order and ring in the new!

As an example, what would happen if your Secretary of Defense were to sit before a Congressional panel and assure them that the few isolated incidents of outrageous overpricing by defense contractors were behind, and that the Pentagon was now running a lean, efficient organization; and, in response, all the Senators simply fell off their chairs with laughter? And if the gallery simply split their sides guffawing? Those seeing through the ruse would feel better, and the man responsible for so enlivening the day of everyone present would perhaps be less likely to offer up such a heap of flapdoodle the next time around.

The best weapon we can recommend, then, as the struggle between old and new orders intensifies, is humor. Can you imagine a political rally at which a presidential candidate found his every line greeted with hysteria? Would he perhaps not change his tune?

Since, as we have said, the new order is already upon you, in attenuated form, let us look at the sundry areas of society we have concentrated on throughout and see how the new order is manifesting itself.

For so long you have been bamboozled into thinking capitalism and Marxism the only economic systems available to the world that you cannot conceive of any other possibility. Yet your species managed to struggle along before *The Wealth of Nations* and *Das Kapital*, did it not? No native culture was ever based on either capitalism or Marxism.

Both philosophies spring from European culture, and both are therefore predicated on a divorce from the natural order.

You see, you have been handed capitalism and Marxism as "package deals" for so long that you cannot see how each is in fact constructed of two layers— one of **premise** and one of **execution**.

The **premise** of capitalism is that the individual must be held supreme, free to follow his own inclinations and talents, and to find the reward for his effort accruing to him.

Who can argue with that?

The **premise** of Marxism is that no man is an island, that yours is a gregarious species given to social structure, and that attention must be given to ensure that no one element of society amasses enormous wealth while others starve.

Who can argue with that?

The premises of both capitalism and Marxism are entirely valid. It is in the execution that the divorce from the natural order manifests, leading both systems to ultimate collapse.

Because you see yourselves as separate from God, as separate from the natural world and as separate from each other, you have been led to believe that the world operates on the Darwinian model of competition among the species, and within each species. The execution of capitalism is thus based on competition— dog-eat-dog.

The basis for capitalism in your culture is competition.

The basis of the natural order is **cooperation**.

You see, you can just as easily construct a new economic order layering the premise of capitalism upon the basis of the natural order.

While the premise of Marxism is valid—you must consider the welfare of others—it is the execution, based on your divorce from the natural order, that leads to its collapse.

For Marxist states are always based on force. It arises from revulsion against the capitalist system's disparities of wealth and privilege, and forces everyone to contribute to the greater good. But who determines that greater good? By what divine right? This system necessarily squashes every semblance of individuality in pursuit of a common good, to be determined in the far reaches of the bureaucracy.

Marxism is based on force.

The natural order is based on **respect**.

In the natural order, no organism, no plant, no animal ever forces its will on another. Even the constant dance of predator and prey is not one of force, for on deepest terms, all organisms understand that as they have partaken of others to sustain their life, so ultimately must they contribute, whether restoring the soil upon decay or more immediately as food.

You can just as easily construct a new economic order layering the premise of Marxism—concern for others—upon the basis of the natural order, respect.

Both capitalism and Marxism must ultimately fall, then, because they are divorced from the natural order. Of the two, capitalism reflects the mechanics of the universe while Marxism betrays both mechanics and foundation. Thus, you find Marxist states—established only in this century—collapsing in a heap of stagnation while your capitalist economy, two hundred years old, still has some steam left.

You see, the new order's economic system will not fall from the sky to dazzle you with its brilliance and novelty. The new order's economic system will simply be the **synthesis** of the **premises** of capitalism and Marxism, layered upon the basis of the natural order.

How does this work?

Again, it is already upon you. There is a concept or phrase gaining a foothold in the society called "right livelihood." Yes, you are to follow your talents and ambitions and profit from them. But you do so with an understanding of the "right"– the natural order. You do not seek to destroy those offering the same services or products. You do not sell products you know to be shabby, poorly made or potentially fatal. You do not decimate the natural world in order to sustain yourself.

The reason you need so many governmental restrictions and regulations on the marketplace is that the execution of your capitalist system, based on divorce from the natural order, leads to companies fouling the air and water, manufacturing products they know to be faulty, potentially lethal, and selling them anyway! Because profit is the bottom line, rather than integrity. So you must construct a welter of regulations designed to protect yourselves from the success of your system!

No monstrous government can persist into the new order. And you can see that **you will not need it** because it would never occur to anyone to destroy the natural world for the sake of profit, to endanger the lives of those sustaining one's livelihood or to pawn off cheap and shabby wares.

Thus you find the synthesis of capitalism and Marxism, their premises joined in the concept of "right livelihood" while it rides on the foundation of the natural order.

That's it.

If, as we maintain, your present government cannot persist into the new order, what will replace it?

Again, your government has grown so enormous because you have projected your personal power outward, have sought to assuage your fears with the second-hand reality of money, have sought to correct the imbalances of the society with reflections of meaning rather than face the root issues. Once such are dismissed from your society, the need for a monstrous central government will evaporate.

Further, note how the country has changed over the course of its life. When first founded, you were thirteen colonies fresh from war with Britain, and it made sense for the colonies to embrace in a cohesion of unity. At that time the population, while engaging in the perennial battles over every little issue, was far more homogeneous than yours is today. It was almost entirely composed of immigrants from England, along with the slaves imported from Africa. There was thus a unity of history, language and culture binding the fledgling country.

Your country now stretches from the Bering Sea to the South Pacific, embracing every race, every culture on earth as all seek to escape the stifling regimes that dominate most societies and seek the relative freedom of your culture. The original purpose of strong federal government is gone, and you thus find yourselves papered over with federalism, burdened with the suffocating paternalism of a government such that you can barely turn your head without bashing up against one more restriction on your life.

This is the result of clinging to a system that made sense in its day but does not in yours, and of your projection of your power onto others, your leaders and the bureaucracy they rule.

For there is an intrinsic unfairness to the way the public's money is doled out, is there not? There is no longer any cohesion of culture, history and purpose among you, so why should one group be forced to underwrite the needs or whims of another? If the AIDS crisis is to be funded by government, why should monogamous Midwestern couples subsidize the compulsive promiscuity of homosexuals on the coasts? Why should New Yorkers, whose subway system belongs in an amusement park as the Hell ride, underwrite the construction of a subway in Los Angeles? Why should those who work support those who choose not to?

And the game of slicing up the treasury's pie is simply a feeding frenzy by the special interest groups and their high-priced lobbyists. For what other way is there to decide who should get what? There is no moral basis for making such decisions, so one bad system is as good as any other bad system.

In the future, those stepping into the new order will return to **community-based government**. As we have seen, those of similar interests, aptitudes and beliefs will gravitate naturally to different parts of the country. It is therefore fairest that local government should be the strongest, with the federal government restricted to policing the borders and other matters best handled at that level.

Again, no new structure of government will fall from the sky to replace the present system. In fact, the new order will be based upon the oldest form of participatory government your country has known: the New England town meeting. Here, at least once a year, the citizens of a town gather to discuss issues of common interest and decide where their money will be spent. Everyone has a chance to speak up, to be heard, to have his voice considered. There is **direct connection** between the governed and the governing. They stand face to face. And while one will not always have one's wishes accepted by the group, one at least has the satisfaction of having one's voice heard in an atmosphere of **respect**. Remember respect, the basis of the natural order, the way you acknowledge Divine Grace in the world?

And if the actions and policies of a given locale are simply too incompatible with one's views, one can always move elsewhere. Thus you ensure the freedom of association, the respect of having one's opinions incorporated into governmental decision making, in a direct fashion between leader and citizen.

Sounds good, doesn't it? How many are willing to step into the new order? And are you willing to send back your Society Security check? To refuse any student loans? To run your farm without handouts? To not consider running to government when your business fails? For of such will the new order be made: those refusing to lay claim to the wages of others.

Once again, there will be no force installing the new order. You will simply turn away from the old order. When you are willing to create your own reality, without laying claim to the efforts of others, then you have chosen to step into the new order.

As far as science and technology are concerned, the only shift that need be made is to instill **respect for the earth** among those in the field. There is no thought of turning back the clock, then, of relinquishing electricity and computers and the other accoutrements of your society, for such aid your life's work. The schism between old and new orders, in the field of science, is caused by those who view the earth as an accident. Who holds respect for an accident?

Science must restore itself to a sense of the **divinity** infusing the earth. Nuclear power, genetic engineering and animal research would never even occur to anyone working in concert with the natural order. They are violations, made possible only by divorce from the natural order, and they will necessarily lead to harm as a means of nudging you back toward the natural order.

The irony is that your quantum physicists are already leaping and bounding into the new order, shattering your notions of linear time, of space, of matter and of energy. This is the cutting edge, and if you find some of our statements throughout this work ridiculous, don't direct your ire toward us—point it at your quantum physicists! For they will find far more areas of agreement than disagreement with what we have said. Space and time are an illusion, and it will not be long before your quantum physicists are like Dorothy meeting the Wizard of Oz, ripping away the curtain—the membrane—to reveal the mechanics responsible for all the smoke and fire.

Science and technology will march right beside you, then, into the new order. They will do so when once again restored to a sense of the divine in the physical earth they explore.

On the other side of the ring, religion will move toward a restoration of your **reason**. As matters now stand, you are asked to believe the most outrageous fairy tales, told that you eat the literal flesh of Christ in communion, and that if you question such doctrine, you are merely paving your own way to Hell.

As you come to see that there is no separation between you and the divine source of your world, you will no longer need a church, a bureaucracy or houses of worship. Your body is your temple, as we believe someone has mentioned before us. You need not look outward to express your unity with the divine, but **inward.** You will no longer invest the caretakers of bureaucratic religion with omniscience, with the power to grant absolution of sin. By going to confession and being absolved, you have escaped responsibility for your acts. Never! in the cosmos can you escape such responsibility. What the process reflects, in deepest terms, is that there are no "good" or "bad" acts, only growth and learning. But on your plane one will certainly be capable of negative influence, and there can be no absolution for this! If the transgression is not redressed in this life, you shall certainly have ample opportunity in the future.

Religion will be seen as the divine source, felt within, upon which you navigate through life with your reason, never—never—accepting another's word on blind faith alone, but insisting on matching **divinity** with **reason.**

This warrants further discussion. You see, you have split the twin pillars of human consciousness—divinity and reason—into two opposing camps. Just as you did with capitalism and Marxism; the cause of this sundering is your divorce from the natural order.

Your species is constructed to explore the earth plane in the **security** of its divine source, using its **reason** to manipulate physical reality. Such are not divorced, not in the natural order. There is never a conflict between reason and divinity in the natural world. It is only in yours, cut off from a sense of the divinity of the world and your species' purpose, that you would split reason and divinity into two camps—one holding reason supreme and wreaking havoc on the natural world, the other claiming divinity supreme and abandoning reason.

Remember the stages of life. Remember that the first stage of life is to establish one's **security**—is the world safe? am I loved?—as a means of creating a **bed of divinity**, of love, upon which all else will be based.

Following that, in the second stage of life one's task is **mastery**—the use of **reason**—to learn to manipulate physical life within the given parameters of your species and world.

There is no divorce between reason and divinity in the child, then. They are meant to work in tandem, always, as one charts a course through life. For the most part, in your culture, one's divinity is beaten out of consciousness—you are taught that the world is not safe; it is an accident; pestilence awaits you around every corner—and thus you are left crippled, with only reason to guide you through life. This results in the maimed culture you now share, the reason for the impending collapse in so many areas of your society.

So you will join the premises of religion and science—reason and divinity—upon a secure cushion of the natural order.

Science will then never consider pursuing any avenue based on disrespect, contempt or hostility for any form of life, or the genetic basis of life. Religion will no longer expect you to surrender your reason to reach salvation.

You see, when we speak of a new order, of what are we speaking? You are simply being **restored** to the oldest order! The natural order, from which you sprang, from which you strayed. You are just being nudged back into your path, that is all. No cosmic intervention, no lightning bolts, no stunning ethereal displays. Simply **restoration**.

Indeed, in the times beyond the restoration of the natural order to your world, there will be growth and expansion of consciousness beyond anything you can presently experience. But this is not the focus of our book. We are simply pointing out the immediate task at hand, restoring yourselves to the natural order, which is simply a return to the world from which you sprang.

You see now how politics, science and religion—your unholy trinity—will change in the time to come. In each case, they will return power to you, the individual, supreme above the mass. Government will shrink. Science will look upon you, your body, with respect. Religion will restore your reason.

And you will be restored.

And that, ladies and gentlemen, is your brave new world.

As we mentioned earlier, although the Christ entity operates this time around by infusing **everyone on earth** with a rush of divinity, there will be those with one foot more firmly rooted in the new order, and those with both feet already there. How will you know them?

As the false profits of television evangelism collapse like a clown pyramid at the circus, who will arise to guide you in the time to come?

Most important of all will be to assume responsibility and control for your own life, independent of others. With your reason and divinity restored, there will be less need to seek wisdom from outside. All wisdom comes from within.

For the time being, however, before your full restoration to the natural order, you may find the words of others to be of help. This is a good time to examine in detail the present rise in the incidence of "channeling"—a subject on which we have some authority—and the reason for its upsurge at this time.

While those able to give voice to spirit entities have always been among you, there is now a surge in that activity, particularly in your decade. This is a result of the Christ entity's returning to your plane, and it is meant as a **bridge** between old and new orders, not the new order itself!

Beginning in the Sixties, there were a few individuals who found themselves suddenly able to drop into trance and allow the discarnate to speak, either through automatic writing or in full voice. This process expanded in the Seventies, with more joining the fold. Now, in the Eighties, you find a veritable explosion, with everybody and his mother chatting with Peter the Great over tea and crumpets.

Notice the characteristics of those channeling. They are almost all of the white race, are they not? A good percentage are male. Our favorite group. The furthest divorced from the natural order. Why should they be channels of wisdom from planes beyond?

Among such individuals, particularly those who have rejected traditional religion and cannot stomach the atrocities of science, there will be a certain questioning, a certain confusion about how to make sense of the world. Reason and divinity can only be joined by the nexus of the natural order, and as these individuals are divorced from that natural order, they are therefore left floundering—as are many of you—seeing the world going to Hell but not knowing how to stop the slide.

Your psyche is a construction of electromagnetic reality, whose configuration is determined, for the most part, before birth but which will change over time, as you pull physical experiences into your store of memory. Those who are, at base, divorced from the natural order but yearning toward the new may therefore cause a fissure in the psyche, a gap that can be used as a **channel**—literally—by those on the spirit plane, to address those on earth.

Remember that your closest links to the natural order are animals and young children.

Have you ever seen the neighborhood dogs gathered humbly around one of their species, as it fell into trance and brought forth messages from Lassie in the Sky?

Have you ever known a young child to fall to the floor in trance and educate his cohorts as to the mysteries of the alphabet and multiplication tables?

You see, animals and young children know nothing of channeling, for they are **channeling nature** every moment of their lives. They have no confusion that would lead to a fissure in the psyche which would permit the entrance of the discarnate.

Our host recently took a trip to the east coast, during which he spent time with his younger sister and a friend. We can predict with utter certainty that neither of these young people will ever channel. Are they spiritually deficient? Precisely the opposite: They are so **firmly, deeply rooted** in the natural order that they have no **need** to hear advice from the spirit plane **restoring** them to the natural order. They are already there!

The same holds true for your great artists or anyone on your plane who lives a life in harmony with the natural order. They are already there.

You see, then, how the increasing polarization of your society lines up vis-à-vis the issue of channeling. Those clinging to the old order are of such a low vibration that they are entirely unable to meet us halfway, so to speak, and form a bond through which we might speak. Those entirely rooted in the new order, living in harmony with the natural world, will also not be prone to channeling, for they don't need it. It is only those **straddling** old and new orders—the white race struggling to return to its natural roots—who can form a **bridge** between new and old orders, a **bridge** between earth and spirit plane.

Further, understand that all information channeled will always be filtered through the beliefs, prejudices and knowledge of the host. No human can speak Ultimate Truth, pure, distilled from the Heart of the Universe. **Neither can we.** In our plane of existence, we are still learning, still growing and still straddling old and new orders, one physical foot in the earth plane, one ectoplasmic foot in the spirit plane.

What we can offer is a version of reality stripped of the limitations of the earth plane, for we have taken a step back into the spiritual plane. We can then filter this through the mind of the host. This explains why you find a strong convergence between the beliefs of the host and the speakings of the entity. It is not that the information is wrong but that it is filtered. As long as the host's beliefs do not contradict the nature of reality, there is no reason why they cannot be employed as the basis for deeper information, you see.

Now, we have had a spat or two with our host during the production of this book, where he was indeed clinging to beliefs that cannot hold in the light of our understanding, and which therefore had to be overridden. But since those channeling at all necessarily have one foot in the new order, there will not be many incidents of genuine conflict between the **beliefs** of the host and the **information** of the spirit guide.

There are those who would "test" channeled entities by insisting they pick the winning lottery number, the next hot stock, the next earthquake. Such challenges usually come from those grounded in the scientific world. And what is the basis of science? The physical world. And what is the basis of physical matter? The atom. And what is the nature of the electron? Unpredictability.

This is no accident. Unpredictability guarantees your free will. If we tell you something will occur, and on the basis of it you change your beliefs or thought patterns, then the predicted event will not occur because you exercised your free will and pulled in a different parallel self at that moment in time. This is why legitimate psychics or channeled entities shy away from making predictions; for not only is it impossible to see the future with utter clarity, but to insist that something will occur robs you of your free will.

What we can see is **potentials, trends,** which if a course is not altered, **may** enter your existence. We can see potential earths, holding the limitless possible outcomes of your struggle to install the new order. There is a parallel earth on which your children are eaten alive by genetic disaster. You need never experience that earth, and you will not if you but turn away from the beliefs that make such a possibility. You are thus **empowered**, not diminished, by our suggesting this possible outcome.

Perhaps we have taken some wind out of the sails of those who channel, and of the spirits coming through. The phenomenon of channeling occurs because you are so desperate for knowledge as to how to right your course that those straddling new and old orders can indeed serve as channels for discarnate information. But once the new order is established, channeling will cease. You will **channel nature**. You will **channel yourselves**, if you can excuse the imagery.

This is why channeling is rising in incidence at this time and will continue to do so until the establishment of the new order. Your psyches are being yanked in two directions; the species cries out for guidance; and it is part of our growth to provide what we can.

We have cast a broad glance around your society and demonstrated how its condition results from your divorce from the natural order. Our entire work can be summed up as follows: You are divine creatures, blessed with reason.

Is this so brilliant, so earth-shattering? Is this the wisdom of the ages? **It is the wisdom of the human infant.**

You see, there is not a thought in this book you were not **born knowing**. As you have read, you may have felt a jump of recognition inside and exclaimed, "Yes! I know that!"

Indeed you do. Indeed you always have.

It is as if, upon birth, someone hacked your legs off. Decades later, as you pull yourself down the sidewalk on your elbows, someone walks up and says, "By the way, here are your legs back." You have not been granted something new; you have simply been restored.

That is our purpose. We're offering you your legs back. And, as always—You choose!

Have we maintained throughout that your closest links with the natural order are the animals and young human children? We refer you to Jesus of Nazareth:

"Observe the birds of the air. . .consider the lilies of the field, how they grow."

"Let the children come to me, and do not hinder them: for to such belongs the kingdom of heaven."

You see, we are world-class plagiarists, shameless ones at that. We are restoring you to knowledge given you two thousand years ago, in your terms.

So do not fall humbled before any channeled entity or any host giving them voice. **Fall humbled before your own divinity. Worship yourselves. Reclaim your proper place in the divine order of nature.**

A few years back, your entire nation watched with riveted concern as a humpback whale made its way through the San Francisco Bay and up the Sacramento

River. You thought the whale was "lost," confused, dazed. Your friend Humphrey knew exactly where he was, and what he was doing.

Any tribe or band finding itself in potentially hostile territory will send out a scout to determine if the area is clear of danger, if the natives are friendly, if it is safe to proceed.

For all your history, the gift of reason has been divided between those exploring the aqueous medium and those living on land—cousins, bound by consciousness, but separated at the beach.

A century ago, the sight of a whale making its way up a river would have been cause for some local curiosity before someone shot it and dragged it up on shore, providing the community with whale steaks to last a year.

As evidence of your progress, such an act was never even considered in your time. Your only concern was to return Humphrey to the safe, saline standard of his birth.

What finally compelled Humphrey to head downstream was the sound of humpback whales feeding, amplified and broadcast from a boat leading him seaward.

While scientists would claim that it was the sound of feeding that attracted Humphrey, this is not the case. Do you not know the difference between someone speaking to you in person and a tape recording of another's voice? Given that sound is the primary sense employed by cetaceans, such discrimination is even more acute among them.

Humphrey followed not the sound but the **intent**. For the first time in the history of the planet, **you spoke to a whale in his language.** You did so out of **concern**, out of **love** for your cetacean cousin.

Thus Humphrey bolted beneath the Golden Gate Bridge to carry his scouting report to his brethren, who waited in suspense and anticipation:

Brothers! They have awakened!

There is only you. You project your thoughts and beliefs upon the fiction of a physical world, to find them reflected back through your senses. That is the sum total of creation. You explore physical life, one of many realms, couched in the security of your divine source, charting a course with the gift of reason.

You have awakened. The time is upon you. Step now into the new order, the ancient order, the eternal order.

There is nothing to fear.

Worship yourself.

Know that you are not alone but are cherished and supported by those from the depths of the ocean to those on the spirit plane beyond your senses.

Reclaim your birthright: divine, unique, eternal.

March forward now, buoyed by divinity, suffused with reason.

To such as you belongs the kingdom of heaven.

Appendix

This book was dictated over the course of 46 sessions, from January 1 through April 30, 1987. During this time, Alexander also held about ten sessions dealing entirely with private matters.

The total time spent in trance during dictation of *Divine Grace* was about 92 hours—slightly less than four days.

As I mentioned in the Preface, *Divine Grace* was delivered as a seamless whole. Only rarely did Alexander indicate new chapters or their headings, leaving such determinations to me.

Each session follows a standard routine. I begin by raising a personal concern—a dream for interpretation, personal or professional issues, an item in the newspaper. I type it on the computer screen, read it aloud and then close my eyes. Alexander normally takes from three to five minutes to come through. He responds to my initial query, sometimes going on for pages at breakneck speed, then without a pause announces, "Now. Lecture," and immediately picks up the next sentence of his book dictation.

Each session lasts three to four hours, including two breaks of at least half an hour.

After he has finished book dictation, Alexander asks for questions and lightens the trance so I can converse with him. I do this by typing my comments on the screen, speaking them aloud as I go. Alexander pours his response through my fingers; I look at the screen to read his words, then shoot another volley in return. These exchanges are more casual, humorous and ribald than Alexander's more formal book dictation work.

While I am in trance, at least two channels seem to be operating. To some extent, my waking consciousness recedes to allow Alexander to manipulate my fingers and the neuronal structures controlling them. On a deeper level, I am aware of the **content** Alexander is delivering, though not always the **words**. On this level I can converse with Alexander while he dictates—both of us operating on two levels at once. Thus we can discuss at length the material he is imparting while the flow of prepared material continues unabated.

I become aware of the English expression of Alexander's thoughts about two sentences before their transcription through my fingers. I can thus urge a new choice of words if his original selection is indelicate or confusing. Sometimes Alexander accepts my suggestions; often he overrides them.

The reader cannot appreciate the differences in speed and force Alexander employed during production of *Divine Grace*. While dredging up historical material, his pace would slow to a crawl, letter by letter. When discussing material of a depth difficult to translate into words, such as the chapter on Divine Grace, delivery would creep so slowly that minutes would pass after one word's production. In contrast, when discussing a topic provoking his ire, the words would flood through my fingers in a furious torrent. Supreme above all such passages was his delivery of the Challenger material. As he denounced NASA and the manufacturer of the O-rings responsible for the explosion, his vehemence pounded my fingers into the keys with such force I feared they would snap off.

I have prepared this Appendix to offer the reader a glimpse of the mechanics and exchanges behind the production of *Divine Grace*.

* * *

Alexander made his first appearance one evening shortly before Christmas 1986. I was in an ebullient mood, making dinner while dancing to the blasting radio. I felt a sudden urge to sit at my home computer. Not knowing what to expect, but having long ago learned to always follow my inner voice, I settled myself before the computer.

My fingers vibrated over the keyboard, as if trying to make sense of the operation. I felt a sudden breakthrough with the corner of my brain responsible for the mechanics of typing. After a string of gibberish, segueing into a series of "hello" salutations, a coherent but stilted message of nine lines was delivered, closing with, "Enjoy your dinner." I did.

The next session brought a page and a half of material regarding the progress of my career. (I am a filmmaker.)

The following session brought another lecture along the same lines, after which, "My name is—but you see, it doesn't matter! Names are meaningless. Therefore, you choose."

I pondered this momentous decision for a bit, then chose Alexander—as in Graham Bell, who had a few things to say about new avenues of communication.

"Fine, Alexander it is, Alexander I am. I have no penis, though, I warn you, if that disqualifies me from bearing that name!

"We have known each other before, you and I, though you do not recognize me flowing out your fingers onto the keyboard. A long time it's been, yes, and ours was an oft-stormy relationship, centered in love but with all kinds of battles to keep life interesting. I trust that this time our relationship can proceed more smoothly—I have no physical arms to hurl furniture at you, in any case!

"You and I were teachers, long, long ago. In a way we still are. I have chosen to communicate with the earth plane at this time both to further my own work and to cast a fond look back at my beloved earth. You are a teacher, also, but a seeker, one impatient for, bursting for, answers. Relax, kid. Life is not so much a series of answers as a series of questions, each leading to a greater and deeper truth. You think I have all the answers, from my lofty perch? Above me, if I could describe it to you, are levels and planes of existence unfathomable to me now, and I look forward to the learning, the growth, the exploration with joy, the joy of learning. So you join me now; we'll work together on this great adventure of life."

After a dream interpretation in our eighth session, Alexander announced: "This is the first of a series of lectures, or chautauquas, we hope to impart through you. You are free to do with them what you wish. Not all of this information will be new to you, due to your reading in this area. But certain things cannot be overstressed." He then launched into what became the Introduction to *Divine Grace*. He did not tell me he was beginning to write a book.

At the close of the next session Alexander offered, "By the way, we enjoy the name 'Alex.' It is the source of some ribbing up here on our plane, since it reminds some more of a dog or a cat, and we hope we evidence higher intellectual skills than those precious creatures. Still, we are fond of our 'pet' name, so to speak."

Having read accounts of people becoming slaves to Ouija boards or other forms of automatic writing, I was determined not to allow Alex to assume supreme importance in my life. I would go for days, deliberately not holding a session, concentrating on my career work. Finally I asked him if there was a rhythm or schedule that would be best for both of us. He replied:

"At this point you seem most comfortable with every other day, so we can stick with that. We could come through more often...understand that there are people who channel every day, for hours on end! So we wish to find a happy medium, and hope its name is Ramón! A little cosmic joke there."

As Alex continued dictating *Divine Grace*, while I still considered it a private lecture series, not a book, I found myself increasingly barraged with his material while going about my everyday life; thoughts, passages and sentences would seep into consciousness. This drove me crazy. I considered ending the sessions entirely if they caused me to lose my focus on my own life. When I raised this issue with him, Alex replied:

"As we have told you, the process of 'anchoring' or solidifying the bonds between us is not one accomplished overnight. You remember how brief the initial sessions were; the anchors weren't strong enough to sustain an exchange any longer than that. Now we have approached a good duration for each session, between two and three hours, with a couple breaks. This allows us to fully explore a given idea or two, without robbing you of your every moment...

"Now, the barrage of information, as you put it, is simply a result of our organizing the material we wish to impart on our plane and poising it for dissemination to you. There was no absolute certainty that a contact with you could be reached or maintained. Now that it has, and we are grateful and pleased, we are sorting through the literally infinite banks of material we could impart to the earth plane to find what could best suit you and others to know at this time...

"At this point the psychological bridge is still permeable on your side, still fresh and new. This is manifested further by the fact that we have yet to achieve the deepest trance states possible. The barrier, then, between our reality and yours is still being constructed, so to speak, and has large gaps where later there will be none. So you do indeed find your head full of bleedthrough ideas. We can only ask that you bear with us, then, and know that every time you do open the channel between us, that channel is automatically strengthened and solidified. It is just a matter of 'time,' so to speak, before you can go about your daily life without hearing little voices in your head that convince you you are cracking up."

By the end of the chapter on Divine Grace, I knew something was up. Alex was referring to me as "our host" instead of calling me by name, as he does in private sessions. At the close of his next chapter I asked, "You're writing a book, aren't you, you sly bastard?"

"Indeed! We did not dare reveal it at the outset as you might have felt such a task to conflict with your film work. As you can see, both can proceed simultaneously for the time being; and when your film work proceeds to the point where it consumes you totally, we shall sit back and wait. There is no 'time' on our plane! We have all the 'time' in the world!

"Now you are free to do what you wish with what we impart, but you have felt stirrings within, urging you to bring our lectures to a wider audience than one. Again we make no demands, and you may do as you wish. There are many on your plane at this time desperately feeling that something is terribly wrong with the state and progress of your world, and perhaps what we say might offer a glimpse into the deeper reality from which you spring. To the extent that you are a member of your species, however much you hate to admit it, you could be doing others a favor through your efforts."

"What occurs in the trance state between you and me is that we construct a psychological bridge between our realities. You send up a vibrational frequency that meets with mine, vibrating at a higher frequency, and together our differing frequencies create a third, unique energy field which you can think of as a psychological bridge. Our information is assembled in nonphysical, nonspoken form; we then send it down across that psychological bridge, and it is at this point that the original intent of the material is translated into English. Your vocabulary is employed, and the grids of intent behind our ideas riffle through your vocabulary as in a dictionary, searching out the precise meaning. Once a grid of intent finds appropriate language to give it expression, it drops out of the psychological bridge into your energy field, where it is transmitted through your neuronal structure into the physical act of typing on the keyboard.

"Understand, then, that when you ask us a question, although you ask the question in English, we do not hear it as such. Language is meaningless on our plane. Your question is passed along the psychological bridge, where it is translated out of English expression, made manifest as a nonverbal grid of intent, which rides the bridge to our reality, where we can perceive and respond to it. So the psychological bridge, a combined force of our disparate vibrational patterns, acts as a cosmic translator. You see now that you could have grown up in any culture, using any language, and we would still be able to communicate with you just the same. We have no idea what the English language is like. If we could suddenly see a page of it, of our own dictated material, we would be as illiterate as a newborn babe in attempting to comprehend it. Like the newborn babe, we exist on a level beyond the reach of the use of earth symbols like language. It is through you, through your eyes, that any knowledge you assume enters; it is across the psychological bridge that the idea behind what you read is stripped of its varnish of English, the naked essence of the thought then transmitted to us for evaluation."

Alex's writing style differs from mine in several important respects. Most annoying to me is his insistence on overriding the inherent chauvinism of English with awkward constructions like "he/she" or referring to children as "it." While wishing along with everyone else that a method could be found to include both sexes without sacrificing economy and eloquence, I am decidedly in the camp employing the masculine pronoun to embrace both sexes until a better system is devised. I asked Alex why he insists on using the all-inclusive but unwieldy "he or she" style.

"There simply is no good way around the intrinsic sexism of your language. You see, our communications are not created in English but are simply funneled through English because that is your native tongue. So we search for the closest approximate meaning in English. When we speak of your race as a whole it is not just men we are referring to. When we speak of adults in your society, it is not just men we are referring to. If we spoke to you in a Romance language, there would be no conflict between our intent and our intent's expression in written form. But it would be incomplete for us to allow our intent to be translated to embrace only the male of the species, when it is the entire race we speak of. Yes, this results in awkward constructions and may impair the flow of words. But we have no choice, for our design is to search your language for the best approximation we can find for our intent. We address the entire human race and must therefore struggle to ensure that the female is not excluded from our expression. Although traditionally the masculine pronoun has allegedly served to embrace both male and female, we don't buy that particular construction. It makes no sense to us. So we do what we have to do to be sure our intent finds its truest expression; and if that results in awkward phrasing, that is the price we will pay, and gladly."

Responding to my concerns about the factual accuracy of some of his material, Alexander said:

"You are not writing this book, though you may be asked to defend it, since we are not quite so readily available! The same holds true for your concern over dates as we launch into our history of religion. We urge you not to worry about it. Remember that the history you know is but one possible line of events out of an infinite swirl of probable earths. There are times when we honestly cannot discern what happened precisely when; for as we have pointed out, even when something does physically occur on your earth, it is then distorted over time by your species! The important thing is not to worry over trivial dates and places but to see how the grand themes of your world are woven through history, providing a vibrant backdrop against which you play out your individual lives.

"You need bear no responsibility for any material in this book; and if challenged, simply retort, 'Alex never was much of an historian.' What more can you do?"

I was deeply upset by parts of Alex's science chapter. It was inconceivable to me that any purpose could be served by disseminating his material on the Challenger explosion, reopening those wounds. During a break, while reviewing what he had dictated to that point, I decided aloud which passages I would delete, finding them too offensive.

At the same time, during his dictation on the disasters that genetic engineering will wreak upon us if unchecked, I felt a wall go up between our two regular channels, deliberately blocking any sight of the catastrophe he viewed. Despite his efforts, I caught a glimpse of a child's face, collapsing with rot, green with putrefaction.

Nothing escapes his notice! After the session he commented:

"We know what you are going to say! You feel we are far too harsh, too strident, too sarcastic for your taste. That we will lose some readers with such an outburst.

"**If you could but see** the disasters your science can wreak upon your planet if left unchecked, you would know we are models of restraint in what we have said tonight! You felt it, when discussing genetic disaster. Those parallel earths are clearly visible to us, and it was only through great force of will that we spared you the unpleasant details! You do not want to know! Nor need you ever.

"We do not wish to come across as a high and mighty passionless observer, divorced from any commitment or concern for the earth plane. It was our home on many, many occasions, and we hold it as a dear memory. We **will not** watch its destruction without raising a voice in protest! If this makes us too **human** for your liking, then remember it is to humans that we must relate. We will not stand apart, calmly appraising the situation. **We love the earth. Your species apparently does not.** Whatever it takes—reason, logic, emotion, sarcasm—we'll use them all! And hope that one or the other will strike a responsive chord!...

"You are, of course, welcome to disagree with our **ideas** at any point, and we welcome the debate. But to state that you will delete passages you find offensive poisons the flow between us. That must remain clear if we are to give truest expression to our thoughts."

I apologized.

"Accepted, of course, and gladly! There is no need to blow the issue out of proportion; it had to happen somewhere along the line, strong-willed as we both are! And we have now reached a satisfactory conclusion: You may disagree with our words whenever you wish, but you understand it can only poison our relationship for you to presume to alter my expression."

Following the chapter on conservatives' hatred of the natural world and passion for weaponry—"passive surrender," in his words—I said, "Thanks, Alex. Now the entire National Rifle Association is going to hunt me down and demonstrate their passive firepower in my general direction!"

Alex replied, "Now, the universe is safe, yours included! You need not worry about the ladies and gentlemen of that club of death. They're too busy shooting each other in the woods to track you down!"

Following the chapter on medicine I said, "Thanks a lot, Alex. Maybe the National Rifle Association is too busy shooting each other in the woods, but now the American Medical Association is certain to come after me."

Alex's reply: "Have you forgotten you carry no health insurance? They won't get anywhere near you!"

Early on in the work I caught glimpses of Alex's outline for the entire volume. It was evident that the book existed in finished form on Alex's plane and simply required my spending sufficient earth hours in trance to bring it to written expression.

Alex's original outline did not include a chapter on AIDS. Feeling that no book purporting to discuss the state of our society would be complete without addressing this issue, I told Alex to do his cosmic research and prepare such a chapter.

In the weeks to come, I would catch glimpses of the material as he organized it. I awoke one morning, fresh from dreams afire with the connection between whale beachings and homosexuals with AIDS.

While camping in Death Valley a month before Alex delivered the AIDS material, I arose early one morning to photograph the sunrise. As I charged up a hill, I suddenly "heard" Alex booming: "The hemophiliac stands as the symbol of a house divided, turning upon itself!"

"Brilliant, Alex," I replied. "Now would you please shut up!"

During a break in dictation of the music chapter, having just delivered the Beatles material, I felt myself drawn to the piano. Naturally, I ran through about twenty minutes of Beatles songs. Inexplicably, I felt myself overcome with emotion, my throat so constricted I could barely sing along. When I returned to trance Alex explained, "Now, what you experienced on the piano bench was a little gift from your friendly ghost, an attenuated experience of the power behind the Beatles' music when fresh. You were too young to participate in such an event at the time, so we yanked you back through time, psychologically, to dip into that feeling of overwhelming intensity experienced at a Beatles concert."

Throughout dictation of *Divine Grace*, I was constantly puzzled by a curious phenomenon. While always receiving bleedthrough information of chapters yet to be imparted, I often found that when the time came for a chapter's dissemination, much of the material I had heard being prepared was not delivered. However long this book is, I heard at least twice as much material being assembled, then not produced. As an example, while the chapter on food was prepared I heard a long dissertation on vegetarianism, which was never delivered. I later asked him his thoughts on the subject—Alex does not embrace the vegetarian philosophy—and he prefaced his remarks by saying:

"We wish we had remembered to discuss vegetarianism in our discussion of food! You have wondered why, since you 'heard' the vegetarian material being prepared for the food chapter, it was not delivered. Our material is not set in stone on our plane, transmitted letter by letter to your computer screen. While we can intend to discuss a certain subject, as you well know, when the 'time' comes to do so, often material is left out. This occurs because each body of thought, or subject we address, has its own swirling electromagnetic reality, and in the process of dictation we try to organize them in a coherent and progressive whole. Lacking omniscience, there can be times when we fail to latch onto a given subject area, or electromagnetic swirl, neglect its presence. Thus the material, while organized, is never delivered. You have experienced this again and again while we work our way through this book, material prepared but not delivered. Consider it your private lecture series, then, unknown to your readers!"

This is Alex's response to my pointing out the contradiction in his holding both literature and film to be the most "realistic" art form:

"Indeed we contradicted ourselves in the chapters on literature and film. Of course it is the case that film is the most 'realistic' of all art forms, most closely replicating your physical reality through moving pictures and sound...Literature was the most 'realistic' of the art forms we discussed up to that point; the film chapter, coming later, represented a progression to an even more 'realistic' art form. We appreciate your catching the error, and perhaps it will serve to take the wind out of our sails, should any reader begin to invest us with omniscience and perfection. Such qualities are only words in the dictionary, on our plane as on yours!"

In one session, Alex finished the chapter on the Sixties, delivered the Seventies and began the Eighties. Afterward I remarked, "Hell of a short chapter on the Seventies, wasn't it?"

"Well, nothing happened."

I was surprised that Alex ended *Divine Grace* when he did. I had heard entire chapters being prepared as he detailed the possible outcomes of the struggle to install the new order—from nuclear war to genetic disaster to mass ecological and economic collapse. None of this was delivered. When I later brought this up, Alex answered:

"You were correct that we left out much material at the end. We always tread a fine line between **alerting** and **alarming** your brethren. The danger in alarming is that it leads to paralysis or despair or withdrawal. What the times call for most is **action**. So by eliminating much of the 'negative' material we hope to leave the reader feeling positive and thus **empowered** to set about creating a new society, one based on a return to the natural order."

As Alex mentioned, during the time this book was being dictated, I visited my sister Monica and the friend to whom this book is dedicated on a trip back east. I close *Divine Grace* as Alex closed his two hours of advice to Paul:

"Let us just affirm that you are a divine creature, that you are rooted in a natural order of absolute security and that there is nothing to fear. . .The only harm that can come to you is when you allow it to come to you by abdicating your reason and your intrinsic sense of your own divinity and your own worth.

"Don't let [feelings of responsibility] stop you from enjoying your life, from pursuing those avenues of pleasure which give your life enrichment. Don't think that you have to save the world. You will automatically help save the world just by being yourself and by being happy with who you are. The happiness comes first; the rest follows."

Ramón Stevens grew up in Mt. Lebanon, Pennsylvania. He holds a degree in psychology from the University of Michigan and attended New York University's Graduate Institute of Film and Television. He lives in Los Angeles.